Advanced Information and Knowledge Processing

Series Editors

Professor Lakhmi Jain
Lakhmi.jain@unisa.edu.au

Professor Xindong Wu
xwu@cs.uvm.edu

T0137744

For further volumes:
http://www.springer.com/series/4738

Tshilidzi Marwala · Monica Lagazio

Militarized Conflict Modeling using Computational Intelligence

 Springer

Tshilidzi Marwala
University of Johannesburg
South Africa
tmarwala@uj.ac.za

Dr. Monica Lagazio
University of Johannesburg
South Africa

ISSN 1610-3947
ISBN 978-1-4471-2701-7   ISBN 978-0-85729-790-7 (eBook)
DOI 10.1007/978-0-85729-790-7
Springer London Dordrecht Heidelberg New York

British Library Cataloguing in Publication Data
A catalogue record for this book is available from the British Library

Cover design: SPi Publisher Services

Printed on acid-free paper

Springer is part of Springer Science+Business Media (www.springer.com)

Foreword

Over the past 20 years enormous progress has been made in predicting and explaining the incidence of violent international conflict. That progress derives from three scientific revolutions. One is the revolution of massively available data. It has been made possible by the effort by thousands of scholars to produce coded information and make it available to the scholarly community. It began with the commitment of scholars like Karl Deutsch and David Singer more than 40 years ago to widen and therefore democratize and internationalize the scientific study of international relations, along with similar efforts in comparative politics to supply reliable data on characteristics of national political systems. This effort soon became an international one, with complementary projects in Europe and elsewhere. It also was interdisciplinary, dependent on similar efforts in economics, anthropology, public health and many other fields, in the private and public sectors of many countries and international organizations. The work in this book draws heavily on their contributions for the systematic coding of national political systems (the democracy-autocracy scale), trade and GDP, alliance ties, relative power, geographical location, and the onset of militarized interstate disputes (MIDs).

The second is the revolution of replication, made imaginable by the data revolution. Although the norm itself is hardly new, it has recently and overwhelmingly become powerful. To be taken seriously, published empirical analyses must be accompanied by posting all relevant data and computational routines on a reasonably permanent website. Such provision is now required by our major journals (see the special feature in the February 2003 issue of *International Studies Perspectives*) and is followed by the authors of this book. These materials then become public information, and it is no longer possible, at least within large and vigorous research programs, to publish material with serious errors in the data or computations without the being exposed. Despite the risk of personal pain, this is an altogether salutary development for a science. Later studies build on and improve other ones, often leading to convergence. The third is the continuing revolution of statistical methods. Within a large class of statistical methods, different analyses may give different answers. But that is unavoidable, not necessarily a fault, since eventually we can expect the most appropriate and competent ones to bring us toward consensus. Formal theory helps in this process, since statistical diagnostics will not suffice if the models are badly specified. But some dispute about what statistical routines are appropriate is unavoidable given the rapid evolution of statistical methods. Analyses that, for example, omitted appropriate controls for endogeneity or temporal and spatial dependence may have been excusable when they were published but are no longer so. Analyses such as those in this book on global networks build on what earlier was a focus on single states, then pairs of states (dyads) and small networks such as triads.

This book stands clearly in the mode of the third revolution, with its application of a wide range of computational intelligence algorithms that have been developed and applied in various disciplines. Many of them exhibit a strong kinship with the neural network analysis of international conflict data earlier employed by Beck, King, and Zeng (2000, 2004) and by Lagazio herself (Lagazio and Russett 2004). For forecasting, all of them have major advantages over the customary logistical regression techniques, producing a much closer fit between predicted conflicts and actual conflicts. They do so by making few assumptions about the functional relationships among all the variables, and permitting the computer algorithm to find the best fit among the often massively complex interactions. Some assumptions of non-linearity and interaction can be built into any logistical regression on good theoretical grounds, but inevitably many others will not be anticipated in such a richly complex reality. It can be useful, for example, to distinguish between influences enabling the use of military force (e.g., contiguity, great economic or military power) and influences that may discourage conflict (shared democracy, economic interdependence). (See Kinsella and Russett 2002, Bennett and Stam 2004.) Neural network and related procedures are very valuable in making predictions, especially when the predictions are made outside the sample of years and events used for establishing the initial results. Also the analyst can carefully scrutinize the results to infer theoretically plausible interactions that were not anticipated initially.

This book should have great appeal to two quite different audiences, among whom there is rather little overlap. The first audience is that in the highly interdisciplinary field of computational intelligence. That is certainly not my field of expertise, though I expect that such specialists can benefit greatly from the meticulous way in which the authors compare the advantages and limitations of the different algorithms, moving more or less progressively through the chain of chapters toward more accurate predictions. The tradeoffs between one algorithm and another can depend on the analyst's particular needs, for example between producing false negatives or positives, and true negatives or positives. For policy predictions, it would seem obvious to want a high ratio of true positives (actual conflicts anticipated) to false ones in time to take for some preventive or ameliorative actions. Yet in the real world of international relations, preventive action, whether through military deterrence, mediation, or economic or political assistance, can be very expensive and deployed only sparingly. Similar tradeoffs of course arise in medical research, between the costs and benefits of identifying and treating every patient who needs it against those of submitting individuals to the costs and pain of treatments for a disease or pathogen with which they are not afflicted. Hence the practical pressures on the analysts to minimize false positives also. Another problem in making practical use of such forecasts is the complexity of the techniques employed in making them. The authors illustrate one such example in Chaps. 6 and 7 where they find a tradeoff between accuracy of forecasts and transparency to the analyst and to the technically-challenged reader. Transparency is a continuing problem in these analyses. Unfortunately, most policy makers and even most international relations scholars are indeed technically-challenged in evaluating the results produced by these models. This means that the ability to move some of these fascinating results into serious policy discussions is limited. But perhaps that may change as the possibilities for productive application, in many disciplines and policy concerns other than international relations, grow. Chapter 12 makes a laudable effort to discuss the practical implications of moving from analytical forecasting to practical applications to controlling and limiting actual conflict. It is a good starting point, though hardly the end of such an effort. To make international relations forecasting more widely accessible and acceptable to policy makers and students of policy, it would be very beneficial for the analyst to display the actual point predictions – by year and dyad – in tables that display the results (false and true positives, false and true negatives) by name. It may not help the medical analyst to display her results that way, since the reader may have little knowledge of the individuals (not to mention legal questions about violating anonymity). But doing so with international relations data to people with often intimate and detailed knowledge about particular countries and conditions could greatly raise the plausibility of the results. Equally important, it could enlist the reader in the common quest for improving the models and data that produce the results. That seems a very logical next step in applying these methods to international relations.

Another and equally important step will be in moving these analyses closer into real time. The datasets in this book do not extend beyond 2001. It is certainly not a criticism to say that, given all the riches in this book. Yet since then there have been not only many more conflict events, but important changes in some of the key predictive variables (countries becoming much more democratic or authoritarian, changes in trade, differential growth in GDP, shifting alliances, etc.) both in the decade or so following the end of the cold war, and the further decade since 2001. That means the ability to forecast particular cases of conflict in 2012 and beyond is limited. That can never be entirely overcome, but it can be substantially reduced. At this time of writing, data on countries' political system (the Polity data) now are available up to 2009, and measures for most of the other independent variables are now available up to very close to 2009, and some (e.g., contiguity) change little. The principal barrier to real-time analysis is the absence of information on the dependent variable, MIDs. A strong effort is underway to bring those data up to 2010, and to have them available on the Correlates of War website (http://www.correlatesofwar.org/datasets.htm).

All in all, I regard this book as a major achievement for the scientific analysis of international relations, and one that deserves the attention of theorists and empirical analysts of world politics.

Beck, N., King, G., Zeng, L.: Improving quantitative studies of international conflict: a conjecture. Am. Polit. Sci. Rev. **94**, 21–36 (2000)

Beck, N., King, G., Zeng, L.: Theory and evidence in international conflict. Am. Polit. Sci. Rev. **98**, 379–389 (2004)

Bennett, D.S., Stam, A.C.: The Behavioral Origins of War. University of Michigan Press, Ann Arbor (2004)

Kinsella, D., Russett, B.: Conflict emergence and escalation in interactive international dyads. J. Polit. **64**(4), 1045–1068 (2002)

Lagazio, M., Russett, B.: A neural network analysis of militarized international disputes, 1885–1992: temporal stability and causal complexity. In Paul, D. (ed.) The Scourge of War: New Extensions on an Old Problem. University of Michigan Press, Ann Arbor (2004)

March 2011   Bruce Russett, PhD
Yale University
New Haven, USA

Preface

Militarized Conflict Modeling using Computational Intelligence introduces the concepts of computational intelligence for militarized interstate conflict modeling. This book is concerned with the analysis of interstate conflicts as a scientific concept, and in particular the methods in which computational intelligence models may help uncover some of the complex behavior that interstate conflicts display. Building on a renowned tradition that goes back to the 1960's, this collection of analyses applies a variety of computational intelligence techniques to war and dispute data. The analyses are driven by a desire to find new ideas and approaches to understanding international conflicts. The objective is to use this improved understanding to build practical platforms and solutions for early warning and conflict management. These warnings can be used by political practitioners to reduce the risk of international conflicts and manage unfolding conflicts. This book introduces computational intelligence techniques to model militarized interstate conflict. The computational intelligence methods used for militarized interstate conflict modeling include neural networks, neuro-fuzzy methods, rough sets which are optimized using particle swarm optimization, simulated annealing and genetic algorithm, neuro-rough models, and control techniques. This book makes an interesting read and it will open new avenues in the use of computational intelligence techniques to militarized interstate modeling.

March 2011   Tshilidzi Marwala, PhD and Monica Lagazio, PhD
University of Johannesburg
Johannesburg

Acknowledgements

We would like to thank the following former and current graduate students for their assistance in developing this manuscript: Ishmael Sibusiso Msiza, Nadim Mohamed, Dr. Brain Leke, Dr. Sizwe Dhlamini, Thando Tettey, Bodie Crossingham, Professor Fulufhelo Nelwamondo, Vukosi Marivate and Eyasu Habtemariam. We also thank colleagues and pratictioners that have collaborated directly and inderectly to writing of the munuscript. In particular, we thank Dr. Ian Kennedy and the anonymous reviewers for their comments and careful reading of the book. We thank Professor Bruce Russett and John Oneal for inspiring our research and guiding our analyses. We owe a great debt to J. David Singer and his immense effort in founding and maintaining the Correlates of War Project.

This book is dedicated to all those people and organizations whose principal objective is to maintain and spread peace in the international context; whether through scholarly research, field work, community activism or political leadership. Let there be more peace!

March 2011   Tshilidzi Marwala and Monica Lagazio
University of Johannesburg

Contents

Chapter 1
Modeling Conflicts Between States: New Developments for an Old Problem

1.1 Introduction

This book is concerned with the analysis of interstate conflicts as a scientific phenomenon, and in particular the ways in which computational intelligence models may help unpack some of the complex behavior that interstate conflicts display (Lagazio and Russett 2004; Chernoff 2004). Building on a distinguished tradition that goes back to the 1960s, this collection of analyses applies a variety of computational intelligence techniques to war and dispute data. The analyses are driven by a desire to find new ideas and approaches to understanding international conflicts. The objective is to use this improved understanding to build practical platforms and solutions for early warning and conflict management. These warnings can be used by political practitioners to reduce the risk of international conflicts and manage unfolding conflicts.

Great progress has been made in predicting and explaining interstate conflict. Improved data, theory, and methods all deserve credit; yet much remains to be done. First, whereas many variables (e.g., geographical proximity, relative power, alliances, political regime type, and economic interdependence) have important effects, even the most successful multivariate analyses leave much of the variance in conflict behavior unaccounted for. This is possibly due to inadequate data, specifications, or theories; complexity or simply random variation. Consequently, questions must arise about the predictive and practical power of such analyses and whether all these research efforts should be used for policy purposes (Geller and Singer 1998).

Second, interstate conflicts are complex phenomena, often displaying non-linear and non-monotonic patterns of interaction. Those complexities are hard to capture and consequently model. Finally, there are questions about whether the causal or predictive relationships are stable across time and space. For instance, one such question is whether democracy and economic interdependence have reduced the risk of interstate conflict throughout the twentieth and the twenty-first century (Thompson and Tucker 1997; Maoz 1998; Russett and Oneal 2001) or their effect

T. Marwala and M. Lagazio, *Militarized Conflict Modeling using Computational Intelligence*, Advanced Information and Knowledge Processing, DOI 10.1007/978-0-85729-790-7_1, © Springer-Verlag London Limited 2011

was limited and spurious (Gowa 1999; Ray 2005). Also doubts exist on the contribution that international organizations may exert on conflict dynamics (Oneal et al. 2003; Oneal and Russett 2006; Boehmer et al. 2004; Pevehouse and Russett 2005).

To uncover enduring conflict dynamics and to shed further light on relationships characterizing conflict outcomes, we have developed and tested several computational intelligence models. Although computational models are not a panacea or always appropriate, we believe they provide a useful methodology that has not been sufficiently exploited in the context of interstate conflict analysis, let alone in political science. Therefore, our first aim is to present a comprehensive survey of research contributions that investigate the use of computational intelligence methods in building interstate models. The provided analysis and comparison of the findings of the different models allows not only an in-depth empirical assessment of the advantages and disadvantages of applying computational intelligence to conflict data, but also for a significant review of possible causal mechanisms at work in warfare. These models also introduce an emphasis on non-linearity, interactive patterns, and multiple causation that is much needed to capture real-world dynamics. In addition, the comparison that we can draw from analyzing the performance of each of the models can also improve on previous attempts to readdress the empirical validity of the theoretical frameworks put forward in the literature. Indeed, claiming to have developed a causal explanation that is a structural feature of the international relations context, but not helping practically in forecasting, is at best of dubious value (Beck et al. 2000).

A second contribution that this book makes is to further improve the methodological tool set that computational models offer, above all in relation to causal interpretation. Often regarded as black boxes, computational models have attracted suspicion from social scientists inclined towards simplicity, easy interpretation, and careful specification in their models (Ray 2005). Political scientists have traditionally shunned forecasting in favor of an emphasis on causal explanation and it is, therefore, important that any proposed new method should allow for causal interpretation as well as improved prediction. This is also paramount for practitioners. Although knowing the risk of a particular conflict can help focus international attention and resources on highly volatile areas, to evaluate alternative foreign policies requires us to know which course of action should be endorsed. For instance, will promoting democracy and economic interdependence encourage peace? Our last aim is to define research challenges that still exist, and to highlight promising new research directions.

The following 13 chapters – from Chap. 2 to 11 – deal with different applications of computational intelligence models to conflict data. Each chapter provides a description of the specific method, which we have applied; an assessment of its strengths and weaknesses for modeling interstate conflicts; and a framework for extracting useful insights from the model results. Furthermore, for each application, we discuss the theoretical and methodological implication of the findings coming from each analysis. Chapter 12 uses all findings from the different models and their underlying causal explanations to develop a practical approach to early warning and conflict management. Finally, the last chapter concerns directions for research and identifies areas and questions that still need further work and answers.

Many of the issues covered by this book are still under development and in dispute among specialists. Therefore, the intention of this book is to promote further debate and an examination of these issues rather than provide conclusive answers. We hope that our work on the subject could inspire further future research and innovative thinking.

1.2 Towards a Consolidation of Theory and Method for Interstate Conflicts

In the first part of the last century, the study of international conflicts was regarded as a sub-discipline of diplomatic history. The researchers' main concern was with describing historical facts and events that led to the two World Wars. One needed to wait for the beginning of the 1960s to witness the adoption of the scientific method by the political science discipline and the emergence of mainstream, quantitative empirical studies of war (Richardson 1960; Deutsch and Singer 1964). During this period, Singer's seminal efforts with the Correlates of War (COW) made a major contribution to the development of the systematic analysis of international conflicts. Singer and Small (1972) collected and integrated several data sets on war events going back to 1816. Singer was also centrally involved in the origin and development of the Militarized International Dispute (MID) dataset, which has proven to be one of the great achievements of the COW project. Singer believed that by focusing on *accuracy* and *replication* in data generation and quantitative data analysis, it was possible to discover empirical patterns and thereby producing generalizations and explanations about international conflicts.

The COW project has adopted several levels of analysis. Singer (1961) initially endorsed the international system, or systemic level, as most promising and expressed skepticism about the power of the nation-state level of investigation – a position shared by a very different kind of scholar, Waltz (1979). Subsequently, Small and Singer (1976) declared their doubts about the emerging attention to a middle level of analysis between the systemic and state levels; that is, on pairs of states, or dyads. Notwithstanding these doubts, Singer was influential in the conceptualization of the MID dataset as bilateral interactions (Leng and Singer 1977), which implies a dyadic approach.

From a methodological standpoint, much of the initial work using the MID dataset was predominantly descriptive, driven by statistical analyses that mapped characteristics and relationships of the international system, which were assumed to be linear. Small and Singer were also cautious in the assessment of the empirical result of their study. It is during this period that the two political scientists questioned the democratic peace hypothesis, which claims the existence of a peace zone between democracies (Babst 1972; Doyle 1983, 1986). The low frequency of democracies in the analyzed time frame could be regarded as a serious flaw in their research design. So, Small and Singer suggested that the low level of war intervention between democracies might be a statistical artifact, caused by the small number of democratic states present in their data set (Small and Singer 1976). From then on, the democratic peace argument *versus* the realist argument tended to play a key role in the methodological and theoretical debate on international war. Subsequent studies, using interstate conflict data, either supported the democratic peace hypothesis, rejecting the statistical artifact argument (Rummel 1979), or failed to find any consistent association between democracy and war, therefore relegating the democratic peace hypothesis to specific time periods or types of warfare (Weede 1984; Domke 1988).[1] Theoretical explanations from a political philosophical angle were also developed (Doyle 1986).

The controversy over the democratic peace findings was beneficial in focusing the democratic argument and, to certain extent, the study of interstate conflicts, both theoretically and empirically, at the dyadic level.[2] Other COW data associates (Maoz and Abdolali 1989; Bremer 1992) have made major innovations in theoretically-driven use of MIDs at the dyadic level. Maoz and Abdolali (1989) focused on three levels of analysis: the individual state level, the dyadic level, and the system level. While no significant evidence supported the link between democracies and peace both at the individual state and system level, the dyadic level presented strong results. The dyadic findings were replicated by a long list of political scientists (Morgan and Howard 1991; Morgan and Schwebach 1992; Weede 1992; Dixon 1993; Moaz and Russett 1992). Some of these studies sought to probe even further the empirical frontiers of the democratic peace proposition. The work of Maoz and Russett (1992) extended the democratic peace argument to militarized conflicts below the level of interstate war. By extending the original concern with war to other types of low-level warfare, Maoz and Russett (1992) dramatically increased the number of positive cases in the dataset. Furthermore, they tested the robustness of the dyadic results by controlling for two other explanatory variables: distance and great power involvement. Their study demonstrates that, when these two factors are controlled for, democracy continues to have a systematic and consistent reducing influence on the probability of interstate conflicts. Bremer's search for the 'dangerous dyads' paralleled Maoz and Russett's (1993) work in their effort to examine the extent to which the democratic results were robust. At the same time, further empirical development was also provided by studies exploring whether the influence of dyadic democracy was limited to the modern period.

Russett and Antholis (1992), Ember et al. (1992), and Weart (1994) offered collateral evidence that the democratic peace zone extends both to primitive societies and the Greek city-state system. In addition, more sophisticated theoretical

---

[1] It is important to notice that all these studies were conducted at the national rather than the dyadic level.

[2] The dyadic hypothesis states that although democracies are not generally less war-prone than non-democracies, they rarely fight each other.

explanations of why such a link exists were put forward. Early efforts fell into two categories: the cultural/normative and the structural/institutional explanations. The former emphasizes the role of shared democratic principles, perceptions, and expectation of the actors' behavior, while the latter focuses on the importance of institutional constraints on the democratic decision making process (Maoz and Russett 1993).

The growing acceptance of the democratic peace proposition within interstate conflict analysis generated a new wave of criticism. Employing a predominantly neo-realist argument, the new studies stressed that the empirical association between the character of political regimes and peace is spurious. They suggest, instead, that peace is the result of shared and transient strategic interests (Layne 1994; Spiro 1994; Farber and Gowa 1995). By emphasizing systemic conditions more than dyadic characteristics, neo-realist argument claims that the bipolar structure of the Cold War period, together with the political leadership provided by the democratic hegemony (US), created the condition for peace among democracies. The enduring conflict of interest between the two major powers, a democracy and an autocracy, generated a pattern of consistent common interest between democratic states. Threatened by a common enemy, democracies responded to the logic of the bipolar system by adopting a balancing behavior, which aimed to form alliances with the other threatened democracies. Furthermore, this common pattern of interest between the democratic states was further strengthened by the benefits and rewards that democracies received from the international system as shaped and directed by the democratic hegemony (Lemke and Reed 1996).

In summary, for the neo-realist the major postwar alliance among democracies indirectly produced the phenomenon of "liberal peace". Faber and Gowa (1995) support the neo-realist position with empirical evidence and statistical analysis. They find that there is no statistically significant relationship between democracy and war before 1914. However, their statistical analysis is problematic since it breaks down the Pre-Cold War period into four sub-periods: The 1816–1913 period, World War I (1914–1918), the period between the two World Wars (1919–1938), and World War II (1939–1945). The statistical implication of this slicing strategy is to reduce the number of democracies in the analyzed samples. Reducing the time frame for the data analysis means that the number of democracies in a given period is so small that any difference between observed and expected frequency becomes statistically insignificant (Faber and Gowa 1995; for rebuff see Maoz 1998).

Even if evidence for the interest-based explanation tends to be mixed, these studies paved the way for new attempts to integrate different theoretical sets of factors and analytical levels into single models of warfare. Vasquez's (1993) work is an example of a compelling empirical investigation, which draws from multiple studies and levels of analysis. Vasquez develops a causal sequence, made of a series of steps, which culminates in war. The initial trigger is provided by territorial disputes, however it is the confluence of different attributes from different levels that conspires to escalate the dispute to violence and finally to world war. Pursing this integration view, game theory has provided a powerful tool to combine the insights of different theories and levels. By examining how different theoretical arguments relate to the menu of options open to decision-makers, diverse constraints from different levels of analysis become part of the more general expected-utility calculation of rational leaders. These constraints represent some of the possible costs that leaders must confront if they choose war-related behavior when faced with interstate crises.

Bueno de Mesquita and Lalman (1992) label this strategic utility calculation the "crisis sub-game" From the sub-game model, it can be deduced that when two democracies interact in a crisis, the most likely outcome would be negotiation, since both states rank war low in their order of preference. Conversely, when a democracy interacts with an autocracy, the most likely result of the strategic interaction would be war. In this case, war is higher in the list of the two states' preferences. Less restrained by structural or normative constraints, authoritarian leaders are more prepared to escalate dispute or launch war; while democratic leaders, predicting war-related behavior from the autocracy, might be prepared to initiate a militarized conflict to pre-empt the anticipated use of force by the opponent (Bueno de Mesquita and Siverson 1995). More recently, Bueno de Mesquita and Lee Ray (2004) have also found evidence that the ratio between the "selectorate", the portion of the population that participates in the selection of political leaders, and the size of the winning coalition is particularly important and has a predictable impact on policy choices, interaction among states, and leaders' attitude towards interstate conflicts.

Further extension of the empirical research on the democratic peace, which focuses on the importance of the three liberal pillars – democracy, economic interdependence, and international law – for keeping peace, has also underlined that wars result from a combination of multiple factors and conditions (Russett and Oneal 2001; Oneal 2006). Particularly, complex is the causal path between economic interdependence and interstate wars. As underlined by the liberal theory, there is a feedback between the two variables. The theory claims not only that trade reduces the likelihood of militarized conflicts, but also that conflicts decrease the level of trade (Russett and Oneal 2001). Consequently, when planning empirical studies, it is important to think carefully about the direction of causality (Stein 1993). Best practice indicates that models of conflict should estimate both impacts simultaneously (Polacheck 1992; Mansfield 1994). Kim (1998) developed rich models to explain both bilateral trade and the risk of dyadic militarized disputes. Her model for the period 1950–1985, shows that the effect of trade on conflict is stronger that the effect of conflict on trade. More recently, Vector Auto-Regression (VAR) or Granger-causality testing has been used to address this circular influence and temporal dependence (Oneal and Russett 2001).

In relation to the impact of other factors on trade, some researchers have shown that a state's security interests, as indicated in the structure of alliances, do influence trade patterns. A state would trade more with allies, since it would not fear that the economic gains derived from the economic interaction would be used against its own security (Gowa and Mansfield 1993). Other more recent work has instead underlined the reverse impact of democracy and economic interdependence on alliance formation. Indeed, alliances reflect not only strategic realities but also shared political and commercial interests (Oneal and Russett 2001). Moreover, distance is also correlated with trade and conflicts. Geographically distant countries trade less with one another. This is because distance increases the cost of trade (Lemke 1995). Furthermore, distance has also an effect on interstate conflicts. Proximity produces opportunities and incentives to fight (Siverson and Starr 1991; Goetz and Diehl 1992; Kocs 1995). Facing with the complexity of the possible interactions and the need to test the robustness of the liberal hypothesis, several researchers have suggested controlling for distance and alliances when developing statistical models (Mansfield 1994; Reuveny and Kang 1996; Oneal and Russett 1997, 2001; Oneal et al. 2003). Their findings show substantial evidence that, when controlling for these two factors, as well as the direction of causality between trade and conflicts, and between democracy, trade, and alliance, the peace-inducing effect of trade on interstate conflicts remains significant.[3]

However, not all recent empirical works support the liberal economic argument. Many have challenged the findings presented by liberal researchers (de Vries 1990; Barbieri 1996; Beck et al. 1998; Green et al. 2001; Barbieri and Peters 2003; Ray 2003). They claim either that economic ties may increase the risk of militarized disputes, that the beneficial influence of economic interdependence is statistically insignificant, or that the impact of democracy and trade has been wrongly estimated. A study by de Vries examines dyads in the Americas and Western Europe between 1950 and 1960. He presents a different measure of interdependence, constructed using political, military, institutional, and diplomatic indicators in addition to the economic ones. Furthermore, he uses as a dependent variable a scale indicating the combined intensity of conflict and co-operation in each dyad. The findings of this analysis reveal that interdependence acts as catalyst, which can intensify both conflict and co-operation, irrespective of the nature of the nation's state (i.e., democracy or autocracy). Although this study may be useful in suggesting the double nature of economic interdependence, we must be aware that de Vries' findings may be the result of the different specifications used.

Barbieri's work follows de Vries and she finds evidence that economic inter-dependence increases the likelihood of conflict rather than reducing it. As in de Vries' case, the discrepancy between her findings and those of previous researches supporting the liberal hypothesis could be the result of the different specifications chosen (Oneal 2006). Barberi's model (Barbieri 1996), which for certain aspects is quite similar to the one developed by Oneal and Russett (1997), differs in the definition and calculation of important bilateral trade, control variables included

---

[3]Some of the studies, which focus on economic interdependence, have argued that asymmetric interdependence increases the probability of conflicts. However, there has been little empirical support for the asymmetrical interdependence argument and more empirical evidence are pointing towards a benefit impact of asymmetrical trade (Gasiorowski and Polachek 1982; Oneal et al. 1996).

in the regression equation and the set of cases analyzed. Barbieri uses trade concentration as a measurement of economic interdependence instead of the value of trade relative to the size of the nation's economy. The latter indicator is more appropriate since economic ties are more influential when playing a key role in the national economy (Russett and Oneal 2001). Moreover, Barbieri does not use a second variable controlling for distance and analyses all dyads rather than focusing only on the politically relevant ones (Barbieri 1996). Even in her more recent analysis, still confirming the initial finding (Barbieri and Peters 2003), a measure of distance has been omitted. As explained previously, distance is correlated both with trade and interstate conflict. Consequently, to avoid spurious associations between economic interdependence and militarized behavior, a second variable controlling for distance should be included in the model (Gleditsch and Hegre 1997; Oneal and Russett 1999).

Focusing more on methodological issues than different specifications, Beck et al. (1998) have also raised doubts on the positive impact of trade. They argue that the presently used statistical models are inappropriate for conflict data because the observations are not temporally independent. This is because the observations for a dyad in 1 year are not independent from the observations in a previous year. Indeed, the probability of dyadic conflict in a given year, for example, is likely to be dependent on the conflict history of that dyad − see Goertz' (1994) work on enduring rivals. In addition, few will deny that what happens between the Iraq-Iran dyad and the US-Iran dyad could have an impact on the US-Iraq dyad. In fact all these three dyads may display a complex dependence structure. To overcome the problem of temporal dependency, they suggest that, in developing a logistic model, a variable controlling for the number of years that have elapsed from the most recent occurrence of a conflict should be used. Adopting the suggested correction, they show that the beneficial influence of economic interdependence becomes statistically insignificant. Although temporal dependence between cases is a serious problem in conflict analysis, this partial solution remains problematic. While solving a problem, the variable *year* opens new issues. The year correction rests on the assumption that the effect of the other explanatory variables and time can be separated (Beck et al. 1998). This seems very unlikely in the case of economic interdependence. As stressed by the liberal theory, economic interdependence falls with the breaking out of a conflict, while rising over time after the end of a conflict.

Green et al. (2001) used a fixed effect model to identify some methodological problems with conflict analysis, namely omitted variable bias (this refers to important factors that could affect the key liberal variables and consequently the probability of conflict, which are not included in the analysis) and the lack of homogeneity of data across space and over time. Their solution is to estimate different regression equations for each individual dyad. However, their analysis also drop all the dyads that have never experienced conflicts (all zero dyads), losing a great deal of information, which is important to explain interstate behavior.

Green et al. (2001) use at most 42 observations for each dyad, which contain very little variation. Their controversial findings indicate that democracy has no effect on militarized disputes as well as on increasing economic interdependence. (See rebuttals by Beck and Katz 2001; King 2001; Bennett and Stam 2000). Finally, Ray (2003, 2005) argues that research on militarized conflict has produced either meaningless results, since too many variables and complex regression analyses have been considered, or that previous approaches (pooled cross-sectional and time-series analyses) have hidden important differences in the relationship of the key variables across space and over time. (A similar critique has been put forward by Green et al. (2001)). To address these issues, which he sees as methodological short falls, one by one he introduces a few explanatory variables and several control variables within the analysis His conclusions show that economically important trade has a beneficial effect only in certain specifications (Ray 2005; for rebuff see Oneal and Russett 2005).

The contribution that inter-governmental organization may exert on promoting peace is less certain (Oneal et al. 2003; Oneal and Russett 2006). It is still theoretically unclear how, when, and which international organizations matter (Mearsheimer 1995; Schweller and Preis 1997), and whether international organizations simultaneously increase or decrease the probability of militarized conflicts. International organizations are both the product of power, as claimed by realists (Mearsheimer 1995), and important international mechanisms to defuse conflicts, as put forward by liberals (Keohane and Nye 1989; Rosenau 1992). In addition international organizations may have important indirect effect on the prospect for peace as well as be correlated with the international power structure. Indeed, international organizations could have important impact on supporting democracy and trade (Russet and Oneal 2001), while at the same time being the product of high level international interactions, which is recognized to increase opportunities for interstate conflicts (the state with the highest number of international interactions is also the state most likely to fight and most likely to join international organizations). More recent support for the benefits of International Government Organizations has come from analyses that have both controlled for these connections with the international system and developed improved measures of International Government Organization's effectiveness (Boehmer et al. 2004; Pevehouse and Russett 2005). However, the relative impact of the three liberal variables still varies from one research work to another depending on the data, specification of the model, spatial and temporal domain, etc.

Formal and empirical research on the relationship among the liberal variables – democracy, economic interdependence and international organizations – has made significant progress in explaining war. Yet, there are still key aspects of these relationships that remain unexplained. The existing division, both theoretical and empirical, is indicative of the complexity of the causal path that leads to war or peace among states.

1.3   Complexity as Multiple and Convergent Paths to War and Peace

The observation that interstate war results from the convergence of multiple conditions and factors is becoming more dominant within the conflict analysis literature.[4] This position has challenged the restrictive linear and fixed-effect assumptions that have previously dominated the field by expanding both our theoretical explanation of international conflicts and methods applied to conflict data.

Ragin (1987) was one of the first to talk about complex causality as the intersection of a set of conditions in time and space that produces a certain types of social phenomena: 'The basic idea is that a phenomenon or a change emerges from the intersection of appropriate preconditions. It is when these multiple factors, which alone are not sufficient conditions for war, come together, that war actually happens. Furthermore, conflict researchers also appear to concur on the notion that not only a single combination of factors or conditions could produce war but multiple combinations and factors could indeed produce the same outcome. As a result, war can occur through several and different causal paths (Levy 2000). In technical terms this is referred to as 'multiple causation' or 'equifinality' (King et al. 1994).

In recognition of these complex dynamics, Russett and Oneal (2001) express doubt that individual causal relationships can be properly considered in isolation. Peace among states may result from multiple and overlapping liberal behaviors, shaped by democracy and interdependence, which interact with the opportunities offered by the realist variables. Their synthesis of Kantian and realist effects emphasizes an interpretation of constraints on a state's willingness and ability to resort to violence. As a result, an understanding of any war will need 'not a uni-causal approach but a multivariate explanation' (Oneal and Russett 1999). Beck et al. (2000) similarly interpret the realist variables as creating a pre-scenario of low or high *ex ante* probability of military conflict into which the influence of the liberal variables is figured. Their conjecture is based on the notion 'that the effects of most explanatory variables are undetectably small for the vast majority of dyads, but they are large, stable, and replicable when the *ex ante* probability of conflict is large.' For instance, they argue that Swaziland and St. Lucia have no chance of going to war today even if they were to become slightly less democratic. On the contrary, if Iran and Iraq were to become more democratic, then the risk of war between the dyad might drop significantly. To model these complex interactions they use a flexible form of neural network model. Even Achen (2002) recognizes that in relation to

---

[4]A recent exception to the complexity approach is Ray's work (2003, 2005), which questions customary procedures for the quantitative analysis of theoretically complex questions in the social sciences. He argues that too many independent variables create unstable models and proposes that researchers should follow Achen's (2002) rule of three — i.e., no more than three independent variables. De Marchi et al. (2004) also find little support for complexity in their analysis. This has been rebutted by Beck et al. (2004).

peace we need to consider that "different groups of people have unique histories, respond to their own special circumstances, and obey distinctive causal patterns". As a result of these unique histories, he suggests the need for political scientists to develop "intimate knowledge of their observations that would constrain our choice of estimators and discipline our formal theories".

Like Russett and Oneal (2001) and Beck et al. (2004), we also share this understanding about complexity and militarized conflict behavior. Indeed, our research over the past years has tried to analyze the influence of competing or confounding variables, while and also look for interactions and non-linearity that characterize different paths to peace and war (Lagazio and Russett 2004; Lagazio and Marwala 2006). Some of our results indicate that a strong positive and reinforcing feedback loop exists between trade and democracy, while a significant interaction effect also runs from democracy and trade to key realist variables (power ratio, allies and geographical proximity).

A sophisticated explanation of how the two liberal variables may interact has been provided by Papayoanou (1996, 1997). Papayoanou develops a formal argument that explicitly incorporates the interaction between democratic political structures and economic interdependence. He argues that political leaders are constrained by the pattern and level of economic ties as well as by the domestic political institutions. The higher the combined constraints, the less likely an interstate conflict is. Another important concept that emerges from Papayoanou's work is related to the positive multiplicative effect that the interaction of the two liberal variables may produce. Although the argument is not fully developed, Papayoanou seems to suggest that in democracies the economic constraints acquire more weight. This is because democratic institutions allow economic interest groups to be powerful in bargaining and coalition formation (Papayoanou 1996, 1997). Indeed, high levels of dyadic trade often create a need for new institutions to manage and stabilize the existing commercial relations. These new institutions within a democratic political competition add more restraints on militarized behavior.

More recently, Gelpi and Grieco (2008) also pay attention to the interaction between democracy and trade. They argue that 'the combined influence of democracy and interdependence may create a powerful web of constraint that reinforces the zone of peace among increasingly interdependent democracies'. To retain their office, democratic leaders will generally have to provide public policy successes, whose benefits are widely shared by the electorate. One example of such a public policy success is that of aggregate economic growth. As result of the high incentive to promote growth, economic constraints in democracies are enhanced and increased (Gelpi and Grieco 2008).

The acceptance of complexity as an attribute of conflict behavior has also triggered other subfields of conflict analysis. Iswaran and Percy (2010) successfully applied a complex model based on Bayesian neural networks and generalized linear models to conflict management. Coppola Jr. and Szidarovszky (2004) developed a highly interactive and non-linear model to capture the relationship between water supply and environmental health risk, while Mubareka and Ehrlich (2010) successfully used ground and satellite data to identify and model environmental indicators to assess population vulnerability to conflict. All these attempts indicate that conflict behaviors, ranging from interstate to intrastate and human security, follow a path of complex and multiple-conjectural causation.

A constant interplay and dialogue between generalization and supporting theory on one hand and the consideration of individual cases on the other, is essential to uncover complex events displaying multiple convergent causal conditions. There is not a single path to war and peace but multiple possibilities. Each possibility represents a different way in which the constraints, for instance provided by democracy and economic interdependence, and the opportunities, offered by proximity, alliance, and power, can interact to influence state behavior in the international context. The power of these complex dynamics can only emerge from theoretical and methodological models especially designed to reveal all the interactions and reciprocal relations existing among the suggested factors. By analyzing some of the most important reciprocal relations, which are deemed to exist between the realist and liberal variables, as well as relations between democracy, economic interdependence and international organizations, we believe that a better understanding of militarized interstate disputes can be achieved. At the same time, we leave to others to investigate additional reciprocal linkages and factors that we have not included in our analysis. More paths to war and peace may need to be uncovered.

1.4   Computational Intelligence in Interstate Conflict Analysis

In the light of the dominance of statistical methods in conflict research, we need to consider the benefits that can result when computational intelligence methodologies are applied to conflict data. Statistically trained political scientists may ask: why computational intelligence? Wouldn't the simpler and more established multivariate statistical techniques do better? Answers to these questions can be articulated both from a methodological and theoretical level. This section addresses these questions by summarizing the key reasons why computational intelligence could provide a valid approach for interstate conflict analysis. A brief explanation of what we mean by Computational Intelligence (CI) will also be provided.

Computational Intelligence is a fairly new research field, which is still in a process of evolution. As a result, competing definitions of CI exist within the literature. At a more general level, CI comprises a set of computing systems with the ability to learn and deal with new events/situations, such that the systems are perceived to have one or more attributes of reason and intelligence. Following this understanding, Poole et al. (1998) defined CI as " ... the study of the design of intelligent agents. ... An intelligent agent is a system that acts intelligently: What it does is appropriate for its circumstances and its goal. It is flexible to changing environments and changing goals, it learns from experience, and it makes appropriate choices given perceptual limitations and finite computation (power)."

This general definition implies that CI is closely related and significantly overlapping with 'soft computing.' In contrast to hard computing, soft computing can tolerate uncertainty and partial truth since its guidance principle is to exploit 'the tolerance for imprecision' (Zadeh 1998). The comparison between soft and hard computing also mirrors another important demarcation that is present in the literature: the difference between traditional Artificial Intelligence (AI) and CI.

Bezdek (1994) argues that CI "... deals with only numerical (low-level) data, has pattern recognition components, does not use knowledge in the artificial intelligence sense; and additionally ... (begins to) exhibit (i) computational adaptability, (ii) computational fault tolerance, (iii) speed approaching human-like turnaround, and (iv) error rates that approximate human performance."

Many computational intelligent researchers agree with Bezdek's distinction. CI is deemed to be different from traditional artificial intelligence (AI). The main differences are:

- AI handles a symbolic knowledge representation, while CI handles a numeric representation;
- AI is concerned with high-level cognitive functions, while CI focuses on the low-level cognitive functions; and
- AI analyzes the structure of a given problem to construct an intelligent system based upon this structure, thus operating in a top-down manner, while CI expects the structure to emerge from an unordered beginning, thus operating in a bottom-up manner (Craenen and Eiben 2002; Duch 2007).

We believe that although traditional AI tends to be more structured and rule-driven than CI, while CI represents a significant subset of AI rather than a different field. Our definition of CI tends to focus more on the adaptation and self-organizing ability of the intelligent computing systems. Therefore we include in the definition any paradigms, algorithms, systems and implementations that enable or facilitate appropriate actions (intelligent behavior) in complex and changing environments. The techniques included in this book — artificial neural network, support vector machines, neuro-fuzzy systems, rough sets, neuro-rough models, evolutionary computation, and swarm intelligence — are all capable of adaptation, self-organization and autonomously acquiring and integrating knowledge. Furthermore, all of them can be used either in a supervised or an unsupervised learning mode. Supervised learning usually produces classifiers from class-labeled training datasets. Classifiers are basically viewed as a function that maps data samples to corresponding class labels. On the other hand, unsupervised learning distinguishes itself from supervised learning by the fact that no class-labeled data is available in the training phase. It groups data points based upon their similarities.

After this brief introduction on the meaning and definition of CI, we can now deal with the theoretical and methodological reasons why CI can provide a useful methodology for the analysis of international conflicts. We believe that this relies on three important features of CI: *Flexibility, Interactivity*, and *Endorsement of Dependency*.

1.4.1 Flexibility

First, CI models impose no *a priori* constraints on the nature of the data examined. The input–output modeling is achieved without any restricting assumption of any particular probabilistic distribution for the independent or dependent variables. Additionally, no rigidly predefined model is superposed on the data structure. Indeed the relationships between dependent and independent variables can be as complex, or as simple, as our general theory of the phenomenon requires. Even when the theory leaves rooms for uncertainty, as an accurate knowledge of the phenomenon may be difficult to achieve, CI can efficiently deal with the unknown. This is because model formulation in CI is shaped not only by theoretical, but also empirical, considerations. (For a recent review of CI see Eberhart and Shi 2007). By learning from the data structure itself, CI models can fill the gap between an initial uncertainty of the assumed nature of the phenomenon and the formulation of an efficient mathematical model, making CI methodology a middle range approach between deductive and inductive model building. Because of their flexible functional form, CI models can support theory and data on international conflicts. For instance, CI can approximate and test models derived from strategic theory on international conflicts to any degree of precision (Beck et al. 2004). This cannot be said about some of the statistical models that have dominated the conflict literature. Signorino and Yilmaz (2003) have proved that the simplest form of strategic interaction among the dyads is violated by the restrictions embedded in logit models, thus making the logit estimates "biased and inconsistent." On the contrary, CI could find, test and confirm flexile and complex patterns indicated by theories on militarized conflict behavior. Furthermore, without de-emphasizing model building based on first principles, CI modelling can also strengthen theory-building by supporting a constant interplay between theory and data.

1.4.2 Interactivity

Second, CI can provide a powerful method to develop non-linear and interactive models of militarized disputes, redressing the restrictive linear and fixed effect assumptions which have dominated the field. As explained in the previous section, recent development in conflict analysis appears to indicate that militarized conflicts display a multiple causation nature. There is not a single path to war and peace but multiple and overlapping behaviors displaying complex interactions. This interactive and non-linear perspective can be fully embraced by CI. By superposing multiple non-linear functions and avoiding *a priori* constraints on the functional nature of the data examined, CI can construct different causal structures in the same model and combine them together in a systematic way (Tiao and Tsay 1994). Indeed, a wide variability of the inputs' effect is allowed, while avoiding the independence assumption of the random effect model (Beck et al. 2000). In practical terms this means that CI models will not estimate that the same change in the explanatory variables between Swaziland and St. Lucia, or Iran and Iraq (for instance caused by an increase in the level of democratization) will produce the same risk of war between these two quite different dyads.

1.4.3   Endorsement of Dependency

Finally, CI models do not require independent observations, and thus can deal with the suspected influences that militarized events exercise on each other across space and time (Sarle 1994). As argued in the previous section, the conflict history of a state can, either positively or negatively, affect the state's willingness to become involved in future conflict (Beck et al. 1998). In addition the history of other dyads may also have an impact on the conflict behavior of a specific dyad, for instance as in the case of Iraq-Iran and Iran-US. As previously argued existing approaches to overcome temporal and space dependency remain problematic, therefore CI could provide a viable ad interesting approach better suited to model conflict data.

The choice of the method should be directed by the researcher's initial theory on conflicts as well as the objective of the exercise. The assumed nature of the process and the theoretical implications embedded in the selected method must match if we aim to produce meaningful results. Since conflict events emerge in the literature as a complex phenomenon characterized by non-linearity, multiple causation, dependency and interaction, CI appears to offer a viable and much needed methodology. Indeed, the conceptual features of CI efficiently complement the needs of conflict research. The case for CI in conflict analysis is then driven by the need to endorse the full spectrum of the nature of international conflicts and to look for tools of greater expressive power that can embrace problems that the research community could not previously define. CI's features of being a flexible, interactive and free of independent assumptions efficiently match the assumed characteristics of conflict events of being highly non-linear, massively interactive, and largely context dependent. The highly flexible approach, which CI models provide, can then establish non-linearity, multiple causation and interaction as characterizing features of conflict behavior, while opening new possibilities for theory building. CI can assist researchers in their effort to formulate more complex theories on conflict behavior moving away from the linear and parsimonious paradigm that has dominated a certain type of discourse in the literature. Ripley's (1993) warning to statisticians that they have worked in a simply structured linear world for too long can also be extend to the international conflict field. As long as our theoretical position can explain the need for additional complexity, there should be no reason to fear, and much to gain by these more sophisticated methods. Indeed, the richness of conflict behavior, which traditional and qualitative international relations study has often emphasized, may finally be expressed in a rigorous manner using a quantitative framework.

One final observation can be made. The search for new methods underlines the creative power of scientific inquiry. Root-Bernstein's (1989) idea of science stresses this important aspect of human analysis: 'Scientific "tools of thought" . . . have been developed not only to reason and test, but to invent.' At some point new questions are formulated. We construct new tools to see what we could not see before with the tools at hand. CI methodology goes a long way towards that objective, and by doing so, allows the development of new ideas for an old problem. Conflict analysis can only progress by applying these new methods.

1.5   Data and Variables

This section describes the data and variables that we have used to develop the CI models. Our data set was the population of politically relevant dyads from 1885 to 2001 (ALL) as described extensively and used by Oneal and Russett (2005).[5] We chose the politically relevant population (contiguous dyads plus all dyads containing a major power) because it sets a hard test for prediction. Omitting all distant dyads composed of weak states means we omit much of the influence that variables not very amenable to policy intervention (distance and national power) would exert in the full data set. By that omission we make our job harder by reducing the predictive power of such variables, but also make it more interesting. By focusing only on dyads that either involve major powers or are contiguous, we test the discriminative power of the CI models on a difficult set of cases. The CI models were fed with only highly informative data since every dyad can be deemed to be at risk of incurring a dispute. Yet it is harder for the models to discriminate between the two classes (dyad-years with disputes and those without disputes) because the politically relevant group is more homogeneous (e.g., closer, more interdependent) than the all-dyad data set.

The dependent variable of the models consisted of a binary variable which indicates the onset of a militarized interstate dispute (MID) of any severity (Maoz 1999). Only dyads with no dispute or with only the initial year of the militarized conflict, ranging from any severity to war, are included, since our concern, related to early warning, is to predict the onset of a conflict rather than its continuation. For dispute or conflict (in this book we use the two words as synonym), we use the extended definition of dispute/conflict meaning a set of interactions between states involving threats to use military force, display of military force or actual use of military force.

We included seven dyadic independent variables. Our theoretical perspective is that of the Kantian research program, addressed to the system of directed and interactive relations among democracy, economic interdependence, international

---

[5]Data have been provided by John Oneal and are posted at http://www.bama.ua.edu/~joneal/CMPS2005.

organizations, and militarized conflict or the lack thereof, as laid out in Russett and Oneal (2001). Consistent with previous works, which also underline the interactive relationships among incentives and constraints, the analysis, included four variables, usually associated with the realist argument, and three "Kantian" variables. The realist variables include *Allies*, a binary measure coded 1 if the members of a dyad are linked by any form of military alliance. *Contingency* is also binary, coded 1 if both states are geographically contiguous, and *Distance* is an interval measure of the distance between the two states' capitals. *Major power* is a binary variable coded 1 if either or both states in the dyad are a major power. The Kantian variable *Democracy* is measured on a scale where 10 is an extreme democracy and −10 is an extreme autocracy. Following the Kantian approach identifying the country with the lowest level of democracy as the weakest link, we have taken the value of the less democratic country in the dyad for our analyses. The Kantian variable *Dependency* is measured as the sum of the countries import and export with its partner divided by the Gross Domestic Product of the stronger country. This is a continuous variable measuring the level of economic interdependence (dyadic trade as a portion of a state's gross domestic product) of the less economically dependent state in the dyad. *Capability* is the logarithm, to the base 10, of the ratio of the total population plus the number of people in urban areas plus industrial energy consumption plus iron and steel production plus the number of military personnel in active duty plus military expenditure in dollars in the last 5 years measured on stronger country to weak country. Most of these measures (e.g., MIDs, alliances, contiguity, major power, and capability) derive from conceptualizations of the COW project and are measured by COW. We lag all independent variables by 1 year to make temporally plausible any inference of causation. There are other variables that can be included but are deemed to be beyond the scope of this book.

1.6 Summary of the Book

Chapter 2 introduces the Bayesian and the evidence frameworks to build the automatic relevance determination technique. These procedures are described in detail, the relevant literature reviews are conducted, and their use is justified. The automatic relevance determination procedure is then applied to determine the relevance of interstate variables that are critical for modeling interstate conflict.

Chapter 3 presents and then compares the multi-layer perceptron neural network to the radial basis function neural network to help comprehend and forecast interstate conflict. These two methods are described in detail and justified with a review of relevant literature and their application to interstate conflict.

In Chap. 4, two Bayesian methods are explained and compared for interstate conflict prediction. The first one is the Bayesian method that applies the Gaussian approximation method to estimate the posterior probability for neural network weights, given the observed data and the evidence framework to train a multi-layer perceptron neural network. The second one treats the posterior probability as is, and then applies the hybrid Monte Carlo procedure to train the multi-layer perceptron neural network.

In Chap. 5, support vector machines are introduced in this chapter for the prediction of militarized interstate disputes and compares this to the hybrid Monte Carlo trained multi-layer perceptron neural networks.

Chapter 6 investigates the level of transparency of the Takagi-Sugeno neuro-fuzzy model by applying it to militarized interstate dispute prediction and comparing these to support vector machine model.

In Chap. 7, the rough set method is applied to model militarized interstate dispute. Two granulization methods for the input data are presented and these are the equal-width-bin and equal-frequency-bin partitioning procedures. The rough set model is also compared to the neuro-fuzzy model which is introduced.

In Chap. 8, approaches to optimally granulize rough set partition sizes using particle swarm optimization and hill climbing techniques, are proposed. The suggested procedures are compared to that based on the equal-width-bin procedure.

Chapter 9 introduces techniques to optimally granulize rough set partition sizes using simulated annealing method. The proposed technique is applied to model the militarized interstate dispute data. The proposed method is compared to the rough set partition technique that is based on particle swarm optimization.

In Chap. 10, technique to optimally granulize rough set partition sizes using genetic algorithm method is proposed. The proposed method is applied to model the militarized interstate dispute data. The suggested method is then compared to the rough set partition technique that is based on simulated annealing.

In Chap. 11 a neuro-rough model which is a combination of a multi-layered perceptron and rough set theory is proposed. The model is formulated using Bayesian framework and trained using Monte Carlo technique and Metropolis criterion. The model is then tested on an ante-natal dataset and is able to combine the accuracy of the Bayesian multi-layer perceptron model and the transparency of rough set model. The proposed technique is then compared to the genetic algorithm optimized rough sets.

In Chap. 12 a practical approach for early warning and conflict management is put forward, which is based on a control system for interstate conflicts. This system makes use of a neural network and a feedback control approach. Controllable variables are identified and assessed with regards to their ability to maximize the occurrence of peace.

References

Achen, C.: Toward a new political methodology: microfoundations and ART. Ann. Rev. Polit. Sci. **5**, 423–450 (2002)

Babst, D.: A force for peace. Ind. Res. **14**, 55 (1972)

Barbieri, K.: Economic interdependence: a path to peace or a source of interstate conflicts? J. Peace Res. **33**, 29–50 (1996)

Barbieri, K., Peters, R.A.: Measure for mis-measure: a response to Gartzke and Li. J. Peace Res. **40**, 713–720 (2003)

Beck, N., Katz, J.: Throwing the baby out with the bathwater: a comment on Green, Kim, and Yoon. Int. Organ. **55**, 487–495 (2001)

Beck, N., Katz, J., Tucker, R.: Taking time seriously in binary time-series-cross-section analysis. Am. J. Polit. Sci. **42**, 1260–1288 (1998)

Beck, N., King, G., Zheng, L.: Improving quantitative studies of international conflict: a conjecture. Am. Polit. Sci. Rev. **94**, 21–35 (2000)

Beck, N., King, G., Zheng, L.: Theory and evidence in international conflict: a response to de Marchi, Gelpi and Grynaviski. Am. Polit. Sci. Rev. **98**, 379–389 (2004)

Bennett, D.S., Stam, A.C.: Research design and estimator choices for analyzing interstate dyads: when decisions matter. J. Conflict Resolut. **44**, 653–679 (2000)

Bezdek, J.C.: What Is Computational Intelligence? Computational Intelligence Imitating Life. IEEE Press, New York (1994)

Boehmer, C., Gartzke, E., Nordstrom, T.: Do intergovernmental organizations promote peace? World Polit. **57**, 1–38 (2004)

Bremer, S.A.: Dangerous dyads: conditions affecting the likelihood of interstate war. J. Conflict Res. **36**, 309–341 (1992)

Bueno de Mesquita, B., Lalman, D.: War and Reason: Domestic and International Imperatives. Yale University Press, New Haven (1992)

Bueno de Mesquita, B., Ray, J.L.: The national interest versus individual political ambition: democracy, autocracy, and the reciprocation of force and violence in militarized interstate dispute. In: Diehl, P.F. (ed.) The Scourge of War: New Extensions on an Old Problem. University of Michigan Press, Ann Arbor (2004)

Bueno de Mesquita, B., Siverson, R.: War and the survival of political leaders: a comparative study of regime types and political accountability. Am. Polit. Sci. Rev. **89**, 841–855 (1995)

Chernoff, F.: The study of democratic peace and progress in international relations. Int. Stud. Perspect. **6**, 49–77 (2004)

Coppola Jr., E., Szidarovszky, F.: Conflict between water supply and environmental health risk: a computational neural network approach. Int. Game Theory Rev. **6**, 475–492 (2004)

Craenen, B., Eiben, A.: Computational Intelligence. Encyclopedia of Life Support Sciences. EOLSS Co. Ltd., Oxford (2002)

De Marchi, S., Gelpi, C.F., Grynaviski, J.D.: Untangling neural nets. Am. Polit. Sci. Rev. **98**, 371–378 (2004)

de Vries, M.: Interdependence, co-operation and conflict: an empirical analysis. J. Peace Res. **27**, 429–444 (1990)

Deutsch, K., Singer, J.D.: Multipolar power systems and international stability. World Polit. **16**, 390–406 (1964)

Dixon, W.: Democracy and the management of international conflict. J. Conflict Resolut. **37**, 42–68 (1993)

Domke, W.: War and the Changing Global System. Yale University Press, New Haven (1988)

Doyle, M.: Kant, liberal legacies, and foreign policy: part 1. Philos. Public Aff. **12**, 205–235 (1983)

Doyle, M.: Liberalism and world politics. Am. Polit. Sci. Rev. **80**, 1151–1169 (1986)

Duch, W.: What is computational intelligence and where is it going? In: Duch, W., Mańdziuk, J. (eds.) Challenges for Computational Intelligence. Springer, Berlin (2007)

Eberhart, R., Shi, Y.: Computational Intelligence: Concepts to Implementations. Morgan Kaufmann, Burlington (2007)

Ember, C., Melvin, E., Bruce, R.: Peace between participatory polities: a cross-national test of the "democracies rarely fight each other" hypothesis. World Polit. **44**, 573–599 (1992)

Farber, H., Gowa, J.: Polities and peace. Int. Security. **20**, 123–146 (1995)

Gasiorowski, M., Polacheck, S.W.: Conflict and interdependence: east-west trade and linkages in the era of détente. J. Conflict Res. **26**, 709–729 (1982)

Geller, D.S., Singer, D.: Nations at War: A Scientific Study of Int Conflicts. Cambridge University Press, Cambridge (1998)

Gelpi, C., Grieco, J.M.: Democracy, trade and the sources of the liberal peace. J. Peace Res. **45**, 327–344 (2008)

Gleditsch, N.P., Hegre, H.: Peace and democracy: three levels of analysis. J. Conflict Resolut. **41**, 283–310 (1997)

Goertz, G.: Contexts of International Politics. Cambridge University Press, Cambridge (1994)

Goetz, G., Diehl, P.: Territorial Changes and International Conflicts. Routledge, London (1992)

Gowa, J.: Democratic states and international disputes. Int. Organ. **49**, 511–522 (1995)

Gowa, J.: Ballots and Bullets: The Elusive Democratic Peace. Princeton University Press, Princeton (1999)

Gowa, J., Mansfield, E.: Power politics and international trade. Am. Polit. Sci. Rev. **87**, 408–420 (1993)

Green, D., Kim, S.Y., Yoon, D.: Dirty pool. Int. Organ. **55**, 441–468 (2001)

Iswaran, N., Percy, D.F.: Conflict analysis using bayesian neural networks and generalized linear models. J. Op. Res. Soc. **61**, 332–341 (2010)

Keohane, R., Nye, J.S.: Power and Interdependence. Scott, Foresman, Glenview (1989)

Kim, S.Y.: Ties that bind: The role of trade in international conflict processes, 1950–1992. Paper presented at the American Political Science Association, Boston, 3–7 Sept 1998

King, G.: Proper nouns and methodological propriety: pooling dyads in international relations data. Int. Organ. **55**, 497–507 (2001)

King, G., Keohane, R., Verba, S.: Designing Social Inquiry: Scientific Inference in Qualitative Research. Princeton University Press, Princeton (1994)

Kocs, S.: Territorial disputes and interstate war, 1945–1987. J. Polit. **57**, 159–175 (1995)

Lagazio, M., Marwala, T.: Assessing different bayesian neural network models for militarised interstate dispute outcome and variable influence. Social Sci. Comput. Rev. **24**, 119–131 (2006)

Lagazio, M., Russett, B.: A neural network analysis of militarized international disputes, 1985–1992: temporal stability and causal complexity. In: Diehl, P.F. (ed.) The Scourge of War: New Extensions on an Old Problem. University of Michigan Press, Ann Arbor (2004)

Layne, C.: Kant or cant: the myth of the democratic peace. Int. Security. **19**, 5–49 (1994)

Lemke, D.: The tyranny of distance: redefining relevant dyads. Int. Interact. **21**, 23–38 (1995)

Lemke, D., Reed, W.: Regime types and status quo evaluations: power transition theory and the democratic peace. Int. Interact. **22**, 143–164 (1996)

Leng, R., Singer, J.D.: A multitheoretical typology of international behavior. In: Bunge, M., Galtun, J., Malitza, M. (eds.) Mathematical Approaches to Intl Relations. Romanian Academy of Social and Political Sciences, Bucharest (1977)

Levy, J.: Reflections on the scientific study of war. In: Vasquez, J.A. (ed.) What Do We Know About War? Rowman and Littlefield, Lanham (2000)

Mansfield, E.: Power, Trade, and War. Princeton University Press, Princeton (1994)

Maoz, Z.: Realist and cultural critiques of the democratic peace: a theoretical and empirical reassessment. Int. Interact. **24**, 1–89 (1998)

Maoz, Z.: Dyadic Militarized Interstate Disputes (DYMID1.1) Dataset-Version 1.1. ftp://spirit.tau.ac.il./zeevmaoz/dyadmid60.xls. Password protected (1999). Last Accessed Aug 2000

Maoz, Z., Abdolali, N.: Regime types and international conflict. J. Conflict Resolut. **33**, 3–35 (1989)

Maoz, Z., Russett, B.: Alliance, contiguity, wealth, and political stability: is the lack of conflict among democracies a statistical artifact? Int. Interact. **17**, 245–268 (1992)

Maoz, Z., Russett, B.: Normative and structural causes of democratic peace, 1946–1986. Am. Polit. Sci. Rev. **87**, 624–638 (1993)

Mearsheimer, J.J.: The false promise of international institutions. Int. Security. **19**, 5–49 (1995)

Morgan, C., Howard, C.S.: Domestic structure, decisional constraints, and war: so why Kant democracies fight. J. Conflict Resolut. **35**, 187–211 (1991)

Morgan, C., Schwebach, V.: Take two democracies and call me in the morning: a prescription for peace? Int. Interact. **17**, 305–320 (1992)

Mubareka, S., Ehrlich, D.: Identifying and modelling environmental indicators for assessing population vulnerability to conflict using ground and satellite data. Ecol. Indic. **10**, 493–503 (2010)

Oneal, J.R.: Confirming the liberal peace with analyses of directed dyads. In: Starr, H. (ed.) Crossing Boundaries: Internal-External Approaches, Levels and Methods of Analysis in International Politics, pp. 1885–2001. Palgrave Macmillan, New York (2006)

Oneal, J., Russett, B.: The classical liberals were right: democracy, interdependence, and conflict, 1950–1985. Int. Stud. Quart. **41**, 267–294 (1997)

Oneal, J., Russett, B.: Is the liberal peace just an artefact of cold war interests? Assessing recent critiques. Int. Interact. **25**, 213–241 (1999)

Oneal, J., Russett, B.: Clear and clean: the fixed effects of democracy and economic interdependence. Int. Organ. **52**, 469–486 (2001)

Oneal, J., Russett, B.: Rule of three, let it be? When more really is better. Conflict Manag. Peace Sci. **22**, 293–310 (2005)

Oneal, J., Russett, B.: Seeking peace in a post-cold war world of hegemony and terrorism. In: Russett, B. (ed.) Policy and Purpose in the Global Community. Palgrave Macmillan, New York (2006)

Oneal, J., Oneal, F., Maoz, Z., Russett, B.: The liberal peace: interdependence, democracy, and international conflict, 1950–1985. J. Peace Res. **33**, 21 (1996)

Oneal, J., Russett, B., Berbaum, M.: Causes of peace: democracy, interdependence, and international organizations, 1985–1992. Int. Stud. Q. **47**, 371–494 (2003)

Papayoanou, P.: Interdependence, institutions, and the balance of power. Int. Security. **20**, 42–76 (1996)

Papayoanou, P.: Economic interdependence and the balance of power. Int. Stud. Quart. **41**, 120–131 (1997)

Pevehouse, J., Russett, B.: Democratic international governmental organizations promote peace. Int. Organ. **60**, 969–1000 (2005)

Polacheck, S.: Conflict and trade: an economics approach to political international interactions. In: Isard, W., Anderton, C.H. (eds.) Economics of Arms Reduction and the Peace Process. North Holland, Amsterdam (1992)

Poole, D., Mackworth, A., Goebel, R.: Computational Intelligence – A Logical Approach. Oxford University Press, Oxford (1998)

Ragin, C.: The Comparative Method: Moving beyond Qualitative and Quantitative Strategies. University of California Press, Berkeley (1987)

Ray, J.L.: Explaining interstate conflict and war: what should be controlled for? Conflict Manag. Peace Sci. **20**, 1–32 (2003)

Ray, J.L.: Constructing multivariate analyses (of dangerous dyads). Conflict Manag. Peace Sci **22**, 277–292 (2005)

Reuveny, R., Kang, H.: International trade, political conflict/cooperation, and Granger causality. Am. J. Polit. Sci. **40**, 943–970 (1996)

Richardson, L.: Statistics of Deadly Quarrel. Boxwood Press, Pittsburgh (1960)

Ripley, B.: Statistical aspects of neural networks. In: Barndorff-Nielsen, O.E., Jensen, J.L., Kendall, W.S. (eds.) Network and Chaos-Statistical and Probabilistic Aspects. Chapman & Hall, London (1993)

Root-Bernstein, R.: How scientists really think. Perspect. Biol. Med. **32**, 472–488 (1989)

Rosenau, J.M.: Citizenship in a changing global order. In: Rosenau, J.M., Czempiel, E. (eds.) Governance Without Government. Cambridge University Press, Cambridge (1992)

Rummel, R.J.: Understanding Conflict and War: War, Power, Peace. Sage, Beverly Hills (1979)

Russett, B., Antholis, W.: Do democracies fight each other? Evidence from the peloponnesian war. J. Peace Res. **29**, 415–434 (1992)

Russett, B., Oneal, J.R.: Triangulating Peace: Democracy, Interdependence, and International Organizations. W. W. Norton, New York (2001)

Sarle, W.: Neural network and statistical models. In: Proceedings of the 19th Annual SAS Users Group International Conference, Dallas. pp. 1–13 (1994)

Schweller, R.L., Priess, D.: A Tale of Two Realisms: Expanding the Institutions Debate. Mershon Int. Stud. Review. **41**, 2 (1997)

Signorino, C.S., Yilmaz, K.: Strategic misspecification in regression models. Am. J. Polit. Sci. **47**, 551–566 (2003)

Singer, J.D.: The level-of-analysis problem in international relations. In: Knorr, K., Verba, S. (eds.) The International System: Theoretical Essays. Princeton University Press, Princeton (1961)

Singer, J.D., Small, M.: The Wages of War, 1816–1965: A Statistical Handbook. Wiley, New York (1972)

Siverson, R., Starr, H.: Diffusion of War: A Study of Opportunity and Willingness. University of Michigan Press, Ann Arbor (1991)

Small, M., Singer, J.D.: The war-proneness of democratic regimes. Jerusalem J. Int. Relat. **1**, 50–69 (1976)

Spiro, D.: The insignificance of the liberal peace. Int. Security. **19**, 50–86 (1994)

Stein, A.: Governments, economic interdependence, and international cooperation. In: Tetlock, P., Husbands, J., Jervis, R., Stern, P., Tilly, C. (eds.) Behavior, Society, and International Conflict. Oxford University Press, Oxford (1993)

Thompson, W.R., Tucker, R.: A tale of two democratic peace critiques. J. Conflict Res. **41**, 428–454 (1997)

Tiao, G.C., Tsay, R.S.: Some advances in non-linear and adaptive modelling in time-series. J. Forecasting. **13**, 109–131 (1994)

Vasquez, J.: The War Puzzle. Cambridge University Press, Cambridge (1993)

Waltz, K.: Theory of International Politics. Addison-Wesley, Reading (1979)

Weart, S.: Peace among democratic and oligarchic republics. J. Peace Res. **31**, 299–316 (1994)

Weede, E.: Democracy and war involvement. J. Conflict Resolut. **28**, 649–664 (1984)

Weede, E.: Some simple calculations on democracy and war involvement. J. Peace Res. **29**, 377–383 (1992)

Zadeh, L.A.: Roles of soft computing and fuzzy logic in the conception, design and deployment of information / intelligent systems. In: Kaynak, O., Zadeh, L.A., Turksen, B., Rudas, I.J. (eds.) Computational Intelligence: Soft Computing and Fuzzy-Neuro Integration with Applications. Springer, Berlin (1998)

Chapter 2
Automatic Relevance Determination for Identifying Interstate Conflict

2.1 Introduction

Current developments in the liberal peace literature has underscored the significance of handling international conflicts as complex phenomena which show non-linear patterns of interactions. In this chapter, militarized interstate disputes (MIDs) is defined as the threat to use military force or a display of military force, which is conducted in an explicit and overtly non-accidental way (Gochman and Maoz 1990). The notion of developing accurate models of interstate disputes has challenged the restrictive linear and fixed effect assumptions that have dominated political science literature. Building on the assumptions and logic of Kantian peace theory (Oneal and Russett 2001) more complex explanations of interstate conflicts have been promoted as well as more complex statistical models that are better capacitated to handle the monotonic features of conflict data. From the explanation side, the relationships between dyadic attributes, which are two states parameters deemed to influence militarized interstate disputes, have been interpreted as highly interdependent. Beck et al. (2000) interpret the dyadic attributes as parameters that generate a pre-scenario probability of military conflict. This point has been confirmed by Lagazio and Russet (2002). Their analysis emphasizes that low levels of the key liberal variables (economic interdependence, democracy, and shared membership in international organizations) together with distance, relative power, and alliances interact to produce multiplicative effects that enhance the likelihood of a dispute, but high levels of those variables do not have the same multiplicative effect on peace. Relative power also seems to exert a strong influence on dispute outcomes when non-democracies are involved, but this influence may be much weaker when democracies settle their disputes (Gelpi and Griesdorf 2001). Special interstate dependency also needs to be taken into consideration. Having states experiencing conflicts as neighbors may increase the negative influence of some of the dyadic attributes, while having democracies as neighbors may reduce it (Gleditsch and Wards 2000). Basically, it is vital that the relevance of each dyadic variable on the prediction of interstate dispute be estimated.

In order to shed further light on the complex relationships that are at work in interstate conflicts, in this chapter the automatic relevance determination method is proposed to estimate the relevance of each dyadic variable.The automatic relevance determination method proposed in this chapter is based on the Bayesian framework. In this chapter, Bayesian neural networks (Neal 1994; MacKay 1991, 1992) are proposed and then utilized to model the relationships between liberal variables and the MID with the aim of estimating the relevance of each variable. Neural networks have been used before to model complex interrelationships between dyadic parameters and the MID (Zeng 1999; Marwala and Lagazio 2004; Neal 1998). With the exception of Marwala and Lagazio (2004), these previous attempts have not used the automatic relevance determination method to assess variable impacts on peace and war. At the core of the automatic relevance determination method are the following mathematical techniques which are described in detail in the next section: neural networks, Bayesian framework, evidence framework, and optimization methods.

2.2 Mathematical Framework

In this chapter, the Automatic Relevance Determination (ARD) method is defined as an efficient method used to determine the relevance of each input variable in its ability to predict interstate conflict. The ARD achieves this by optimizing the hyperparameters to maximize the evidence. Because this book is primarily on the prediction of interstate conflict, models have been used to estimate the risk of two countries entering a militarized interstate conflict. In this chapter the ARD method is a method that determines the relevance of each input variable with respect to its ability to estimate the risk of two countries entering into militarized disputes. Wang and Lu (2006) successfully implemented the ARD method to estimate influential variables in modeling the ozone layer. Nummenmaa et al. (2007) successfully applied the ARD to a dataset where a male subject was presented with uncontaminated tone and checker board reversal stimuli, individually and in combination, in employing a MRI-based cortical surface model. Fu and Browne (2007) succesfully applied an ensemble of neural networks to create a more dependable ARD method.

Ulusoy and Bishop (2006) applied ARD to identify relevant features for object recognition of 2D images. Other applications of the ARD include the work of Smyrnakis and Evans (2007), where they successfully applied the ARD method to rank the variables to determine ischaemic episodes. Other successful applications of the ARD include identifying regions of the thalamus implicated in schizophrenia (Browne 2006). Lisboa et al. (2009) used the partial logistic artificial neural network for estimating risks, Wu et al. (2010) used the ARD to estimate relevant variables in multichannel EEG, and Van Calster et al. (2006) used the ARD to estimate relevant variables in classifying ovarian tumors. One component of the ARD is neural networks, which is the subject of the next section.

2.2.1 Neural Networks

This section gives a summary of neural networks in the context of interstate conflict modelling (Habtemariam et al. 2005). A neural network is an information processing technique that is motivated by the way biological nervous systems, like the human brain, process information. It is a computer-based machine that is intended to model the manner in which the brain processes a particular task or function of interest (Haykin 1999).

It is a remarkably powerful mechanism that has found successful use in mechanical engineering (Marwala and Hunt 1999; Vilakazi and Marwala 2007), civil engineering (Marwala 2000, 2001), aerospace engineering (Marwala 2003), biomedical engineering (Mohamed, et al. 2006), finance (Patel and Marwala 2006), statistics (Marwala 2009), and political science (Lagazio and Marwala 2005). In this chapter, neural networks are viewed as generalized regression models that can model any data, linear or non-linear. A neural network consists of four main components (Haykin 1999):

- the processing units u_j, where each u_j has a certain activation level $a_j(t)$ at any point in time;
- weighted inter-connections between various processing units. These inter-connections determine how the activation of 1 unit leads to the input for another unit;
- an activation rule, which acts on the set of input signals at a unit to produce a new output signal; and
- a learning rule that specifies how to adjust the weights for a given input/output pair (Haykin 1999; Freeman and Skapura 1991).

Because of their capacity to derive meaning from complex data, neural networks are used to extract patterns and detect trends that are too complicated to be observed by many other computer methods (Hassoun 1995). A trained neural network can be considered as an expert in the class of information it has been given to explore (Yoon and Peterson 1990; Lunga and Marwala 2006). This expert can then be used to provide predictions given new situations. Because of their ability to adapt to non-linear data, neural networks have been used to model various non-linear applications (Leke et al. 2007).

The structure of neural processing units and their inter-connections can have a profound impact on the processing abilities of neural networks. Consequently, there are many different connections that define how data flows between the input, hidden, and output layers.

There are a number of types of neural network architectures, some of which will be considered later, for example, the multi-layer perceptron (MLP) and the radial basis function (RBF) (Bishop 1995). For this chapter, the MLP was used to map dyadic interstate variables to a militarized interstate dispute class. The reason for using MLP was because it provides a distributed representation with

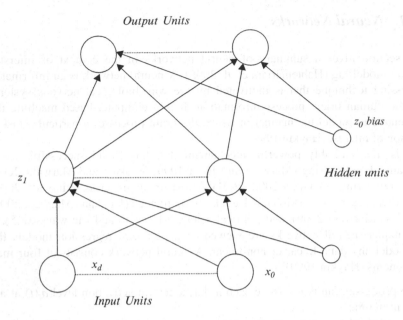

Output Units

z_0 *bias*

Hidden units

z_1

x_d

x_0

Input Units

Fig. 2.1 Feed-forward multi-layer perceptron network having two layers of adaptive weights (Marwala 2009)

respect to the input space due to cross-coupling between hidden units, while the RBF provides only local representation (Bishop 1995).

Ghate et al. (2010) successfully used the MLP neural network classifier to detect faults in three phase induction motors, while Zhang et al. (2008) used the MLP network to study gene association to diagnose diseases. Ebrahimzadeh and Khazaee (2010) applied the MLP to detect premature ventricular contractions, while Kim et al. (2010) applied the MLP for feature selection in HIV-1 protease cleavage site analysis, whereas Chiddarwar et al.(2010) used the MLP neural networks in robotics to solve kinematics problems. In this chapter, the MLP architecture contains a hyperbolic tangent basis function in the hidden units, and a logistic basis functions in the output units (Bishop 1995). A schematic diagram of the MLP is shown in Fig. 2.1.

This network architecture contains hidden units and output units and has one hidden layer. The bias parameters in the first layer are shown as mapping weights from an extra input having a fixed value of $x_0 = 1$. The bias parameters in the second layer are shown as weights from an extra hidden unit, with the activation fixed at $z_0 = 1$. The model in Fig. 2.1 can take into account the intrinsic dimensionality of the data. Models of this form can approximate any continuous function to arbitrary accuracy if the number of hidden units M is sufficiently large. The MLP may be expanded by considering several layers but it has been demonstrated by the Universal Approximation Theorem (Cybenko 1989) that a two-layered architecture is adequate for the MLP. As a result of this theorem, for this chapter, the two-layered network shown in Fig. 2.1 was selected. The relationship between MID class, y, and dyadic variables, x, may be written as follows (Bishop 1995):

$$y_k = f_{outer}\left(\sum_{j=1}^{M} w_{kj}^{(2)} f_{inner}\left(\sum_{i=1}^{d} w_{ji}^{(1)} x_i + w_{j0}^{(1)}\right) + w_{k0}^{(2)}\right) \quad (2.1)$$

Here, $w_{ji}^{(1)}$ and $w_{ji}^{(2)}$ indicate neural network weights in the first and second layers, respectively, going from input i to hidden unit j, M is the number of hidden units, d is the number of output units while $w_{j0}^{(1)}$ indicates the bias for the hidden unit j. This book used a hyperbolic tangent function for the function $f_{inner}(\bullet)$. The function $f_{outer}(\bullet)$ is logistic because the problem we are dealing with is a classification problem and, therefore, a logistic function should be used instead of a linear function (Bishop 1995). The logistic function is defined as follows (Bishop 1995):

$$f_{outer}(v) = \frac{1}{1 + e^{-v}} \quad (2.2)$$

The training of conventional neural networks identifies the network weights, while the training of probabilistic neural networks identifies the distributions of the network weights. A cost function must be chosen to identify the weights in Eq. 2.1. A *cost function* is a mathematical representation of the overall objective of the problem. For this chapter, the main objective was to identify a set of neural network weights, given the dyadic variables and conflict classes.

If the training set $D = \{x_k, y_k\}_{k=1}^{N}$ is used – where superscript N is the number of training examples, and assuming that the targets y are sampled independently given the kth inputs x_k and the weight parameters w_{kj} then the cost function, E, may be written using the cross-entropy cost function (Rosenblatt 1961; Bishop 1995):

$$E_D = -\beta \sum_{n=1}^{N} \sum_{k=1}^{K} \{t_{nk} \ln(y_{nk}) + (1 - t_{nk}) \ln(1 - y_{nk})\} \quad (2.3)$$

Here, t_{nk} is the target vector for the nth output and k^{th} training example, N is the number of training examples, K is the number of network output units, n is the index for the training pattern, β is the data contribution to the error, and k is the index for the output units.

The cross-entropy function was chosen because it has been found to be more suited to classification problems than the sum-of-square of error cost function (Bishop 1995). This function is inspired by the postulation that desired outputs are independent, binary, random variables, and the required output network response represents the conditional probability that these variables would be one. The cross-entropy cost function is based on the idea of having the value of the output represent the probability $P(C1 | x)$ for class C1. Equation 2.3 can be regularized by introducing extra information to the objective function with a penalty function to solve an ill-posed problem or to prevent over-fitting by ensuring smoothness of the solution to balance complexity and accuracy using (Bishop 1995):

$$E_W = -\frac{\alpha}{2} \sum_{j=1}^{W} w_j^2 \qquad (2.4)$$

Here α is the prior contribution to the regularization error, and W is the number of network weights. This regularization parameter penalises weights of large magnitudes (Bishop 1995; Tibshirani 1996). To solve for the weights in Eq. 2.1, the backpropagation method described in the next section was adopted.

By combining Eqs. 2.3 and 2.4, the overall fitness function can be written as follows (Bishop 1995):

$$E = \beta E_D + \alpha E_W$$

$$= -\beta \sum_{n=1}^{N} \sum_{k=1}^{K} \{t_{nk} \ln(y_{nk}) + (1 - t_{nk}) \ln(1 - y_{nk})\} - \frac{\alpha}{2} \sum_{j=1}^{W} w_j^2 \qquad (2.5)$$

2.2.1.1 Back-Propagation Method

The backpropagation method is a technique of training a neural networks which was proposed by Bryson and Ho and promoted by Rumelhart, Hinton and Williams (Rumelhart et al. 1986; Russell and Norvig 1995; Bryson and Ho 1989). Backpropagation belongs to supervised learning techniques and is essentially an application of the Delta rule. Backpropagation necessitates that the activation function (seen in Eq. 2.1) can be differentiated. The backpropagation method is divided into the propagation and weight update. The propagation aspect has these steps (Bishop 1995):

- produce the propagation's output activations by forward propagating the training pattern's input into the neural network,
- calculate the deltas of all output and hidden neurons by backpropagating the output activations in the neural network by using the training pattern's target.

The weight update feature uses the output delta and input activation to obtain the gradient of the weight. Then the weight in the opposite direction of the gradient is used by subtracting a proportion of it from the weight and then this proportion impacts the performance of the learning process. The sign of the gradient of a weight describes the direction where the error increases and this is the reason that the weight is updated in the opposite direction (Bishop 1995), and this process is repeated until convergence.

In simple terms, back-propagation is applied to identify the network weights given the training data, using an optimization method. In general, the weights can be identified using the following iterative method (Werbos et al. 1974; Zhao et al. 2010):

$$\{w\}_{i+1} = \{w\}_i - \eta \frac{\partial E}{\partial \{w\}}(\{w\}_i) \tag{2.6}$$

In Eq. 2.6, the parameter η is the learning rate while $\{\}$ represents a vector. The minimization of the objective function, E, is achieved by calculating the derivative of the errors in Eq. 2.3 with respect to the network's weight. The derivative of the error is calculated with respect to the weight which connects the hidden layer to the output layer and may be written, using the chain rule (Bishop 1995):

$$\frac{\partial E}{\partial w_{kj}} = \frac{\partial E}{\partial a_k} \frac{\partial a_k}{\partial w_{kj}}$$

$$= \frac{\partial E}{\partial y_k} \frac{\partial y_k}{\partial a_k} \frac{\partial a_k}{\partial w_{kj}}$$

$$= \sum_n f'_{outer}(a_k) \frac{\partial E}{\partial y_{nk}} z_j \tag{2.7}$$

In Eq. 2.7, $z_j = f_{inner}(a_j)$ and $a_k = \sum_{j=0}^{M} w_{kj}^{(2)} y_j$. The derivative of the error with respect to weight which connects the hidden layer to the output layer may also be written using the chain rule (Bishop 1995):

$$\frac{\partial E}{\partial w_{kj}} = \frac{\partial E}{\partial a_k} \frac{\partial a_k}{\partial w_{kj}}$$

$$= \sum_n f'_{inner}(a_j) \sum_k w_{kj} f'_{outer}(a_k) \frac{\partial E}{\partial y_{nk}} \tag{2.8}$$

In Eq. 2.8, $a_j = \sum_{i=1}^{d} w_{ji}^{(1)} x_i$. The derivative of the cost function in Eq. 2.3 may thus be written as (Bishop 1995):

$$\frac{\partial E}{\partial y_{nk}} = \frac{t_{nk}}{y_{nk}} + (1 - t_{nk})(1 - y_{nk}) \tag{2.9}$$

while that of the hyperbolic tangent function is (Bishop 1995):

$$f'_{inner}(a_j) = \sec h^2(a_j) \tag{2.10}$$

Now that it has been determined how to calculate the gradient of the error with respect to the network weights using back-propagation algorithms, Eq. 2.6 can be used to update the network weights using an optimization process until some pre-defined stopping condition is achieved. If the learning rate in Eq. 2.6 is fixed, then this is known as the *steepest descent optimization* method (Robbins and Monro 1951). On the other hand, the steepest descent method is not computationally efficient and, therefore, an improved method needs to be found. In this chapter, the scaled conjugate gradient method was implemented (Møller 1993), the subject of the next section.

2.2.1.2   Scaled Conjugate Gradient Method

The technique in which the network weights are estimated from the data is through the use of some non-linear optimization method (Mordecai 2003). In this chapter the scaled conjugate gradient method (Møller 1993) was used. Before the scaled conjugate gradient method is described, it is important to understand how it works. As indicated before, the weight vector, which gives the minimum error, is computed by taking successive steps through the weight space as shown in Eq. 2.8 until some stopping criterion is attained. Different algorithms choose this learning rate differently. In this section, the gradient descent method is discussed, followed by how it is extended to the conjugate gradient method (Hestenes and Stiefel 1952). For the gradient descent method, the step size is defined as $-\eta \partial E / \partial w$, where the parameter η is the learning rate and the gradient of the error is calculated using the back-propagation technique described in the previous section.

If the learning rate is sufficiently small, the value of the error decreases at each successive step until a minimum value for the error between the model prediction and training target data is obtained. The disadvantage with this approach is that it is computationally expensive when compared to other techniques. For the conjugate gradient method, the quadratic function of the error is minimized at every step over a progressively expanding linear vector space that includes the global minimum of the error (Luenberger 1984; Fletcher 1987; Bertsekas 1995).

For the conjugate gradient procedure, the following steps are followed (Haykin 1999; Marwala 2009; Babaie-Kafaki et al. 2010):

1. Choose the initial weight vector $\{w\}_0$.
2. Calculate the gradient vector $\frac{\partial E}{\partial \{w\}}(\{w\}_0)$.
3. At each step, n, use the line search to find $\eta(n)$ that minimizes $E(\eta)$ representing the cost function expressed in terms of η for fixed values of w and $-\frac{\partial E}{\partial \{w\}}(\{w_n\})$.
4. Check that the Euclidean norm of the vector $-\frac{\partial E}{\partial w}(\{w_n\})$ is sufficiently less than that of $-\frac{\partial E}{\partial w}(\{w_0\})$.
5. Update the weight vector using Eq. 2.5.
6. For w_{n+1}, compute the updated gradient $\frac{\partial E}{\partial \{w\}}(\{w\}_{n+1})$.
7. Use the Polak-Ribiére method to calculate:

$$\beta(n+1) = \frac{\nabla E(\{w\}_{n+1})^T (\nabla E(\{w\}_{n+1}) - \nabla E(\{w\}_n))}{\nabla E(\{w\}_n)^T \nabla E(\{w\}_n)}$$

8. Update the direction vector

$$\frac{\partial E}{\partial \{w\}}(\{w\}_{n+2}) = \frac{\partial E}{\partial \{w\}}(\{w\}_{n+1}) - \beta(n+1)\frac{\partial E}{\partial \{w\}}(\{w\}_n).$$

9. Set $n = n + 1$ and go back to step 3.
10. Stop when the following condition is satisfied:

$$\varepsilon = \frac{\partial E}{\partial \{w\}}(\{w\}_{n+2}) - \frac{\partial E}{\partial \{w\}}(\{w\}_{n+1}) \text{ where } \varepsilon \text{ is a small number.}$$

The scaled conjugate gradient method differs from the conjugate gradient method in that it does not involve the line search described in step 3. The step-size (see step 3) is calculated directly by using the following formula (Møller 1993):

$$\eta(n) = 2\left(\eta(n) - \left(\frac{\partial E(n)}{\partial \{w\}}(n)\right)^T H(n)\left(\frac{\partial E(n)}{\partial \{w\}}(n)\right)\right.$$

$$\left. + \eta(n)\left\|\left(\frac{\partial E(n)}{\partial \{w\}}(n)\right)\right\|^2 \middle/ \left\|\left(\frac{\partial E(n)}{\partial \{w\}}(n)\right)\right\|\right)^2 \qquad (2.11)$$

where H is the Hessian of the gradient. The scaled conjugate gradient method is used because it has been found to solve the optimization problems encountered when training an MLP network more computationally efficient than the gradient descent and conjugate gradient methods (Bishop 1995).

2.2.2 Bayesian Framework

For this chapter, multi-layered neural networks were deemed as parameterized classification models that make probabilistic assumptions about the data. The probabilistic outlook of these models was facilitated by the use of the Bayesian framework. Learning algorithms were viewed as methods for finding parameter values that look probable in the light of the data. The learning process was conducted by dividing the data into training, validation, and testing sets. This was done for model selection and to ensure that the trained network was not biased towards the training data it had seen. Another way of achieving this is through the use of the regularization framework, which comes naturally from the Bayesian formulation and is now discussed in detail in this chapter.

Thomas Bayes (1702–1761) was the first person to prove a particular case of the Bayes' theorem. Pierre-Simon Laplace (1749–1827) generalized the theorem and applied it to problems such as celestial mechanics, medical statistics, and reliability (Stigler 1986; Fienberg 2006; Bernardo 2005). In the early days, the

Bayesian technique used uniform priors and was called "inverse probability" and later supplanted by a technique called "frequentist statistics". Frequentist statistics, also called the maximum-likelihood approach, are aimed at finding the most likely solution without regard to the probability distribution of that solution. The frequentist approach is basically a special case of Bayesian results representing the most probable solution in the distribution of the posterior probability function.

In summary, Bayesian techniques are comprised of the following ideas (Bishop 1995):

- The usage of hierarchical models and the marginalization over the values of irrelevant parameters using methods such as the Markov chain Monte Carlo techniques.
- The progressive application of the Bayes' theorem as data points are obtained and after estimating a posterior distribution, the posterior equals the following prior.
- In the frequentist approach, a hypothesis is a proposition which must be proven right or wrong while in a Bayesian technique, a hypothesis has a probability.

The Bayesian technique has been applied to many complex problems, including those of finite element model updating (Marwala and Sibisi 2005; Marwala 2010), missing data estimation (Marwala 2009), probabilistic risk assessment (Kelly and Smith 2009), modelling integrated river basin management (Barton et al. 2008), modeling behaviors for mobile robots (Lazkano et al. 2007), diagnosis of airplane engines (Sahin et al. 2007), and for environmental modelling (Uusitalo 2007).

The problem of identifying the weights (w_i) and biases (with subscripts 0 in Fig. 2.1) in the hidden layers may be posed in the Bayesian form as (Box and Tiao 1973):

$$P(\{w\}|[D]) = \frac{P([D]|\{w\})P(\{w\})}{P([D])} \qquad (2.12)$$

where $P(w)$ is the probability distribution function of the weight-space in the absence of any data, also known as the prior distribution and $D \equiv (y_1, \ldots, y_N)$ is a matrix containing the identity of damage data. The quantity $P(w|D)$ is the posterior probability distribution after the data have been seen and $P(D|w)$ is the likelihood function.

2.2.2.1   Likelihood Function

The likelihood function is the concept that shows the probability of the model which depends on the free parameters of a model to be correct. It is essentially the probability of the observed data, given the free parameters of the model. The likelihood can be written mathematically as follows, by using the cross entropy error (Edwards 1972):

$$P([D]|\{w\}) = \frac{1}{Z_D} \exp(-\beta E_D)$$

$$= \frac{1}{Z_D} \exp \left(\beta \sum_n^N \sum_k^K \{t_{nk} \ln(y_{nk}) + (1 - t_{nk}) \ln(1 - y_{nk})\} \right)$$

(2.13)

In Eq. 2.13, E_D is the cross-entropy error function which is described in Eq. 2.3, β represents the hyperparameters, and Z_D is a normalization constant which can be estimated as follows:

$$Z_D = \int_{-\infty}^{\infty} \exp \left(\beta \sum_n^N \sum_k^K \{t_{nk} \ln(y_{nk}) + (1 - t_{nk}) \ln(1 - y_{nk})\} \right) d\{w\} \quad (2.14)$$

2.2.2.2 Prior Function

The prior probability distribution is the assumed probability of the free parameters. A *prior* is frequently a subjective estimation by a knowledgeable expert (Jaynes 1968; Bernardo 1979). There are different kinds of priors and these include informative and uninformative priors. An *informative prior* shows precise, certain information about a variable while an *uninformative prior* states ambiguous or general information about a variable. A prior distribution that assumes that model parameters (also known as free parameters) are of the same order of magnitude, can be written as follows (Bishop 1995):

$$P(\{w\}) = \frac{1}{Z_w} \exp(-E_W)$$

$$= \frac{1}{Z_w} \exp \left(-\frac{\alpha}{2} \sum_j^W w_j^2 \right)$$

(2.15)

Parameter α represents the hyperparameters, and Z_W is the normalization constant which can be estimated as follows:

$$Z_w = \int_{-\infty}^{\infty} \exp \left(-\frac{\alpha}{2} \sum_j^W w_j^2 \right) d\{w\}$$

(2.16)

The prior distribution of a Bayesian approach is the regularization parameter in Eq. 2.3. As indicated before, regularization comprises introducing extra information to the objective function, through a penalty function, to solve an ill-posed problem or to prevent overfitting to ensure the smoothness of the solution to balance complexity with accuracy.

2.2.2.3 Posterior Function

In this chapter, the posterior probability is the probability of the network weights given the observed data. In essence it is a conditional probability allocated after the pertinent evidence, that is, the probability distribution of the observed data, is factored (Lee 2004). It is calculated by multiplying the likelihood function with the prior function and dividing it by a normalization function which is also called the evidence. By combining Eqs. 2.12 and 2.15, the posterior distribution can be written as (Bishop 1995):

$$P(w|D) = \frac{1}{Z_s} \exp\left(\beta \sum_{n}^{N} \sum_{k}^{K} \{t_{nk} \ln(y_{nk}) + (1 - t_{nk}) \ln(1 - y_{nk})\} - \frac{\alpha}{2} \sum_{j}^{W} w_j^2 \right)$$

(2.17)

where

$$Z_E(\alpha, \beta) = \int \exp\left(-\beta E_D - \alpha E_W\right) dw$$

$$= \left(\frac{2\pi}{\beta}\right)^{N/2} + \left(\frac{2\pi}{\alpha}\right)^{W/2}$$

(2.18)

The distribution in Eq. 2.17 is a canonical distribution (Haykin 1999). Training the network using a Bayesian approach yields an identification of the probability distribution of the weights in Eq. 2.1. The Bayesian approach automatically penalizes highly complex models and can, therefore, select an optimal model without applying independent methods such as cross-validation (Bishop 1995).

2.2.3 Automatic Relevance Determination

An automatic relevance determination method was constructed by associating the hyperparameters of the prior with each input variable. This, therefore, required Eq. 2.15 to be generalized to form (MacKay 1991; 1992):

$$E_W = \frac{1}{2} \sum_{k} \alpha_k \{w\}^T [I_k]\{w\}$$

(2.19)

Here, superscript T is the transpose, k is the weight group and $[I]$ is the identity matrix. By using the generalized prior in Eq. 2.19, the posterior probability in Eq. 2.17 becomes:

$$P(\{w\}|[D], H_i) = \frac{1}{Z_s} \exp\left(\beta \sum_n \{t_n \ln y(\{x\}_n) + (1 - t_n)In(1 - y(\{x\}_n\}\right)$$
$$-\frac{1}{2} \sum_k \alpha_k \{w\}^T [I_k]\{w\}\right)$$
$$= \frac{1}{Z_E} \exp(-E(\{w\})) \tag{2.20}$$

where

$$Z_E(\alpha, \beta) = \left(\frac{2\pi}{\beta}\right)^{N/2} + \prod_k \left(\frac{2\pi}{\alpha_k}\right)^{W_k/2} \tag{2.21}$$

Here W_k is the number of weights in group k.

Using the Taylor expansion, the error in Eq. 2.20 becomes

$$E^*(\{w\})$$
$$= -\sum_n \beta \{t_n In(y\{x\}_n) + (1 - t_n)In(1 - y(\{x\}_n\} + \frac{1}{2} \sum_k \alpha_k \{w\}^T [I]_k\{w\}$$

$$\approx E(\{w\}_{MP}) + \frac{1}{2}(\{w\} - \{w\}_{MP})^T [A](\{w\} - \{w\}_{MP}) \tag{2.22}$$

where

$$[A] = \beta \nabla \nabla E_D + \sum_k \alpha_k [I_k] \tag{2.23}$$

Here, the subscript MP indicates the Most Probable weights, superscript T stands for the transpose and $[A]$ stands for the Hessian matrix.

The evidence can be written as follows (Bishop 1995):

$$p([D]|\alpha, \beta) = \frac{1}{Z_D Z_W} \int \exp(-E(\{w\})) \, d\{w\}$$

$$= \frac{Z_E}{Z_D Z_W}$$

$$= \frac{\left(\frac{2\pi}{\beta}\right)^{N/2} + \prod_k \left(\frac{2\pi}{\alpha_k}\right)^{W_k/2}}{\left(\frac{2\pi}{\beta}\right)^{N/2} \prod_k \left(\frac{2\pi}{\alpha_k}\right)^{W_k/2}} \tag{2.24}$$

Maximization of the log evidence gives the following estimations for the hyperparameters:

$$\beta^{MP} = \frac{N - \gamma}{2E_D \left(\{w\}^{MP}\right)} \qquad (2.25)$$

$$\alpha_k^{MP} = \frac{\gamma_k}{2E_{W_k} \left(\{w\}^{MP}\right)} \qquad (2.26)$$

where $\gamma = \sum_k \gamma_k$, $2E_{W_k} = \{w\}^T [I_k]\{w\}$ and

$$\gamma_k = \sum_j \left(\frac{\pi_j - \alpha_k}{\eta_j} \left([V]^T [I_k][V]\right)_{jj} \right) \qquad (2.27)$$

and η_j are the eigenvalues of [A], and [V] are the eigenvalues such that $[V]^T [V] = [I]$.

To determine the relevance of each input variable, the α_k^{MP}, β^{MP}, and the Most Probable weight, $\{w\}^{MP}$, is determined using the evidence framework (MacKay 1991):

1. Randomly select the initial values for the hyperparameters.
2. Train the neural network using the scaled conjugate gradient algorithm to minimize the cost function in Eq. 2.5 to obtain $\{w\}^{MP}$.
3. Apply the evidence framework to estimate the hyperparameters using Eqs. 2.25 and 2.26.
4. Repeat steps 2 and 3 until convergence.

2.3　Application to Interstate Conflict

This chapter implements the ARD to understand the influence of the input parameters on the MID. As indicated before, the ARD model (MacKay 1992; Neal 1998) is Bayesian in nature, and is used to determine the relevance of each input on the output. The ARD is constructed by assigning a different hyperparameter to each input variable and estimating the hyperparameters using a Bayesian framework. The input weights that have higher hyperparameters are not influential and have less effect on the output than the lower hyperparameters.

Before implementing the ARD, this section describes the liberal variables and MID data that are used. As described in Chap. 1, we use four variables associated with realist analysis and three "Kantian" variables (Anonymous 2010). The first variable is *Allies*, a binary measure coded 1 if the members of a dyad are linked by any form of military alliance, and 0 in the absence of military alliance. *Contingency* is also binary, coded 1 if both states share a common boundary and 0 if they do not, and *Distance* is the logarithm, to the base 10, of the distance in kilometers between the two states' capitals. *Major Power* is a binary variable, coded 1 if either or both states in the dyad is a major power and 0 if neither are super powers. *Capability* is the logarithm, to the base 10, of the ratio of the total population plus the number of people in urban areas plus industrial energy consumption plus iron and steel production plus the number of military personnel in active duty plus military expenditure in dollars in the last 5 years measured on stronger country to weak country. The variable *Democracy* is measured on a scale where the value of 10 is an extreme democracy and a value of -10 is an extreme autocracy and taking the lowest value of the two countries. The variable *Dependency* is measured as the sum of the countries import and export with its partner divided by the Gross Domestic Product of the stronger country. It is a continuous variable measuring the level of economic interdependence (dyadic trade as a portion of a state's gross domestic product) of the less economically dependent state in the dyad. These measures were derived from conceptualizations and measurements conducted by the Correlates of War (COW) project.

We chose the politically relevant population (all dyads containing a major power) because it sets a hard test for prediction. Omitting all distant dyads composed of weak states means that we omit much of the influence with variables that are not very amenable to policy intervention (distance and national power). By that omission, we make our job harder by reducing the predictive power of such variables, but it also makes it more interesting. By applying the training and validation sampling technique we show that a strong performance is achieved even when the analysis is restricted to the politically relevant group. By focusing only on dyads that either involve major powers or are contiguous, we test the discriminative power of the neural network on a difficult set of cases. The neural network system is fed with only highly informative data since every dyad can be deemed to be at risk of incurring a dispute, yet it is harder for the network to discriminate between the two classes (dyad-years with disputes and those without disputes) because the politically relevant group is more homogeneous (e.g., closer, more inter-dependent) than the all-dyad data set.

The COW data are used to generate training and testing sets. The training data set consists of 500 conflicts and 500 non-conflict cases, and the test data consists of 392 conflict data and 392 peace data. We use a balanced training set, with a randomly selected equal number of conflicts and non-conflicts cases, to produce robust classifications and stronger insights on the reasons of conflicts. The data are normalized to fall between 0 and 1. This is done to improve the effectiveness of neural networks modeling (Bishop 1995). The MLP architecture was chosen using $M = 10$, a logistic function in the output layer, and a hyperbolic function in the hidden layers as the optimal architecture.

In this book, the ARD is used to rank liberal variables with regards to their influence on the MID. The ARD is implemented, the hyperparameters calculated, and then the inverse of the hyperparameters is calculated, and the results are shown in Fig. 2.2. Figure 2.2 indicates that the *Dependency* variable has the highest influence, followed by *Capability*, followed by *Democracy* and then *Allies*. The remaining three variables, that is, *Contingency*, *Distance*, and *Major Power*, have

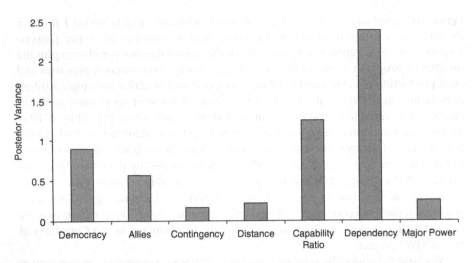

Fig. 2.2 Relevance of each liberal variable with regards to the classification of MIDs

similar impact although it is much smaller in comparison with the other two liberal variables, democracy and economic interdependence, and the two realist variables, allies and difference in capabilities.

The results in Fig. 2.2 indicate that all the liberal variables used in this book influence the conflict and peace outcome. However, alliance, and power ratio play a part in providing opportunities and incentives for interstate action and therefore they have also an important effects on promoting peace or conflict between states. Overall, the results, first, support the theory of democratic peace, which claims that democracies never go to war. Secondly it also indicates the importance of economic interdependence and economic ties for promoting peace. In addition, once again this result underlines that the relationship between peace and the Kantian factors is not bi-directional. Economic interdependence interacts with democracy to enhance its own influence as well as democracy's influence on peace. Furthermore, the impact of the two Kantian factors is also significantly mediated by both the dyadic balance of power and alliances.

However, the three remaining realist variables, *Distance*, *Contingency*, and *Major Power*, cannot be completely ignored. They still provide the ex-ante conditions for war to happen. For example, Swaziland and Bahamas have a lower probability of going to war, primarily because they are so far apart and as result they have no incentives to go to war. The same cannot be said in relation to major powers. Great powers have the capacity to engage in distant conflicts as well as the incentives to do so. In summary, the constrains that high level of economic interdependence, democracy, allies as well as difference in capability ratio exert on interstate behavior, are activated when the opportunities for conflicts, provided by geographical proximity and/or great power interests, are in place.

2.4 Conclusion

This chapter introduced the Bayesian technique to deal with the question of ranking relevant variables for the prediction of the MID. This automatic relevance method was based on the Bayesian framework and used the evidence framework as well as the scaled conjugate gradient method. When the automatic relevance determination was used to rank the importance of each input variable, it was found that *Dependency* carries the most weight, then *Capability*, then *Democracy*, and then *Allies*.

2.5 Further Work

This chapter applied the neural networks ARD to rank variables for the prediction of the MID. In the future, support vector machines should be applied to study the relevance of each variable and this should be compared to neural networks. Furthermore, a hybrid of these methods should be applied to rank the input variables.

References

Anonymous.: Correlates of war project. http://www.correlatesofwar.org/Last (2010). Accessed 20 Sept 2010
Babaie-Kafaki, S., Ghanbari, R., Mahdavi-Amiri, N.: Two new conjugate gradient methods based on modified secant equations. J. Comput. Appl. Math. **234**, 1374–1386 (2010)
Barton, D.N., Saloranta, T., Moe, S.J., Eggestad, H.O., Kuikka, S.: Bayesian belief networks as a meta-modelling tool in integrated river basin management – pros and cons in evaluating nutrient abatement decisions under uncertainty in a Norwegian River Basin. Ecol. Econ. **66**, 91–104 (2008)
Beck, N., King, G., Zeng, L.: Improving quantitative studies of international conflict: a conjecture. Am. Polit. Sci. Rev **94**, 21–35 (2000)
Bernardo, J.M.: Reference posterior distributions for Bayesian inference. J. R. Stat. Soc. **41**, 113–147 (1979)
Bernardo, J.M.: Reference analysis. Handb. Stat. **25**, 17–90 (2005)
Bertsekas, D.P.: Non-linear Programming. Athenas Scientific, Cambridge (1995)
Bishop, C.M.: Neural Networks for Pattern Recognition. Oxford University Press, Oxford (1995)
Box, G.E.P., Tiao, G.C.: Bayesian Inference in Statistical Analysis. Wiley, Hoboken (1973)
Browne, A.: Using neural networks with automatic relevance determination to identify regions of the thalamus implicated in Schizophrenia. In: Proceedings of the IEEE International Joint Conference on Neural Networks. pp. 97–101, Vancouver (2006)
Bryson, A.E., Ho, Y.C.: Applied Optimal Control: Optimization, Estimation, and Control. Xerox College Publishing, Kentucky (1989)
Chiddarwar, S.S., Babu, N.R.: Comparison of RBF and MLP neural networks to solve inverse kinematic problems for 6R serial robots by a fusion approach. Eng. Appl. Artif. Intel **23**, 1083–1092 (2010)
Cybenko, G.: Approximations by superpositions of sigmoidal functions. Math.Control. Signal. Syst **2**, 303–314 (1989)

Ebrahimzadeh, A., Khazaee, A.: Detection of premature ventricular contractions using mlp neural networks: a comparative study. Measurement **43**, 103–112 (2010)

Edwards, A.W.F.: Likelihood. Cambridge University Press, Cambridge (1972)

Fienberg, S.E.: When did Bayesian inference become "Bayesian"? Bayesian. Anal **1**, 1–40 (2006)

Fletcher, R.: Practical Methods of Optimization. Wiley, New York (1987)

Freeman, J., Skapura, D.: Neural Networks: Algorithms, Applications and Programming Techniques. Addison-Wesley, Reading (1991)

Fu, Y., Browne, A.: Using ensembles of neural networks to improve automatic relevance determination. In: Proceeding of the IEEE International Joint Conference on Neural Networks, pp. 1590–1594, Orlando (2007)

Gelpi, C., Griesdorf, M.: Winners and losers? Democracies in international crisis, 1918–94. Am. Polit. Sci. Rev **95**, 633–647 (2001)

Ghate, V.N., Dudul, S.V.: Optimal MLP neural network classifier for fault detection of three phase induction motor. Expert Syst. Appl. **37**, 3468–3481 (2010)

Gleditsch, K.S., Wards, M.D.: Peace and war in time and space: the role of democratization. Int. Stud. Q. **43**, 1–29 (2000)

Gochman, C., Maoz, Z.: Militarized interstate disputes 1816–1976. In: Singer, D., Diehl, P. (eds.) Measuring the Correlates of War. University of Michigan Press, Ann Arbor (1990)

Habtemariam, E., Marwala, T., Lagazio, M.: Artificial intelligence for conflict management. In: Proceedings of the IEEE International Joint Conference on Neural Networks, pp. 2583–2588, Montreal (2005)

Hassoun, M.H.: Fundamentals of Artificial Neural Networks. MIT Press, Cambridge (1995)

Haykin, S.: Neural Networks. Prentice-Hall, Englewood Cliffs (1999)

Hestenes, M.R., Stiefel, E.: Methods of conjugate gradients for solving linear systems. J. Res. Nat. Bur. Stand **6**, 409–436 (1952)

Jaynes, E.T.: Prior probabilities. IEEE Trans. Syst. Sci. Cyb. **4**, 227–241 (1968)

Kelly, D.L., Smith, C.L.: Bayesian inference in probabilistic risk assessment – the current state of the art. Reliab. Eng. Syst. Saf. **94**, 628–643 (2009)

Kim, G., Kim, Y., Lim, H., Kim, H.: An MLP-based feature subset selection for HIV-1 protease cleavage site analysis. Artif. Intell. Med. **48**, 83–89 (2010)

Lagazio, M., Marwala, T.: Assessing different bayesian neural network models for militarized interstate dispute. Soc. Sci. Comput. Rev. **24**, 1–12 (2005)

Lagazio, M., Russet, B.: A neural network analysis of MIDs, 1885–1992: are the patterns stable? In: Diehl, P. (ed.) Toward a Scientific Understanding of War: Studies in Honor of J. David Singer. University of Michigan Press, Ann Arbor (2002)

Lazkano, E., Sierra, B., Astigarraga, A., Martínez-Otzeta, J.M.: On the use of Bayesian networks to develop behaviours for mobile robots. Robot. Auton. Syst. **55**, 253–265 (2007)

Lee, P.M.: Bayesian Statistics, an Introduction. Wiley, Hoboken (2004)

Leke, B., Marwala, T., Tettey, T.: Using inverse neural network for HIV adaptive control. Int. J. Comput. Intell. Res. **3**, 11–15 (2007)

Lisboa, P.J.G., Etchells, T.A., Jarman, I.H., Arsene, C.T.C., Aung, M.S.H., Eleuteri, A., Taktak, A.F.G., Ambrogi, F., Boracchi, P., Biganzoli, E.: Partial logistic artificial neural network for competing risks regularized with automatic relevance determination. IEEE Trans. Neural. Nets **20**, 1403–1416 (2009)

Luenberger, D.G.: Linear and Non-linear Programming. Addison-Wesley, Reading (1984)

Lunga, D., Marwala, T.: On-line forecasting of stock market movement direction using the improved incremental algorithm. Lecture Notes in Computer Science, vol. 4234, pp. 440–449, Springer Heidelberg (2006)

MacKay, D.J.C.: Bayesian methods for adaptive models. PhD thesis, California Institute of Technology (1991)

MacKay, D.J.C.: A practical Bayesian framework for back propagation networks. Neural Comput. **4**, 448–472 (1992)

Marwala, T.: On damage identification using a committee of neural networks. J. Eng. Mech. **126**, 43–50 (2000)

Marwala, T.: Probabilistic fault identification using a committee of neural networks and vibration data. J. Aircraft **38**, 138–146 (2001)

Marwala, T.: Fault classification using pseudo modal energies and neural networks. Am. Inst. Aeronaut. Astronaut. J. **41**, 82–89 (2003)

Marwala, T.: Computational Intelligence for Missing Data Imputation, Estimation and Management: Knowledge Optimization Techniques. IGI Global Publications, New York (2009)

Marwala, T.: Finite Element Model Updating Using Computational Intelligence Techniques: Applications to Structural Dynamics. Springer, Heidelberg (2010)

Marwala, T., Hunt, H.E.M.: Fault identification using finite element models and neural networks. Mech. Syst. Signal. Process **13**, 475–490 (1999)

Marwala, T., Lagazio, M.: Modelling and controlling interstate conflict. In: Proceedings of the IEEE International Joint Conference on Neural Networks, pp. 1233–1238, Budapest (2004)

Marwala, T., Sibisi, S.: Finite element model updating using bayesian framework and modal properties. J. Aircraft **42**, 275–278 (2005)

Mohamed, N., Rubin, D., Marwala, T.: Detection of epileptiform activity in human EEG signals using bayesian neural networks. Neural Info. Process Lett. Rev. **10**, 1–10 (2006)

Møller, A.F.: A scaled conjugate gradient algorithm for fast supervised learning. Neural Nets **6**, 525–533 (1993)

Mordecai, A.: Non-linear Programming: Analysis and Methods. Dover Publishing, New York (2003)

Neal, R.M.: Bayesian learning for neural networks. PhD thesis, University of Toronto (1994)

Neal, R.M.: Assessing the relevance determination methods using DELVE. In: Bishop, C.M. (ed.) Neural Nets and Machine Learn. Springer, Berlin (1998)

Nummenmaa, A., Auranen, T., Hämäläinen, M.S., Jääskeläinen, I.P., Sams, M., Vehtari, A., Lampinen, J.: Automatic relevance determination based hierarchical Bayesian MEG inversion in practice. NeuroImage **37**, 876–889 (2007)

Oneal, J.R., Russett, B.: Clear and clean: the fixed effects of democracy and economic interdependence. Int. Organ **3**, 469–486 (2001)

Patel, P., Marwala, T.: Neural networks, fuzzy inference systems and adaptive-neuro fuzzy inference systems for financial decision making. Lecture Notes in Computer Science, vol. 4234, pp. 430–439, Springer Heidelberg (2006)

Robbins, H., Monro, S.: A stochastic approximation method. Ann. Math. Stat. **22**, 400–407 (1951)

Rosenblatt, F.: Principles of Neurodynamics: Perceptrons and the Theory of Brain Mechanisms. Spartan, Washington, DC (1961)

Rumelhart, D.E., Hinton, G.E., Williams, R.J.: Parallel Distributed Processing: Explorations in the Microstructure of Cognition. MIT Press, Cambridge (1986)

Russell, S., Norvig, P.: Artificial Intelligence: A Modern Approach. Prentice Hall, Englewood Cliffs (1995)

Sahin, F., Yavuz, M.Ç., Arnavut, Z., Uluyol, Ö.: Fault diagnosis for airplane engines using Bayesian networks and distributed particle swarm optimization. Parallel Comput. **33**, 124–143 (2007)

Smyrnakis, M.G., Evans, D.J.: Classifying ischemic events using a Bayesian inference multilayer perceptron and input variable evaluation using automatic relevance determination. Comput. Cardiol. **34**, 305–308 (2007)

Stigler, S.M.: The History of Statistics. Harvard University Press, Cambridge (1986)

Tibshirani, R.: Regression shrinkage and selection via the lasso. J. R. Stat. Soc. **58**, 267–288 (1996)

Ulusoy, I., Bishop, C.M.: Automatic relevance determination for the estimation of relevant features for object recognition. In: Proceedings of the IEEE 14th Signal Processing and Communication Applications, pp. 1–4, Antalya (2006)

Uusitalo, L.: Advantages and challenges of Bayesian networks in environmental modelling. Ecol. Model. **203**, 312–318 (2007)

Van Calster, B., Timmerman, D., Nabney, I.T., Valentin, L., Van Holsbeke, C., Van Huffel, S.: Classifying ovarian tumors using Bayesian multi-layer perceptrons and automatic relevance determination: a multi-center study. In: Proceedings of the Engineering in Medicine and Biology Society, pp. 5342–5345, New York (2006)

Vilakazi, B.C., Marwala, T.: Condition monitoring using computational intelligence. In: Laha, D., Mandal, P. (eds.) Handbook on Computational Intelligence in Manufacturing and Production Management, illustrated edn. IGI Publishers, New York (2007)

Wang, D., Lu, W.Z.: Interval estimation of urban ozone level and selection of influential factors by employing automatic relevance determination. Model. Chemosphere **62**, 1600–1611 (2006)

Werbos, P.J.: Beyond regression: new tool for prediction and analysis in the behavioral sciences. Ph.D. thesis, Harvard University (1974)

Wu, W., Chen, Z., Gao, S., Brown, E.N.: Hierarchical Bayesian modeling of inter-trial variability and variational Bayesian learning of common spatial patterns from multichannel EEG. In: Proceedings of the 2010 IEEE International Conference on Acoustics Speech and Signal Processing, pp. 501–504, Montreal (2010)

Yoon, Y., Peterson, L.L.: Artificial neural networks: An emerging new technique. In: Proceedings of the ACM SIGBDP Conference on Trends and Directions in Expert Systems, pp. 417–422, Orlando (1990)

Zeng, L.: Prediction and classification with neural network models. Soc. Method Res. **27**, 499–524 (1999)

Zhang, J., Liu, S., Wang, Y.: Gene association study with SVM, MLP, and cross-validation for the diagnosis of diseases. Prog. Nat. Sci. **18**, 741–750 (2008)

Zhao, Z., Xin, H., Ren, Y., Guo, X.: Application and comparison of BP neural network algorithm in MATLAB. In: Proceedings of the International Conference on Measurement Technology and Mechatron Automat, pp. 590–593, New York (2010)

Chapter 3
Multi-layer Perceptron and Radial Basis Function for Modeling Interstate Conflict

3.1 Introduction

Finding a suitable way of modeling conflict has been a subject of research for the last 30 years. In spite of many techniques being proposed for modeling international conflict, the results of the different models are frequently in conflict with each other. However, Iswaran and Percy (2010) successfully applied Bayesian neural networks and generalized linear models to modeling conflict.

Coppola and Szidarovszky (2004) applied neural networks to model the conflict between water supply and environmental health risk while Kowalski (1992) applied adaptive neural networks for low and high intensity conflict and in battlefield formations. Neural networks were able to successfully identify battlefield formations and frequently occurring events from terrorist activity reports.

Schrodt (1991) used a neural network model to predict interstate conflict and compared it with discriminant analysis, logit analysis, and rule-based decision trees. The neural network was observed to outperform both discriminant analysis and decision trees and gave similar accuracy to a multinomial logit. In the study, the neural network gave worse results than the discriminant and logit models for predicting non-modal values of the dependent variable.

Mubareka and Ehrlich (2010) successfully used ground and satellite data to identify and model environmental indicators to assess the population's vulnerability to conflict. Masci and Tedeschi (2009) applied game-theory for conflict resolution in air-traffic while Moffat and Medhurst (2009) used experimental games to model human decision-making in simulation models. They demonstrated that these games offer robust support for fast planning.

Crossingham et al. (2008) applied optimized rough sets for modeling interstate conflict. They showed that all of the proposed optimized methods produced higher forecasting accuracies than those of the two static methods and that a genetic algorithm approach produced the highest accuracy. The rules generated from the rough set were linguistic and easy-to-interpret. Tettey and Marwala (2007) applied a Takagi-Sugeno neuro-fuzzy model and a neural network model for conflict

T. Marwala and M. Lagazio, *Militarized Conflict Modeling using Computational Intelligence*, Advanced Information and Knowledge Processing,
DOI 10.1007/978-0-85729-790-7_3, © Springer-Verlag London Limited 2011

management. It was found that the neural network model could forecast conflict with an accuracy of 77.3%. The Takagi-Sugeno Neuro-fuzzy model was optimized to forecast conflict and gave an accuracy of 80.36%. Knowledge from the Takagi-Sugeno neuro-fuzzy model was extracted by interpreting the model's fuzzy rules and their outcomes. It was found that both models offer some transparency which helped in understanding conflict management.

Hipel and Meister (1994) proposed a conflict analysis method to model coalitions in multilateral negotiations. Two proposed metrics were implemented for an international conflict and then compared to predict coalitions that were likely to form in a given dispute. The results demonstrated the manner in which coalitions affect resolving the trading conflict. Yolles (1993) proposed a decision table for modeling conflict processes in groups with a critical size.

In the next part of this chapter, the multi-layer neural network for classification will be introduced. In particular, a Bayesian network with Gaussian approximation will be introduced to classify conflict. Techniques such as the evidence framework will be introduced not in the context of the maximum likelihood approach but rather in the general framework of the Bayesian technique. Concepts such as moderated outputs will also be introduced.

In the remaining part of this chapter, the radial basis function neural-network will be introduced. The radial basis function will be trained using a two- stage process. The first stage involves the use of the k-means technique to identify the centers of the radial basis function. The second stage involves the use of the pseudo-inverse function to identify the network weights. Both the multi-layer perceptron and the radial basis function networks will be applied to model interstate conflict and the results obtained will then be compared. Finally, future and emerging research questions will be identified.

3.2 Mathematical Framework

In this section the mathematical background of neural networks – the multi-layer perceptron and the radial basis function networks – will be described. This includes a review of the background literature of successful implementations, an explanation of architectures, and a description of the techniques that are used to train these networks.

A neural network is an information processing paradigm that is inspired by the way biological nervous systems, like the human brain, process information. It is a computer based machine, designed to model the way in which the brain performs a particular task or function of interest (Haykin 1999). It is an exceptionally powerful instrument that has found successful use in mechanical engineering (Marwala and Hunt 1999; Vilakazi and Marwala 2007), civil engineering (Marwala 2000), aerospace engineering (Marwala 2001, 2003), biomedical engineering (Marwala 2007), and finance (Patel and Marwala 2006). In this chapter, neural networks are viewed as generalized regression models that can model both linear and non-linear data. According to the textbook, a neural network consists of four main parts:

- the processing units u_j, where each u_j has a certain activation level $a_j(t)$ at any point in time;
- weighted inter-connections between various processing units. These inter-connections determine how the activation of one unit leads to the input for another unit;
- an activation rule, which acts on the set of input signals at a unit to produce a new output signal; and
- a learning rule that specifies how to adjust the weights for a given input or output pair (Freeman and Skapura 1991).

Because of their ability to gather meaning from complicated data, neural networks are employed to extract patterns and detect trends that are too complex to be noticed by many other computer techniques (Hassoun 1995). A trained neural network can be considered as an expert in the category of information that it has been given to analyze (Yoon and Peterson 1990). This expert can then be used to provide predictions, when presented with new situations. Because of their ability to adapt to non-linear data, neural networks have been used to model various non-linear applications (Hassoun 1995; Leke et al. 2007).

The configuration of neural processing units and their inter-connections can have a profound impact on the processing capabilities of neural networks. Consequently, there are many different connections that define how data flows between the input, hidden and output layers. The next section gives details on the architecture of the two neural networks employed in this chapter.

3.2.1 Multi-layer Perceptrons (MLP) for Classification Problems

The multi-layer perceptron (MLP) network has been successfully applied, in the past, in both classification and regression problems. Narasinga-Rao et al. (2010) successfully used the MLP for predicting the quality of life in diabetes patients using age, gender, weight, and fasting plasma glucose as a set of inputs. Ikuta et al. (2010) proposed that a chaos glial network be connected to a multi-layer perceptron (MLP) to solve a two-spiral problem and found that the proposed method performed better than the conventional MLP.

Zadeh et al. (2010) proposed using a MLP to predict daily flows from Khosrow Shirin watershed, and observed that precipitation and discharge with 1 day time lag best predicts daily flows. Pasero et al. (2010) applied the MLP for a time series analysis, while Sug (2010) applied a MLP for task classification. Zhang and Li (2009) applied a hybrid of the Hidden Markov Model (HMM) and the MLP for speech recognition and demonstrated that the hybrid model performed better than the HMM.

He et al. (2009) applied the MLP for short-term demand forecasting using graphics processing units. Bernardo-Torres and Gómez-Gil (2009) used the MLP to forecast seismograms while Sug (2009) applied the MLP to pilot sampling. Kushwaha and Shakya (2009) successfully applied the MLP for predicting the helical content of proteins while Karami et al. (2009) successfully applied it to decoding low-density parity-check codes.

Other successful applications for the MLP include the work by Achili et al. (2009) in robotics, Sancho-Gómez et al. (2009) for decision support systems with missing data, Krishna (2009) in an air data system, Hu and Weng (2009) in image processing, Duta and Duta (2009) in turbo-machinery optimization, Pontin et al. (2009) in predicting the occurrence of stinging jellyfish, Yazdanmehr et al. (2009) for the modeling of nanocrystals, Watts and Worner (2009) for predicting the distribution of fungal crop diseases as well as Yilmaz and Özer (2009) for pitch angle control in wind turbines above the rated wind speed.

In this book, neural networks are regarded as a broad structure for describing non-linear mappings between multi-dimensional spaces where the form of the mapping is overseen by a set of free parameters (Bishop 1995; Mohamed 2003; Mohamed et al. 2006) to be estimated from the data. There are two ways in which neural networks can be trained: supervised and unsupervised learning. We consider only supervised learning. In supervised learning, the training data involves both the input to the neural networks and a corresponding target output. In this chapter, the input is a set of features that are deemed to influence interstate conflict as described in earlier chapters and the target output is binary, where a value of 1 represents the *conflict* pattern class and a value of 0 represents the *peace* pattern class.

3.2.1.1 Architecture

For this chapter, the MLP neural network architecture was chosen for mapping the relationship between conflict variables and the Militarized Interstate Dispute (MID) class. Each link between inputs and neurons was weighted by adjustable weight parameters, also known as free parameters. Additionally, each neuron has an adjustable bias weight parameter which is denoted by a link from a constant input $x_0 = 1$ and $z_0 = 1$ for the hidden neurons and the output neuron, respectively. This category of two-layer MLP models is capable of estimating any continuous function with arbitrary accuracy, as long as the number of hidden neurons is adequately large (Bishop 1995; Mohamed 2003).

The advantage of an MLP network is the interconnected cross-coupling that exists between the input variables and the hidden nodes, and the hidden nodes and the output variables. If we assume that x is the input to the MLP and y is the output of the MLP, a mapping function between the input and the output may be written as follows (Bishop 1995):

$$y = f_{output} \left(\sum_{j=1}^{M} w_j \, f_{hidden} \left(\sum_{i=0}^{N} w_{ij} x_i \right) + w_0 \right) \tag{3.1}$$

where N is the number of inputs units, M is the number of hidden neurons, x_i is the ith input unit, w_{ij} is the weight parameter between input i and hidden neuron j and w_j is the weight parameter between hidden neuron j and the output neuron. The activation function $f_{output}(\cdot)$ is sigmoid and can be written as follows (Bishop 1995):

$$f_{output}(a) = \frac{1}{1 + e^{-a}} \tag{3.2}$$

For this chapter, we use a neural network to classify the MID. In modeling complex problems, care must be taken in the choice of the output activation function. For classification problems, as is the case in this chapter, the sigmoid function indicated in Eq. 3.2 has been observed to be ideal. For regression problems, however, the linear activation function is ideal. The activation function $f_{hidden}(\cdot)$ is a hyperbolic tangent can be written as follows (Bishop 1995):

$$f_{hidden}(a) = \tan(a) \tag{3.3}$$

3.2.1.2 Training of the Multi-layer Perceptron

Once the activation function in Eq. 3.1 is defined and the sizes of the hidden nodes are chosen, what remains is to estimate the network weights. These network weights are, in Statistics, referred to as free parameters. These network weights are estimated from the observed data through a process called training. There are a number of crucial issues that need to be taken into account in training the networks. These include ensuring that, on identifying the network weights, the resulting network should not just memorize the data but learn from it. There are techniques that have been proposed to deal with this particular issue, and they include cross-validation, early-stopping, and regularization.

There are two general approaches that can be used to train a neural network. The approaches are the maximum likelihood method and the Bayesian approach. The maximum likelihood method identifies the network weights that maximize the ability of a trained network to better predict the observed data, while the Bayesian approach builds the probability distribution of the network model given the observed data. It should be noted here that the maximum likelihood method and Bayesian approach are the same thing and the difference is, really, that the maximum likelihood method identifies the network vector of weights that is most likely in the posterior probability distribution function. The first task to do on identifying a vector of network weights to maximize the predicting ability of the neural network is to construct an objective function, which is also described as a fitness function in the evolutionary programming mindset. The objective function is, in essence, a measure of the difference between the predictions of the model and the observed data.

In a two-class classification problem, the objective function is the difference between the neural network's predicted output and the target output, t, given in

Eq. 3.1 for all training patterns. E is the cross-entropy error function given by (Bishop 1995):

$$E = - \sum_{p=1}^{P} \{t_p \ln(y_p) + (1 - t_p) \ln(1 - y_p)\} \qquad (3.4)$$

There are many advantages of the cross-entropy function and one of these include the fact that it allows the output to be interpreted probabilistically without the need to apply a Bayesian approach. Neural networks are trained by iteratively adjusting the weight parameters, w, to minimize the objective function given by Eq. 3.4. This is achieved by randomly initializing the network weights and then adjusting the weight parameters using the scaled conjugate gradient technique (Moller 1993), which was described in Chap. 2. The scaled conjugate gradient method was chosen over other optimization approaches because of its efficient convergence properties.

Generalization is the ability of a trained neural network model to classify input patterns that were not seen during the training of the neural network. In essence, on seeking a network that generalizes, one identifies a balance between the ability of a network to recall the training data *i.e.*, training it with the ability of the network to predict unseen data *i.e.*, validity. The generalization of performance is a true reflection of the capacity of a neural network to accomplish a classification duty. This can only be proven by dividing the data into training and testing data sets.

Bishop (1995) showed that a minimization of the cross-entropy objective function in the neural network training with the activation function of a neural network represented by Eq. 3.2, results in the output of a neural network estimating the posterior probability of membership to a particular class, given the input $\{x\}$. In the present case of modeling interstate conflict, the output estimates the posterior probability of conflict. If this class is represented by C_1 and the pattern class for not containing conflict activity is represented by C_2, the relations for the posterior probability of class membership can be written as follows (Bishop 1995):

$$P(C_1 | \{x\}) = y \qquad (3.5)$$

$$P(C_2 | \{x\}) = 1 - y \qquad (3.6)$$

Equations 3.5 and 3.6 provide a probabilistic interpretation to the neural network output. On the basis of these relationships, it is evident that the input vector has a high probability of being an element of class C_1 when y is close to 1 and C_2 when y is close to 0. If y is close to 0.5, then there is uncertainty in the class membership of the input vector. A basic technique to increase the effectiveness of the classifier is to implement an upper and lower rejection threshold to the neural network output (Bishop 1995; Mohamed 2003). This classification decision rule can be written as follows (Mohamed 2003):

$$\text{Choose } C_1 \text{ if } y > \gamma$$
$$\text{Choose } C_2 \text{ if } y < (1 - \gamma)$$
$$\text{Otherwise do not classify } \{x\} \tag{3.7}$$

The parameter γ sets the level of the rejection threshold and allows the user to decide the level at which a decision can be made.

3.2.1.3 Bayesian Formulation

A neural network trained with the maximum likelihood method makes the assumption that weight parameters have a fixed, unknown value and an estimation of this value is performed by minimizing an appropriate objective function. In this chapter, it is the cross-entropy function described in Eq. 3.4. Nevertheless, as the vector of weight parameters, $\{w\}$, is estimated from a finite set of observed data, there is always some degree of uncertainty associated with the value of this weight vector. For example, if a single training pattern of data is removed from the training set, the weight vector that was learned during training will differ from the weight vector that was learned when the same training pattern was present in the training set. Therefore, in the light of this observation, it is important to ask which weight vector is the correct one, given the sensitivity of the identified weight vector to parameters such as the initial weight vector during training, as well as the data included in the training.

Bayesian learning assigns a probability distribution to the weight vector that represents the relative degrees of believability of the values of the weight vector and, therefore, circumvents the choice of which weight vector is the correct one. As described in Chap. 2, a multi-layer perceptron model structure with the number of hidden layer neurons is defined as H, and a prior distribution $p(\{w\}|H)$ is allocated to the weight vector to reveal any initial beliefs regarding the distribution of the weight parameters. When a set of training data, $[D]$, is observed, the prior distribution is converted into a posterior distribution of network weights using Bayes' theorem as follows (Bishop 1995; Mohamed 2003):

$$p(\{w\}|[D], H) = \frac{p([D]|\{w\}, H)p(\{w\}|H)}{p([D]|H)} \tag{3.8}$$

Here $p([D]|\{w\},H)$ is the *likelihood* distribution function and $p([D]|H)$ is the *evidence* of model H. MacKay (1992) used the Gaussian prior which can be written as follows (Bishop 1995):

$$p(\{w\}|H) = \frac{1}{(2\pi/\alpha)^{W/2}} \exp\left(-\frac{\alpha}{2} \sum_i w_i^2\right) \tag{3.9}$$

As described in Chap. 2, α is the regularization coefficient and W is the number of weight parameters in the neural network. The distribution in Eq. 3.9 is a Gaussian with variance $1/\alpha$. When w is large, $p(\{w\}|H)$ will be small. This prior distribution, which is called the sum of squares of weights, ensures smaller values for weight parameters. By using the prior distribution in Eq. 3.9, and applying Bayes' theorem, the posterior probability of the weight vector, given the training data in Eq. 3.8, may be written as follows (MacKay 1991):

$$p(\{w\}|[D], H) = \frac{1}{Z_S(\alpha)} \exp(-E(\{w\})) \tag{3.10}$$

where

$$E(\{w\}) = -\sum_{p=1}^{P} \{t_P \ln(y_P) + (1 - t_P) \ln(1 - y_P)\} + \frac{\alpha}{2} \sum_i w_i^2 \tag{3.11}$$

and

$$Z_S(\alpha) = \int -E(\{w\})d\{w\} \tag{3.12}$$

In Eq. 3.10, the Weight vector corresponding to the Maximum of the Posterior distribution, $\{w_{MP}\}$, can be estimated by minimizing the negative logarithm of the posterior distribution. This corresponds to minimizing the objective function in Eq. 3.11 which is comprised of the cross-entropy objective in Eq. 3.4 and the weight decay regularizer, described in Chap. 2.

Assessing the posterior probability in Eq. 3.10 cannot be done analytically because it involves integration over a high dimensional weight space. A technique of conducting these computations in a more tractable way is to approximate the posterior function. MacKay (1992) introduced the evidence framework and Buntine and Weigend (1991) approximated the posterior distribution, which is canonical, with a Gaussian distribution centered on one of its modes at $\{w_{MP}\}$. Neal (1992) proposed a more general and exact approach, where the hybrid Monte Carlo, the subject of Chap. 4, is used to estimate integrations over weight space. The technique of MacKay (1992) was implemented for this chapter because it is computationally cheaper than the hybrid Monte Carlo method and because the evidence approximation should produce superior results over Buntine and Weigend's (1991) technique when estimating regularization coefficients.

MacKay's evidence framework gives principled methods for model selection, prediction, and estimating the regularization coefficients with no validation data set. This permits more data to be used for training the neural network, which is advantageous when only limited data is accessible for training. The evidence framework is described as follows:

1. *Estimating Regularization Coefficients*: As described in Chap. 2, the evidence of α is evaluated by integrating over network weight parameters as:

$$p([D]|\alpha, H) = \int p([D]|\{w\}, H) p(\{w\}|\alpha) d\{w\} \qquad (3.13)$$

Using Eq. 3.13, MacKay (1992) derived an expression for the most probable regularization coefficient α_{MP} that maximizes $p([D]|\alpha, H)$. This has the form (Bishop 1995):

$$\alpha_{MP} = \frac{\gamma}{\sum w_i^2} \qquad (3.14)$$

where

$$\gamma = \sum_{i=1}^{W} \frac{\lambda_i}{\lambda_i + \alpha} \qquad (3.15)$$

and λ_i are eigenvectors of the Hessian matrix $[A]$ or second derivative of the objective function in Eq. 3.11 with respect to weight parameters. The Hessian is computed using the Pearlmutter method (Pearlmutter 1994; Bishop 1995).

Training the network is conducted by minimizing Eq. 3.11 and by initializing α to a small random number. The weighted parameters are adjusted by using the scaled conjugate gradient algorithm described in Chap. 2. When a minimum value is attained, then α_{MP} is estimated using Eq. 3.14 by maintaining $\{w\}$ constant. This technique is repeated again until α and $\{w\}$ converge to stable levels.

2. *Model Order Selection*: The evidence framework is a technique that is used to compare neural network models of varying complexity by calculating the evidence of the model. For a neural network model, H_i, the evidence is given by (MacKay 1992):

$$p([D]|H_i) = \int p([D]|\alpha, H_i) p(\alpha|H_i) d\{w\} \qquad (3.16)$$

The logarithm of Eq. 3.16 can, by following the argument of MacKay (1992), be written:

$$\ln p([D]|H_i) = -E(\{w\}) - \frac{1}{2} \ln \det([A]) + \frac{W}{2} \ln \alpha$$
$$+ \ln \left(2^N N!\right) + \frac{1}{2} \ln \left(\frac{4\pi}{\gamma}\right) \qquad (3.17)$$

Previous research has revealed a distinct correlation between the model evidence and generalization capacity of a neural network (Bishop 1995). Equation 3.17 permits the model with the highest evidence to be chosen without the need to segment the data into training and validation sets.

3. *Moderated Outputs*: Neural networks approximate a mapping function by inter-
polating in areas of a function space estimated by a finite set of training data.
Therefore, the error in the predictions within this space is higher than predictions
outside of this space. Moderated outputs were formulated by MacKay (1992)
to fine-tune the neural network output by an amount that is a function of the
uncertainty of the weight parameters. An equation for the moderated output can
be derived by assuming that the activation function of the output neuron, a, is
a linear function of the neural network weights which can be written as follows
(MacKay 1992):

$$P(C_1|\{\mathbf{x}\}) = g\left(K(s)a_{MP}\right) \tag{3.18}$$

where

$$K(s) = \left(1 + \frac{\pi s^2}{8}\right)^{-\frac{1}{2}} \tag{3.19}$$

and

$$s^2(x) = \{g\}^T[A]^{-1}\{g\} \tag{3.20}$$

Here, a_{MP} is the activation of the output neuron when $\{w\} = \{w_{MP}\}$ and $\{g\}$ is
the derivative of a with respect to $\{w\}$.

3.2.2   Radial-Basis Function (RBF)

The other neural network architecture used for this chapter was the Radial-Basis
Function (RBF) which is a feed-forward network, trained using a supervised training
algorithm (Haykin 1999; Buhmann and Ablowitz 2003; Marwala 2009). The RBF
is usually arranged with a single hidden layer of units whose activation function is
selected from a class of functions called *basis functions*. The activation of the hidden
units, in an RBF neural network, is given by a non-linear function of the distance
between the input vector and a prototype vector (Bishop 1995).

Garg et al. (2010) successfully evolved an RBF network using a genetic
algorithm to obtain an optimal architecture and applied these to predict drill flank
wear. The results obtained gave a more accurate network which was computationally
efficient. Fisch et al. (2010) successfully applied the RBF neural network for
intrusion detection and compared this to other techniques such as the MLP, neuro-
fuzzy networks and decision trees, and observed that the RBF was capable of
detecting novel attacks.

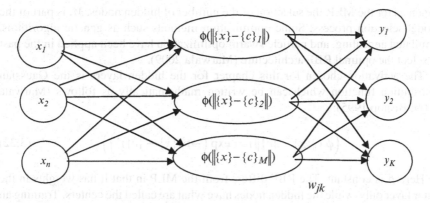

Fig. 3.1 Radial basis function network architecture

Goel and Stander (2009) compared three error criteria to select RBF network attributes such as activation functions and coordinates of centers. The results demonstrated that this selection criterion gave the best results. Baddari et al. (2009) applied the RBF to inverting seismic data and Li et al. (2010) applied the RBF to forecast ecological footprints. Kumar et al. (2010) applied the RBF for parameter estimation in rotorcraft and showed that the RBF gave better results than the finite difference approach. Wu et al. (2010) applied the RBF to predict the onset of Parkinson's disease tremor and Kagoda et al. (2010) applied RBF networks to forecasting stream flows.

Some of the successful applications of the RBF include applications in magneto hydrodynamic simulations by Colaco et al. (2009), image registration and warping by Siddiqui et al. (2009), the estimation of the biophysical parameters in rice by Yang et al. (2009), and the estimation of the orbit of global positioning systems by Preseren and Stopar (2009), as well as the discrimination of cover crops in olive orchards by Hervas-Martinez et al. (2010).

While similar to the MLP networks in a number of ways, RBF networks have several advantages. They usually train much faster than the MLP networks, and are less prone to problems with non-stationary inputs due to the behavior of the radial basis function (Bishop 1995). The RBF network can thus be described as shown in Fig. 3.1 and can be described mathematically as follows (Buhmann and Ablowitz 2003; Marwala 2009; Hervas-Martinez et al. 2010):

$$y_k(\{x\}) = \sum_{j=1}^{M} w_{jk} \phi_j \left(\| \{x\} - \{c\}_j \| \right) \qquad (3.21)$$

In Eq. 3.21, w_{jk} represents the output weights, each corresponding to the connection between a hidden unit and an output unit, M represents the number of hidden units, $\{c\}_j$ is the center for the jth neuron, $\phi_j(\{x\})$ is the jth non-linear activation function, $\{x\}$ the input vector, and $k = 1, 2, 3, ..., M$ (Bishop 1995).

Again as for the MLP, the selection of the number of hidden nodes, M, is part of the model selection process. Some optimization methods such as genetic algorithms, simulated annealing, and particle swarm optimization have been applied in the past to select the optimal RBF architecture (Marwala 2009).

The activation chosen for this chapter for the hidden layers is the Gaussian distribution function which can be written mathematically as follows (Marwala 2009; Bishop 1995):

$$\left(\phi \left(\| \{x\} - \{c\} \| \right) = \exp \left(-\beta (\{x\} - \{c\})^2 \right) \right) \tag{3.22}$$

Here β is constant. The RBF differs from the MLP in that it has weights in the outer layer only, while the hidden nodes have what are called the centers. Training an RBF network entails identifying two sets of parameters: the centers and the output weights which can both be viewed as free parameters in a regression framework. The centers and network weights can both be determined simultaneously using the full Bayesian method or can alternatively be identified using the maximization of expectation technique (Bishop 1995). For this chapter, a two-stage training process was used to first identify the centers, followed by a determination of the network weights. The first stage is the use of a self-organizing map technique called the *k-means* clustering method to determine the centers (Hartigan 1975). The step of identifying the centers only considers the input space, while the identification of the network weights considers both the input and output space.

The *k-means* procedure is aimed at clustering objects based on attributes into k segments. In this chapter, k is equal to the number of centers, M, in the RBF network. The objective of the *k-means* algorithm is to discover the centers of natural clusters in the data and assumes that the object attributes form a vector space. It achieves this objective by minimizing the total intra-cluster variance, or, the squared error function which can be written as follows (Hartigan and Wong 1979; Marwala 2009):

$$E = \sum_{i=1}^{C} \sum_{x_j \in S_i} \left(\{x\}_j - \{c\}_i \right)^2 \tag{3.23}$$

In Eq. 3.23, C is the number of clusters in S_i, $i = 1, 2, ..., M$ and $\{c\}_i$ is the center of all the points $x_j \in S_i$.

For this chapter, the Lloyd's classic (Lloyd 1982) algorithm is used to identify the cluster centers. Lloyd's algorithm was initialized by randomly dividing the input space into k initial sets or using heuristic data. The mean point is calculated for each set and then a new partition is constructed by associating each point with the closest center. The centroids are then re-calculated for the new clusters, and the process is repeated by changing these two steps until convergence. Convergence is achieved when the centroids no longer change or the points no longer switch clusters.

The technique in which the centers are identified has been described. So, the next undertaking is to calculate the network weights in Eq. 3.23 given the training data and the identified centers. To undertake this task, the Moore-Penrose pseudo inverse

(Moore 1920; Penrose 1955; Golub and Van Loan 1996) was used. It should be noted that once the centers have been identified, then the estimation of the network weights becomes a linear process (Golub and Van Loan 1996). Given the training data and the centers identified, then Eq. 3.21 can be rewritten as:

$$[y_{ij}] = [\phi_{ik}][w_{kj}] \qquad (3.24)$$

Here, $[y_{ij}]$ is the output matrix, with i represents the number of training examples and j represents the number of outputs. Parameter $[\phi_{ik}]$ is the activation function matrix in the hidden layer, i represents the training examples, k is the number of hidden neurons while $[w_{kj}]$ is the weight matrix.

From Eq. 3.24 it can be observed that to solve for the weight matrix, $[w_{kj}]$, what ought to happen is the inversion of the activation function matrix $[\phi_{ik}]$. However, this matrix is not square and therefore it cannot be inverted using standard matrix techniques. Fortunately, this matrix can be inverted using the Moore-Penrose pseudo-inverse method which is written mathematically as follows (Penrose 1955):

$$[\phi_{ik}]^* = \left([\phi_{ik}][\phi_{ik}]^T\right)^{-1}[\phi_{ik}]^T \qquad (3.25)$$

This, therefore, implies that the weight matrix may be estimated by using the pseudo inverse factor as:

$$[w_{kj}] = [\phi_{ik}]^*[y_{ij}] \qquad (3.26)$$

The NETLAB® toolbox (Nabney 2001) that runs in MATLAB® was used to implement the RBF neural network of this chapter.

3.2.3 Model Selection

After identifying the weights through training the RBF model with a segment of the data labeled 'training data set', an appropriate model, given by the size of the hidden nodes, was obtained from the segment of the validation data set. As explained before, to successfully conduct an interstate conflict modeling process, it is important to identify the correct model, whether it is the MLP or the RBF. The process of selecting an appropriate model is known as model selection (Burnham and Anderson 2002). The process of deriving a model from data is a non-unique problem. This is because many models can fit the training data and, therefore, it becomes impossible to identify the most appropriate model.

The general approach to selecting a model is based on two principles: the goodness of fit and the model's complexity. Essentially, goodness of fit implies that a good model should predict the validation data which it has not seen during the training stage. The complexity of the model is based on Occam's principle which states that the best model, the preferred model in this chapter, is the simplest one.

In selecting the best model, there are crucial questions that need to be taken into account and two of these questions are:

• What is the best balance between the goodness of fit and the complexity of the model?
• How are these attributes actually implemented?

For this chapter, goodness of fit was measured by the error between the model's prediction and the validation set, while the complexity of the model was measured by the number of free parameters in the data. As stated before, free parameters in the MLP model are defined as the network weights and biases, while in the RBF network they are defined as the network centers and weights. In this chapter, model selection is viewed as the mechanism for selecting a model that has a good probability of estimating the validation data set that it has not seen during the training stage, and the bias and variance are measures of the ability of this model to operate in an acceptable way.

For this chapter, the cross-validation method (Devijver and Kittler 1982; Chang et al. 1992; Kohavi 1995) was used. The way in which cross-validation is conducted is to divide the data into three segments. The first segment is called the training set, which is used to train the RBF networks. For this chapter, for the RBF, *k-means* and pseudo-inverse techniques were used to estimate the free parameters (centers and weights in Eq. 3.21).

The way in which this training process was conducted was to train several models (with a different number of hidden nodes). The second set of data is called the validation data set, and was used for this chapter to select the best RBF models – this is the model selection stage. Finally, the third data set of data called the testing set was used to evaluate the effectiveness of the selected models.

3.3   A Comparison Between the MLP and the RBF Paradigms

One important task is to investigate which of the two paradigms *i.e.*, the MLP and RBF is better in terms of accuracy, simplicity, and efficiency. Mehrabi et al. (2009) applied the MLP and RBF neural networks to differentiate chronic obstructive pulmonary from congestive heart failure diseases. They used a Bayesian regularization framework, described in Chap. 2, to increase the generalization ability of the MLP network, while they applied the K-Means clustering technique to choose the RBF centers to identify the optimum size for the radial basis functions. When they applied the 10-fold cross-validation technique, the MLP gave a sensitivity of 83.9%, a specificity of 86%, and an Area Under the receiver operating characteristic Curve (AUC) of 0.889; while the RBF network gave a sensitivity of 81.8%, a specificity of 88.4%, and AUC of 0.924. From these results it is unclear which technique – the MLP or the RBF – is better.

Janghel et al. (2010) applied a number of techniques including the MLP and RBF for breast cancer diagnosis and observed that the MLP network performs better than

Table 3.1 A comparison between the MLP and the RBF paradigms

Attribute	MLP	RBF
Structure	Activation functions, biases, weights in all layers	Activation functions, centers, weights only in the second layer
Architecture	Cross-coupled connections on the first and second layers	Cross-coupled connections on the second layer only
Data processing	Requires normalization	Does not require normalization
Training	Weights and biases are identified simultaneously	Two stage: identifying the centers followed by an identifying weights (this is a linear programming exercise)
Computational Efficiency	Computationally expensive	Computationally cheap

the RBF network. Ghomi and Mahdi-Goodarzi (2010) applied and compared the MLP and the RBF for the forecasting of peak loads of electric utilities and observed that the MLP gave more accuracy than the RBF.

Msiza et al. (2007) applied and compared the MLP and the RBF for forecasting the short-term and long-term water demand in the Gauteng Province, Republic of South Africa. The RBF converged to a solution faster than the MLP and it was the most accurate and the most reliable tool in processing large amounts of non-linear, non-parametric data in this investigation. Other comparisons where the two methods give similar results include that by Yilmaz and Özer (2009) for pitch angle control in wind turbines.

These comparisons between the MLP and the RBF are summarized in Table 3.1. In this table, several attributes were used to compare the two methods: these were the structures, architectures, data processing requirements, training characteristics, and computational efficiency of both methods. From this comparison, it can be concluded that RBF networks generally have a smaller number of free parameters, and are also less topologically complex than the MLP paradigm. Furthermore, the RBF is generally more computationally efficient in training than the MLP.

3.4 Application to Interstate Conflict

The MLP and the RBF were employed to classify the MID data. The main focus was to look at the percentage of correct MID prediction of the test data set by each technique. Previous research has shown that a balanced set, *i.e.*, an equal number of conflict and peace dyads give more consistent conclusions than studies that do not follow this practice. The same principle was adhered to in this study. The training set for this chapter contained 1,000 randomly chosen dyads, 500 from each group. The test set contained 392 dyads which were conflict dyads and 392 which were non-conflict dyads.

Table 3.2 Classification results

Method	True conflicts TC	False peaces FP	True peaces TP	False conflicts FC
RBF	278	114	288	104
MLP	295	97	299	93

The MLP and the RBF neural networks require one to choose the best architecture to give good classification results. The best combination of the number of hidden units, activation function, training algorithm and training cycles that result in a network best able to generalize the test data was searched for during the model selection process. This helped to avoid the risk of over or under training. Logistic and hyperbolic activation functions were chosen for the output and hidden layers respectively. The number of hidden units was 10 for the Gaussian activation function and 10 hidden units were chosen as activation functions for the RBF network.

Table 3.2 gives the confusion matrix for the results. Although the MLP network performed slightly better than the RBF network in predicting True Conflicts (true positives), this was achieved at the expense of reducing the number of False Peaces (true negatives) predicted. Also, MLP picked up on the True Peaces (true positives) better than the RBF without reducing the number of False Conflicts (false negatives). Overall, the RBF network predicted conflict and peace with merit figures of 71% and 73%, respectively. The corresponding results for the MLP are better at 75% and 76%, respectively for conflict and peace. The averaged results for correct predictions are 72% for the RBF and 75.5% for the MLP.

The performance of the classifiers was also evaluated using the Receiver Operating Characteristics (ROC) curve. The ROC curve is a graphical depiction of the sensitivity of the classifier, also called the true positive rate, against the sensitivity also called the false positive rate. The sensitivity was calculated as the difference between 1 and the specificity.

The ROC curve is a valuable tool that has been used for a wide range of applications. Lasko et al. (2005) used ROC curves in the classification of biomedical informatics and Lind et al. (2002) used the ROC curves to evaluate methods of predicting radiation-induced symptomatic lung injury. Mohamed (2006) used ROC curves for dynamic protein classification, and furthermore Yonelinas and Parks (2007) used ROC curves in recognition memory work. Further information on ROC curves can be found in the work of Beiden et al. (2000), Dorfman et al. (1995), and Halpern et al. (1996).

The ROC graphs for the MLP and the RBF appear in Fig. 3.2. The Area Under the Curve (AUC) was used as a measure to compare the performance of each classifier. The Areas Under the Curves for MLP and RBF were 0.84 and 0.82, respectively thus giving a very good classifier in accordance with ROC curves (Au et al. 2004; Metz 2006; Brown and Davis 2006). Thus MLP is clearly better in predicting the conflicts without affecting the prediction of peace.

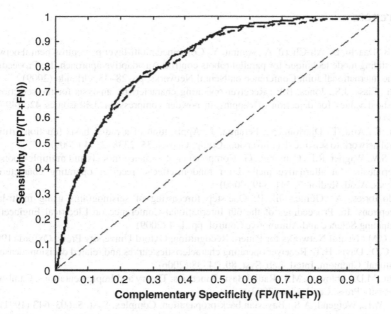

Fig. 3.2 A graph showing the relevance of each liberal variable with regard to MIDs classification (solid curve is MLP while dashed curve is the RBF)

3.5 Conclusion

For this chapter the MLP and RBF techniques were implemented for modeling interstate conflict. The MLP was formulated using the evidence framework within the context of a Bayesian network and was trained using the scaled conjugate gradient method. The RBF network was trained using the *k-means* algorithm to identify the centers and the pseudo-inverse technique was used to estimate the output layer weights. The results obtained indicate that the MLP technique was better at predicting interstate conflict than the RBF technique.

3.6 Further Work

For further work, a combination of the RBF and MLP networks within the context of a committee of networks, should be used and compared to the individual methods for interstate conflict modeling. In particular, an optimal combination of these two techniques should be identified.

References

Achili, B., Daachi, B., Ali-Cherif, A., Amirat, Y.: Combined multi-layer perceptron neural network and sliding mode technique for parallel robots control: An adaptive approach. In: Proceedings of the International Joint Conference on Neural Networks, pp. 28–35, Orlando (2009)

Au, Y.H., Eissa, J.S., Jones, B.E.: Receiver operating characteristic analysis for the selection of threshold values for detection of capping in powder compression. Ultrasonics **42**, 149–153 (2004)

Baddari, K., Aifa, T., Djarfour, N., Ferahtia, J.: Application of a radial basis function artificial neural network to seismic data inversion. Comp. Geosci. **35**, 2338–2344 (2009)

Beiden, S.V., Wagner, R.F., Campbell, G.: Components-of-variance models and multiple-bootstrap experiments: An alternative method for random-effects, receiver operating characteristic analysis. Acad. Radiol. **7**, 341–349 (2000)

Bernardo-Torres, A., Gómez-Gil, P.: One-step forecasting of seismograms using multi-layer perceptrons. In: Proceedings of the 6th International Conference on Electrical Engineering, Computing Science and Automotive Control, pp. 1–4 (2009)

Bishop, C.M.: Neural Networks for Pattern Recognition. Oxford University Press, Oxford (1995)

Brown, C.D., Davis, H.T.: Receiver operating characteristics curves and related decision measures: A tutorial. Chemom. Intell. Lab. Syst. **80**, 24–38 (2006)

Buhmann, M.D., Ablowitz, M.J.: Radial Basis Functions: Theory and Implementations. Cambridge University Press, Cambridge (2003)

Buntine, W.L., Weigend, A.S.: Bayesian back-propagation. Complex. Syst. **5**, 603–643 (1991)

Burnham, K.P., Anderson, D.R.: Model Selection and Multimodel Inference: A Practical-Theoretic Approach. Springer, Berlin (2002)

Chang, J., Luo, Y., Su, K.: GPSM: A generalized probabilistic semantic model for ambiguity resolution. In: Proceedings of the 30th Annual Meeting on Association for Computing, pp. 177–184 (1992)

Colaco, M.J., Dulikravich, G.S., Orlande, H.R.B.: Magnetohydrodynamic simulations using radial basis functions. Int. J. Heat Mass Transf. **52**, 5932–5939 (2009)

Coppola Jr., E., Szidarovszky, F.: Conflict between water supply and environmental health risk: A computational neural network approach. Int. Game Theory Rev. **6**, 475–492 (2004)

Crossingham, B., Marwala, T., Lagazio, M.: Optimised rough sets for modelling interstate conflict. In: Proceedings of the IEEE International Conference on Systems, Man and Cybernetics, pp. 1198–1204 (2008)

Devijver, P.A., Kittler, J.: Pattern Recognition: A Statistical Approach. Prentice-Hall, London (1982)

Dorfman, D.D., Berbaum, K.S., Lenth, R.V.: Multireader, multicase receiver operating characteristic methodology: A bootstrap analysis. Acad. Radiol. **2**, 626–633 (1995)

Duta, M.C., Duta, M.D.: Multi-objective turbomachinery optimization using a gradient-enhanced multi-layer perceptron. Int. J. Numer. Methods Fluid. **61**, 591–605 (2009)

Fisch, D., Hofmann, A., Sick, B.: On the versatility of radial basis function neural networks: A case study in the field of intrusion detection. Inf. Sci. **180**, 2421–2439 (2010)

Freeman, J., Skapura, D.: Neural Networks: Algorithms, Applications and Programming Techniques. Addison-Wesley, Reading (1991)

Garg, S., Patra, K., Khetrapal, V., Pal, S.K., Chakraborty, D.: Genetically evolved radial basis function network based prediction of drill flank wear. Eng. Appl. Artif. Intell. **23**, 1112–1120 (2010)

Ghomi, M.G., Mahdi-Goodarzi, M.: Peak load forecasting of electric utilities for west province of IRAN by using neural network without weather information. In: Proceedings of the 12th International Conference on Computer Modelling and Simulation, pp. 28–32 (2010)

Goel, T., Stander, N.: Comparing three error criteria for selecting radial basis function network topology. Comput. Methods Appl. Mech. Eng **198**, 2137–2150 (2009)

Golub, G.H., van Loan, C.F.: Matrix Computation. Johns Hopkins University Press, Baltimore (1996)

Halpern, E.J., Albert, M., Krieger, A.M., Metz, C.E., Maidment, A.D.: Comparison of receiver operating characteristic curves on the basis of optimal operating points. Acad. Radiol. **3**, 245–253 (1996)

Hartigan, J.A.: Clustering Algorithms. Wiley, Englewood Cliffs (1975)

Hartigan, J.A., Wong, M.A.: A K-Means clustering algorithm. Appl. Stat. **28**, 100–108 (1979)

Hassoun, M.H.: Fundamentals of Artificial Neural Networks. MIT Press, Cambridge (1995)

Haykin, S.: Neural Networks. Prentice-Hall, Englewood Cliffs (1999)

He, T., Dong, Z.Y., Meng, K., Wang, H., Oh, Y.T.: Accelerating multi-layer perceptron based short-term demand forecasting using graphics processing units. Trans & Distr Conf & Expo: Asia and Pacific: 1–4 (2009)

Hervas-Martinez, C., Gutierrez, P.A., Pena-Barragan, J.M., Jurado-Exposito, M., Lopez-Granados, F.: A logistic radial basis function regression method for discrimination of cover crops in olive orchards. Expert Syst. Appl. **37**, 8432–8444 (2010)

Hipel, K.W., Meister, D.B.: Conflict analysis methodology for modelling coalitions in multilateral negotiations. Inf. Decis. Technol. Amsterdam **19**, 85–103 (1994)

Hu, X., Weng, Q.: Estimating impervious surfaces from medium spatial resolution imagery using the self-organizing Map and Multi-layer Perceptron Neural Networks. Remote Sens. Environ **113**, 2089–2102 (2009)

Ikuta, C., Uwate, Y., Nishio, Y.: Chaos glial network connected to multi-layer perceptron for solving two-spiral problem. In: Proceeding of IEEE International Symposium on Circuits and Systems: Nano-Bio Circuit Fabrics and Systems, pp. 1360–1363 (2010)

Iswaran, N., Percy, D.F.: Conflict analysis using bayesian neural networks and generalized linear models. J. Oper. Res. Soc. **61**, 332–341 (2010)

Janghel, RR., Shukla, A., Tiwari, R., Kala, R.: Breast cancer diagnosis using artificial neural network models. In: Proceedings of the 3rd International Conference on Information Science and Interaction Science, pp. 89–94 (2010)

Kagoda, P.A., Ndiritu, J., Ntuli, C., Mwaka, B.: Application of radial basis function neural networks to short-term streamflow forecasting. Phys. Chem. Earth **35**, 571–581 (2010)

Karami, A.R., Ahmadian-Attari, M., Tavakoli, H.: Multi-layer perceptron neural networks decoder for LDPC codes. In: Proceeding of the 5th International Conference on Wireless Communications, Networking and Mobile Computing, pp. 1–4 (2009)

Kohavi, R.: A study of cross-validation and bootstrap for accuracy estimation and model selection. In: Proceedings of the 4th International Joint Conference on Artificial Intelligence, pp. 1137–1143 (1995)

Kowalski, C.: Using adaptive neural networks for situation recognition in high- and low-intensity conflict. In: Proceedings of the International Joint Conference on Neural Networks, 912p (1992)

Krishna, H.S.: Highly accurate multi-layer perceptron neural network for air data system. Defence Sci. J. **59**, 670–674 (2009)

Kumar, R., Ganguli, R., Omkar, S.N.: Rotorcraft parameter estimation using radial basis function neural network. Appl. Math. Comput. **216**, 584–597 (2010)

Kushwaha, SK., Shakya, M.: Multi-layer perceptron architecture for tertiary structure prediction of helical content of proteins from peptide sequences. In: Proceedings of the International Conference on Advances in Recent Technologies in Communication and Computing, pp. 465–467 (2009)

Lasko, T.A., Bhagwat, J.G., Zou, K.H., Ohno-Machado, L.: The use of receiver operating characteristic curves in biomedical informatics. J. Biomed. Inform. **38**, 404–415 (2005)

Leke, B., Marwala, T., Tettey, T.: Using inverse neural network for HIV adaptive control. Int. J. Comput. Intell. Res **3**, 11–15 (2007)

Li, X.M., Xiao, R.B., Yuan, S.H., Chen, J.A., Zhou, J.X.: Urban total ecological footprint forecasting by using radial basis function neural networks: A case study of Wuhan city, China. Ecol. Indic. **10**, 241–248 (2010)

Lind, P.A., Marks, L.B., Hollis, D., Fan, M., Zhou, S.M., Munley, M.T., Shafman, T.D., Jaszczak, R.J., Coleman, R.E.: Receiver operating characteristic curves to assess predictors of radiation-induced symptomatic lung injury. Int. J. Radiat. Oncol. Biol. Phys. **54**, 340–347 (2002)

Lloyd, S.O.: Least squares quantization in PCM. IEEE Trans. Inf. Theory **28**, 129–137 (1982)

MacKay, D.: Bayesian methods for adaptive models. PhD thesis, California Institute of Technology (1991)

MacKay, D.J.C.: Bayesian methods for adaptive models, 2nd edn. PhD thesis, California University of Technology (1992)

Marwala, T.: On damage identification using a committee of neural networks. J. Eng. Mech. **126**, 43–50 (2000)

Marwala, T.: Probabilistic fault identification using a committee of neural networks and vibration data. J. Aircraft **38**, 138–146 (2001)

Marwala, T.: Fault classification using pseudo modal energies and neural networks. Am. Inst. Aeronaut. Astronaut. J. **41**, 82–89 (2003)

Marwala, T.: Bayesian training of neural network using genetic programming. Pattern Recognit. Lett. **28**, 1452–1458 (2007)

Marwala, T.: Computational Intelligence for Missing Data Imputation, Estimation and Management: Knowledge Optimization Techniques. IGI Global Publications, New York (2009)

Marwala, T., Hunt, H.E.M.: Fault identification using finite element models and neural networks. Mech. Syst. Signal Process. **13**, 475–490 (1999)

Masci, P., Tedeschi, A.: Modelling and evaluation of a game-theory approach for airborne conflict resolution in omnet++. In: Proceedings of the 2nd International Conference on Dependability, pp.162–165 (2009)

Mehrabi, S., Maghsoudloo, M., Arabalibeik, H., Noormand, R., Nozari, Y.: Application of multilayer perceptron and radial basis function neural networks in differentiating between chronic obstructive pulmonary and congestive heart failure diseases. Expert Syst. Appl. **36**, 6956–6959 (2009)

Metz, C.E.: Receiver operating characteristic analysis: A tool for the quantitative evaluation of observer performance and imaging systems. J. Am. Coll. Radiol. **3**, 413–422 (2006)

Moffat, J., Medhurst, J.: Modelling of human decision-making in simulation models of conflict using experimental gaming. Eur. J. Oper. Res. **196**, 1147–1157 (2009)

Mohamed, N.: Detection of epileptic activity in the EEG using artificial neural networks M.Sc. (Electrical Engineering) thesis University of the Witwatersrand (2003)

Mohamed, S.: Dynamic protein classification: Adaptive models based on incremental learning strategies. Unpublished Master's Thesis, University of the Witwatersrand, Johannesburg (2006)

Mohamed, N., Rubin, D., Marwala, T.: Detection of epileptiform activity in human EEG signals using Bayesian neural networks. Neural Inf. Process – Lett. Rev. **10**, 1–10 (2006)

Moller, M.F.: A scaled conjugate gradient algorithm for fast supervised learning. Neural Netw. **6**, 525–533 (1993)

Moore, E.H.: On the reciprocal of the general algebraic matrix. Bull. Am. Math. Soc. **26**, 394–395 (1920)

Msiza, I.S., Nelwamondo, F.V., Marwala, T.: Water demand forecasting using multi-layer perceptron and radial basis functions. In: Proceedings of the IEEE International Conference on Neural Networks, pp. 13–18 (2007)

Mubareka, S., Ehrlich, D.: Identifying and modelling environmental indicators for assessing population vulnerability to conflict using ground and satellite data. Ecol. Indic. **10**, 493–503 (2010)

Nabney, I.T.: Netlab: Algorithms for Pattern Recognition. Springer, Cambridge (2001)

Narasinga-Rao, M.R., Sridhar, G.R., Madhu, K., Rao, A.A.: A clinical decision support system using multi-layer perceptron neural network to predict quality of life in diabetes. Diabetes Metab. Syndr.: Clin. Res. Rev. **4**(1), 57–59 (2010)

Neal, R.M.: Bayesian training of back-propagation networks by the hybrid monte carlo method. Technical Report CRG-TR-92-1, Department of Computer Science, University of Toronto (1992)

Pasero, E., Raimondo, G., Ruffa, S.: MULP: A multi-layer perceptron application to long-term, out-of-sample time series prediction. Lect. Notes Comput. Sci. **6064**, 566–575 (2010)

Patel, P., Marwala, T.: Neural networks, fuzzy inference systems and adaptive-neuro fuzzy inference systems for financial decision making. Lect. Notes Comput. Sci. **4234**, 430–439 (2006)

Pearlmutter, B.A.: Fast exact multiplication by the Hessian. Neural Comput. **6**, 147–160 (1994)

Penrose, R.: A generalized inverse for matrices. Proc. Camb. Philos. Soc. **51**, 406–413 (1955)

Pontin, D.R., Worner, S.P., Watts, M.J.: Using time lagged input data to improve prediction of stinging jellyfish occurrence at New Zealand beaches by multi-layer perceptrons. Lect. Notes. Comput. Sci. **5506**, 909–916 (2009)

Preseren, P.P., Stopar, B.: GPS orbit approximation using radial basis function networks. Comput. Geosci. **35**, 1389–1396 (2009)

Sancho-Gómez, J.L., García-Laencina, P.J., Figueiras-Vidal, A.R.: Combining missing data imputation and pattern classification in a multi-layer perceptron. Intell. Autom. Soft Comput. **15**, 539–553 (2009)

Schrodt, P.A.: Prediction of interstate conflict outcomes using a neural network. Soc. Sci. Comput. Rev **9**, 359–380 (1991)

Siddiqui, A.M., Masood, A., Saleem, M.: A locally constrained radial basis function for registration and warping of images. Pattern Recognit. Lett. **30**, 377–390 (2009)

Sug, H.: A pilot sampling method for multi-layer perceptrons. In: Proceedings of the 13th WSEAS International Conference on Computers, pp. 629–633 (2009)

Sug, H.: Investigating better multi-layer perceptrons for the task of classification. WSEAS Trans. Comput. **9**, 475–485 (2010)

Tettey, T., Marwala, T.: Conflict modelling and knowledge extraction using computational intelligence methods. In: Proceedings of the 11th International Conference on Intelligence Engineering Systems, pp. 161–166 (2007)

Vilakazi, B.C., Marwala, T.: Condition monitoring using computational intelligence. In: Laha, D., Mandal, P. (eds.) Handbook on Computational Intelligence in Manufacturing and Production Management, illustrated edn. IGI Publishers, New York (2007)

Watts, M.J., Worner, S.P.: Predicting the distribution of fungal crop diseases from abiotic and biotic factors using multi-layer perceptrons. Lect. Notes Comput. Sci. **5506**, 901–908 (2009)

Wu, D., Warwick, K., Ma, Z., Burgess, J.G., Pan, S., Aziz, T.Z.: Prediction of parkinson's disease tremor onset using radial basis function neural networks. Expert Syst. Appl. **37**, 2923–2928 (2010)

Yang, X.H., Wang, F.M., Huang, J.F., Wang, J.W., Wang, R.C., Shen, Z.Q., Wang, X.Z.: Comparison between radial basis function neural network and regression model for estimation of rice biophysical parameters using remote sensing. Pedosphere **19**, 176–188 (2009)

Yazdanmehr, M., Anijdan, S.H.M., Samadi, A., Bahrami, A.: Mechanical behavior modeling of nanocrystalline NiAl compound by a feed-forward back-propagation multi-layer perceptron ANN. Comput. Mater. Sci. **44**, 1231–1235 (2009)

Yilmaz, A.S., Özer, Z.: Pitch angle control in wind turbines above the rated wind speed by multi-layer perceptron and radial basis function neural networks. Expert Syst. Appl. **36**, 9767–9775 (2009)

Yolles, M.I.: Towards simulation of the conflict modelling cycle. In: Proceedings of the IEEE International Conference on System, Man and Cybernetics, pp. 401–411 (1993)

Yonelinas, A.P., Parks, C.M.: Receiver operating characteristics (ROCs) in recognition memory: A review. Psychol. Bull. **133**, 800–832 (2007)

Yoon, Y., Peterson, L.L.: Artificial neural networks: An emerging new technique. In: Proceedings of the ACM SIGBDP Conference on Trends and Directions in Expert Systems, pp. 417–422 (1990)

Zadeh, M.R., Amin, S., Khalili, D., Singh, V.P.: Daily outflow prediction by multi layer perceptron with logistic sigmoid and tangent sigmoid activation functions. Water Res. Manag. **24**, 2673–2688 (2010)

Zhang, P., Li, H.: Hybrid model of continuous hidden markov model and multi-layer perceptron in speech recognition. In: Proceedings of the 2nd International Conference on Intelligent Computing Technology and Automotive, pp. 62–65 (2009)

Chapter 4
Bayesian Approaches to Modeling Interstate Conflict

4.1 Introduction

Chapter 2 presented a method of identifying the relevance of variables for the prediction of Militarised Interstate Disputes (MIDs), which is called the automatic relevance determination. This method applies Bayesian theory and the evidence framework to construct the automatic relevance determination method. The automatic relevance determination method was used to determine the relevance of interstate variables that are essential for modeling of MIDs. It was found that the two liberal variables, economic interdependence and democracy, and two realist variables, capability ratio and allies, were particularly important for explaining ad predicting the MIDs.

In Chap. 3, the Multi-Layer Perceptron (MLP) neural network and the Radial Basis Function (RBF) neural network were introduced and applied to model MIDs. The results obtained demonstrated that the MLP is better at predicting MIDs than the RBF neural network. This is mainly because structurally the MLP cross-couples the input variables better than the RBF does. Because of this observation that the MLP is better than the RBF, this chapter will only consider the MLP.

With the frequency at which wars are occurring, it has become imperative that more research effort be directed towards early warning and conflict management. The main aim of conducting this research is to further understand the occurrence and management of international conflict. A significant amount of research effort has been channeled towards conducting empirical studies of international conflict. These empirical studies are advancing on two fronts. Firstly, there has been significant effort dedicated to improving the explanatory variables in interstate interactions. Secondly, there have been efforts to find a suitable model which to accurately forecast international conflict. A successful outcome in quantitative analysis is therefore been defined as the ability to accurately forecast international conflict and, at the same time, provide a causal explanations for dispute outcomes

T. Marwala and M. Lagazio, *Militarized Conflict Modeling using Computational Intelligence*, Advanced Information and Knowledge Processing, DOI 10.1007/978-0-85729-790-7_4, © Springer-Verlag London Limited 2011

(Beck et al. 2000). Improved results, both on the predication and explanation side, can then be used to specify early warning and conflict management tools, which will contribute to decision making and policy formulation.

Recent developments in data collection have allowed a significant improvement in the prediction of militarized interstate disputes. In this chapter, MIDs are defined as disputes between sovereign states below the threshold of war. MIDs include: explicit threats to use force, display of force, mobilization of force, or the use of force just short of war (Gochman and Maoz 1990). This allows studies to include a broad scope of conflicts that pose a grave threat to international peace and security but which have political effects and complications comparable to that of full warfare.

On the forecasting side, there is a need to find more accurate ways of predicting international conflict. This has seen a shift from statistical techniques to neural networks in an attempt to avoid the problems experienced with statistical models (Lagazio and Marwala 2005). However, neural networks have the disadvantage of not being transparent. For this reason, neural networks are not able to readily offer a causal explanation for any result obtained through their use. Up to now, in the field of interstate conflict, no studies have dealt with the issue of non-linear control for interstate disputes through the use of non-linear prediction models, such as neural networks, to build effective decision support systems for conflict prevention. Although some attempts have been made to use control theory in political science (Gillespie et al. 1977), these efforts rely on traditional control mechanisms, which are still based on a linear plant model. However, we know that this is not an accurate method for conflict data since the relationships among key variables are highly interdependent and non-linear (Russett et al. 2003; Lagazio and Russett 2004).

In an attempt to assess non-linear control methodologies for the MIDs, this chapter applies the Bayesian framework to produce a neural network model which predicts militarized interstate disputes (Marwala 2001; MacKay 1991, 1992; Zeng 1999). In particular, this chapter applies the hybrid Monte Carlo to sample the posterior probability function of the network weight, given the data.

Yu and van Engelen (2010) applied the arc refractor technique and the evidence framework for adaptive importance sampling on large networks and observed a substantial enhancement of reflector methods when compared to other adaptive importance sampling methods. Coles et al. (2009) successfully applied a grazing mobility strategy, which is inspired by the foraging behavior of herbivores grazing pastures, in Bayesian networks for mobile wireless sensor networks.

The neural networks developed were applied to model the relationships between the dyadic attributes and the MIDs, and then the HMC and Gaussian approximation result sets are compared against each other. Neural networks have been applied before to model the complex interrelationships between dyadic parameters and the MIDs (Thompson and Tucker 1997), however, the HMC has not yet been used to model the MIDs. It is therefore important to assess whether this less restrictive Bayesian framework, the HMC, which does not use the Gaussian approximation technique to calculate the model parameters, can in fact improve the prediction accuracy in conflict analysis. The results and conclusions obtained from these investigations are then reported.

4.2 Neural Networks

In this chapter, as in the previous chapter, multi-layer perceptron neural network models are expressed in the Bayesian context and trained through applying the evidence framework based on Gaussian approximation and hybrid Monte Carlo methods. These models are applied for dispute classification in conflict analysis, hence this section gives an over-view of neural networks within the context of classification problems. In this chapter, a multi-layer perceptron is applied to map the seven dyadic variables (x) and the militarized interstate disputes (y). The relationship between the kth MID, y_k, and the dyadic variables, x, may be written as follows (Bishop 1995; Marwala 2009):

$$y_k = f_{outer} \left(\sum_{j=1}^{M} w_{kj}^{(2)} f_{inner} \left(\sum_{i=1}^{d} w_{ji}^{(1)} x_i + w_{j0}^{(1)} \right) + w_{k0}^{(2)} \right) \tag{4.1}$$

Here, $w_{ji}^{(1)}$ and $w_{ji}^{(2)}$ indicate the weights in the first and second layers, respectively, going from input i to hidden unit j, M is the number of hidden units, d is the number of output units, while $w_{j0}^{(1)}$ indicates the bias for the hidden unit j and $w_{k0}^{(2)}$ indicates the bias for the output unit k.

Selecting suitable network architecture is a vital aspect of model building. For this chapter, the structure selected was the MLP trained by applying the scaled conjugate gradient method (Moller 1993). Furthermore, in selecting the suitable MLP model, another significant decision lies in the choice of the right number of hidden units (M), and the category of functional transformations that they achieve. This is because a large value of M will yield very flexible networks, which may learn not only the data structure but also the fundamental noise in the data. As an alternative, a small value of M will create networks that are incapable of modeling complex relationships. To recognize the optimal MLP structure, the network was trained numerous times through applying the scaled conjugate gradient method. The problem of identifying the weights and biases in neural networks may be posed in the Bayesian framework as (Bishop 1995; Marwala 2009):

$$P(w|[D]) = \frac{P([D]|w) P(w)}{P([D])} \tag{4.2}$$

where $P(w)$ is the probability distribution function of the weight-space in the absence of any data, also known as the prior distribution function and $[D] \equiv (y_1, \ldots, y_N)$ is a matrix containing the MID data. The expression $P(w|[D])$ is the posterior probability distribution function after the data have been observed, $P([D]|w)$ is the likelihood function and $P([D])$ is the normalization function, also known as the "evidence". For the MLP, Eq. 4.2 may be expanded by applying the cross-entropy error function to give (Bishop 1995; Marwala 2009):

$$P(w|[D]) = \frac{1}{Z_s} \exp \left(\beta \sum_n^N \sum_k^K \{t_{nk} \ln(y_{nk}) + (1 - t_{nk}) \ln(1 - y_{nk})\} - \sum_j^W \frac{\alpha_j}{2} w_j^2 \right)$$

(4.3)

where

$$Z_S(\alpha, \beta) = \left(\frac{2\pi}{\beta} \right)^{N/2} + \left(\frac{2\pi}{\alpha} \right)^{W/2}$$

(4.4)

The cost-entropy function was applied because of its classification advantages and a weight-decay was assumed for the prior distribution because it penalizes the weights with large magnitudes. In Eq. 4.3, n is the index for the training pattern, hyperparameter β is the data contribution to the error, k is the index for the output units, t_{nk} is the target output corresponding to the nth training pattern and kth output unit and y_{nk} is the corresponding predicted output. The parameter α_j is another hyperparameter, which determines the relative contribution of the regularization term on the training error. In Eq. 4.3, the hyperparameters may be set for groups of weights. Equation 4.3 can be solved in two ways: by using the Taylor expansion and through approximating it as a Gaussian distribution as in Chap. 3 and applying the evidence framework; or by numerically sampling posterior probability applying methods such as Monte Carlo method, simulated annealing, genetic Monte Carlo method, or the hybrid Monte Carlo. The next section describes some of these sampling methods.

4.3 Sampling Methods

This section sucessively describes the following sampling methods: the Monte Carlo Method, the Markov Chain Monte Carlo Method, the Genetic Markov Chain Monte Carlo Sampling, Simulated Annealing and Gibbs Sampling.

4.3.1 Monte Carlo Method

Monte Carlo methods are a type of numerical techniques that depend on repetitive random sampling to estimate the results. Monte Carlo methods are frequently used to simulate complex systems. Due to their dependence on repeated computation of random or simulated random numbers, these techniques are ideally suitable for estimation by applying computers and tend to be used when it is impractical or impossible to estimate a solution with a deterministic approach (Kandela et al. 2010).

The Monte Carlo method is a computational method that applies repeated random sampling to calculate a result (Mathe and Novak 2007; Akhmatskaya et al. 2009; Ratick and Schwarz 2009). Monte Carlo methods have been applied for simulating physical and mathematical systems. For example, Lai (2009) applied the Monte Carlo method to solving matrix and integral problems while McClarren and Urbatsch (2009) applied a modified Monte Carlo method for modeling time-dependent radiative transfer with adaptive material coupling.

Other recent applications of the Monte Carlo method include its use in particle coagulation (Zhao and Zheng 2009), in diffusion problems (Liu et al. 2009), for the design of radiation detectors (Dunn and Shultis 2009), for modeling bacterial activities (Oliveira et al. 2009), for vehicle detection (Jia and Zhang 2009), for modeling the bystander effect (Xia et al. 2009), and for modeling nitrogen absorption (Rahmati and Modarress 2009).

Kandela et al. (2010) applied Monte Carlo technique to study the movement of tablets in a pan coater by applying video imaging. They applied the technique to track the motion of tablets and used coating variables including circulation time, surface time, projected surface area and surface velocity of a tablet. These parameters were derived from video imaging experiments. Other successful applications of Monte Carlo including Padilla Cabal et al. (2010) who applied the technique to estimate the efficiency of an n-type HPGe detector as well as Fefelov et al. (2009) who applied Monte Carlo to study the self-assembled monolayer with several different orientations of organic molecules.

Martin and Ayesa (2010) applied the Monte Carlo method to calibrate water quality models while Roskilly et al. (2010) applied the Monte Carlo method to investigate the effect of shape on particle separation. Do et al. (2010) applied Monte Carlo methods to simulate the vapor-liquid equilibrium properties of R134a and its liquid microscopic structure and observed that the simulations agreed with experimental data. Ozaki et al. (2010) applied the Monte Carlo method to develop a framework for data analysis including a mechanism to connect and control data processing modules.

Monte Carlo simulation methods are advantageous in analyzing systems with a large number of degrees of freedom and uncertain inputs in varied fields such as fluid dynamics, materials science, and solid mechanisms (Robert and Casella 2004). The Monte Carlo method generally follows the following procedure (Robert and Casella 2004):

- Define the input space.
- Randomly generate inputs from the input space by applying a chosen probability distribution.
- Use the generated input for the deterministic computation.
- Integrate the results of the individual computations to estimate the final result.

A simple example that has been applied many times to explain the Monte Carlo method is the estimation of π by drawing a square and putting a circle inside it. The area of the square is $4r^2$ while the area of the circle inside it is πr^2. The ratio of the area of the circle to the area of the square is $\pi/4$. By applying the Monte Carlo method described above the input space is any point inside the square. If data points are randomly generated to fall inside the square, the ratio of the number of points that fall inside the circle to the ratio of the points that fall inside the square is equal to $\pi/4$.

4.3.2 Markov Chain Monte Carlo Method

Another way of sampling the posterior probability is to use the Markov Chain Monte Carlo (MCMC) method, which is a random walk Monte Carlo method. It is conducted through creating a Markov chain to identify an equilibrium distribution. The MCMC consists of a Markov process and a Monte Carlo simulation (Liesenfeld and Richard 2008). After many random walk steps, the retained states will converge to a desired posterior distribution. In principle, as the number of steps approach infinity, the accuracy of the estimated probability distribution becomes ideal. Rodina et al. (2010) applied the MCMC to estimate renal disease, while Drugan and Thierens (2010) proposed the evolutionary MCMC where evolutionary techniques were applied to exhange information between states. Wang et al. (2010b) applied the MCMC for spectrum sensing in cognitive radio while Wang and Harrison (2010) applied the MCMC to characterize a water distribution system.

Jing and Vadakkepat (2009) applied a Markov Chain Monte Carlo process to the tracking of maneuvering objects while Gallagher et al. (2009) applied the Markov Chain Monte Carlo process to identify optimal models, model resolution, and model choice for earth science problems and Curran (2008) applied the MCMC process in DNA profiling. Other successful applications of the Markov Chain Monte Carlo process include its use in environmental modeling (Gauchere et al. 2008), in medical imaging (Jun et al. 2008), in lake-water quality modeling (Malve et al. 2007), in economics (Jacquier et al. 2007) and in statistics (Lombardi 2007).

In the implementing the MCMC process, a system is considered whose evolution is represented by a stochastic process comprised of random variables $\{x_1, x_2, x_3, \ldots, x_i\}$. A random variable x_i inhabits a state x at discrete time i. The collection of all possible states that all random variables can inhabit is known as a *state space*. If the probability that the system is in state x_{i+1} at time $i+1$ depends completely on the fact that it was in state x_i at time i, then the random variables $\{x_1, x_2, x_3, \ldots, x_i\}$ form a Markov chain. In the Markov Chain Monte Carlo, the transition between states is achieved by adding a random noise (ε) to the current state as follows (Marwala 2010):

$$x_{i+1} = x_i + \varepsilon \tag{4.5}$$

When the current state has been achieved, it is either accepted or rejected. In this chapter the acceptance of a state is decided by applying the Metropolis algorithm (Bedard 2008; Meyer et al. 2008).

This algorithm which was invented by Metropolis et al. (1953) has been applied extensively to solve problems of statistical mechanics. Bazavov et al. (2009) successfully applied biased Metropolis algorithms for protein simulation. Other applications of the Metropolis algorithms are in nuclear power plants (Sacco et al. 2008), in protein chains simulation (Tiana et al. 2007), and for the prediction of free Co-Pt nano-clusters (Moskovkin and Hou 2007).

In summary, in the MCMC implementation, on sampling a stochastic process $\{x_1, x_2, x_3, \ldots, x_i\}$ consisting of random variables, random changes to x are introduced by applying Eq. 4.5 and they are either accepted or rejected, according to the following Metropolis et al. (1953) criterion (Marwala 2009, 2010):

$$if\ E_{new} < E_{old}\ accept\ state\ (s_{new})$$

$$else$$

$$accept\ (s_{new})\ with\ probability$$

$$\exp\{-(E_{new} - E_{old})\} \tag{4.6}$$

By carefully examining Eq. 4.6, it may be observed that states with high probability form the majority of the Markov chain, and those with low probability form the minority of the Markov chain.

4.3.3 Genetic Markov Chain Monte Carlo Sampling

Another way of sampling the posterior probability is to use a genetic MCMC (Marwala 2007). The Genetic Algorithm (GA) is a type of genetic programming and a technique that is inspired by genetic algorithm as explained in this section. The implementation of genetic programming is inspired by the realization that it efficiently samples through the parameter space, and thereby increases the likelihood that a global posterior distribution will be attained rather than a local sub-optimal solution. In this technique there is no need to compute partial derivatives as is the case in techniques such as the Hybrid Monte Carlo (Neal 1993); and the dynamics of sampling in binary space ensures that probable parameters are sampled more frequently than less probable ones.

The genetic algorithm technique was inspired by Darwin's theory of natural evolution (Marwala 2010) where the principles of the survival of the fittest and natural selection are used to explain the evolution of species. It has been successfully applied to complex problems such as in the automatic control of vehicles (Onieva et al. 2011), modeling of road traffic noise (Rahmani et al. 2011), in flight control (El-Mahallawy et al. 2011) and in mechanical engineering (Esat et al. 2011). In natural evolution, members of the population compete with each other to survive and reproduce and evolutionarily successful individuals reproduce while weaker members die. As a consequence, the genes that are successful have a higher probability of spreading within the population than less successful ones. This natural optimization technique has effectively been applied to optimize complex problems (Holland 1975; Goldberg 1989). This technique applies a population of binary-string chromosomes. Each of these strings is the discretized representation of a point in the search. On generating a new population three operators are performed: (1) crossover; (2) mutation; (3) and reproduction. All of these operators are implemented in genetic MCMC sampling.

The *crossover* operator mixes genetic information in the population by cutting pairs of chromosomes at random points along their length and exchanging the cut sections. This has the effect of joining successful operators together. Crossover occurs with a certain probability. In most natural systems, the probability of crossover occurring is higher than the probability of mutation occurring. A simple crossover technique is applied in this chapter (Goldberg 1989; Kaya 2011). For simple crossover, one crossover point is selected, a binary string from the beginning of chromosome to the crossover point is copied from one parent, and the rest is copied from the second parent. For example, when a parameter **11001**011 undergoes a simple crossover with 11011**111** it becomes **11001111.**

The *mutation* operator picks a binary digit of the chromosomes at random and inverts it. This has a potential of introducing new information to the population. Mutation occurs with a set probability. In many natural systems, the probability of mutation is low (*i.e.*, less than 1%). One example of mutation is binary mutation (Goldberg 1989). When binary mutation is applied a number written in binary form is chosen and its value is inverted. For an example: 11001011 may become 11000011.

Reproduction takes successful chromosomes and reproduces them in accordance with their fitness functions. Metropolis et al. (1953) criteria is applied as a reproduction technique. In so doing, the least fit members are gradually driven out of the population of states that form a Markov chain. The procedure for the genetic MCMC technique is (Marwala 2009):

- Generate an initial sample weight vector $\{w\}_n$.
- Convert the sample into binary form by applying the Gray technique (Michalewicz 1996).
- Mutate the sample to form a new sample vector $\{w\}_{n+1}$.
- The new weight vector $\{w\}_{n+1}$ undergoes a crossover with its predecessor $\{w\}_n$ and mutates again to form a new network weight vector $\{w\}_{n+2}$.
- Convert the weight vector $\{w\}_{n+2}$ into floating-point and then calculate the probability.
- Accept or reject the network weight vector by applying the Metropolis et al. (1953) criterion.
- States $\{w\}_{n+2}$ and $\{w\}_{n+1}$ in binary form undergo a crossover and are mutated to form $\{w\}_{n+3}$.
- Reproduce the state $\{w\}_{n+3}$ by applying the Metropolis et al. (1953) criterion.

The genetic MCMC is different to the traditional genetic algorithm technique in the following ways (Marwala 2009):

(a) The genetic MCMC does not generate a new population of genes at any given iteration, unlike genetic algorithm, but it generates one sample during each iteration.

(b) The fitness function applies the Metropolis criterion, while in the genetic algorithm this is not the case.

(c) The genetic MCMC has a higher mutation rate than genetic algorithm.

The genetic MCMC is different to the standard MCMC in the following ways (Marwala 2009):

(a) The random walk in the classical MCMC is replaced by a procedure inspired by Darwin's theory of evolution which entails crossover, mutation and reproduction.

(b) It operates in floating-point space.

4.3.4 Simulated Annealing

Simulated Annealing is a Monte Carlo technique that is inspired by the process of annealing where matter, such as metals, recrystallize or liquids freeze which can be used to sample a probability distribution. It has been successfully applied to scheduling (Torabzadeh and Zandieh 2010), for modeling ashphalt (Ozgan and Saruhan 2010) and in cellular manufacturing (Paydar et al. 2010). Naderi et al. (2009) introduced an improved simulated technique for scheduling flow-shops that minimizes the entire completion time and the total tardiness. A technique based on simulated annealing was successfully designed to achieve a trade-off between intensification and diversification mechanisms.

Kannan and Zacharias (2009) successfully applied simulated annealing to improve and optimize protein structures, while Dafflon et al. (2009) successfully applied simulated annealing for the classification of heterogeneous aquifers. Cretu and Pop (2009) designed acoustic structures by applying simulated annealing, while Wei-Zhong and Xi-Gang (2009) applied simulated annealing for the optimal synthesis of heat-integrated distillation sequences. Cosola et al. (2008) introduced a universal structure to identify hyper-elastic membranes using multi-point simulated annealing. This technique was used for mechanically characterizing hyper-elastic materials. Pedamallu and Ozdamar (2008) studied a hybrid simulated annealing and local search algorithm for constrained optimization and their numerical experiments demonstrated good results.

In the annealing process, a material such as metal is heated until it is molten and then its temperature is slowly decreased such that the metal is virtually in thermodynamic equilibrium. As the temperature of the object drops, the system becomes more ordered and approaches a *frozen* state at $T = 0$. If the cooling technique is directed inefficiently or the initial temperature of the object is not adequately high, the system may become quenched, forming defects or freezing out in meta-stable states, indicating that the system is trapped in a local minimum energy state.

The procedure that is followed to simulate the annealing procedure was proposed by Metropolis et al. (1953) and it encompasses selecting an initial state and temperature, and maintaining the temperature the same, disturbing the initial formation and calculating the probability of the new state. If the new probability is higher than the old probability then the new state is accepted, otherwise if the opposite is the case, then this state is accepted with a low probability. Simulated annealing replaces a current solution with a "nearby" random solution using a probability that depends on the difference between the differences in probability. The temperature reduces throughout the process, so as temperature approaches zero, there are less random changes in the solution. As it is the case in greedy search techniques, simulated annealing keeps moving towards the best solution, except that it has the advantage of reversal in fitness. That means it can move to a solution with worse fitness than it has currently achieved, but the advantage of this is that it ensures that the solution is not a local optimum distribution, but a global optimum posterior distribution. This is a vital advantage that simulated annealing has over other techniques but, once again, its drawback is its potentially high computational time. The probability of accepting the reversal is given by Boltzmann's equation (Bryan et al. 2006; Marwala 2010):

$$P(\Delta E) = \frac{1}{Z} \exp\left(-\frac{\Delta E}{T}\right) \tag{4.7}$$

Here ΔE is the difference in error between the old and new states. The state indicates the possible updated finite element models. T is the temperature of the system; Z is a normalization factor that ensures that when the probability function is integrated to infinity it becomes 1.

4.3.5 Gibbs Sampling

Gibbs sampling is a procedure to create a sequence of samples from the joint probability distribution of at least two random variables in order to (Casella and George 1992):

- approximate a joint distribution;
- estimate the marginal distribution of one of the variables;
- calculate an integral that estimates the expected value of a variable.

Gibbs sampling, which can be viewed as a type of Markov Chain Monte Carlo technique, is a mechanism for statistical inference and it is a random procedure which is a substitute for deterministic techniques. Hossein-Zadeh and Ardalan (2010a) applied Gibbs sampling for Bayesian approximations of genetic parameters for metritis, retained placenta, milk illness, and mastitis in Holstein dairy cows. They analyzed 57,301 dairy cows by applying the Gibbs sampling technique and observed the significance of the health traits in Holstein dairy cows. Furthermore, Hossein-Zadeh and Ardalan (2010b) applied Gibbs sampling to approximate the genetic parameters for body weight and litter size of Moghani sheep and observed that genetic correlations among the growth traits and litter size were negative for direct genetic and maternal genetic effects. Natesan et al. (2010) successfully applied Gibbs sampling to estimate graded response multilevel models and ordinary graded response models. Other successful applications of Gibbs sampling include the mapping of ambiguous short-sequence tags by Wang et al. (2010a) and in the decentralized coordination of autonomous swarms by Tan et al. (2010).

Gibbs sampling is appropriate in the case when the joint distribution is not known clearly or is challenging to directly sample but the conditional distribution of each variable is known and is easy to sample. The Gibbs sampling procedure produces an example from the distribution of each variable, conditional on the present values of the other variables. The series of samples creates a Markov chain, and the stationary distribution of the Markov chain is the joint distribution (Gelman et al. 1995). Gibbs sampling is implemented as follows by supposing that we intend to obtain k samples of $X = \{x_1, \ldots, x_n\}$ from a joint distribution $p(x_1, \ldots, x_n)$ and denoting the ith sample by $X^{(i)} = \{x_1^{(i)}, \ldots, x_n^{(i)}\}$ (Gelman et al. 1995):

- Begin with an initial value $X^{(0)}$ for each variable.
- For each sample $i = \{1 \ldots k\}$, sample each variable $x_j^{(i)}$ from the conditional distribution $p\left(x_j^{(i)} \middle| x_1^{(i)}, \ldots, x_{j-1}^{(i)}, x_{j+1}^{(i-1)}, \ldots, x_n^{(i-1)}\right)$. This means we must sample each variable from the distribution of that variable conditional to all other variables and apply the latest values and update the variable with a fresh value once it has been sampled.

These samples then estimate the joint distribution of all the variables and the marginal distribution of any variable can be estimated by investigating the samples of those variables and disregarding the others.

4.4 Gaussian Approximation

The Bayesian training of a multi-layer perceptron neural networks is fundamentally about calculating the posterior distribution. One technique of attaining this objective is to accept a Gaussian approximation of the posterior probability by using a Taylor expansion. If this hypothesis is assumed, the posterior probability of the MIDs can be calculated by maximizing the evidence. The evidence framework calculates the values of the hyperparameters that are most probable, and then integrates them over the weights by applying an approximation around the most likely weights. The consequential evidence is then maximized over the hyperparameters. The evidence framework is implemented by following these steps as described in Chap. 3:

- Infer the parameters w for a given value of α. This is calculated in this chapter by applying the scaled conjugate gradient optimization technique.
- Infer the value of α using a Gaussian distribution and maximizing the evidence given the most likely weights.

This chapter reviews and then applies a technique of sampling through a posterior distribution of weights called the hybrid Monte Carlo technique (Neal 1993). Distributions of this nature have been studied extensively in statistical mechanics. In statistical mechanics, the macroscopic thermodynamic properties are derived from the state space, *i.e.*, the position and momentum of miniscule objects such as molecules. The number of degrees of freedom that these objects have is enormous, so the only way to solve this problem is to formulate it in a probabilistic framework.

4.5 Hybrid Monte Carlo

This chapter applies the hybrid Monte Carlo technique to identify the posterior probability of the weight vectors given the training data. This Monte Carlo technique applies the gradient of the error that is calculated by applying back-propagation method as described in Chap. 2. The use of the gradient method ensures that the simulation samples throughout the regions of higher probabilities and thus increases the time it takes to converge on a stationary probability distribution function. This technique is viewed as a type of a Markov chain with transition between states achieved by alternating the 'stochastic' and 'dynamic moves'. The 'stochastic' moves allow the procedure to explore states with different total energy while the 'dynamic' moves are attained by applying the Hamiltonian dynamics and permitting the procedure to explore states with the total energy approximately constant. In its simplest form, the hybrid Monte Carlo method can be viewed as a combination of Monte Carlo sampling procedure which is guided by the gradient of the probability distribution function at each state.

Ghoufi and Maurin (2010) applied hybrid Monte Carlo method to forecast the structural transitions of a porous Metal-organic framework material and demonstrated that hybridizing the hybrid osmotic Monte Carlo method with a "phase mixture" model is an effective method to forecast the adsorption behavior accurately. Rei et al. (2010) applied a hybrid Monte Carlo in a single vehicle routing problem with stochastic demands and the results obtained demonstrated that this method is effective. Aleksandrov et al. (2010) applied a hybrid Monte Carlo to study the vapor-liquid equilibria of copper and observed that the results of the simulation and experiment were close. Zhang et al. (2010) applied hybrid Monte Carlo method to simulate stress-induced texture evolution and use this result to construct an internal variable rate equation which could predict the time evolution. Bogaerts (2009) applied hybrid Monte Carlo technique to study the effects of oxygen addition to argon glow discharges and Qian et al. (2011) applied a hybrid Monte Carlo method to approximate the animal population affected by an environmental catastrophe. Kulak (2009) applied a hybrid Monte Carlo method to simulate fluorescence anisotropy decay whereas Suzuki et al. (2010) applied this procedure in fluoride ion-water cluster.

4.6 Stochastic Dynamics Model

In statistical mechanics the positions and the momentum of all molecules at a given time in a physical system describe the state space of the system. The positions of the molecules define the potential energy of the system and the momentum defines the kinetic energy of the system. In this chapter, what is referred to in statistical mechanics as the canonical distribution of the 'potential energy' is the posterior distribution. The canonical distribution of the system's kinetic energy is (Neal 1993; Marwala 2009):

$$P(\{p\}) = \frac{1}{Z_K} \exp(-K(\{p\})) = (2\pi)^{-n/2} \exp\left(-\frac{1}{2}\sum_i p_i^2\right) \quad (4.8)$$

In molecular dynamics p_i is the momentum of the ith molecule. Here p is not to be confused with, P, which specifies probability. In neural networks, p_i is a fictional parameter that is used to provide the technique with molecular dynamics characteristics. It must be borne in mind that the weight vector, $\{w\}$, and momentum vector, $\{p\}$, are of the same dimension and accordingly the superscript W is applied in Eq. 4.3. The sum of the kinetic and potential energy is called the Hamiltonian of the system and can be mathematically described as follows (Neal 1993; Bishop 1995; Marwala 2009):

$$H(w, p) = \beta \sum_{N}^{N} \sum_{k}^{K} \{y_{nk} - t_{nk}\}^2 + \frac{\alpha}{2}\sum_{j=1}^{W} w_j^2 + \frac{1}{2}\sum_i^{W} p_i^2 \quad (4.9)$$

In Eq. 4.9, the first two expressions are the potential energy of the system, which is the exponent of the posterior distribution, and the last term is the kinetic energy. The canonical distribution over the phase space, *i.e.*, position and momentum, can be mathematically described as follows (Neal 1993; Bishop 1995; Marwala 2009):

$$P(w, p) = \frac{1}{Z} \exp(-H(w, p)) = P(w|D)P(p) \quad (4.10)$$

By sampling through the weight and momentum space, the posterior distribution of weight is achieved by overlooking the distribution of the momentum vector, p. The dynamics in the phase space may be stated in terms of the Hamiltonian dynamics by articulating the derivative of the 'position' and 'momentum' in terms of fictional time τ. It should be remembered that the expression 'position' applied here is identical to the network weights. The dynamics of the system may thus be expressed through applying the Hamiltonian dynamics as follows (Neal 1993; Bishop 1995; Marwala 2009):

$$\frac{dw_i}{d\tau} = +\frac{\partial H}{\partial p_i} = p_i \quad (4.11)$$

$$\frac{dp_i}{d\tau} = +\frac{\partial H}{\partial w_i} = -\frac{\partial E}{\partial p_i} \tag{4.12}$$

The dynamics, stated in Eqs. 4.11 and 4.12, cannot be attained precisely. As a result these equations are discretized by applying a 'leapfrog' technique. The leapfrog discretization of Eqs. 4.11–4.12 may be defined as follows (Neal 1993; Bishop 1995; Marwala 2009):

$$\hat{p}_i\left(\tau + \frac{\varepsilon}{2}\right) = \hat{p}_i(\tau) - \frac{\varepsilon}{2}\frac{\partial E}{\partial w_i}(\hat{w}(\tau)) \tag{4.13}$$

$$\hat{w}_i(\tau + \varepsilon) = \hat{w}_i(\tau) + \varepsilon\hat{p}_i\left(\tau + \frac{\varepsilon}{2}\right) \tag{4.14}$$

$$\hat{p}_i(\tau + \varepsilon) = \hat{p}_i\left(\tau + \frac{\varepsilon}{2}\right) - \frac{\varepsilon}{2}\frac{\partial E}{\partial w_i}(\hat{w}(\tau + \varepsilon)) \tag{4.15}$$

By applying Eq. 4.11, the leapfrog takes a slight half step for the momentum vector, $\{p\}$, and, applying Eq. 4.12, takes a full step for the 'position', $\{w\}$, and, by applying Eq. 4.13, takes a half step for the momentum vector, $\{p\}$. The combination of these three steps generate a single leapfrog iteration that computes the 'position' and 'momentum' of a system at time $\tau + \varepsilon$ from the network weight vector and 'momentum' at time τ. The above discretization is reversible in time. It nearly conserves the Hamiltonian, representing the total energy, and preserves the volume in the phase space, as necessisated by Liouville's theorem (Neal 1993). The volume preservation is attained since the moves that the leapfrog takes are shear transformations.

One subject that should be taken into account is that following Hamiltonian dynamics does not sample through the canonical distribution ergodically because the total energy stays the same, but at most samples through the micro-canonical distribution for a given energy. One method applied to guarantee that the simulation is ergodic, is by applying 'stochastic' moves by altering the Hamiltonian, H, through the simulation and this is attained by substituting the 'momentum' vector, $\{p\}$, before the next leapfrog iteration is achieved. In this chapter, a normally distributed vector with a zero-mean substitutes for the 'momentum' vector. The dynamic steps presented in this section use the gradient of the error with respect to the 'position' which is the network weight vector. The technique used to move from one state to another called the hybrid Monte Carlo which applies Hamiltonian dynamics to achieve dynamic moves and randomly changes the 'momentum' vector to attain stochastic moves. Simulating a distribution by perturbing a single vector, $\{w\}$ as is done in the MCMC is not practical due to high dimensional nature of the state space and the variation of the posterior probability of the weight vector. A technique that applies the gradient of the Hamiltonian with respect to the weight vector, $\{w\}$, was applied to improve the Metropolis algorithm, explained earlier in the chapter, and is the subject of the next section. The Hybrid Monte Carlo technique combines the stochastic dynamics model with the Metropolis algorithm and by so doing removes the bias resulting from the use of a non-zero step size. The Hybrid Monte Carlo technique operates by taking a series of trajectories from an initial state, *i.e.*, 'positions' and 'momentum', and moving in some direction in the state space for a given length of time and accepting the final state by applying the Metropolis algorithm. The validity of the hybrid Monte Carlo rests on three properties of the Hamiltonian dynamics. These properties are (Neal 1993; Marwala 2009):

- Time reversibility: it is invariant under $t \rightarrow -t$, $p \rightarrow -p$.
- Conservation of energy: the $H(w,p)$ is the same at all times.
- Conservation of state space volumes due to Liouville's theorem (Neal 1993).

For a given leapfrog step size, ε_0, and the number of leapfrog steps, L, the dynamic transition of the hybrid Monte Carlo procedure is conducted as follows (Neal 1993; Marwala 2009):

1. Randomly choose the direction of the trajectory, λ, to be either -1 for a backwards trajectory or $+1$ for forwards trajectory.
2. Starting from the initial state, $(\{w\}, \{p\})$, perform L leapfrog steps with the step size $\varepsilon = \varepsilon_0(1 + 0.1k)$ resulting in state $(\{w\}^*, \{p\}^*)$. Here ε_0 is a chosen fixed step size and k is a number chosen from a uniform distribution and which lies between 0 and 1. The reason why this step size is implemented is explained later in this chapter.
3. Reject or accept $(\{w\}^*, \{p\}^*)$ by applying the Metropolis criterion. If the state is accepted then the new state becomes $(\{w\}^*, \{p\}^*)$. If rejected the old state, $(\{w\}, \{p\})$, is retained as the new state.

Subsequent to applying step (3) the momentum vector is re-started before moving on to produce the subsequent state. In this chapter, the momentum vector was sampled from a Gaussian distribution before generating the following state. This guarantees that the stochastic dynamics model samples are not limited to the micro-canonical ensemble. By changing the momentums the total energy is permitted to change since the momentums of the particles are refreshed.

A comment about the hybrid Monte Carlo technique is that it uses the gradient information in step (2) above by applying the leapfrog steps. The advantages of using this gradient information is that the hybrid Monte Carlo trajectories move in the direction of high probabilities, resulting in an improved probability that the resulting state be accepted and that the accepted states are not highly correlated. In neural networks the gradient is calculated using back-propagation (Bishop 1995).

The number of leapfrog steps, L, must be significantly higher than one to allow a fast exploration of the state space. The choice of ε_0 and L affects the speed at which the simulation converges to a stationary distribution and the correlation between the states accepted. The leapfrog discretization does not introduce systematic errors due to occasional rejection of states that result with the increase of the Hamiltonian. In step (2) of the application of the hybrid Monte Carlo technique, the step size $\varepsilon = \varepsilon_0(1 + 0.1k)$ where k is uniformly distributed between 0 and 1 is not fixed. In effect this guarantees that the definite step size for each trajectory is changed so that the accepted states do not have a high correlation. The same effect can be achieved by varying the leapfrog steps. In this chapter only the step size was varied.

The application of the Bayesian approach to neural networks results in weight vectors that have a mean and standard deviation. As a result, the output parameters have a probability distribution. Following the rules of probability theory, the distribution of the output vector $\{y\}$ for a given input vector $\{x\}$ may be written in the following form (Bishop 1995: Marwala 2009):

$$p(\{y\} \Big| \{x\}, D) = \int p(\{y\} | \{x\}, \{w\}) \, p(\{w\} | D) d\{w\} \qquad (4.16)$$

In this chapter, the hybrid Monte Carlo technique was employed to determine the distribution of the weight vectors, and subsequently, of the output parameters. The integral in Eq. 4.16 may be approximated as follows (Bishop 1995; Neal 1993; Marwala 2009):

$$I \equiv \frac{1}{L} \sum_{i=1}^{L} f(\{w\}_i) \qquad (4.17)$$

In Eq. 4.17, L is the number of retained states and f is the MLP network. The application of a Bayesian framework to the neural network results, with the mapping weight vector between the input and output having a probability distribution.

4.7 Comparison of Sampling Methods

In this section the Markov chain Monte Carlo, the genetic MCMC, simulated annealing, Gibbs sampling and the hybrid Monte Carlo are compared. This comparison is summarized in Table 4.1. The table demonstrates that the hybrid Monte Carlo is advantageous over the other techniques. Consequently, this chapter will compare the hybrid Monte Carlo to the Gaussian approximation technique, which was discussed in detail in Chap. 2. The hybrid Monte Carlo is essentially an MCMC technique where the transition between states is facilitated by the knowledge of the gradient and its characteristics. For this reason it is better than the classical MCMC.

4.8 Interstate Conflict

Neural networks methods were implemented and the classification of conflict results were obtained. To assess the performance of the classification results, the area under the Receiver Operating Characteristics (ROC) graphs was used. This measurement of performance was chosen since the ROC curves investigate the tradeoffs between

Table 4.1 Comparison of techniques

Technique	Advantages	Disadvantages
Markov Chain Monte Carlo (MCMC)	It is easy to analyze and implement. The random walk often explores space already explored.	It explores the space in comparatively small steps; It can take a long time to converge
Genetic MCMC	It can explore the space efficiently in binary form.	Scaling this technique to a higher dimension is difficult.
Simulated annealing	It is relatively easy to implement.	It is computationally expensive. It requires carefully selected tunable parameters.
Gibbs sampling	It necessitates that all the conditional distributions of the target distribution be sampled precisely. It is less reliant on the initial parameters. More adaptable, easier to improve with heuristics	It is more reliant on all sequences. It is less methodical in exploring of the initial parameter space.
Gaussian approximation	It is mathematically tractable.	It approximates the posterior probability. It only works for a specific class of problems.
Hybrid Monte Carlo	It circumvents the random walk behaviour by introducing an auxiliary momentum. It samples the space in larger steps. It rapidly converges to a solution.	Calculating the gradient and Hessian can be a problem for certain classes of problems.

false positive and false negative for a variety of predictive thresholds, and do not penalize models whose prediction is biased too high or too low.

In the ROC curves, the x-axis gives the proportion of disputes correctly predicted, while the y-axis provides the proportion of non-disputes correctly predicted for different thresholds. The general idea is that any threshold applied as cut-off value between disputes and non-disputes will correspond to a single point on the ROC curve. The area under the ROC curve indicates how good the classifier is. If the area under the ROC curve is 1 then the classifier has classified all cases correctly, while if it is 0 then the classifier has classified all cases incorrectly. The results indicate that both the Gaussian and the HMC approach give the same level of classification accuracy.

When a confusion matrix was applied to analyze the classification results of the two Bayesian methods, the results in Table 4.2 were obtained. The confusion matrix contains information about actual and predicted classifications given by a classification system. When the accuracies of the two methods were calculated

Table 4.2 Classification results

Method	True conflicts TC	False peaces FP	True peaces TP	False conflicts FC
Gaussian approximation	278	114	290	102
Hybrid Monte Carlo	286	106	290	102

on the basis of the true positive rate (the proportion of disputes that are correctly identified), the HMC performed marginally better than the GA. As shown in Table 4.2, the HMC provided a true positive rate of 73%, while the Gaussian approximation gave a rate of 71%. With respect to the true negative rate (the proportion of non-disputes that are classified correctly) both methods performed the same with 74% accuracy. Overall, the HMC gave a true detection rate of 73.5% while the Gaussian approximation gave that of 72.5%. The area under the ROC curve was 0.86 for the HMC technique and 0.84 for the Gaussian approximation method.

On the basis of these results, the HMC appears to be more accurate than the Gaussian approximation. This is mainly due to the fact that the Gaussian approximation is usually not as valid as the Monte Carlo method. The explanations for HMC performing better than Gaussian approximation can be understood by comparing with the two literature texts by Neal (1993) and MacKay (1991). The application of Bayesian neural networks necessitates integration over high dimensional weight spaces. To make these integration steps more tractable, approximations are presented which streamline their computation. On condition that that the assumptions made are valid the computation of the integrals will be fairly accurate. Nevertheless, the use of Markov Chain Monte Carlo approaches suggested by Neal (1993) do not necessitate any approximations and are consequently more general than the Gaussian approximation technique. It is should be noted that since the HMC is better at predicting disputes, this improvement is reasonably significant from a policy perspective. HMC decreases the false positive rate compared to the Gaussian approximation.

4.9 Conclusion

This chapter applied Bayesian neural networks to model the relationships between democracy, allies, contiguity, distance, capability as well as dependency and militarized disputes. Gaussian approximation and hybrid Monte Carlo (HMC) method were applied to train the Bayesian neural networks. The HMC attempts to circumvent the random walk behaviour of the Markov Chain Monte Carlo simulation by presenting a supplementary momentum vector and applying Hamiltonian dynamics, where the potential function is the targeted probability distribution function. The MCMC has the advantage that it samples across the sample space in larger steps and are consequently less correlated and converges more quickly to the posterior probability. It was found that the HMC was more accurate than the Gaussian approximation.

4.10 Further Work

For future work, more complicated versions of the hybrid Monte Carlo method which can alternate between a Gibbs sampling and hybrid Monte Carlo method should be explored. Furthermore, a realistic prior distribution should be explored and the results compared.

References

Akhmatskaya, E., Bou-Rabee, N., Reich, S.: A comparison of generalized hybrid Monte Carlo methods with and without Momentum Flip. J. Comput. Phys. **228**, 2256–2265 (2009)

Aleksandrov, T., Desgranges, C., Delhommelle, J.: Vapor-liquid equilibria of copper using hybrid Monte Carlo Wang-Landau simulations. Fluid Phase Equilib. **287**, 79–83 (2010)

Bazavov, A., Berg, B.A., Zhou, H.: Application of biased metropolis algorithms: from protons to proteins. Math. Comput. Simul. (2009). doi:doi:10.1016/j.matcom.2009.05.005

Beck, N., King, G., Zeng, L.: Improving quantitative studies of international conflict: a conjecture. Am. Politic Sci. Rev. **94**, 21–35 (2000)

Bedard, M.: Optimal acceptance rates for metropolis algorithms: moving beyond 0.234. Stoch. Process Appl. **118**, 2198–2222 (2008)

Bishop, C.M.: Neural Networks for Pattern Recognition. Oxford University Press, London (1995)

Bogaerts, A.: Effects of oxygen addition to Argon glow discharges: a hybrid Monte Carlo-fluid modeling investigation. Spectro. Acta. Part B Atomic. Spectro. **64**, 1266–1279 (2009)

Bryan, K., Cunningham, P., Bolshkova, N.: Application of simulated annealing to the biclustering of gene expression data. IEEE Trans. Inf. Technol. Biomed. **10**, 519–525 (2006)

Casella, G., George, E.I.: Explaining the Gibbs sampler. Am. Stat. **46**, 167–174 (1992)

Coles, M.D., Azzi, D., Haynes, B.P., Hewitt, A.: A Bayesian network approach to a biologically inspired motion strategy for mobile wireless sensor networks. Ad. Hoc. Nets. **7**, 1217–1228 (2009)

Cosola, E., Genovese, K., Lamberti, L., Pappalettere, C.: A general framework for identification of hyper-elastic membranes with Moire techniques and multi-point simulated annealing. Int. J. Solids Struct. **45**, 6074–6099 (2008)

Cretu, N., Pop, M.: Acoustic behavior design with simulated annealing. Comput. Mater. Sci. **44**, 1312–1318 (2009)

Curran, J.M.: A MCMC method for resolving two person mixtures. Sci. Justice **48**, 168–177 (2008)

Dafflon, B., Irving, J., Holliger, K.: Simulated-annealing-based conditional simulation for the local-scale characterization of heterogeneous aquifers. J. Appl. Geophys. **68**, 60–70 (2009)

Do, H., Wheatley, R.J., Hirst, J.D.: Microscopic structure of liquid 1-1-1-2-Tetrafluoroethane (R134a) from Monte Carlo simulation. Phys. Chem. Chem. Phys. **12**, 13266–13272 (2010)

Drugan, M.M., Thierens, D.: Recombination operators and selection strategies for evolutionary Markov Chain Monte Carlo algorithms. Evol. Intell. **3**, 79–101 (2010)

Dunn, W.L., Shultis, J.K.: Monte Carlo methods for design and analysis of radiation detectors. Radiat. Phys. Chem. **78**, 852–858 (2009)

El-Mahallawy, A.A., Yousef, H.A., El-Singaby, M.I., Madkour, A.A., Youssef, A.M.: Robust flight control system design using H∞ loop-shaping and recessive trait crossover genetic algorithm. Expert Syst. Appl. **38**, 169–174 (2011)

Esat, I.I., Saud, M., Naci Engin, S.: A novel method to obtain a real-time control force strategy using genetic algorithms for dynamic systems subjected to external arbitrary excitations. J. Sound Vib. **330**, 27–48 (2011)

Fefelov, V.F., Gorbunov, V.A., Myshlyavtsev, A.V., Myshlyavtseva, M.D.: The simplest self-assembled Monolayer model with different orientations of complex organic molecules – Monte Carlo and transfer-matrix techniques. Chem. Eng. J. **154**, 107–114 (2009)

Gallagher, K., Charvin, K., Nielsen, S., Sambridge, M., Stephenson, J.: Markov Chain Monte Carlo (MCMC) sampling methods to determine optimal models, model resolution and model choice for earth science problems. Mar. Pet. Geol. **26**, 525–535 (2009)

Gauchere, C., Campillo, F., Misson, L., Guiot, J., Boreux, J.J.: Parameterization of a process-based tree-growth model: comparison of optimization. MCMC and particle filtering algorithms. Environ. Model. Softw. **23**, 1280–1288 (2008)

Gelman, A., Carlin, J.B., Stern, H.S., Rubin, D.B.: Bayesian Data Analysis. Chapman & Hall, London (1995)

Ghoufi, A., Maurin, G.: Hybrid Monte Carlo simulations combined with a phase mixture model to predict the structural transitions of a porous metal-organic framework material upon adsorption of guest molecules. J. Phys. Chem. C **114**, 6496–6502 (2010)

Gillespie, J.V., Zinnes, D.A., Tahim, G.S., Schrodt, P.A., Rubison, R.M.: An optimal control model of arms race. Am. Politic Sci. Rev. **71**, 226–244 (1977)

Gochman, C., Maoz, Z.: Militarized interstate disputes 1816–1976. In: Singer, D., Diehl, P. (eds.) Measuring the Correlates of War. University of Michigan Press, Ann Arbor (1990)

Goldberg, D.E.: Genetic Algorithms in Search, Optimization and Machine Learning. Addison-Wesley, Reading (1989)

Holland, J.: Adaptation in Natural and Artificial Systems. University of Michigan Press, Ann Arbor (1975)

Hossein-Zadeh, N.G., Ardalan, M.: Bayesian estimates of genetic parameters for metritis, retained placenta, milk fever, and clinical mastitis in holstein dairy cows via Gibbs sampling. Res. Vet. Sci. **90**, 146–149 (2010a)

Hossein-Zadeh, N.G., Ardalan, M.: Estimation of genetic parameters for body weight traits and litter size of Moghani sheep, using a Bayesian approach via Gibbs sampling. J. Agric. Sci. **148**, 363–370 (2010b)

Jacquier, E., Johannes, M., Polson, N.: MCMC maximum likelihood for latent state models. J Econ. **137**, 615–640 (2007)

Jia, Y., Zhang, C.: Front-view vehicle detection by Markov Chain Monte Carlo method. Pattern Recognit. **42**, 313–321 (2009)

Jing, L., Vadakkepat, P.: Interacting MCMC particle filter for tracking maneuvering target. Dig. Signal Process (2009). doi:10.1016/j.dsp. 2009.08.011

Jun, S.C., George, J.S., Kim, W., Pare-Blagoev, J., Plis, S., Ranken, D.M., Schmidt, D.M.: Bayesian brain source imaging based on combined MEG/EEG and fMRI using MCMC. NeuroImage **40**, 1581–1594 (2008)

Kandela, B., Sheorey, U., Banerjee, A., Bellare, J.: Study of tablet-coating parameters for a pan coater through video imaging and Monte Carlo simulation. Powder Technol. **204**, 103–112 (2010)

Kannan, S., Zacharias, M.: Simulated annealing coupled replica exchange molecular dynamics–an efficient conformational sampling method. J. Struct. Biol. **166**, 288–294 (2009)

Kaya, M.: The effects of two new Crossover operators on genetic algorithm performance. Appl. Soft Comput. J. **11**, 881–890 (2011)

Kulak, L.: Hybrid Monte-Carlo simulations of fluorescence anisotropy decay in three-component donor-mediator-acceptor systems in the presence of energy transfer. Chem. Phys. Letts. **467**, 435–438 (2009)

Lagazio, M., Marwala, T.: Assessing different Bayesian neural network models for militarized interstate dispute. Soc. Sci. Comp. Rev. **2005**, 1–12 (2005)

Lagazio, M., Russett, B.: A neural network analysis of MIDs, 1885–1992: are the patterns stable? In: Diehl, P. (ed.) The Scourge of War: New Extensions on an Old Problem. University of Michigan Press, Ann Arbor (2004)

Lai, Y.: Adaptive Monte Carlo methods for matrix equations with applications. J. Comput. Appl. Math. **231**, 705–714 (2009)

Liesenfeld, R., Richard, J.: Improving MCMC, using efficient importance sampling. Comput. Stat. Data Anal. **53**, 272–288 (2008)

Liu, X., Newsome, D., Coppens, M.: Dynamic Monte Carlo simulations of binary self-diffusion in ZSM-5. Microp. Mesop. Mater. **125**, 149–159 (2009)

Lombardi, M.J.: Bayesian inference for [Alpha]-stable sistributions: a random walk MCMC approach. Comput. Stat. Data Anal. **51**, 2688–2700 (2007)

MacKay, D.J.C.: A practical Bayesian framework for backpropagation networks. Neural Comp. **4**, 448–472 (1992)

MacKay, D.J.C.: Bayesian methods for adaptive models. Ph.D. thesis, California Institute of Technology (1991)

Malve, O., Laine, M., Haario, H., Kirkkala, T., Sarvala, J.: Bayesian modelling of algal mass occurrences – using adaptive MCMC methods with a lake water quality model. Environ. Model. Softw. **22**, 966–977 (2007)

Martin, C., Ayesa, E.: An integrated Monte Carlo methodology for the calibration of water quality models. Ecol. Model. **221**, 2656–2667 (2010)

Marwala, T.: Bayesian training of neural network using genetic programming. Pattern Recognit. Lett. (2007). doi:org/10.1016/j.patrec.2007.034

Marwala, T.: Computational Intelligence for Missing Data Imputation, Estimation and Management: Knowledge Optimization Techniques. IGI Global Publications, New York (2009)

Marwala, T.: Finite Element Model Updating Using Computational Intelligence Techniques. Springer, London (2010)

Marwala, T.: Fault identification using neural networks and vibration data. Ph.D. thesis, University of Cambridge (2001)

Marwala, T., Lagazio, M., Tettey, T.: An integrated human-computer system for controlling interstate disputes. Int. J. Comp. Appl. **31**, 239–246 (2009)

Mathe, P., Novak, E.: Simple Monte Carlo and the Metropolis algorithm. J. Complex. **23**, 673–696 (2007)

McClarren, R.G., Urbatsch, T.J.: A modified implicit Monte Carlo method for time-dependent radiative transfer with adaptive material coupling. J. Comput. Phys. **228**, 5669–5686 (2009)

Metropolis, N., Rosenbluth, A., Rosenbluth, M., Teller, A., Teller, E.: Equation of state calculations by fast computing machines. J. Chem. Phys. **21**, 1087–1092 (1953)

Meyer, R., Cai, B., Perron, F.: Adaptive rejection metropolis sampling using lagrange interpolation polynomials of degree 2. Comput. Stat Data Anal. **52**, 3408–3423 (2008)

Michalewicz, Z.: Genetic Algorithms + Data Structures = Evolution Programs. Springer, New York (1996)

Moller, M.: A scaled conjugate gradient algorithm for fast supervised learning. Neural Nets. **6**, 525–533 (1993)

Moskovkin, P., Hou, M.: Metropolis Monte Carlo predictions of free Co-Pt nanoclusters. J. Alloy Compd. **434–435**, 550–554 (2007)

Naderi, B., Zandieh, M., Khaleghi, A., Balagh, G., Roshanaei, V.: An improved simulated annealing for hybrid flowshops with sequence-dependent setup and transportation times to minimize total completion time and total tardiness. Expert Syst. Appl. **36**, 9625–9633 (2009)

Natesan, P., Limbers, C., Varni, J.W.: Bayesian estimation of graded response multilevel models using Gibbs sampling: formulation and illustration. Educ. Psychol. Meas. **70**, 420–439 (2010)

Neal, R.M.: Probabilistic inference using Markov Chain Monte Carlo methods, University of Toronto Technical Report CRG-TR-93-1, Toronto (1993)

Oliveira, R.G., Schneck, E., Quinn, B.E., Konovalov, O.V., Brandenburg, K., Seydel, U., Gill, T., Hanna, C.B., Pink, D.A., Tanaka, M.: Physical mechanisms of bacterial survival revealed by combined grazing-incidence X-ray scattering and Monte Carlo simulation. Comptes Rendus Chimie **12**, 209–217 (2009)

Onieva, E., Naranjo, J.E., Milanés, V., Alonso, J., García, R., Pérez, J.: Automatic lateral control for unmanned vehicles via genetic algorithms. Appl. Soft Comput. J. **11**, 1303–1309 (2011)

Ozaki, M., Ohno, M., Terada, Y., Watanabe, S., Mizuno, T., Takahashi, T., Kokubun, M., Tsujimoto, M., Yamasaki, N.Y., Odaka, H., Takei, Y., Yuasa, T., Furuzawa, A., Mori, H., Matsumoto, H., Okajima, T., Kilbourne, C.A., Tajima, H., Ishisaki, Y.: The Monte Carlo simulation framework of the ASTRO-H X-Ray observatory. In: Proc of SPIE – The Intl Soc for Optical Eng:7732, Art No 773239 (2010)

Ozgan, E., Saruhan, H.: Modeling of Asphalt concrete via simulated annealing. Adv. Eng. Softw. **41**, 680–683 (2010)

Padilla Cabal, F., Lopez-Pino, N., Luis Bernal-Castillo, J., Martinez-Palenzuela, Y., Aguilar-Mena, J., D'Alessandro, K., Arbelo, Y., Corrales, Y., Diaz, O.: Monte Carlo based geometrical model for efficiency calculation of an N-type HPGe detector. Appl. Radiat. Isotopes **68**, 2403–2408 (2010)

Paydar, M.M., Mahdavi, I., Sharafuddin, I., Solimanpur, M.: Applying simulated annealing for designing cellular manufacturing systems using MDmTSP. Comp. Ind. Eng. **59**, 929–936 (2010)

Pedamallu, C.S., Ozdamar, L.: Investigating a hybrid simulated annealing and local search algorithm for constrained optimization. Eur. J. Oper. Res. **185**, 1230–1245 (2008)

Qian, G., Li, N., Huggins, R.: Using capture-recapture data and hybrid Monte Carlo sampling to estimate an animal population affected by an environmental catastrophe. Comput. Stat. Data Anal. **55**, 655–666 (2011)

Rahmani, S., Mousavi, S.M., Kamali, M.J.: Modeling of road-traffic noise with the use of genetic algorithm. Appl. Soft Comput. J. **11**, 1008–1013 (2011)

Rahmati, M., Modarress, H.: Nitrogen adsorption on nanoporous zeolites studied by Grand Canonical Monte Carlo simulation. J. Mol. Struct. THEOCHEM **901**, 110–116 (2009)

Ratick, S., Schwarz, G.: Monte Carlo simulation. In: Kitchin, R., Thrift, N. (eds.) International Encyclopedia of Human Geography. Elsevier, Oxford (2009)

Rei, W., Gendreau, M., Soriano, P.: A hybrid Monte Carlo local branching algorithm for the single vehicle routing problem with stochastic demands. Trans. Sci. **44**, 136–146 (2010)

Robert, C.P., Casella, G.: Monte Carlo Statistical Methods. Springer, London (2004)

Rodina, A., Bliznakova, K., Pallikarakis, N.: End stage renal disease patients' projections using Markov Chain Monte Carlo simulation. In: Proceedings of IFMBE, pp. 796–799 (2010)

Roskilly, S.J., Colbourn, E.A., Alli, O., Williams, D., Paul, K.A., Welfare, E.H., Trusty, P.A.: Investigating the effect of shape on particle segregation using a Monte Carlo simulation. Powder Technol. **203**, 211–222 (2010)

Russett, B., Oneal, J.R., Berbaum, M.: Causes of peace: democracy, interdependence, and international organizations, 1885–1992. Int. Stud. Q. **47**, 371–393 (2003)

Sacco, W.F., Lapa, C.M.F., Pereira, C.M.N.A., Filho, H.A.: A Metropolis algorithm applied to a nuclear power plant auxiliary feedwater system surveillance tests policy optimization. Prog. Nucl. Energy **50**, 15–21 (2008)

Suzuki, K., Tachikawa, M., Shiga, M.: Efficient Ab Initio path integral hybrid Monte Carlo based on the fourth-order Trotter expansion: application to fluoride ion-water cluster. J. Chem. Phys. **132**, 1–7, Art No 144108 (2010)

Tan, X., Xi, W., Baras, J.S.: Decentralized coordination of autonomous Swarms using parallel Gibbs sampling. Automatica **46**, 2068–2076 (2010)

Thompson, W.R., Tucker, R.M.: A tale of two democratic peace critiques. J. Conflict Res. **41**, 428–454 (1997)

Tiana, G., Sutto, L., Broglia, R.A.: Use of the Metropolis algorithm to simulate the dynamics of protein chains. Phys. A Stat. Mech. Appl. **380**, 241–249 (2007)

Torabzadeh, E., Zandieh, M.: Cloud theory-based simulated annealing approach for scheduling in the two-stage assembly flowshop. Adv. Eng. Softw. **41**, 1238–1243 (2010)

Wang, H., Harrison, K.W.: Adaptive Bayesian contaminant source characterization in water distribution systems via a parallel implementation of Markov Chain Monte Carlo (MCMC). In: Proceedings of the World Environmental and Water Resources Congress, pp. 4323–4329 (2010)

Wang, J., Huda, A., Lunyak, V.V., Jordan, I.K.: A Gibbs sampling strategy applied to the mapping of ambiguous short-sequence tags. Bioinformatics **26**, 2501–2508 (2010b)

Wang, X.Y., Wong, A., Ho, P.-H.: Spectrum sensing in cognitive radio using a Markov-Chain Monte-Carlo scheme. IEEE Commun. Lett. **14**, 830–832 (2010c)

Wei-Zhong, A., Xi-Gang, Y.: A simulated annealing-based approach to the optimal synthesis of heat-integrated distillation sequences. Comput. Chem. Eng. **33**, 199–212 (2009)

Xia, J., Liu, L., Xue, J., Wang, Y., Wu, L.: Modeling of radiation-induced bystander effect using Monte Carlo methods. Nucl. Instrum. Methods Phys. Res. Sect. B Beam Interact Mater. Atoms **267**, 1015–1018 (2009)

Yu, H., van Engelen, R.: Arc refractor methods for adaptive importance sampling on large Bayesian networks under evidential reasoning. Int. J. Approx. Reason. **51**, 800–819 (2010)

Zeng, L.: Prediction and classification with neural network models. Sociol. Methods Res. **27**, 499–524 (1999)

Zhang, L., Bartel, T., Lusk, M.T.: Parallelized hybrid Monte Carlo simulation of stress-induced texture evolution. Comput. Mater. Sci. **48**, 419–425 (2010)

Zhao, H., Zheng, C.: Correcting the multi-Monte Carlo method for particle coagulation. Powder Technol. **193**, 120–123 (2009)

Chapter 5
Support Vector Machines for Modeling Interstate Conflict

5.1 Introduction

Chapter 2 presented and implemented a technique to identify the relevance of variables for the prediction of militarized interstate disputes. This technique applied Bayesian theory and an evidence framework to create an automatic relevance-determination method. The automatic relevance-determination method was applied to determine the relevance of interstate variables that are essential for modeling the militarized interstate disputes. Consistently with the Kantian peace theory, it was found that economic interdependence and democracy are important factors for maintaining peace together with power difference and memberships in international alliances.

In Chap. 3, the multi-layer perceptron neural-network and the radial basis function neural-network were introduced and applied to model the militarized interstate disputes. The results obtained demonstrated that the multi-layer perceptron was better at predicting militarized interstate disputes than was the radial basis function network. This was mainly because structurally the input variables to the multi-layer perceptron neural networks were more cross-coupled than in the radial basis function. Because the multi-layer perceptron neural-network was better than the radial basis function, this chapter only considers the multi-layer perceptron neural-network.

Chapter 4 described two Bayesian techniques and compared them for interstate conflict. The first one was the Bayesian technique that applied a Gaussian approximation approach to estimate the posterior probability of the neural network weights, given the observed data and the evidence framework to train the multi-layer perceptron neural-network. The second technique involved treating the posterior probability as formulated and then applying the hybrid Monte Carlo technique to train the multi-layer perceptron neural-network. When these techniques were applied to model militarized interstate disputes, it was observed that training the neural network with the posterior probability as formulated, and applying the hybrid

T. Marwala and M. Lagazio, *Militarized Conflict Modeling using Computational Intelligence*, Advanced Information and Knowledge Processing,
DOI 10.1007/978-0-85729-790-7_5, © Springer-Verlag London Limited 2011

Monte Carlo technique gave better results than estimating the posterior probability with a Gaussian approximation function and then applying the evidence framework to train the neural network.

The concept of militarized interstate disputes – as defined by Gochman and Maoz (1984) and by Marwala and Lagazio (2004) – refers to an extended definition of disputes/conflicts, which starts with the threat of using military force between sovereign states in an explicit way. In other words, a militarized interstate dispute is a state that results from interactions between two states, which may result into peace or conflict. These interactions are expressed in the form of dyadic attributes, which are the two states' parameters considered to influence the probability of military conflict (Beck et al. 2000). In this study, seven dyadic variables were used to predict the militarized interstate disputes outcome.

Interstate conflict is a complex phenomenon that encompasses non-linear pattern of interactions (Beck et al. 2000; Lagazio and Russett 2003; Marwala and Lagazio 2004). Various efforts have and are still in progress to improve the militarized interstate disputes data, the underlying theory, and statistical modeling techniques for interstate conflict (Beck et al. 2000.) Previously, linear statistical methods were used for quantitative analysis of conflicts and were far from satisfactory. The results obtained showed a high variance, which make them difficult to rely upon (Beck et al. 2000).

Results have to be taken cautiously and their interpretation requires prior knowledge of the problem domain. This makes it inevitably necessary to look for techniques other than traditional statistical methods to quantitatively analyze international conflicts. Artificial intelligence techniques have proved to be very good in modeling complex and nonlinear problems without any *a priori* constraints about the underlying functions that assumed to govern the distribution of the militarized interstate dispute data (Beck et al. 2000). It thus makes sense to model interstate conflicts using artificial intelligence techniques.

Neural networks were previously used by Marwala and Lagazio (2004), Beck et al. (2000), and Lagazio and Russett (2003) to model militarized interstate disputes. In this chapter, two artificial intelligence techniques, the hybrid Monte Carlo trained multi-layer perceptron neural networks and support vector machines are used for the same purpose and their results were compared. These two techniques were compared for applications such as text texture verification, done by Chen and Odobez (2002), and option pricing done by Pires and Marwala (2004). Their findings show that support vector machines outperformed neural networks, which is the motivation to use support vector machines to model interstate conflict.

5.2   Background

This section presents three methods for conflict modelling: learning machines, artificial neural networks, and support vector machines.

5.2.1 Learning Machines

Many different types of learning machines have been applied for different purposes. The two major applications of learning machines are for classification and regression analysis. A *learning problem for classification* can be defined as finding a rule that assigns objects into different classes (Müller et al. 2001). The rule that governs the classification is devised based on an acquired knowledge about the object. The process of knowledge acquisition is called *training*. In this chapter, we look at two different types of learning machines for the purpose of predicting militarized interstate disputes. Both these techniques learn an underlying pattern based on training using militarized interstate dispute data to predict previously unseen (test) militarized interstate dispute data.

5.2.2 Artificial Neural Networks

A neural network is a processor that is modeled to resemble the functioning of the brain in its ability to acquire knowledge from its environment and store the information in some synaptic weights (Haykin 1999). It is composed of simple neurons that are capable of processing information in a massively parallel fashion and can also make generalizations once it is trained using training data. This property gives neural networks the ability to solve complex non-linear problems (Haykin 1999).

The most widely used neural network is a feed-forward multi-layer perceptron network with two layers of adaptive weights (Bishop 1995). As was demonstrated in earlier chapters, a neural network has input, hidden, and output layers. The input layer represents the independent variables, while the hidden and output layers represent the latent and dependent variables respectively (Zeng 1999). Feed-forward multi-layer perceptron neural networks provide a framework to represent a nonlinear functional mapping of a set of d input variables $x_i, i = 1, ..., d$ into a set of c output variables y_j $j = 1, ..., c$ (Bishop 1995).

The mathematical relationship between the input and output units of the neural network is represented by the following function (Bishop 1995; Marwala and Lagazio 2004):

$$y_k = f_{outer}\left(\sum_{j=1}^{M} w_{kj}^{(2)} f_{inner}\left(\sum_{i=1}^{d} w_{ji}^{(1)} x_i + w_{j0}^{(1)}\right) + w_{k0}^{(2)}\right) \quad (5.1)$$

where $w_{ji}^{(1)}$ and $w_{kj}^{(2)}$ are the first and second layer weights going from input i to hidden unit j and hidden unit j to output unit k, respectively. M is the number of the hidden units, d is the number of input units, while $w_{j0}^{(1)}$ and $w_{k0}^{(2)}$ represent biases of the hidden and output units, respectively. The output activation function is given by f_{outer}, while f_{inner} represents the activation function of the hidden unit. In this chapter, the Bayesian approach was used to formulate the solution to estimate the network weights of Eq. 5.1, and the resulting solution was obtained through the use of the hybrid Monte Carlo method. These techniques were explained in detail in earlier chapters.

5.2.3   Support Vector Machines (SVMs)

Support vector machines are supervised learning methods used mainly for classi-fication, are derived from statistical learning theory and were first introduced by Vapnik (1998). The application of SVMs to model complex systems has been a subject of research for many years. For example, Shen et al. (2005) proposed using the SVMs based color image watermarking technique that operates by applying the information supplied by the reference positions and the watermark which was adaptively embedded into the blue channel of the host image by taking the human visual system into account. Other successful implementations of SVMs to model complicated systems include Marwala et al. (2006) who applied SVMs in the fault classification of mechanical systems and Msiza et al. (2007) who used SVMs in forecasting water demand time series.

Chen et al. (2011) applied SVMs to estimate monthly solar radiation and the results demonstrated that SVMs perform better than traditional approaches, such as neural networks, for predicting solar radiation. Yeh et al. (2011) applied SVMs in the recognition of counterfeit banknotes. Each banknote was separated into segments and the luminance histograms of the segments were used as the inputs to the SVM model and each segment was paired with its own kernels. When the procedure was tested on Taiwanese banknotes, it was shown that the proposed method performed better than methods such as the single-kernel SVM.

Tellaeche et al. (2009) successfully applied support vector machines and com-puter vision for weed identification whereas Lin et al. (2011) applied SVMs to predict business failure, based on previous financial data. The results obtained showed that the proposed method gave a good classification rate. Li-Xia et al. (2011) implemented SVMs and particle swarm optimization for tax forecasting and the results showed that the SVM model performs well.

The use of SVMs has also been extended to regression analysis problems, thus resulting in the term Support Vector Regression (SVR) (Gunn 1997; Chang et al. 2007; Chuang 2008). Pires and Marwala (2004) used SVMs for option pricing and further extended these to the Bayesian framework, while Gidudu et al. (2007) applied SVMs in image classification. Jayadeva and Chandra (2007) used the regularized least squares fuzzy SVMs for financial time series forecasting, while Zhang et al. (2006) used SVMs for the on-line health monitoring of large-scale structures.

Thissen et al. (2004) used SVMs for spectral regression applications. Xi et al. (2007) used support vector machines, successfully, for predictive control on an air conditioned plant. One of the problems with SVMs is the computational load needed to train them. Researchers such as Guo and Zhang (2007) have developed methods for accelerating SVMs, while Üstün et al. (2007) visualized and interpreted SVM models.

Other applications of SVMs include non-linear time series prediction (Lau and Wu 2007), the prediction of jet penetration depth (Wang et al. 2010), tool wear identification (Tao and Tao 2010), ozone concentration (Ortiz-García et al. 2010), the identification of people (Palanivel and Yegnanarayana 2008), chemical compound analysis (Zhou et al. 2006), response modeling (Kim et al. 2008), the estimation of software project effort (Oliveira 2006) and the real-time prediction of order flow times (Alenezi et al. 2007). In a drive to improve the performance of SVMs, some innovative approaches have been introduced, including the approach of Üstün et al. (2006) who applied Pearson VII function based kernels.

In this chapter, SVMs were used to classify interstate conflict data into *conflict* and *peace*. For SVMs, a data point is conceptualized as a *p*-dimensional vector. The aim is to separate such points with a *p*-1-dimensional hyperplane, known as a linear classifier. There are numerous hyperplanes that can be used. One of these includes the one that exhibits the largest separation, also called margin, between the two classes. The selected hyperplane can be chosen so that the distance from it to the nearest data point on both sides is maximized. This is then known as the *maximum-margin hyperplane*. The classification problem can be stated as approximating a function $f : R^N \rightarrow \{-1, 1\}$ dependent on input-output training data which are produced from an independently and identically distributed unknown probability distribution $P(\{x\}, y)$ in such a way that f is able to classify unseen $(\{x\}, y)$ data (Müller et al. 2001; Habtemariam 2006). The preferred function minimizes the expected error (risk) and can be mathematically written as follows (Habtemariam 2006; Habtemariam et al. 2005):

$$R[f] = \int l(f(\{x\}), y) dP(\{x\}, y) \tag{5.2}$$

where l indicates a loss function (Müller et al. 2001). Because the fundamental probability distribution P is not known, Eq. 5.2 cannot be solved implicitly. The best course of action is to identify an upper bound for the risk function which is given mathematically as follows (Vapnik 1995; Müller et al. 2001):

$$R[f] = R[f]_{emp} + \sqrt{\frac{h \left(\ln \frac{2n}{h} + 1 \right) - \ln \left(\frac{\delta}{4} \right)}{n}} \tag{5.3}$$

where $h \in N^+$ is the Vapnik-Chervonenkis (VC) dimension of $f \in F$ and $\delta > 0$. The VC dimension of a function class F is defined as the biggest number of h coordinates that can be divided in all possible ways by means of functions of that class (Vapnik 1995). The empirical error $R[f]_{emp}$ is a training error given by (Habtemariam 2006):

$$R[f]_{emp} = \frac{1}{n} \sum_{i+1}^{n} l(f(x_i), y_i) \tag{5.4}$$

Fig. 5.1 A linear support
vector machine classifier and
margins: A linear classifier is
defined by a hyperplane's
normal vector {x} and an
offset b, i.e., the decision
boundary is
$\{\{x\}|\{w\}.\{x\} + b = 0\}$ (*thick
line*). Each of the two half
spaces defined by this
hyperplane corresponds to
one class, i.e.,
$f(x) = sign((\{w\}.\{x\}) + b)$
(Müller et al. 2001)

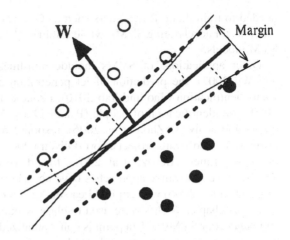

Assuming that the training sample is linearly separable by a hyperplane of the
form (Habtemariam 2006):

$$f(x) = \langle w, \{x\}\rangle + b \quad with \quad w \in \chi, \quad b \in \Re \tag{5.5}$$

where $\langle .,.\rangle$ denotes the dot product, $\{w\}$ is an adjustable weight vector and $\{b\}$ is
an offset and the classification problem looks like Fig. 5.1 (Müller et al. 2001).
The objective of the learning process as proposed by Vapnik and Lerner (1963)
is to discover the hyperplane with maximum margin of separation from the class
of dividing hyperplanes. Nevertheless, because practical data frequently display
complex properties which cannot be divided linearly, more complex classifiers are
essential. To circumvent the complexity of the nonlinear classifiers, the concept of
linear classifiers in a feature space can be introduced. SVMs attempt to discover
a linear separating hyperplane by initially mapping the input space into a higher
dimensional feature space F. This suggests that each training example x_i be
substituted by $\Phi(x_i)$ to give (Habtemariam 2006):

$$Y_i \left((\{w\}.\Phi(\{x\}_i) + b\right), i = 1, 2, ..., n \tag{5.6}$$

The *VC* dimension h in the feature space F is constrained subject to $h \leq$
$||W||^2 R^2 + 1$ where R is the radius of the smallest sphere around the training data
(Müller et al. 2001; Habtemariam 2006). Therefore, minimizing the expected risk
can be framed as an optimization problem as follows (Burges 1998; Müller et al.
2001; Schölkopf and Smola 2003):

$$\text{Minimize } (\{w\}, b) \frac{1}{2}||\{w\}||^2 \tag{5.7}$$

Subject to:

$$c_i \left(\{w\}.\{x\}_i - b \right) \geq 1, i = 1, ..., n \tag{5.8}$$

Equations 5.7 and 5.8 are collectively known as the *quadratic programming problem* because it is the problem of optimizing a quadratic function of several variables subject to linear constraints on these variables (Schölkopf and Smola 2003). From the expressions:

$$\| \{w\} \|^2 = w.w \tag{5.9}$$

$$\{w\} = \sum_{i=0}^{n} \alpha_i c_i \{x\}_i \tag{5.10}$$

It can be demonstrated that the dual of the support vector machines can, by maximizing in α_i, be written in Lagrangian form as follows (Schölkopf and Smola 2003):

$$L(\alpha) = \sum_{i=1}^{n} \alpha_i - \frac{1}{2} \sum_{i,j} \alpha_i \alpha_j c_i c_j \{x\}_i^T \{x\}_j$$

$$= \sum_{i=1}^{n} \alpha_i - \frac{1}{2} \sum_{i,j} \alpha_i \alpha_j c_i c_j k \left(\{x\}_i, \{x\}_j \right), i = 1, ..., n \tag{5.11}$$

Subject to:

$$\alpha_i \geq 0, i = 1, ..., n \tag{5.12}$$

and to the constraint from the minimization in b:

$$\alpha_i \geq 0, i = 1, ..., n \tag{5.13}$$

and subject to the following constraints:

$$\sum_{i=1}^{n} \alpha_i c_i = 0 \tag{5.14}$$

Here the kernel is (Müller et al. 2001):

$$k \left(\{x\}_i, \{x\}_j \right) = \{x\}_i \cdot \{x\}_j \tag{5.15}$$

(a) Soft margin

Cortes and Vapnik (1995) proposed an improved maximum margin notion that permits mislabeled data points. If there is no hyperplane that can exactly divide the "yes" and "no" data points, the *Soft Margin* technique will select a hyperplane that divides the data points as efficiently as possible, still maximizing the distance to the nearest neatly divided data points. The technique proposes slack variables, γ_i which quantify the degree of misclassification of the data point as follows (Cortes and Vapnik 1995):

$$c_i\left(\{w\} \cdot \{x\}_i - b\right) \geq 1 - \gamma_i, 1 \leq i \leq n \tag{5.16}$$

A function which penalizes non-zero γ_i augments the objective and, therefore, the optimization exhibits a compromise between a large margin and a small error penalty. If a linear penalty function is assumed, the optimization problem then can be written by minimizing $\{w\}$ and γ_i through the following function (Cortes and Vapnik 1995):

$$\frac{1}{2}\|\{w\}\|^2 + C \sum_{i=1}^{n} \gamma_i \tag{5.17}$$

subject to:

$$c_i\left(\{w\} \cdot \{x\}_i - b\right) \geq 1 - \gamma_i, \gamma_i \geq 0, i = 1,...,n \tag{5.18}$$

In Eq. 5.17, C is the capacity. Equations 5.17 and 5.18 can be written in Lagrangian form by optimizing the following equation in terms of $\{w\}, \gamma, b, \alpha$ and β as follows (Cortes and Vapnik 1995):

$$\min_{\{w\},\gamma,b} \max_{\alpha,\beta}$$

$$\left\{\frac{1}{2}\|\{w\}\|^2 + C \sum_{i=1}^{n} \gamma_i - \sum_{i=1}^{n} \alpha_i \left[c_i\left(\{w\} \cdot \{x\}_i - b\right) - 1 + \gamma_i\right] - \sum_{i=1}^{n} \beta_i \gamma_i\right\} \tag{5.19}$$

where $\alpha_i, \beta_i \geqslant 0$.

The main benefit of a linear penalty function is that the slack variables are automatically removed from the dual problem and therefore C only appears as a supplementary constraint on the Lagrange multipliers. The use of non-linear penalty functions to lessen the impact of outliers on the classifier has been applied in the past but it had a consequence of making the optimization problem non-convex and difficult identify a global solution.

(b) Non-linear classification

To apply the linear SVM procedure for producing non-linear classifiers, the kernel trick was applied (Aizerman et al. 1964) to the maximum-margin hyperplanes (Boser et al. 1992). In this technique the, dot product is replaced by a non-linear kernel function to fit the maximum-margin hyperplane in a transformed feature space. While this dot product transformation may be non-linear, the transformed space may be in high dimensions. For example, when a Gaussian radial basis function kernel is used, the resultant feature space is a Hilbert space of infinite dimension. Some useful kernel functions include (Vapnik 1995; Müller et al. 2001):

The Radial Basis Function:

$$k\left(\{x\}_i, \{x\}_j\right) = \exp\left(-\gamma \|x\}_i - \{x\}_j\|^2\right), \gamma > 0 \tag{5.20}$$

The Polynomial (homogeneous):

$$k\left(\{x\}_i, \{x\}_j\right) = \left(\{x\}_i \cdot \{x\}_j\right)^d \tag{5.21}$$

The Polynomial (inhomogeneous):

$$k\left(\{x\}_i, \{x\}_j\right) = \left(\{x\}_i \cdot \{x\}_j + 1\right)^d \tag{5.22}$$

The Hyperbolic tangent:

$$k\left(\{x\}_i, \{x\}_j\right) = \tanh\left(\varepsilon\{x\}_i \cdot \{x\}_j + b\right), \varepsilon > 0; b < 0 \tag{5.23}$$

The variables of the maximum-margin hyperplane were identified by optimizing the objective equation. This was done by using an interior point method that identifies a solution for the Karush-Kuhn-Tucker (KKT) conditions of the primal and dual problems (Kuhn and Tucker 1951; Karush 1939). To circumvent solving a linear system, including the large kernel matrix, a low rank estimate to the matrix was applied to implement the kernel trick. The Karush–Kuhn–Tucker conditions were necessary for optimizing a non-linear programming problem, for the satisfaction of a particular regularity condition. For the given problem listed below:

$$Minimize: f(\{x\}) \tag{5.24}$$

subject to:

$$g_i(\{x\}) \leq 0; h_j(\{x\}) = 0 \tag{5.25}$$

Here, g_i is the ith inequality constraint and h_i is the ith equality constraint. The Karush-Kuhn-Tucker technique permits the inequality constraints by generalizing the technique of Lagrange multipliers which permit only equality constraints. The necessary conditions for the KKT are:

Table 5.1 Comparison of methods

Attributes	Support vector machines	Neural networks
General philosophy	Structural risk minimization Computational complexity does not depend on the size of the input variables Practice derived from theory	Empirical risk minimization Computational complexity depends on the size of the input variables Theory derived from practice
Optimization	Global optimum	Local optimization
Generalization	The margin is important for generalization purposes	Weight decay regularization is important to ensure network generalization
Model selection	Automatically select the model size by selecting the support vectors	Model is usually selected by using methods such as genetic algorithm or Bayesian formulation

Stationary:

$$\nabla f\left(\{x^*\}\right) + \sum_{i=1}^{m} \mu_i \nabla g_i\left(\{x^*\}\right) + \sum_{j=1}^{l} \lambda_j \nabla h_j\left(\{x^*\}\right) = 0, i = 1,...,m;$$

$$j = 1,...,l \hspace{6cm} (5.26)$$

Primal and dual feasibility as well as complementary slackness:

$$g_i\left(\{x^*\}\right) \leq 0, i = 1,...,m$$
$$h_j\left(\{x^*\}\right) = 0; j = 1,...,l$$
$$\mu_i \geq 0, i = 1,...,m$$
$$\mu_i g_i\left(\{x^*\}\right) = 0, i = 1,...,m \hspace{3cm} (5.27)$$

The KKT technique can be viewed as a generalized version of the Lagrangian approach by setting $m = 0$. In certain circumstances, the necessary conditions are also sufficient for optimization. However, in many situations the necessary conditions are not sufficient for optimization and further information, such as the second derivative, is necessary. The necessary conditions are sufficient for optimization if the objective function f and the inequality constraints g_j are continuously differentiable convex functions and the equality constraints g_j are functions which have constant gradients.

A comparison was made between SVMs and neural networks. This comparison is in Table 5.1.

5.2.4 Conflict Modelling

In this chapter, the modelling of international disputes has consisted of numerical and experimental investigations based on dyadic information for pairs of countries. In our perspective a Dyad-year denoted a pair of states in a specific year. Political scientists implement dyadic variables as a measure of the likelihood that two countries will experience a militarized conflict. Even though wide-ranging data gathering has been performed, much research is in progress to derive acceptable and consistent conflict models. A consistent reason of why conflict modelling is not an easy task, in accordance with (Beck et al. 2000), is that an international dispute is an infrequent event and the procedures and paths that produce it differ for each occurrence.

A minor alteration made on the explanatory parameters significantly affects the militarized interstate dispute consequence. This causes the modeling of militarized interstate disputes to be a greatly nonlinear, exceedingly interrelated, and situation-reliant. In modeling interstate disputes, Marwala and Lagazio (2004) as well as Lagazio and Russett (2003) applied seven dyadic variables and used militarized interstate dispute data (Russett and Oneal 2001). Since the same variables as discussed in (Marwala and Lagazio 2004; Lagazio and Russett 2003; Oneal and Russett 1999; Oneal and Russett 2001), were used for this book, their description appears in Chap. 1.

5.3 Results and Discussion

In this chapter, a multi-layer perceptron neural-network based on a Bayesian framework was implemented for the prediction of interstate conflict (MacKay 1991, 1992). The Bayesian framework was applied to estimate the posterior probability of the network weights, given the observed data from the likelihood probability function of the network observed data, the network weights, the probability of the network weight, and the probability of the observed data. The hybrid Monte Carlo method was applied to sample the posterior probability function of the network weight given the data (Marwala et al. 2009; Neal 1993). The attributes assumed for Chap. 4 were also assumed for this chapter in constructing and training the multi-layer perceptron neural-network.

A support vector machine method, which was implemented in this chapter, is a technique of mapping the input into a feature space of higher dimensionality by identifying a linear separating hyperplane with a maximum margin of separation between the two classes. In this chapter, the two classes were *peace* and *conflict*. There are numerous mapping functions, which are also called *kernel functions* that were used. These include the linear, polynomial, radial basis functions, and sigmoid function. The selection of a kernel function was determined by the type of problem that was under consideration. As an example, the radial basis functions dealt better with non-linear data than the linear kernel functions. Furthermore, the polynomial kernel has a number of hyperparameters which impact on the complexity of the

Table 5.2 Classification results

Method	True conflicts TC	False peaces FP	True peaces TP	False conflicts FC
Support vector machines	297	95	290	102
Hybrid Monte Carlo	286	106	290	102

model and, at times, its values may approach infinity or zero as the point becomes large. The radial basis function is a popular technique to implement as a kernel function for the application of support vector machines.

Similar to the neural network, support vector machines also require a choice of a model that yields an optimal outcome. Preliminary investigation in this chapter demonstrated that radial basis function offers the best results for the classification of interstate conflict. When a radial basis function is implemented as a kernel function, two parameters are necessarily tuned to provide the best result. These parameters are the *penalty parameter* of the error term C and the $\gamma parameter$ of the RBF kernel function. Cross-validation and grid-search are two methods which are used to identify an optimal model. In this chapter, a tenfold cross-validation method and a simple grid-search for the variables C and γ were used. The parameters $C = 1$ and $\gamma = 16.75$ were found to give the best results (Habtemariam 2006).

As indicated before, multi-layer perceptron neural networks based on the Bayesian framework and support vector machines were employed to classify the militarized interstate dispute data. The focus of the research was to look at the percentage of correct militarized interstate conflict prediction for the test data set, which had not been used in the training, for each technique.

Table 5.2 depicts the confusion matrix (i.e., true positives, true negatives, false positives, and false negatives) for the results. Support vector machines predicted true conflict cases (true positives) with a detection rate of 76% whereas the hybrid Monte Carlo trained multi-layer perceptron neural-network predicted true positive cases with a detection rate of 73%. Support vector machine and the hybrid Monte Carlo trained multi-layer perceptron neural-network were both able to correctly predict peace (true negatives) with a detection rate of 74%. Overall, the support vector machines and the neural networks could predict peace and conflict with rates of 75% and 73.5% respectively. Support vector machines gave the area under the Receiver Operating Characteristics (ROC) curve as 0.87 compared to 0.86 given by a neural network trained using the hybrid Monte Carlo method.

For the purpose of observing the effect of each variable on the militarized interstate dispute results, two distinct sensitivity analyses were conducted for neural networks and support vector machines. The two analyses demonstrated similar results in identifying the influences of several parameters while they showed different results in others.

The first investigation, assigning each variable to its possible maximum value while maintaining the rest at their possible minimum levels and *vice versa,* assesses changes in the militarized interstate dispute outcome. The outcomes for neural-network demonstrated that *democracy levels* and *capability ratios* are capable of bringing a peaceful consequence when all the other variables are maintained at a minimal level, which is favorable to war. This means that democracy and difference in dyadic power can still constrained states even when all the other factors, economic interdependence, geographical proximity and allies, are providing incentives to go to war. In addition, this indicates that dyadic power preponderance has a significant deterring effect on conflict, as does the joint democracy of the states involved. Alternatively, maintaining all the parameters at their maximum levels, which means high democracy, high level of economic interdependence, high difference in power ratio, high number of shared alliances and high geographical distance, while assigning one parameter to its minimum level, lead to a peaceful consequence. Put differently, there is no single variable which can alter the result when all the other variables are put to their possible maximum level, which is favorable to peace. This means that when the majority of all the realist or liberal factors are constraining state behavior, no single liberal or realist variable can provide on its own enough incentives to go to war. The same investigation conducted for support vector machines demonstrates that vector machine is not capable of identifying the influence of a parameter using the same tactic, as was possible with neural networks. With support vector machine the parameters can be put to their minimum or maximum and the result offered will be in both cases a *peace* outcome.

The second investigation was conducted to assess the sensitivity of the parameters within the context of partial derivatives as conducted by Zeng (1999). The notion is essentially to understand the change in the output as a consequence of a change in one of the input variables. The investigation assesses as to how the militarized interstate dispute changes when one variable is allocated its possible maximum and minimum values while maintaining all the other variables the same. The results demonstrate that *democracy level* has the maximum effect in reducing conflict while *capability ratio* is second in conformance with the first experiment. Permitting *democracy* to have its possible maximum value for the whole data set could circumvent conflict completely. *Capability ratio* reduced the incidence of conflict by 97%. Maximizing *alliance* between the dyads reduced the number of conflicts by 22%. Maximizing *dependency* has a 7% effect in reducing possible conflicts. Reducing *major power* could reduce the number of conflicts by 2%. Minimizing the *contiguity* of the dyads to their possible lower values and maximizing the *distance* reduced the number of conflicts by 45% and 30%, respectively. This last result is in line with the realist theory that says further apart countries have less reasons to have conflicts (Oneal and Russett 1999).

These results seem to indicate that the path to war is triggered by more complex interactions among the realist and liberal variables than the path to peace. While very high level of democracy and power ratio can still produce peace, when all the other conditions are calling for war, no single factor, either realist or liberal, can push a state to war when all the others are calling for peace. The results of the experiment are somehow difficult to interpret and a final conclusion should not be drawn. Evidently further examination is essential to understand the influence of each variable (e.g., by exploring with other sensitivity analysis techniques) as well as the different impact that the same variables may have on peace and war.

Consequently, a substitute sensitivity-analysis that includes only one explanatory variable to predict the militarized interstate disputes should be used and its accuracy should be measured.

5.4 Conclusion

In this chapter, two artificial intelligence techniques, neural networks and support vector machines, were applied to predict militarized interstate disputes. The independent/ input variables were *Democracy*, *Allies*, *Contingency*, *Distance*, *Capability*, *Dependency* and *Major Power* while the dependent/output variable was the *MID* result which was either *peace* or *conflict*. A neural network trained with a scaled-conjugate gradient-algorithm and the SVM with a radial basis kernel function together with grid-search and cross-validation techniques were studied to find the optimal model.

The results show that the SVM model is better than the neural network model at forecasting conflicts without affecting the correct peace prediction. Two separate experiments were conducted to see the influence of each variable on the militarized interstate dispute outcome. The first one assigned each variable its possible highest value, while keeping the rest to their lowest possible values. The neural networks results show that both *democracy level* and *capability ratio* can influence the outcome to be *peace*. On the other hand, none of the variables could influence the militarized interstate dispute outcome to be *conflict* when all the other variables were at a maximum. The SVM could not predict the effects of the variable for this experiment.

The second experiment assigned each variable its highest or lowest possible value while keeping the other variables fixed at their original values. The results agree with the previous experiment. If we group the variables in terms of their effect and rank them, *democracy level* and *capability ratio* are first, *contiguity*, *distance*, and *alliance* second and *dependency*, *major power* are ranked third using militarized interstate dispute. Although the SVM performed better at militarized interstate dispute prediction than the neural network, the predicted results of militarized interstate disputes can be easily interpreted by an analysis of the influence of individual variables.

5.5 Further Work

This chapter implemented a standard support vector machine with an arbitrarily chosen kernel function. The results demonstrated a marginal improvement of the support vector machines over the neural network trained using the hybrid Monte Carlo method. In the future, a support vector machine which automatically chooses the kernel functions must be developed and implemented.

References

Aizerman, M., Braverman, E., Rozonoer, L.: Theoretical foundations of the potential function method in pattern recognition learning. Autom. Rem. Contr. **25**, 821–837 (1964)

Alenezi, A., Moses, S.A., Trafalis, T.B.: Real-time prediction of order flowtimes using support vector regression. Comp. Oper. Res. **35**, 3489–3503 (2007)

Beck, N., King, G., Zeng, L.: Improving quantitative studies of international conflict: a conjecture. Am. Politic Sci. Rev. **94**, 21–33 (2000)

Bishop, C.: Neural Networks for Pattern Recognition. Oxford University Press, Oxford (1995)

Boser, B.E., Guyon, I.M., Vapnik, V.N.: A training algorithm for optimal margin classifiers. In: Haussler, D. (ed.) Proceedings of the 5th Annual ACM Workshop on COLT, pp. 144–152. ACM Press, Pittsburgh (1992)

Burges, C.: A tutorial on support vector machines for pattern recognition. Data Min. Knowl. Disc. **2**, 121–167 (1998)

Chang, B.R., Tsai, H.F., Young, C.-P.: Diversity of quantum optimizations for training adaptive support vector regression and its prediction applications. Expert Syst. Appl. **34**, 2612–2621 (2007)

Chen, D., Odobez, J.: Comparison of support vector machine and neural network for text texture verification. Technical report IDIAP-RR-02 19. Martigny, IDIAP Research Institute (2002)

Chen, J.L., Liu, H.B., Wu, W., Xie, D.T.: Estimation of monthly solar radiation from measured temperatures using support vector machines – a case study. Renew. Eng. **36**, 413–420 (2011)

Chuang, C.-C.: Extended support vector interval regression networks for interval input–output data. Info. Sci. **178**, 871–891 (2008)

Cortes, C., Vapnik, V.: Support-vector networks. Mach. Learn. **20**, 273–297 (1995)

Gidudu, A., Hulley, G., Marwala, T.: Image classification using SVMs: one-against-one vs one-against-all. In: Proceedings of the 28th Asian Conference on Remote Sensing. CD-Rom (2007)

Gochman, C., Maoz, Z.: Militarized interstate disputes 1816–1976. J. Confl. Res. **28**, 585–615 (1984)

Gunn, S.R.: Support vector machines for classification and regression. ISIS technical report. University of Southampton (1997)

Guo, G., Zhang, J.S.: Reducing examples to accelerate support vector regression. Pattern Recognit. Letts. **28**, 2173–2183 (2007)

Habtemariam, E.: Artificial intelligence for conflict management. Master thesis, University of the Witwatersrand, Johannesburg (2006)

Habtemariam, E., Marwala, T., Lagazio, M.: Artificial intelligence for conflict management. In: Proceedings of the IEEE International Joint Conference on Neural Networks, pp. 2583–2588. IEEE, Montreal (2005)

Haykin, S.: Neural Networks: A Comprehensive Foundation. Prentice-Hall, Upper Saddle River (1999)

Jayadeva, R.K., Chandra, S.: Regularized least squares fuzzy support vector regression for financial time series forecasting. Expert Syst. Appl. **178**, 3402–3414 (2007)

Karush, W.: Minima of functions of several variables with inequalities as side constraints. MSc thesis, University of Chicago (1939)

Kim, D., Lee, H., Cho, S.: Response modeling with support vector regression. Expert Syst. Appl. **34**, 1102–1108 (2008)

Kuhn, H.W., Tucker, A.W.: Nonlinear programming. In: Proceedings of 2nd Berkeley symposium, pp. 481–492 (1951)

Lagazio, M., Russett, B.: A Neural Network Analysis of Militarized Disputes, 1885–1992: Temporal Stability and Causal Complexity. University of Michigan Press, Ann Arbor (2003)

Lau, K.W., Wu, Q.H.: Local prediction of non-linear time series using support vector regression. Pattern Recognit. **41**, 1539–1547 (2007)

Lin, F., Yeh, C.C., Lee, M.Y.: The use of hybrid manifold learning and support vector machines in the prediction of business failure. Knowledge-Based Syst. **24**, 95–101 (2011)

Li-Xia, L., Yi-Qi, Z., Liu, X.Y.: Tax forecasting theory and model based on SVM optimized by PSO. Expert Syst. Appl. **38**, 116–120 (2011)

MacKay, D.J.C.: Bayesian methods for adaptive models. Ph.D. thesis. California Institute of Technology (1991)

MacKay, D.J.C.: A practical Bayesian framework for backpropagation networks. Neural Comput. **4**, 448–472 (1992)

Marwala, T., Lagazio, M.: Modelling and controlling interstate conflict. In: Proceedings of the IEEE International Joint Conference on Neural Networks, pp. 1233–1238. IEEE, Budapest (2004)

Marwala, T., Chakraverty, S., Mahola, U.: Fault classification using multi-layer perceptrons and support vector machines. Int. J. Eng. Simul. **7**, 29–35 (2006)

Marwala, T., Lagazio, M., Tettey, T.: An integrated human-computer system for controlling interstate disputes. Int. J. Comput. Appl. **31**, 239–246 (2009)

Msiza, I.S., Nelwamondo, F.V., Marwala, T.: Artificial neural networks and support vector machines for water demand time series forecasting. In: Proceedings of the IEEE International Conference on Systems, Man, and Cybernetics, pp. 638–643. IEEE, Montreal (2007)

Müller, K.R., Mika, S., Ratsch, G., Tsuda, K., Scholkopf, B.: An introduction to Kernel-based learning algorithms. IEEE Trans. Neural Nets. **12**, 181–201 (2001)

Neal, R.M.: Probabilistic inference using Markov Chain Monte Carlo methods. University of Toronto technical teport CRG-TR-93-1. Toronto (1993)

Oliveira, A.L.I.: Estimation of software project effort with support vector regression. Neurocomput. **69**, 1749–1753 (2006)

Oneal, J., Russett, B.: The Kantian peace: the Pacific benefits of democracy, interdependence, and international organization. World Politics **1**, 1–37 (1999)

Oneal, J., Russett, B.: Clear and clean: the fixed effects of liberal peace. Int. Org. **52**, 469–485 (2001)

Ortiz-García, E.G., Salcedo-Sanz, S., Pérez-Bellido, Á.M., Portilla-Figueras, J.A., Prieto, L.: Prediction of hourly O_3 concentrations using support vector regression algorithms. Atmos. Environ. **44**, 4481–4488 (2010)

Palanivel, S., Yegnanarayana, B.: Multimodal person authentication using speech, face and visual speech [modalities]. Comp. Vis. Image Underst. **109**, 44–55 (2008)

Pires, M., Marwala, T.: Option pricing using neural networks and support vector machines. In: Proceedings of the IEEE International Conference on Systems, Man, and Cybernetics, pp. 1279–1285. IEEE, The Hague (2004)

Russett, B., Oneal, J.: Triangulating Peace: Democracy, Interdependence, and International Organizations. W.W. Norton, New York (2001)

Schölkopf, B., Smola, A.J.: A short introduction to learning with Kernels. In: Mendelson, S., Smola, A.J. (eds.) Proceedings of the Machine Learning Summer School, pp. 41–64. Springer, Berlin (2003)

Shen, R., Fu, Y., Lu, H.: A novel image watermarking scheme based on support vector regression. J. Syst. Softw. **78**, 1–8 (2005)

Tao, X., Tao, W.: Cutting tool wear identification based on wavelet package and SVM. In: Proceedings of the World Congress on Intelligent Control and Automation, pp. 5953–5957 (2010)

Tellaeche, A., Pajares, G., Burgos-Artizzu, X.P., Ribeiro, A.: A computer vision approach for weeds identification through support vector machines. Appl. Soft Comput. J. **11**, 908–915 (2009)

Thissen, U., Pepers, M., Üstün, B., Melssen, W.J., Buydens, L.M.C.: Comparing support vector machines to PLS for spectral regression applications. Chemomet. Intell. Lab. Syst. **73**, 169–179 (2004)

Üstün, B., Melssen, W.J., Buydens, L.M.C.: Facilitating the application of support vector regression by using a universal pearson VII function based Kernel. Chemomet. Intell. Lab. Syst. **81**, 29–40 (2006)

Üstün, B., Melssen, W.J., Buydens, L.M.C.: Visualisation and interpretation of support vector regression models. Anal. Chim. Acta. **595**, 299–309 (2007)

Vapnik, V.: The Nature of Statistical Learning Theory. Springer Verlag, New York (1995)

Vapnik, V.: Statistical Learning Theory. Wiley-Interscience, New York (1998)

Vapnik, V., Lerner, A.: Pattern recognition using generalized portrait method. Automat. Rem. Contr. **24**, 774–780 (1963)

Wang, C.-H., Zhong, Z.-P., Li, R., J-Q, E.: Prediction of jet penetration depth based on least square support vector machine. Powder Technol. **203**, 404–411 (2010)

Xi, X.-C., Poo, A.-N., Chou, S.-K.: Support vector regression model predictive control on a HVAC plant. Contr. Eng. Prac. **15**, 897–908 (2007)

Yeh, C.Y., Su, W.P., Lee, S.J.: Employing multiple-kernel support vector machines for counterfeit Banknote recognition. Appl. Soft Comput. J. **11**, 1439–1447 (2011)

Zeng, L.: Prediction and classification with neural network models. Soc. Method. Res. **27**, 499–524 (1999)

Zhang, J., Sato, T., Iai, S.: Support vector regression for on-line health monitoring of large-scale structures. Struct. Saf. **28**, 392–406 (2006)

Zhou, Y.-P., Jiang, J.-H., Lin, W.-Q., Zou, H.-Y., Wu, H.-L., Shen, G.-L., Yu, R.-Q.: Boosting support vector regression in QSAR studies of bioactivities of chemical compounds. Eur. J. Pharm. Sci. **28**, 344–353 (2006)

Chapter 6
Fuzzy Sets for Modeling Interstate Conflict

6.1 Introduction

In Chap. 2, a technique for identifying the relevance of variables on the prediction of militarized interstate disputes was proposed and implemented. This technique applied Bayesian theory and the evidence framework to create the automatic relevance determination method. The automatic relevance determination technique was applied to determine the relevance of interstate variables that are essential for modeling the militarized interstate disputes, and it was found that all the input variables considered were important in the prediction of the militarized interstate dispute.

In Chap. 3, a multi-layer perceptron neural network and a radial basis function neural network were introduced and applied to model militarized interstate disputes. The results obtained demonstrated that the multi-layer perceptron neural network is better at predicting militarized interstate disputes, when compared to the radial basis function neural network. This is mainly because of the fact that, structurally, the input variables to the multi-layer perceptron are more cross-coupled than the radial basis function.

In Chap. 4, two Bayesian techniques were described and compared for interstate conflict modeling. The first one was a Bayesian technique that applied the Gaussian approach to approximate the posterior probability of the neural network weights, given the observed data, and the evidence framework to train the multi-layer perceptron neural network. The second technique involved treating the posterior probability in full and then applying the hybrid Monte Carlo technique to train the multi-layer perceptron neural network. When these techniques were applied to model militarized interstate disputes, it was observed that training the neural network with the posterior probability, as is, and applying the hybrid Monte Carlo technique gives better results than approximating the posterior probability with a Gaussian approximation function and then applying the evidence framework to train the neural network.

In Chap. 5, support vector machines were introduced for the prediction of militarized interstate dispute and compared to the Bayesian formulated and hybrid

T. Marwala and M. Lagazio, *Militarized Conflict Modeling using Computational Intelligence*, Advanced Information and Knowledge Processing, DOI 10.1007/978-0-85729-790-7_6, © Springer-Verlag London Limited 2011

Monte Carlo trained neural networks. The results demonstrated that support vector machines predict militarized interstate disputes better than neural networks, while neural networks give more consistent and easy to interpret sensitivity analysis than support vector machines.

In this chapter, a neuro-fuzzy network is applied to model interstate disputes, primarily due to the thesis that states that fuzzy systems are better able to give rules that define interrelationships that exist in a data set than neural networks and support vector machines. The results obtained are compared to the support vector machines which were found to give more accurate results than neural networks in Chap. 5.

Demirli and Khoshnejad (2009) applied a neuro-fuzzy controller for autonomous parallel parking of a car-like mobile robot using the data from three sonar sensors and the turning angle. The fuzzy model was identified using a subtractive clustering algorithm and the results demonstrated success in deciding the direction of the motion. Zhou et al. (2010) applied an adaptive-network-based fuzzy inference system for analyzing the capturing process of carbon. The obtained results were informative and revealed knowledge about the parameters involved in the carbon dioxide capturing process.

Kurtulus and Razack (2010) applied a neuro-fuzzy system for modeling daily discharge responses of a large karstic aquifer and the results demonstrated that neural networks and the neuro-fuzzy system give good predictions of the karst daily discharges. Talei et al. (2010) applied a neuro-fuzzy model for modeling rainfall and the results demonstrated that the neuro-fuzzy method is able to estimate peak flow with good accuracy.

When modeling complex real world systems, two main approaches have been applied in the past: "White Box" and "Black Box" modeling. On one hand, white box modeling refers to the derivation of an expression describing a system using physical laws, *i.e.*, from first principles (Jang et al. 1997). On the other hand, black box modeling – which is more common to machine intelligence – is the approximation of an unidentified complex function using a configuration which is not anyhow linked to the system being modeled. An example of black box modeling is neural network technique to model the input-output relationship of some complex process (Nelwamondo et al. 2006).

Much has been written about the lack of transparency of neural networks when it comes to modeling systems. The first criticism lies with the fact that the use of neural networks has been found to be limited in some applications (Tettey 2007). For most applications, a neural network is required to use inputs, from a given process, in order for it to arrive at a corresponding output. In certain applications, an inverse neural network has been used, where the network is trained to provide the inputs to a process, given the outputs (Bishop 1995; Leke et al. 2007). One major shortcoming, which has been identified, is that the neural network is able to give output results without offering a chance for one to obtain a causal interpretation of the results (Marwala 2009; Patel and Marwala 2006). The lack of transparency of the model restricts the confidence in applying neural networks to problems. The sole reason for this is that the lack of transparency does not allow the model to be validated against human expert knowledge.

Neuro-fuzzy models have been viewed as an alternative to bridging the gap between white box and black box modeling (Haykin 1999; Patel and Marwala 2010). This is because of the neuro-fuzzy model's ability to combine available knowledge of a process with data obtained from the process. The advantage of these types of neuro-fuzzy models is that, not only do they facilitate the incorporation of expert knowledge into the modeling process, but they also allow knowledge discovery to take place. The Takagi-Sugeno (TS) neuro-fuzzy model is a universal approximator (Bih 2006) that has found widespread use in data-driven identification, and is considered to be a gray box modeling approach (Marwala 2007).

This chapter applies both support vector machines and neuro-fuzzy modeling to the problem of interstate conflict management. By using data-driven identification, this chapter aims to demonstrate the interpretability of these models. The chapter focuses mainly on the type of knowledge that analysts can be able to extract from both models. The importance of this knowledge extraction lies in the fact that international conflict management studies are centered on finding accurate methods of forecasting conflict and, at the same time, providing causal interpretation of results (Tettey and Marwala 2006a).

With the rate at which wars are occurring, it has become necessary that tools which assist in the avoidance of interstate conflict be developed and that these tools be used to understand the causes of this conflict. Predicting the onset of conflict is important, however, understanding the reason why different states go to war is just as significant. A successful interstate conflict decision support tool is, therefore, the one which is able to forecast dispute outcomes fairly accurately and, at the same time, allow for an intuitive causal interpretation of interstate relations (Tettey and Marwala 2006b). Such a tool would also allow for improved confidence in causal hypothesis testing.

Improvements in conflict management have been on two fronts. On the one hand, there has been effort to improve the collected data measures which are used to study interstate interactions. An important step forward has been in the definition of militarized interstate disputes as a set of interactions between or among states that can result in the actual use, display, or threat of using military force in an explicit way (Beck et al. 2000). This has led to collection and development of militarized interstate dispute data (MIDs), which allows us not only to analyze intense violent interactions among states but also the initial stages of a conflict, where militarized behavior occurs without escalation to full violence or war, as these may be very important in exploring mediation issues before full violence breaks up. As described in Chap. 1, the explanatory variables we use in our militarized interstate dispute studies are *Democracy, Dependency, Capability, Alliance, Contiguity, Distance* and *Major power*. Projects such as the Correlates of War (COW) facilitate the accurate and reliable collection and dissemination of such data measures (Jones et al. 1996). Any set of measures/variables describing a particular dyadic interstate interaction has a dispute outcome attached to it. The dispute outcome is either a *peace* or *militarized disputes*.

On the forecasting side, statistical methods have been used for a long time to predict conflict and it has been found that no conventional statistical model can predict international conflict with probability of more than 0.5 (Tettey 2007; Habtemariam and Marwala 2005). The use of conventional statistical models has led to fragmentary conclusions and results that are not in unison and significantly change when model specifications are slightly modified. An example of this can still be found in the sometime different views that political scientist hold in relation to the impact of democracy on peace. For example, in their work, Thompson and Tucker (1997) concluded that if the explanatory variables indicate that countries are democratic, the chances of war are then reduced. However, Mansfield and Snyder (1997) oppose this notion and suggest that if we focus on processes of democratization, which means when democracy is not yet consolidated, the likelihood of war increases. Another example of contradictory findings is on the role of trade in preventing conflict (Oneal and Russet 1997, 1999; Barbieri 1996; Beck et al. 1998). Lagazio and Russet (2004) point out that the reason for the failure of statistical methods might be attributed to the fact that the interstate variables, which are deemed to relate to the militarized interstate dispute, are non-linear, highly interdependent and context dependent. This, therefore, calls for the use of more suitable techniques. Neural networks, particularly multi-layer perceptrons, have been applied to the modeling of interstate conflict. Neuro-fuzzy modeling has also been successfully applied to the modeling of interstate conflict (Tettey and Marwala 2006b). The advantage of using such models is that they are able to capture complex input-output relationships without the need for a priori knowledge or assumptions about the problem domain.

It is found that the use of neural networks yields results expressed in the form of classification accuracy. The interpretation of this predictive accuracy is also found to be unambiguous compared to previous methods. However, the resulting neural network model, which supports the prediction accuracy, is regarded as a black box. This is due to the fact that models developed by the neural networks do not provide an easy way of obtaining a causal interpretation of dispute outcomes. The weights, which are the model parameters, extracted from the neural network offer no clear understanding as to why two states go to war.

Marwala and Lagazio (2004) proposed the use of Automatic Relevance Detection as a means to making the neural network more transparent. The result of automatic relevance detection reveals the importance of the two key liberal variables, economic interdependence and democracy, in predicting and explaining dispute outcomes. However, two realist variables, power ratio and allies, are also found to exert an important and significant impact on peace. From this work on neural networks, we can conclude that neural network models have a fairly strong forecasting ability, but only a limited amount of knowledge on the causal relationships identified by the neural network can be extracted.

Habtemariam and Marwala (2005) introduced support vector machines to the study of conflict management and found that support vector machines offer an improved forecasting ability over neural networks. However, a sensitivity analysis which aims to determine the influence of each variable on a dispute outcome reveals that results obtained from neural networks are much more intuitive and aligned with our theories on interstate conflicts. This, therefore, implies that while support vector machines offer better forecasting performance, they lack the ability to give an intuitive and logical causal interpretation of the results. As stated earlier on in the chapter, the main focus of international conflict studies has been both on the ability of a model to accurately forecast dispute outcomes and, at the same time, to provide political practitioners with insights on the reasons why a conflict may occur.

In the next section, a neuro-fuzzy model is proposed as a method of modeling interstate relations which has a fairly accurate forecasting ability and, at the same time, offers intuitive causal interpretations. This approach may help increase our ability to extract more knowledge about conflicts from the internal model developed by neural networks.

6.2 Computational Intelligence

6.2.1 Basic Fuzzy Logic Theory

Fuzzy logic is a technique of mapping an input space to an output space by means of a list of linguistic rules that consist of the if-then statements (Bih 2006). Fuzzy logic consists of four components: fuzzy sets, membership functions, fuzzy logic operators, and fuzzy rules (Von Altrock 1995; Biacino and Gerla 2002; Cox 1994).

In conventional set theory, an object is either an element or is not an element of a specific set (Devlin 1993; Ferreirós 1999; Johnson 1972). Consequently, it is possible to define if an object belongs to a specific set because a set has distinct boundaries, as long as an object cannot realize partial membership. An alternative approach of discerning this is that an object's belonging to a set is either true or false. A characteristic function for a classical set has a value of 1 if the object belongs to the set and a value of zero if the object doesn't belong to the set (Cantor 1874). For instance, if a set X is defined to represent all possible weights of people, one could define a "fat" subset for any person who is above or equal to a specific weight x, and anyone below x doesn't belong to the "fat" subset but to a "thin" subset. This is clearly intransigent as a person just below the boundary is labeled as being thin when they are obviously fat to some degree. Consequently, in-between values such as legitimately fat are not allowed. In addition, these clear cut defined boundaries can be very subjective in terms of what a person may define as belonging to a specific set.

The key objective of fuzzy logic is to permit a more flexible representation of sets of objects by using a fuzzy set. A fuzzy set does not have as clear cut boundaries as a classical set and the objects are characterized by a degree of membership to a specific set (Hájek 1995, 1998; Halpern 2003; Wright and Marwala 2006). Consequently, intermediate values of objects can be represented in a way that is closer to the way the human brain thinks, as opposed to the clear cut-off boundaries in classical sets.

A membership function defines the degree that an object belongs to a certain set or class. The membership function is a curve that maps the input space variable to a number between 0 and 1, representing the degree that a specific input variable belongs to a specific set (Klir and Folger 1988; Klir et al. 1997; Klir and Yuan 1995). A membership function can be a curve of any shape. Using the example above, there would be two subsets one for fat and one for thin that would overlap. In this way, a person can have a partial participation in each of these sets, therefore, determining the degree to which the person is both fat and thin.

Logical operators are defined to generate new fuzzy sets from the existing fuzzy sets. In classical set theory, there are three key operators used, permitting logical expressions to be defined: intersection, union, and the complement (Kosko 1993; Kosko and Isaka 1993). These operators are used in fuzzy logic, and have been adapted to deal with partial memberships. The intersection (AND operator) of two fuzzy sets is given by a minimum operation, and the union (OR operator) of two fuzzy sets is given by a maximum operation (Novák 1989, 2005; Novák et al. 1999). These logical operators are used in the rules and determination of the final output fuzzy set.

Fuzzy rules formulate the conditional statements which are used to model the input-output relationships of the system, and are expressed in natural language. These linguistic rules are in the form of if-then statements which use the logical operators and membership functions to produce an output. An important property of fuzzy logic is the use of linguistic variables. Linguistic variables are variables that take words or sentences as their values instead of numbers (Zadeh 1965; Zemankova-Leech 1983; Zimmermann 2001). Each linguistic variable takes a linguistic value that corresponds to a fuzzy set, and the set of values that it can take is called the term set. For example, a linguistic variable *weight* could have the following term set {*very fat, fat, medium, thin, very thin*}. A single fuzzy rule is of the form:

$$\textbf{if } x \textbf{ is } A \textbf{ then } y \textbf{ is } B \tag{6.1}$$

where A and B are fuzzy sets defined for the input and output space respectively. Both x and y are linguistic variables, while A and B are the linguistic values or labels represented by the membership functions. Each rule consists of two parts: the antecedent and the consequent. The antecedent is the component of the rule falling between the if-then, and maps the input x to the fuzzy set A, using a membership function. The consequent is the component of the rule after the then, and maps the output y to a membership function. The input membership values act like weighting factors to determine their influence on the fuzzy output sets. A fuzzy system consists of a list of these if-then rules which are evaluated in parallel. The antecedent can have more than one linguistic variable, these inputs are combined using the AND operator.

Each of the rules is evaluated for an input set, and corresponding output for the rule obtained. If an input corresponds to two linguistic variable values then the rules associated with both these values will be evaluated. Also, the rest of the rules will be evaluated, however they will not have an effect on the final result as the linguistic variable will have a value of zero. Therefore, if the antecedent is true to some degree,

Fig. 6.1 Showing the steps
involved in the application
of fuzzy logic to a problem
(Wright and Marwala 2006)

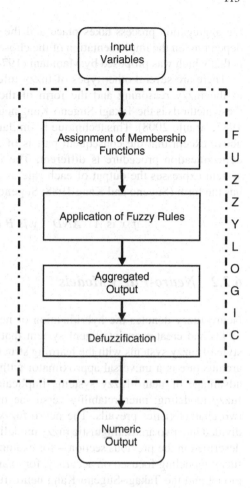

the consequent will have to be true to some degree (Zadeh 1965). The degree of each linguistic output value is then computed by performing a combined logical sum for each membership function (Zadeh 1965) after which all the combined sums for a specific linguistic variable can be aggregated. These last stages involve the use of an inference method which will map the result onto an output membership function (Zadeh 1965).

Finally defuzzification process is performed where a single numeric output is produced. One method of computing the degree of each linguistic output value is to take the maximum of all rules describing this linguistic output value, and the output is taken as the center of gravity of the area under the effected part of the output membership function. There are other inference methods such as averaging and sum mean square. Figure 6.1 shows the steps involved in creating an input-output mapping using fuzzy logic.

The use of a series of fuzzy rules, and inference methods to produce a defuzzified output constitute a Fuzzy Inference System (FIS). The final configuration in which the aggregation process takes place and the method of defuzzification can differ depending on the implementation of the chosen FIS. The approach discussed above is that which was proposed by Mamdani (1974).

There are several other types of fuzzy inference systems which vary according to the fuzzy reasoning and the form of the if-then statements applied. One of these methods is the Takagi-Sugeno-Kang neuro-fuzzy method (Takagi and Sugeno 1985; Araujo 2008). This technique is similar to the Mamdani approach described above except that the consequent part is of a different form and, as a result, the defuzzification procedure is different. The if-then statement of a Sugeno fuzzy system expresses the output of each rule as a function of the input variables and has the form (Sugeno and Kang 1988; Sugeno 1985):

$$if \ x \ \text{is} \ A \quad \textbf{AND} \quad y \ is \ B \ \textbf{then} \ z = f\ (x, y) \tag{6.2}$$

6.2.2 Neuro-Fuzzy Models

Neuro-fuzzy denotes the hybridization of neural networks and fuzzy logic (Jang 1993) and creates an intelligent system that combines the human-like reasoning style of fuzzy systems with the learning structure of neural networks. The resulting architecture is a universal approximator with an interpretable IF-THEN rule. The advantage of neuro-fuzzy systems implicates two conflicting characteristics in fuzzy modeling: interpretability versus accuracy and, in reality, only one of the two characteristics prevails. The neuro-fuzzy in fuzzy modeling research field is divided into two areas: linguistic fuzzy modeling focused on interpretability and was described in the previous section – for example, the Mamdani model – and precise fuzzy modeling focused on accuracy, for example, the Takagi-Sugeno neuro-fuzzy model and the Takagi-Sugeno-Kang neuro-fuzzy model (Sugeno and Kang 1988; Sugeno 1985; Takagi and Sugeno 1985; Araujo 2008).

Hsu and Lin (2009) implemented a recurrent wavelet-based neuro-fuzzy system with a reinforcement group cooperation-based symbiotic evolution for solving various control problems. The results obtained indicated that the proposed method was good. Kwong et al. (2009) applied a neuro-fuzzy network to model customer satisfaction for new product development of a notebook computer. The experimental results of mean absolute errors and variance of errors demonstrated that the neuro-fuzzy network has superior performance when measured against statistical regression. Iplikci (2010) applied support vector machines based neuro-fuzzy control for nonlinear systems. The results demonstrated that the proposed controller reveals significantly high performance and gives small transient- and steady-state tracking errors even in the presence of noise.

Montazer et al. (2010) applied a neuro-fuzzy inference method to recognize Farsi numeral characters. The proposed method was applied to a dataset of unknown numeral characters of 33 different Farsi fonts and the recognition rates averaging

97% was obtained. Cetisli (2010) developed an adaptive neuro-fuzzy classifier which used linguistic hedges and the results, in the form of recognition rates, showed that of the proposed technique was superior to the other fuzzy-based classification approaches with less fuzzy rules.

Other successful implementations of neuro-fuzzy systems include the work of Abiyev et al. (2011) on the application of a type-2 neuro-fuzzy system based on clustering and gradient techniques for system identification and channel equalization; Cano-Izquierdo et al. (2010) on the application of a neuro-fuzzy model to control systems; Khajeh and Modarress (2010) on the application of an adaptive neuro-fuzzy inference system and a radial basis function neural network to predict solubility of gases in polystyrene; Kucuk et al. (2011) on the application of an adaptive neuro-fuzzy inference system to predict the performance of the impact hammer; and Ata and Kocyigit (2010) on the application of an adaptive neuro-fuzzy inference system to predict tip speed ratio in wind turbines. Cabalar et al. (2010) applied a neuro-fuzzy technique to constitutively model response of Leighton Buzzard Sand mixtures, while El-Sebakhy (2010) applied the technique to identify flow regimes and predict liquid-holdup in horizontal multiphase flow. Shiri and Kisi (2010) applied a hybrid wavelet and neuro-fuzzy model for predicting short-term and long-term stream flow, while Mashrei et al. (2010) applied neural networks model and adaptive neuro-fuzzy inference system to predict the moment capacity of Ferro-cement members.

As explained before, fuzzy logic concepts provide a method of formulating imprecise models of reasoning, such as common sense reasoning, for uncertain and complex processes. It resembles human reasoning in its use of approximate information and uncertainty to generate decisions. The ability of fuzzy logic to approximate human reasoning is a motivation for considering fuzzy systems in this work. In fuzzy systems, the evaluation of the output is performed by a computing framework called, as mentioned before, the fuzzy inference system. The fuzzy inference system maps fuzzy or crisp inputs to the output – which is usually a fuzzy set. This fuzzy inference system performs a composition of the inputs using fuzzy set theory, fuzzy *if-then* rules, and fuzzy reasoning to arrive at the output. More specifically, the fuzzy inference process involves the fuzzification of the input variables (i.e. partitioning of the input data into fuzzy sets), evaluation of rules, aggregation of the rule outputs and, finally, the defuzzification (i.e. extraction of a crisp value which best represents a fuzzy set) of the result.

There are two popular fuzzy models: the Mamdani model and the Takagi-Sugeno neuro-fuzzy model. The Takagi-Sugeno neuro-fuzzy model is more popular when it comes to data-driven identification and has been proven to be a universal approximator (Tettey and Marwala 2007). The Takagi-Sugeno neuro-fuzzy model has been proven to have the ability to approximate any non-linear function arbitrarily given that the number of rules is not limited. It is for these reasons that it is used in this chapter. The most common form of the Takagi-Sugeno neuro-fuzzy model is the first order one. A diagram of a two-input and single output Takagi-Sugeno neuro-fuzzy model is shown in Fig. 6.2 (Babuska and Verbruggen 2003).

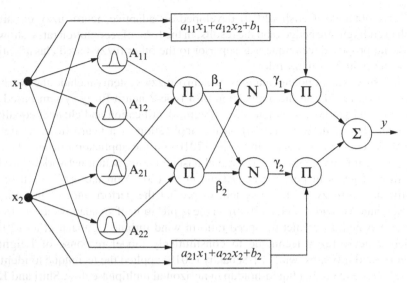

Fig. 6.2 An example of a two-input first order Takagi-Sugeno fuzzy model

In the Takagi-Sugeno neuro-fuzzy model, the antecedent part of the rule is a fuzzy proposition and the consequent function is an affine linear function of the input variables as shown as follows (Takagi and Sugeno 1985):

$$R_i : \text{If } x \text{ is } A_i \quad \text{then} \quad y_i = a_i^T x + b_i \qquad (6.3)$$

where R_i is the ith fuzzy rule, x is the input vector, A_i is a fuzzy set, a_i is the consequence parameter vector, b_i is a scalar offset and $i = 1, 2, ..., K$. The parameter K is the number of rules in the fuzzy model. If there are too few rules in the fuzzy model, it may not be possible to accurately model a process. Too many rules may lead to an overly complex model with redundant fuzzy rules which compromises the integrity of the model (Sentes et al. 1998). In this chapter, the optimum number of rules is empirically determined using a cross-validation process (Bishop 1995). The optimum number of rules is chosen from the model with the lowest error and standard deviation. The final antecedent values in the model describe the fuzzy regions in the input space in which the consequent functions are valid.

The first step in any inference procedure is the partitioning of the input space in order to form the antecedents of the fuzzy rules. The shapes of the membership functions of the antecedents can be chosen to be Gaussian or triangular. The Gaussian membership function of the following form is chosen in this chapter (Zadeh 1965).

$$\mu^i(x) = \prod_{j=1}^{n} e^{-\frac{\left(x_j - c_j^i\right)^2}{\left(b_j^i\right)^2}} \qquad (6.4)$$

Here, μ^i is the combined antecedent value for the ith rule, n is the number of antecedents belonging to the ith rule, c is the center of the Gaussian function, and b describes the variance of the Gaussian membership function.

The consequent function in the Takagi-Sugeno neuro-fuzzy model can either be constant or linear. In this chapter, it is found that the linear consequent function gives a more accurate result. The form of the linear consequent function is shown below (Babuska and Verbruggen 2003):

$$y_i = \sum_{j=1}^{n} p_{ij} x_j + p_{i0} \tag{6.5}$$

where p_{ij} is the jth parameter of the ith fuzzy rule. If a constant is used as the consequent function, i.e. $y_i = p_i$, the zero-order Takagi-Sugeno neuro-fuzzy model becomes a special case of the Mamdani inference system (Mamdani 1974). The output y of the entire inference system is computed by taking a weighted average of the individual rules' contributions as shown in (Babuska and Verbruggen 2003):

$$y = \frac{\sum_{i=1}^{K} \beta_i(x) y_i}{\sum_{i=1}^{K} \beta_i(x)} = \frac{\sum_{i=1}^{K} \beta_i(x) \left(a_i^T x + b_i\right)}{\sum_{i=1}^{K} \beta_i(x)} \tag{6.6}$$

where $\beta_i(x)$ is the activation of the ith rule. The $\beta_i(x)$ can be a complicated expression but, in our work, it will be equivalent to the degree of fulfilment of the ith rule. The parameters a_i are then approximate models of the non-linear system under consideration (Babuska 1991).

When setting up a fuzzy rule-based system we are required to optimize parameters such as membership functions and consequent parameters. In order to optimize these parameters, the fuzzy system relies on training algorithms inherited from artificial neural networks such as gradient descent-based learning. It is for this reason that they are referred to as neuro-fuzzy models. There are two approaches to training neuro-fuzzy models (Babuska and Verbruggen 2003):

1. Fuzzy rules may be extracted from expert knowledge and used to create an initial model. The parameters of the model can then be fine-tuned using data collected from the operational system being modelled.
2. The number of rules can be determined from collected numerical data using a model selection technique. The parameters of the model are also optimized using the existing data.

The major motivation for using a Takagi-Sugeno neuro-fuzzy model in this work is that, not only is it suitable for data-driven identification, but it is also considered to be a gray box. Unlike other computational intelligence methods, once optimized, it is possible to extract information which allows one to understand the process being modeled. Later in this chapter, we explore the interpretability of this model to see what kind of information can be explored.

6.2.3 Support Vector Machines

The fuzzy results obtained from this chapter are compared to the support vector machine results which were observed to be successful in Chap. 5 and in many other research studies (Marwala et al. 2006). The fundamental motive behind support vector machines is to map the input space to an output (1 or 0) by identifying a hyperplane that represents the largest separation, or margin, between the two classes.

The optimization problem solved in the support vector machine training is then set up to be a quadratic programming problem by first finding the Lagrangian multiplier and applying the Karush-Kuhn Tucker conditions (Schölkopf and Smola 2002). The function can then be determined so that the linear function needed to fit the training data can be found explicitly.

Successful implementations of support vector machines include the development of a structural health monitoring system by Hagiwara and Mita (2002); the analysis of stochastic mechanics by Hurtado (2003); the segmentation of remote sensing images by Mitra et al. (2004); bankruptcy prediction by Min and Lee (2005), web service quality control based on text mining by Lo (2008); climate change analysis by Tripathi et al. (2006); as well as gene extraction in cancer diagnosis by Huang and Kecman (2005).

Support vector machines employ a technique of mapping the input into a feature space of higher dimensionality and then find a linear hyperplane which separates classes with a maximum margin of separation. There are various mapping or kernel functions in use, the most common of which are linear, polynomial, radial basis function, and sigmoid. The choice of a kernel function depends on the type of problem at hand and the radial basis function: $K(x_i, x_j) = \exp(-\gamma||x_i - x_j||^2, \gamma > 0$ can handle non-linear data better than the linear kernel function. Moreover, the polynomial kernel has a number of hyperparameters which influences the complexity of the model and sometimes its values may become infinity or zero as the degree becomes large. This makes radial basis functions to be a common choice for use.

Analogous to the neural network, a support vector machine also requires selection of a model that gives an optimal result. The conducted experiments demonstrate that a radial basis function offers best results, in less time, for the classification of militarized interstate dispute data. When a radial basis function is used as the kernel function, there are two parameters that are required to be adjusted to give the best result. These are the penalty parameter of the error term C and the γ parameter of the radial basis kernel function. For this experiment, as in Chap. 5, a simple grid-search for the variables C and γ were used. The parameters $C = 1$ and $\gamma = 16.75$ gave the best results.

6.3 Knowledge Extraction

6.3.1 Classification Results

The forecasting ability of the Takagi-Sugeno neuro-fuzzy and support vector machine models are evaluated. The support vector machine training was conducted as it was done in Chap. 5. Both the models are trained with a balanced training set containing 1,000 instances. This is to ensure that both *conflict* and *peace* outcomes are given equal importance. The models are then tested on the selected balanced set which contains 392 peace cases and 392 conflict cases. The confusion matrices for both the Takagi-Sugeno neuro-fuzzy and Bayesian neural support vector machine models with a cut-off of 0.5 are shown in Table 6.1.

The results obtained demonstrate that detection rate of conflict was 77% when using the Takagi-Sugeno neuro-fuzzy model whereas when using the support vector machine the detection rate was 76%. The detection rate for peace was 73% when using the Takagi-Sugeno neuro-fuzzy model while it is 74% when the support vector machine is used. Overall the detection rate of a correct outcome was 75% when both these methods were implemented. Furthermore, the area under the receiver operating characteristics curves when both these methods are used is 0.86 for Takagi-Sugeno neuro-fuzzy method and 0.87 for support vector machine.

6.3.2 Fuzzy Rule Extraction

The Takagi-Sugeno neuro-fuzzy model used for forecasting can also be used for rule extraction. Two fuzzy rules can be extracted from the model and these are shown below.

If u_1 is A_{11} and u_2 is A_{12} and u_3 is A_{13} and u_4 is A_{14} and u_5 is A_{15} and u_6 is A_{16} and u_7 is A_{17} then:

$$y_1 = -1.9 \times 10^{-1} u_1 - 1.3 \times 10^{-1} u_2 + 0.0 \times 10^0 u_3 - 6.1 \times 10^{-1} u_4$$

$$- 1.3 \times 10^{-1} u_5 - 1.3 \times 10^0 u_6 + 4.7 \times 10^{-1} u_7 + 9.0 \times 10^{-1}$$

Table 6.1 Classification results

Method	True conflicts (TC)	False peaces (FP)	True peaces (TP)	False conflicts (FC)
Takagi-Sugeno neuro-fuzzy	303	89	288	104
Support vector machine	297	95	290	102

If u_1 is A_{21} **and** u_2 is A_{22} **and** u_3 is A_{23} **and** u_4 is A_{24} **and** u_5 is A_{25} **and** u_6 is A_{26} **and** u_7 is A_{27} **then:**

$$y_2 = -2.8 \times 10^{-1} u_1 + 6.3 \times 10^{-2} u_2 + 2.5 \times 10^{-1} u_3 - 7.6 \times 10^{-1} u_4$$
$$- 8.9 \times 10^{-1} u_5 - 9.0 \times 10^{0} u_6 + 0.0 \times 10^{0} u_7 + 3.7 \times 10^{-1}$$

The symbols from $u1$ to $u7$ are the input vector which consists of *Democracy, Dependency, Capability, Alliance, Contiguity, Distance,* and *Major Power.*

It is clear that the rules are quite complex and need to be simplified in order to obtain a didactic interpretation. In fact, it is often found that when automated techniques are applied to obtain fuzzy models, unnecessary complexity is often present (Sentes et al. 1998).

In our case, the Takagi-Sugeno fuzzy model contains only two fuzzy rules. The removal of a fuzzy set similar to the universal set leaves only one remaining fuzzy set. The result of this is that the input is being partitioned into only one fuzzy set and therefore introduces difficulty when expressing the premise in linguistic terms. To simplify the fuzzy rules and avoid the redundant fuzzy sets, the number of inputs into the Takagi-Sugeno neuro-fuzzy model has been pruned down to four variables. These variables are *Democracy, Dependency, Alliance,* and *Contiguity.* The rules extracted can then be converted so that they are represented in the commonly used linguistic terms. However it is only possible to translate the antecedent of the fuzzy statement into English. The consequent part, together with the firing strength of the rule, is still expressed mathematically. The translated fuzzy rules, with the firing strengths omitted, can be written as shown below:

If Democracy Level is low **and** Alliance is strong **and** Contiguity is true **then**

$$y_1 = -3.87 \times 10^{-1} u_1 - 9.19 \times 10^{-1} u_3 - 7.95 \times 10^{-1} u_4 + 3.90 \times 10^{-1}$$

If Democracy Level is high **and** Alliance is weak **and** Contiguity is false **then**

$$y_2 = -1.25 \times 10^{-1} u_1 - 5.62 \times 10^{-1} u_3 - 2.35 \times 10^{-1} u_4 + 4.23 \times 10^{-1}$$

From observing the above rules, it is clear to see that the model is not quite as transparent as we would like it to be. This is because the consequent of each of the rules is still a mathematical expression. To validate the model, we still have to apply expert knowledge of the problem domain. For instance from the combination of the two statements, we can extrapolate that if the level of *Democracy* of two countries is *low,* they have an *strong* alliance and they *share a border,* there is a reasonable chance that the countries can find themselves in a conflict situation. This seems to indicate that the opportunities, provided by geographical proximity, must be in place for an interstate interaction to degenerate into conflict when democracy is lacking. Also it appears to indicate that when this dangerous combination is in place (lack of democracy and proximity), economic interdependence or share alliances cannot alone prevent a dispute between two countries to occur, regardless of the level of economic ties or alliances that may exist between them. This result appears to strongly support democratic peace theory and democracy as a key and necessary factor for peace. If we find values of *Democracy, Alliance,* and *Contiguity* which have a membership value of one, which means very low democracy, shared membership in alliances as well as geographical proximity, we can then use these as inputs to the model to see if it confirms our extracted knowledge. It is found that by using these values and an arbitrary *Dependency* value the model gives an output decision value $y = 0.6743$, which means it predicts a conflict will occur. By validating the model with similar statements, we can get insight for how much confidence we can put in the system. The model can further be used to test hypothetical scenarios in a similar way to which it is validated. The neuro-fuzzy model, therefore, offers a method of forecasting international conflict while also catering for the cases where causal interpretations are required.

6.4   Conclusion

The transparency of the neuro-fuzzy models has been investigated. The model has been applied to the modelling of interstate conflict, an application in which obtaining causal interpretation of interstate interactions is just as important as forecasting dispute outcomes. It is found that the model does offer some transparency, however it is limited due to the fact that the result of the fuzzy rules is expressed as a mathematical statement. In spite of this, the Takagi-Sugeno neuro-fuzzy model seems more suitable for hypothesis testing. A hypothesis stated linguistically can easily be verified using this model. The Takagi-Sugeno neuro-fuzzy model was compared to the support vector machine method and it was found that even though a support vector machine shows marginal advantage over the Takagi-Sugeno neuro-fuzzy model in terms of predictive capacity, the Takagi-Sugeno neuro-fuzzy model allows for linguistic interpretation.

6.5   Further Work

The Takagi-Sugeno neuro-fuzzy model was implemented for modeling interstate conflict and it was found that it gives results that are more transparent than the support vector machine. For future work, more advanced neuro-fuzzy systems such as the brain-inspired evolving neuro-fuzzy system should be implemented and the results be compared to the Takagi-Sugeno neuro-fuzzy system.

References

Abiyev, R.H., Kaynak, O., Alshanableh, T., Mamedov, F.: A type-2 neuro-fuzzy system based on clustering and gradient techniques applied to system identification and channel equalization. Appl. Soft Comput. **11**, 1396–1406 (2011)

Araujo, E.: Improved Takagi-Sugeno fuzzy approach. In: Proceedings of the IEEE International Conference on Fuzzy Systems, pp. 1154–1158, Hong Kong (2008)

Ata, R., Kocyigit, Y.: An adaptive neuro-fuzzy inference system approach for prediction of tip speed ratio in wind turbines. Expert Syst. Appl. **37**, 5454–5460 (2010)

Babuska, R.: Fuzzy modeling and identification. Ph.D. thesis, Technical University of Delft, Delft (1991)

Babuska, R., Verbruggen, H.: Neuro-fuzzy methods for nonlinear system identification. Annu. Rev. Control **27**, 73–85 (2003)

Barbieri, K.: Economic interdependence – a path to peace or a source of interstate conflict. J. Peace Res. **33**, 29–49 (1996)

Beck, N., Katz, J., Tucker, R.: Taking time seriously: time-series cross-section analysis with a binary dependent variable. Am. J. Polit. Sci. **42**, 1260–1288 (1998)

Beck, N., King, G., Zeng, L.: Improving quantitative studies of international conflict: a conjecture. Am. Polit. Sci. Rev. **94**, 21–35 (2000)

Biacino, L., Gerla, G.: Fuzzy logic, continuity and effectiveness. Arch. Math. Log. **41**, 643–667 (2002)

Bih, J.: Paradigm shift – an introduction to fuzzy logic. IEEE Potential. **25**(1), 6–21 (2006)

Bishop, C.: Neural Networks for Pattern Recognition. Oxford University Press, Oxford (1995)

Cabalar, A.F., Cevik, A., Gokceoglu, C., Baykal, G.: Neuro-fuzzy based constitutive modeling of undrained response of Leighton Buzzard Sand mixtures. Expert Syst. Appl. **37**, 842–851 (2010)

Cano-Izquierdo, J., Almonacid, M., Ibarrola, J.J.: Applying neuro-fuzzy model dFasArt in control systems. Eng. Appl. Artif. Intell. **23**, 1053–1063 (2010)

Cantor, G.: Über eine Eigenschaft des Inbegriffes aller reellen algebraischen Zahlen. Crelle. J. F. Math. **77**, 258–262 (1874)

Cetisli, B.: Development of an adaptive neuro-fuzzy classifier using linguistic hedges: part 1. Expert Syst. Appl. **37**, 6093–6101 (2010)

Cox, E.: The Fuzzy Systems Handbook: A Practitioner's Guide to Building, Using, Maintaining Fuzzy Systems. AP Professional, Boston (1994)

Demirli, K., Khoshnejad, M.: Autonomous parallel parking of a car-like mobile robot by a neuro-fuzzy sensor-based controller. Fuzzy Set. Syst. **160**, 2876–2891 (2009)

Devlin, K.: The Joy of Sets. Springer, Berlin (1993)

El-Sebakhy, E.A.: Flow regimes identification and liquid-holdup prediction in horizontal multiphase flow based on neuro-fuzzy inference systems. Math. Comp. Simulat. **80**, 1854–1866 (2010)

Ferreirós, J.: Labyrinth of Thought: A History of Set Theory and Its Role in Modern Mathematics. Birkhäuser, Basel (1999)

Habtemariam, E.A., Marwala, T.: Artificial intelligence for conflict management. In: Proceedings of the IEEE International Joint Conference on Neural Networks, pp. 2583–2588, Montreal (2005)

Hagiwara, H., Mita, A.: Structural health monitoring system using support vector machine. Adv. Build. Technol. **28**, 481–488 (2002)

Hájek, P.: Fuzzy logic and arithmetical hierarchy. Fuzzy Set. Syst. **3**, 359–363 (1995)

Hájek, P.: Metamathematics of Fuzzy Logic. Kluwer, Dordrecht (1998)

Halpern, J.Y.: Reasoning About Uncertainty. MIT Press, Cambridge (2003)

Haykin, S.: Neural Networks: A Comprehensive Foundation. Prentice Hall, Englewood Cliffs (1999)

Hsu, Y.-C., Lin, S.-F.: Reinforcement group cooperation-based symbiotic evolution for recurrent wavelet-based neuro-fuzzy systems. J. Neurocomput. **72**, 2418–2432 (2009)

Huang, T.M., Kecman, V.: Gene extraction for cancer diagnosis by support vector machines – an improvement. Artif. Intell. Med. **35**, 185–194 (2005)

Hurtado, J.E.: Relevance of support vector machines for stochastic mechanics. Comput. Fluid. Solid. Mech. **20**, 2298–2301 (2003)

Iplikci, S.: Support vector machines based neuro-fuzzy control of nonlinear systems. J. Neurocomput. **73**, 2097–2107 (2010)

Jang, J.-S.R.: ANFIS: Adaptive-network-based Fuzzy Inference System. IEEE Trans. Syst. Man Cybern. **23**, 665–685 (1993)

Jang, J.S.R., Sun, C.T., Mizutani, E.: Neuro-Fuzzy and Soft Computing: A Computational Approach to Learning and Machine Intelligence. Prentice Hall, Toronto (1997)

Johnson, P.: A History of Set Theory. Prindle, Weber & Schmidt, Boston (1972)

Jones, D., Bremer, S., Singer, J.: Militarized interstate disputes, 1816–1992 rationale, coding rules and empirical patterns. Conflict Manag. Peace Sci. **15**, 585–615 (1996)

Khajeh, A., Modarress, H.: Prediction of solubility of gases in polystyrene by adaptive neuro-fuzzy inference system and radial basis function neural network. Expert Syst. Appl **37**, 3070–3074 (2010)

Klir, G.J., Folger, T.A.: Fuzzy Sets, Uncertainty, and Information. Prentice Hall, Englewood Cliffs (1988)

Klir, G.J., Yuan, B.: Fuzzy Sets and Fuzzy Logic: Theory and Applications. Prentice Hall, Upper Saddle River (1995)

Klir, G.J., St Clair, U.H., Yuan, B.: Fuzzy Set Theory: Foundations and Applications. Prentice Hall, Upper Saddle River (1997)

Kosko, B.: Fuzzy Thinking: The New Science of Fuzzy Logic. Hyperion, New York (1993)

Kosko, B., Isaka, S.: Fuzzy logic. Sci. Am. **269**, 76–81 (1993)

Kucuk, K., Aksoy, C.O., Basarir, H., Onargan, T., Genis, M., Ozacar, V.: Prediction of the performance of impact hammer by adaptive neuro-fuzzy inference system modelling. Tunn. Undergr. Sp. Tech. **26**, 38–45 (2011)

Kurtulus, B., Razack, M.: Modeling daily discharge responses of a large karstic aquifer using soft computing methods: artificial neural network and neuro-fuzzy. J. Hydrol. **381**, 10–111 (2010)

Kwong, C.K., Wong, T.C., Chan, K.Y.: A methodology of generating customer satisfaction models for new product development using a neuro-fuzzy approach. Expert Syst. Appl **36**, 11262–11270 (2009)

Lagazio, M., Russett, B.: A Neural Network Analysis of MIDs, 1885–1992: Are the Patterns Stable? In the Scourge of War: New Extensions on an Old Problem, ch. Towards a Scientific Understanding of War: Studies in Honor of J. David Singer. University of Michigan Press, Ann Arbor (2004)

Leke, B., Marwala, T., Tettey, T.: Using inverse neural network for HIV adaptive control. Intl. J. Comput. Intell. Res. **3**, 11–15 (2007)

Lo, S.: Web service quality control based on text mining using support vector machine. Expert Syst. Appl. **34**, 603–610 (2008)

Mamdani, E.H.: Application of fuzzy algorithms for the control of a dynamic plant. Proc. IEEE. **121**, 1585–1588 (1974)

Mansfield, E.D., Snyder, J.: A tale of two democratic peace critiques: a reply to Thompson and Tucker. J. Confl. Res. **41**, 457–461 (1997)

Marwala, T.: Computational Intelligence for Modelling Complex Systems. Research India Publications, Delhi (2007)

Marwala, T.: Computational Intelligence for Missing Data Imputation, Estimation and Management, Knowledge Optimization Techniques. IGI Global Publications, New York (2009)

Marwala, T., Lagazio, M.: Modelling and controlling interstate conflict. In: Proceedings of the IEEE International Joint Conference on Neural Networks, pp. 1233–1238, Budapest (2004)

Marwala, T., Chakraverty, S., Mahola, U.: Fault classification using multi-layer perceptrons and support vector machines. Intl. J. Eng. Simul. **7**, 29–35 (2006)

Mashrei, M.A., Abdulrazzaq, N., Abdalla, T.Y., Rahman, M.S.: Neural networks model and adaptive neuro-fuzzy inference system for predicting the moment capacity of ferrocement members. Eng. Struct. **32**, 1723–1734 (2010)

Min, J.H., Lee, Y.-C.: Bankruptcy prediction using support vector machine with optimal choice of kernel function parameters. Expert Syst. Appl. **28**, 603–614 (2005)

Mitra, P., Shankar, B.U., Pal, S.K.: Segmentation of multispectral remote sensing images using active support vector machines. Pattern Recogn. Lett. **25**, 1067–1074 (2004)

Montazer, G.A., Saremi, H.Q., Khatibi, V.: A neuro-fuzzy inference engine for farsi numeral characters recognition. Expert Syst. Appl. **37**, 6327–6337 (2010)

Nelwamondo, F.V., Marwala, T., Mahola, U.: Early classifications of bearing faults using hidden Markov models, Gaussian mixture models, mel-frequency cepstral coefficients and fractals. Int. J. Innov. Comput., Info. Control **2**, 1281–1299 (2006)

Novák, V.: Fuzzy Sets and Their Applications. Adam Hilger, Bristol (1989)

Novák, V.: On fuzzy type theory. Fuzzy Set. Syst. **149**, 235–273 (2005)

Novák, V., Perfilieva, I., Močkoř, J.: Mathematical Principles of Fuzzy Logic. Kluwer, Dordrecht (1999)

Oneal, J., Russet, B.: The classical liberals were right: democracy, interdependence and conflict, 1950–1985. Int. Stud. Quart. **41**, 267–294 (1997)

Oneal, J., Russet, B.: Prediction and classification with neural network models. Sociol. Method. Res. **4**, 499–524 (1999)

Patel, P.B., Marwala, T.: Forecasting closing price indices using neural networks. In: Proceedings of the IEEE International Conference on Systems, Man and Cybernetics, pp. 2351–2356, Taipei, Taiwan (2006)

Patel, P.B., Marwala, T.: Caller behaviour classification using computational intelligence methods. Int. J. Neural Syst. **20**, 87–93 (2010)

Schölkopf, B., Smola, A.J.: Learning with Kernels. MIT Press, Cambridge (2002)

Sentes, M., Babuska, R., Kaymak, U., van Nauta, L.H.: Similarity measures in fuzzy rule base simplification. IEEE Trans. Syst. Man Cybern. B Cybern. **28**, 376–386 (1998)

Shiri, J., Kisi, O.: Short-term and long-term streamflow forecasting using a wavelet and neuro-fuzzy conjunction model. J. Hydrol. **394**, 486–493 (2010)

Sugeno, M.: Industrial Applications of Fuzzy Control. Elsevier, Amsterdam (1985)

Sugeno, M., Kang, G.: Structure identification of fuzzy model. Fuzzy Set. Syst. **28**, 15–33 (1988)

Takagi, T., Sugeno, M.: Fuzzy identification of systems and its applications to modeling and control. IEEE Trans. Syst. Man Cybern. **15**, 116–132 (1985)

Talei, A., Hock, L., Chua, C., Quek, C.: A novel application of a neuro-fuzzy computational technique in event-based rainfall-runoff modeling. Expert Syst. Appl. **37**, 7456–7468 (2010)

Tettey, T.: A computational intelligence approach to modelling interstate conflict: Conflict and causal interpretations. MSc thesis, University of the Witwatersrand, Johannesburg (2007)

Tettey, T., Marwala, T.: Controlling interstate conflict using neuro-fuzzy modeling and genetic algorithms. In: Proceedings of the 10th International Conference on Intelligent Engineering Systems, pp. 30–34, London (2006a)

Tettey, T., Marwala, T.: Neuro-fuzzy modeling and fuzzy rule extraction applied to conflict management. Lect. Note. Comp. Sci. **4234**, 1087–1094 (2006b)

Tettey, T., Marwala, T.: Conflict modelling and knowledge extraction using computational intelligence methods. In: Proceedings of the 11th IEEE International Conference on Intelligent Engineering Systems, pp. 161–166, Budapest (2007)

Thompson, W., Tucker, R.: A tale of two democratic peace critiques. J. Confl. Res **41**, 428–454 (1997)

Tripathi, S., Srinivas, V.V., Nanjundiah, R.S.: Downscaling of precipitation for climate change scenarios: a support vector machine approach. J. Hydrol. **330**, 621–640 (2006)

Von Altrock, C.: Fuzzy Logic and NeuroFuzzy Applications Explained. Prentice Hall, Englewood Cliffs (1995)

Wright, S., Marwala, T.: Artificial intelligence techniques for steam generator modelling. arXiv:0811.1711 (2006)

Zadeh, L.A.: Fuzzy sets. Info. Control **8**, 338–353 (1965)

Zemankova-Leech, M.: Fuzzy relational data bases. Ph.D. dissertation, Florida State University, Tallahassee (1983)

Zhou, Q., Chan, C.W., Tontiwachwuthikul, P.: An application of neuro-fuzzy technology for analysis of the CO_2 capture process. Fuzzy Set. Syst. **161**, 2597–2611 (2010)

Zimmermann, H.: Fuzzy Set Theory and Its Applications. Kluwer Academic Publishers, Boston (2001)

Chapter 7
Rough Sets for Modeling Interstate Conflict

7.1 Introduction

Rough set theory, introduced by Pawlak (1991), is a mathematical tool which deals with vagueness and uncertainty. It allows for the approximation of sets that are difficult to describe with available information. This chapter applies rough set theory to the modeling of militarized interstate disputes to assess whether this approach can improve both prediction of conflict and interpretation of the reasons why two states go to war. The advantages of rough sets, as with many other computational intelligence techniques, are that they do not require rigid *a priori* assumptions about the mathematical nature of such complex relationships, as commonly used multivariate statistical techniques do (Machowski and Marwala 2005; Crossingham et al. 2008). Rough set theory is based on the assumption that the information of interest is associated with some information of its universe of discourse (Crossingham and Marwala 2008b; Tettey et al. 2007; Marwala and Crossingham 2008, 2009; Crossingham and Marwala 2008a, 2007).

Xie et al. (2011) applied variable precision rough set for land use / land cover retrieval from remote sensing images. The results demonstrated a retrieval accuracy of 87.32%. Chen et al. (2011) applied a rough set approach for the prediction of protein interaction hot spots. Their results revealed that four features – namely – the change of accessible surface area, percentage of the change of accessible surface area, size of a residue, and atomic contacts were important in predicting the hot spots. Salamó and López-Sánchez (2011) successfully applied rough sets for feature selection in Case-Based Reasoning classifiers. Lin et al. (2011) applied a hybrid of rough set theory and flow network graphs to predict the customer churn in credit card accounts using 21,000 customer samples equally divided into three classes (survival, voluntary churn, and involuntary churn). The input data included demographic, psychographic, and transactional variables for studying and classifying customer characteristics. The results obtained indicated that rough sets can forecast customer churn and offer valuable information for decision-makers.

T. Marwala and M. Lagazio, *Militarized Conflict Modeling using Computational Intelligence*, Advanced Information and Knowledge Processing, DOI 10.1007/978-0-85729-790-7_7, © Springer-Verlag London Limited 2011

Other successful applications of rough set theory include the work by Azadeh et al. (2011) who used a rough set method for assessing the efficiency of personnel, Zou et al. (2011) who applied rough sets for distributor selection in a supply chain management system, Huang et al. (2011) who applied rough sets in patent development with emphasis on resource allocation, Wang et al. (2010) who applied rough sets and a Tabu search for credit scoring, Gong et al. (2010) for a rare-earth extraction process, Zhang et al. (2010) in controlling reagents in an ionic reverse flotation process, Yan et al. (2010) in predicting soil moisture, Chen et al. (2010) for creating a diagnostic system based on Chinese traditional medicine for the elderly pneumonia, and Liao et al. (2010) for a model to evaluate brand trust. The main concept of rough set theory is an indiscernibility relation, where indiscernibility means indistinguishable from one another. For knowledge acquisition from data with numerical attributes, special techniques are applied. Most frequently a step called *discretization* is taken before the main step of rule induction or decision tree generation is used (Crossingham and Marwala 2007). Several methods to perform the task of discretization are: Boolean reasoning, equal-width-bin (EWB) partitioning and equal-frequency-bin (EFB) partitioning (Jaafar et al. 2006; Fayyad and Irani 1993; Yao and Yao 2002).

This chapter applies EWB and EFB partitioning techniques to discretize the rough set partitions. The results are compared to those of the more commonly used methods, as well as those from the neuro-fuzzy model implemented in Chap. 6. In this chapter, rough set theory is first explained, then the EWB and EFB methods are implemented and compared, then the methods are applied to the militarized interstate dispute data set.

7.2 Rough Sets

The main goal of rough sets is to synthesize approximations of concepts from the acquired data. Unlike other methods used to handle uncertainty, rough set theory has its own unique advantages (Crossingham 2007) in that it does not require:

- any preliminary or additional information about the empirical training data such as the statistical probability; and
- basic probability assignment or the value of possibility in fuzzy set theory (Pawlak and Munakata 1996).

Rough set theory deals with the approximation of sets that are difficult to describe with the available information (Ohrn and Rowland 2000). It deals predominantly with the classification of imprecise, uncertain, or incomplete information. Two approximations, namely the upper and lower approximation, are formed to deal with inconsistent information. The data are represented using an information table.

Rough set theory is based on a set of rules, which are expressed in terms of linguistic variables. Rough sets are of fundamental importance to computational intelligence and cognitive science, and are highly applicable to the tasks of machine learning and decision analysis, especially in the analysis of decisions in which there are inconsistencies. As a consequence of the fact that they are rule-based, rough sets are very transparent but they are not as accurate. Certainly, they are not good as universal approximators, as other machine learning tools such as neural networks are in their predictions. It can thus be summarized that, in machine learning, there is always a trade-off between prediction accuracy and transparency.

Crossingham and Marwala (2007) presented an approach to optimize the rough set partition sizes using various optimization techniques. Three optimization techniques were implemented to perform the granularization process – namely – the genetic algorithm, hill climbing, and simulated annealing. These optimization methods maximize the classification accuracy of the rough sets. The proposed rough set partition methods were tested on a demographic set. The three techniques were compared for their computational time, accuracy, and number of rules produced when applied to the HIV data set. The optimized method results were then compared to a non-optimized discretization method, using Equal-Width-Bin (EWB) partitioning. The accuracies achieved after optimizing the partitions using a genetic algorithm (GA), hill climbing, and simulated annealing (SA) were 66.89%, 65.84%, and 65.48% – respectively – compared to the accuracy of the EWB partitioning of 59.86%. In addition to rough sets providing the plausibility of the estimated HIV status, they also provided the linguistic rules describing how the demographic parameters drive the risk of HIV.

Rough set theory provides a technique of reasoning from vague and imprecise data (Goh and Law 2003). The technique is based on the assumption that some observed information is somehow associated with some information in the universe of the discourse (Komorowski et al. 1999; Yang and John 2006; Kondo 2006). This implies that if some aspects of the data are missing, then they can be estimated from the part of the information in the universe of discourse which is similar to the observed part of that particular data. Objects with the same information are indiscernible in the view of the available information. An elementary set consisting of indiscernible objects forms a basic granule of knowledge. A union of an elementary set is referred to as a *crisp set*; otherwise, the set is considered to be *rough*. The next sub-sections briefly introduce concepts that are common to rough set theory.

7.2.1 Information System

An information system (Λ), is defined as a pair (U, A) where U is a finite set of objects called the universe and A is a non-empty finite set of attributes as shown in Eq. 7.1 below (Crossingham 2007; Yang and John 2006; Nelwamondo 2008; Marwala 2009).

$$\Lambda = (U, A) \tag{7.1}$$

Every attribute $a \in A$ has a value, which must be a member of a value set V_a of the attribute a (Dubois 1990; Crossingham 2007):

$$a : U \rightarrow V_a \qquad (7.2)$$

A rough set is defined with a set of attributes and the indiscernibility relation between them. Indiscernibility is discussed in the next sub-section.

7.2.2 The Indiscernibility Relation

The indiscernibility relation is one of the fundamental ideas of rough set theory (Grzymala-Busse and Siddhaye 2004; Zhao et al. 2007; Pawlak and Skowron 2007). *Indiscernibility* simply implies similarity (Goh and Law 2003) and, therefore, these sets of objects are indistinguishable. Given an information system Λ and subset $B \subseteq A$, B the indiscernibility determines a binary relation $I(B)$ on U such that (Pawlak et al. 1988; Ohrn 1999; Wu et al. 2003; Ohrn and Rowland 2000):

$$(x, y) \in I(B)$$

if and only if

$$a(x) = a(y) \qquad (7.3)$$

for all $a \in A$ where $a(x)$ denotes the value of attribute a for element x. Equation 7.3 implies that any two elements that belong to $I(B)$ should be identical from the point of view of a. Suppose U has a finite set of N objects $\{x_1, x_2,..,x_N\}$. Let Q be a finite set of n attributes $\{q_1, q_2,...,q_n\}$ in the same information system Λ then (Inuiguchi and Miyajima; 2007; Crossingham 2007):

$$\Lambda = \langle U, Q, V, f \rangle \qquad (7.4)$$

where f is the total decision function, called the *information function*. From the definition of the indiscernibility relation given in this section, any two objects have a similarity relation to attribute a if they have the same attribute values everywhere.

7.2.3 Information Table and Data Representation

An information table is used in rough sets theory as a way of representing the data. Data in the information table are arranged based on their condition attributes and decision attribute (D). *Condition attributes* and *decision attributes* are analogous to the independent variables and dependent variable (Goh and Law 2003). These attributes are divided into $C \cup D = Q$ and $C \cup D = 0$.

Table 7.1 An example of an information table with missing values

	B_1	B_2	B_3	D
1	1	1	0.2	P
2	1	2	0.3	A
3	0	1	0.3	P
4	?	?	0.3	P
5	0	3	0.4	A
6	0	2	0.2	P
7	1	4	?	A

An information table can be classified into *complete* and *incomplete classes*. All objects in a complete class have known attribute values *B*, whereas an information table is considered incomplete if at least one attribute variable has a missing value. An example of an incomplete information table is given in Table 7.1. Data is represented in the table where each row represents an instance, sometimes referred to as an object. Every column represents an attribute which is a measured variable. This kind of table is also referred to as an *Information System* (Komorowski et al. 1999; Leung et al. 2006).

7.2.4 Decision Rules Induction

Rough sets also involve generating decision rules for a given information table. The rules are normally based on condition attributes values (Bi et al. 2003; Slezak and Ziarko 2005; Ziarko 1998). The rules are presented in an '*if CONDITION(S)-then DECISION*' format. Stefanowski (1998) successfully used a rough set approach for inference in decision rules.

Wang et al. (2006) used rough set theory to deal with vagueness and uncertainty and, thereby reduced the redundancy in assessing the degree of malignancy in brain glioma, based on Magnetic Resonance Imaging (MRI) findings as well as the clinical data before an operation. These data included inappropriate features at the same time as uncertainties and missing values. The rough set rules that were extracted from these data were used to forecast the degree of malignancy. Rough set based feature selection algorithms were used to choose features so that classification accuracy based on decision rules could be improved. These chosen feature subsets were used to produce decision rules for the classification task. The results obtained demonstrated that the presented method identified reducts that generated decision rules with higher classification rates than conventional approaches.

7.2.5 The Lower and Upper Approximation of Sets

The lower and upper approximations of sets are defined on the basis of the indiscernibility relation as it was discussed above. The *lower approximation* is defined as the collection of cases whose equivalent classes are contained in the cases that need to be approximated whereas the *upper approximation* is defined as the collection of classes that are partially contained in the set that need to be approximated (Rowland et al. 1998; Degang et al. 2006; Witlox and Tindemans 2004). Let concept X be defined as a set of all cases defined by a specific value of the decision. Any finite union of elementary set, associated with B is called a *B-definable set* (Grzymala-Busse and Siddhaye 2004). The set X is approximated by two B-definable sets, referred to as the B-lower approximation denoted by $\underline{B}X$. and B-upper approximation $\overline{B}X$. The B-lower approximation is defined as (Bazan et al. 2004; Crossingham 2007):

$$\underline{B}X = \{x \in U \,|[x]_B \subseteq X\} \tag{7.5}$$

and the B-upper approximation is defined as (Crossingham 2007):

$$\overline{B}X = \{x \in U \,|[x]_B \cap X \neq 0\} \tag{7.6}$$

There are other methods that have been reported for defining the lower and upper approximations for a completely specified decision table. Some of the common ones include approximating the lower and upper approximation of X using Eqs. 7.7 and 7.8, as follows (Grzymala-Busse 2004; Crossingham 2007):

$$\cup\{[x]_B \,|x \in U, [x]_B \subseteq X\} \tag{7.7}$$

$$\cup\{[x]_B \,|x \in U, [x]_B \cap X \neq 0\} \tag{7.8}$$

The definition of definability is modified in cases of incompletely specified tables. In this case, any finite union of characteristic sets of B is called a *B-definable set*. Three different definitions of approximations have been discussed by Grzymala-Busse and Siddhaye (2004). Again letting B be a subset of A of all attributes and $R(B)$ be the characteristic relation of the incomplete decision table with characteristic sets $K(x)$, where $x \in U$, the following are defined (Grzymala-Busse 2004; Crossingham 2007):

$$\underline{B}X = \{x \in U \,|K_B(x) \subseteq X\} \tag{7.9}$$

and

$$\overline{B}X = \{x \in U \,|K_B(x) \cap X \neq 0\} \tag{7.10}$$

Equations 7.9 and 7.10 are referred to as *singletons*. The subset lower and upper approximations of incompletely specified data sets are then defined as:

$$\cup\{K_B(x) \,|x \in U, K_B(x) \subseteq X\} \tag{7.11}$$

and

$$\cup \{K_B(x) \,|\, x \in U, K_B(x) \cap X = 0\} \tag{7.12}$$

More information on these methods can be found in (Grzymala-Busse and Hu 2001; Grzymala-Busse and Siddhaye 2004; Crossingham 2007). It follows from these properties that a crisp set is only defined if $\underline{B}(X) = \overline{B}(X)$. *Roughness* is therefore defined as the difference between the upper and the lower approximation.

7.2.6 Set Approximation

Various properties of rough sets have been presented in the work of Pawlak (1991). One property of rough set theory is the definability of a rough set (Quafafou 2000). This was discussed briefly above for the case when the lower and upper approximations are equal. Otherwise if this is not the case, then the target set is un-definable. Some of the special cases of definability are (Pawlak et al. 1988; Crossingham 2007; Nelwamondo 2008; Marwala 2009):

- *Internally definable* set: Here, $\underline{B}X \neq 0$ and $\overline{B}X = U$. The attribute set B has objects that certainly are elements of the target set X, even though there are no objects that can definitively be excluded from the set X.
- *Externally definable* set: Here, $\underline{B}X = 0$ and $\overline{B}X \neq U$. The attribute set B has no objects that certainly are elements of the target set X, even though there are objects that can definitively be excluded from the set X.
- *Totally un-definable* set: Here, $\underline{B}X = 0$ and $\overline{B}X = U$. The attribute set B has no objects that certainly are elements of the target set X, even though there are no objects that can definitively be excluded from the set X.

7.2.7 The Reduct

Another property of rough sets is the reduct. An interesting analysis is whether there are attributes B in the information system that are more important to the knowledge represented in the equivalence class structure than other attributes. It is essential to find out if there is a subset of attributes which, by itself, could completely describe the knowledge in the database. This attribute set is known as the *reduct*.

Beynon (2001) observed that the elementary feature of the variable precision rough set model entailed an exploration for subsets of condition attributes which give identical information for classification functions as the complete set of given attributes. Beynon labeled these subsets *approximate reducts* and described these for an identified classification error represented by β and then identified specific anomalies and fascinating implications for identifying β-reducts were suggested which guaranteed a general knowledge similar to that obtained from the full set of attributes.

Terlecki and Walczak (2007) described the relations between rough set reducts and emerging patterns. From this study, a practical application for these observations to the minimal reduct problem using these to test the differentiating factor of an attribute set was established. Shan and Ziarko (1995) formally defined a *reduct* as a subset of attributes $RED \subseteq B$ such that:

- $[x]_{RED} = [x]_B$. That is, the equivalence classes that were induced by reducing the attribute set RED are identical to the similar class structure that was induced by the full attribute set B.
- Attribute set RED is minimal because $[x]_{(RED-A)} \neq [x]_B$ for any attribute $A \in RED$. In simple form, there is no attribute that can be taken away from the set RED without altering the equivalence classes $[x]_B$.

Thus a reduct can be visualized as an adequate set of features that can sufficiently well express the category's structure. One characteristic of a reduct in an information system is that it is not unique because there may be other subsets of attributes which may still preserve the equivalence class structure conveyed in the information system. The set of characteristics that are common in all reducts is called a *core*.

7.2.8   Boundary Region

The boundary region, which can be written as the difference $\overline{B}X - \underline{BX}$, is a region which is composed of objects that cannot be included nor excluded as members of the target set X. In simple terms, the lower approximation of a target set is an approximation which consists only of those objects which can be positively identified as members of the set. The upper approximation is a loose approximation and includes objects that may be members of the target set. The boundary region is the region in between the upper approximation and the lower approximation.

7.2.9   Rough Membership Functions

Rough membership function is a function $\mu_A^x : U \rightarrow [0, 1]$ that, when applied to object x, quantifies the degree of overlap between set X and the indiscernibility set to which x belongs. The rough membership function is used to calculate the plausibility and can be defined as (Pawlak 1991; Crossingham 2007):

$$\mu_A^x(X) = \frac{|[x]_B \cap X|}{|[x]_B|} \tag{7.13}$$

The rough membership function can be viewed as a fuzzification with rough approximation. It ensures the translation from rough approximation into membership function. The outstanding feature of a rough membership function is that it is derived from data (Hoa and Son 2008; Crossingham 2007).

7.3 Discretization Methods

The methods which allow continuous data to be processed involve discretization. There are several methods available to perform discretization, but the two popularly ones – equal-width-bin (EWB) partitioning and equal-frequency-bin (EFB) partitioning – were investigated by Crossingham (2007). Details are given below.

7.3.1 Equal-Width-Bin (EWB) Partitioning

EWB partitioning divides the range of observed values of an attribute into k equal sized bins (Crossingham et al. 2009). In this chapter, k is taken as four. One notable problem of this method is that it is vulnerable to outliers that may drastically skew the data range. This problem was eliminated through the pre-processing step of cleaning the data. The manner in which data can be discretized using EWB follows (Crossingham et al. 2009):

- Evaluate the Smallest and Largest value for each attribute and label these values S and L.
- Write the width of each interval, W, as:

$$W = \frac{L - S}{4} \qquad (7.14)$$

- The interval boundaries can be determined as: $S + W, S + 2W, S + 3W$. These boundaries can be determined for any number of intervals k, up to the term $S + (k - 1)W$.

7.3.2 Equal-Frequency-Bin (EFB) Partitioning

EFB partitioning sorts the values of each attribute in ascending order and divides them into k bins where (given m instances) each bin contains m/k adjacent values. In most instances there probably exist duplicated values. The EFB partitioning can be implemented as follows (Crossingham 2007):

- Arrange the values of each attribute $(v_1^a, v_2^a, v_3^a, ..., v_m^a)$ into intervals whereby m is the number of instances.

- Each interval therefore is made of the following sequential values:

$$\lambda = \frac{m}{4} \tag{7.15}$$

- The cut-off points may be computed using the following equation which is valid for $i = 1, 2, 3$ where k intervals can be calculated for $i = 1, \ldots, k - 1$:

$$c_i = \frac{v_{i\lambda} + v_{i\lambda+1}}{2} \tag{7.16}$$

7.4 Rough Set Formulation

The process of modeling the rough set can be classified into these five stages (Crossingham 2007):

1. The first stage is to select the data.
2. The second stage involves pre-processing the data to ensure that it is ready for analysis. This stage involves discretizing the data and removing unnecessary data (cleaning the data).
3. If reducts are considered, the third stage is to use the cleaned data to generate reducts. A *reduct* is the most concise way in which we can discern object classes. In other words, a reduct is the minimal subset of attributes that enables the same classification of elements of the universe as the whole set of attributes. To cope with inconsistencies, lower and upper approximations of decision classes are defined in this stage.
4. Stage four is where the rules are extracted or generated. The rules are usually determined based on condition attribute values. Once the rules are extracted, they can be presented in an '*if* CONDITION(S)-*then* DECISION' format.
5. The fifth and final stage involves testing the newly created rules on a test set. The accuracy must be noted and sent back into the optimization method used in step 2 and the process will continue until the optimum or highest accuracy is achieved.

The procedure for computing rough sets and extracting rules is given in Algorithm 1 (Crossingham 2007). Once the rules are extracted, they can be tested using a set of testing data. The classification output is expressed as a decision value which lies between 0 and 1. The accuracy of the rough set is determined using the Area Under the receiver operating characteristic Curve (AUC).

7.5 Neuro-Fuzzy System

As explained in Chap. 6, a fuzzy inference system is a model that takes a fuzzy set as an input and performs a composition to arrive at the output, based on the concepts of fuzzy set theory, fuzzy '*if-then*' rules and fuzzy reasoning (Jang et al. 1997). A fuzzy

Algorithm 1: Procedure to generate a rough set model (Crossingham 2007)
Input: Condition and Decision Attributes
Output: Certain and Possible Rules
1   Obtain the data set to be used;
2   **Repeat**
3   **for** *conditional_attribute* ← 1 to *size_of_training_data* **do**
4   Pre-process data to ensure that it is ready for analysis;
5   Discretize the data according to the optimization technique;
6   Compute the lower approximation, as defined in Eq. 7.5;
7   Compute the upper approximation, as defined in Eq. 7.6;
8   From the general rules, calculate plausibility measures for an object x belonging to set X, as defined by Eq. 7.13;
9   From the general rules, calculate plausibilityExtract the *certain* rules from the lower approximation generated for each subset;
10   Similarly, extract the *possible* rules from the upper approximation of each subset;
11   Remove the generated rules for the purposes of testing on unseen data;
12   Compute the classifier performance using the AUC;
13   **End**
14   **until** Optimization technique termination condition;

inference procedure involves the fuzzification of the input variables, an evaluation of rules, an aggregation of the rule outputs and, finally, the defuzzification of the result. There are two common types of fuzzy models: the Mamdani model and the Takagi-Sugeno model. The Takagi-Sugeno model is popular when it comes to data-driven identification and is used in this chapter. In this model, the antecedent part of the rule is a fuzzy proposition and the consequent is an affine linear function of the input variables as shown in (Babuska and Verbruggen 2003):

$$R_i : \text{ If } x \text{ is } A_i(x) \text{ then } y_i = a_i^T x + b_i, [w_i] \qquad (7.17)$$

where a_i is the consequence parameter vector, b_i is a scalar offset and $i = 1, 2 ..., K$. The symbol K represents the number of fuzzy rules in the model and $w_i \in [0, 1]$ is the weight of the rule. The antecedent propositions in the model describe the fuzzy regions in the input space in which the consequent functions are valid and can be stated in the following conjunctive form (Araujo 2008; Wright and Marwala 2006):

$$R_i : \text{ If } x_1 \text{ is } A_{i,1}(x_1) \text{ and} ... \text{ and } x_n \text{ is } A_{i,n}(x_n) \text{ then } \hat{y} = a_i^T x + b_i, [w_i] \qquad (7.18)$$

The degree of fulfillment of the ith rule is calculated as the product of the individual membership degrees and the rule's weight (Araujo 2008; Wright and Marwala 2006):

$$\beta_i(x) = w_i A_i(x) = w_i \prod_{j=1}^{n} A_{i,j}(x_j) \qquad (7.19)$$

The output y is then computed by taking a weighted average of the individual rules' contributions as shown below (Wright and Marwala 2006; Araujo 2008; Babuska and Verbruggen 2003):

$$\hat{y} = \frac{\sum\limits_{i=1}^{K} \beta_i(x) y_i}{\sum\limits_{i=1}^{K} \beta_i(x)} = \frac{\sum\limits_{i=1}^{K} \beta_i(x)(a_i^T x + b_i)}{\sum\limits_{i=1}^{K} \beta_i(x)} \qquad (7.20)$$

where $\beta_i(x)$ is the degree of fulfillment of the ith rule. The parameters a_i are then approximate models of the considered nonlinear system. A fuzzy rule-based system with learning ability, also known as a neuro-fuzzy network, is referred to here as a *neuro-fuzzy system* and it was implemented as documented in Chap. 6.

7.6   Rough Sets Versus Fuzzy Sets

Fuzzy sets are sets that have elements with degrees of membership. In other words, in fuzzy logic an element of a set has a degree of belonging or membership to that particular set. Zadeh (1965) introduced fuzzy sets as an expansion of the classical concept of sets. In classical set theory, the membership of elements in a set is evaluated in binary terms, that is, it is either a member of that set or it is not a member of that particular set. Fuzzy set theory allows the steady evaluation of the membership of elements in a set. This is illustrated with the help of a membership function scaled to fall within the interval [0, 1]. Thus a fuzzy set is a generalized version of a classical set and conversely a classical set is a special case of the membership function of a fuzzy set which only permits the values 0 or 1. Thus far, fuzzy set theory has not generated any results that differ from the results from a probability or classical set theory.

Zhang and Shao (2006) developed a self-learning method to identify a fuzzy model and extrapolate missing rules. This was done using the modified gradient descent method and a confidence measure. Their method can simultaneously identify a fuzzy model, revise its parameters and establish optimal output fuzzy sets. Their results showed the usefulness and accuracy of the advanced method when tested on a classical truck control problem.

Coulibaly and Evora (2007) investigated a multilayer perceptron network, a time-lagged feed-forward network, a generalized radial basis function network, a recurrent neural network, a time delay recurrent neural network, and a counter-propagation fuzzy-neural network along with different optimization methods for estimating the daily missing total precipitation records and daily extreme temperature series. The results revealed that the multi-layer perceptron, the time-lagged feed-forward network, and the counter-propagation fuzzy-neural network offered the highest accuracy in estimating missing precipitation values. The multi-layer

Table 7.2 Comparison of methods

Attributes	Rough sets	Fuzzy sets
General philosophy	Designed to deal with vagueness of data. Lower and upper approximation. Discretization of the input variables	Fuzzy sets have fuzzification of the input variables
Optimization	Optimization through the discretization	Optimization through the selection of membership functions
Generalization	Reducts are used to generalize	'If-then' rules are used to generalize

perceptron was found to be successful at imputing missing daily precipitation values. In addition, the multi-layer perceptron showed itself to be the most suitable for imputing missing daily maximum and minimum temperature values. The counter-propagation fuzzy-neural network was similar to the multi-layer perceptron at imputing missing daily maximum temperatures; nevertheless, it was less useful for estimating the minimum temperatures. The recurrent neural network and time delay recurrent neural network were found to be the least appropriate for imputing both the daily precipitation and the extreme temperature records, while the radial basis function was good at approximating the maximum and minimum temperatures.

A *rough set* is defined as a proper estimation of a classical crisp set through a pair of sets which offer the lower and the upper approximation of the original set. The lower approximation of sets are similar to sets that have already been observed in the information system, while higher approximation sets are sets that can only be inferred – whether strongly or weakly – from the information system. These lower and upper approximation sets are crisp sets in the classical description of rough set theory (Pawlak 1991), but in other variants, the approximating sets may also be fuzzy sets. The distinguishing features of fuzzy sets and rough sets, as Table 7.2 shows, is that – while fuzzy sets operate via membership functions – rough sets operate through upper and lower approximation sets (Chanas and Kuchta 1992).

The similarity between the two approaches is that they are both designed to deal with the vagueness and uncertainty in the data. For example, Jensen and Shen (2004) introduced dimensionality reduction that retained semantics using both rough and fuzzy-rough based approaches. Some researchers such as Deng et al. (2007) introduced a method that combines both rough and fuzzy sets. The reasoning for this hybridization process is that, although these techniques are similar, each offers unique advantages. Such a hybrid fuzzy rough set scheme was applied to model problems such as breast cancer detection. Furthermore, Liu et al. (2011) studied the distribution of center location using a hybrid of rough set method and fuzzy logic. Bilski (2010) applied an unsupervised learning method to compare the quality of the soft computing algorithms in analog systems diagnostics.

7.7   Interstate Conflict

Recent developments in the conflict literature have emphasized the importance of treating international conflicts as complex phenomena often displaying nonlinear and non-monotonic patterns of interactions (Crossingham 2007). Various methods have been implemented and there are still efforts underway to further study interstate interactions and militarized interstate disputes. *Militarized interstate disputes* are defined as a set of interactions between or among states involving threats to use military force, displays of military force, or actual uses of military force (Crossingham et al. 2009). As outlined in earlier chapters, militarized interstate disputes are conflicts between states that do not just lead to full-scale war since they also include state interactions that are conflicting but not violent. The traditional level of analysis chosen for militarized disputes is at dyadic level (a pair of states), therefore the variables associated with the analysis of conflicts are referred to as *dyadic variables*. Research has shown (Crossingham et al. 2009) that no legitimate statistical model has managed to forecast an international conflict with a probability of greater than 0.5. Statistical models have also produced results that are conflicting. Although political scientists have long eschewed the forecasting of conflicts in favor of causal interpretations, forecasting remains an important factor in early warning, since practitioners need accurate predictions of conflicts in order to plan interventions. Furthermore, forecasts can be used to verify claims about the causal structure or, at least in part (Crossingham et al. 2009). Indeed, accurate forecasting will aid in the interpretation and explanation of the conflict. The practical concern towards early warning has produced a shift from statistical methods to computational intelligence techniques, leading to several computational intelligence methods been applied to conflict management.

Neural networks have been used to model the complex interrelationships between the dyadic parameters and the militarized interstate disputes as described in Chaps. 2–4. Other methods that have been implemented include support vector machines in Chap. 5, and neuro-fuzzy techniques in Chap. 6.

Although political scientists are less likely to evaluate conflict models per se than, say economists, forecasting underlines all evaluations of such a model, and it is this information that will be of significant use (Crossingham et al. 2009). The militarized interstate dispute data was modeled as explained in Chap. 2, and the results are shown in Table 7.3.

The training process resulted in 125 rules for the equal-width-bin (EWB) rough set model and 90 rules for the equal-frequency-bin (EFB) rough set model. The

Table 7.3 Classification results

Method	True Conflicts (TC)	False Peaces (FP)	True Peaces (TP)	False Conflicts (FC)
Rough sets: equal-width-bin	272	120	291	99
Rough sets: equal-freq-bin	292	100	268	124
Takagi-Sugeno neuro-fuzzy	303	89	288	104

results show that the detection rate of conflict was 74% when the EFB rough set model was used, 69% when the EWB rough set model was used, and 77% when using the Takagi-Sugeno neuro-fuzzy model. The detection rate for peace was 68% when the EFB rough set model was used, 75% when the EWB rough set model was used, and 73% when the Takagi-Sugeno neuro-fuzzy model was used.

Overall, the detection rate for a correct outcome was 71% when the EFB rough set model was used, 72% when the EWB rough set model was used, and 75% when using the Takagi-Sugeno neuro-fuzzy model. Furthermore, the Area Under the receiver operating characteristics Curves (AUC), was 0.86 for the Takagi-Sugeno neuro-fuzzy method, 0.77 for the EWB rough set model, and 0.76 for the EFB rough set model. The rough set rules obtained when the EWB was used are listed below:

If *Allies* = 1 (True) and *Contiguity* = 0 (False) and *Major Powers* = 1 (True) and *Distance* = 8 (High) and *Capability* = 9 (High) and *Democracy* = 10 (High) and *Dependency* = 0.17 (High) Then *Outcome* = Most Probably Peace.

This statement, although stating the obvious context for peace, is consistent with both the realist and liberal theory. Indeed, the rule obtained refers to the perfect conditions when both realist and liberal variables are providing strong state constrains for war, therefore strongly inciting peaceful relationships.

If u_1 is A_{21} and u_2 is A_{22} and u_3 is A_{23} and u_4 is A_{24} and u_5 is A_{25} and u_6 is A_{26} and u_7 is A_{27} then $y = -0.28 u_1 + 6.3 \times 10^{-2} u_2 + 0.25 u_3 - 0.76 u_4 - 0.89 u_5 - 9.0 u_6 + 0 u_7 + 0.4$

The symbols from u_1 to u_7 are the input vector which consists of *Democracy*, *Dependency*, *Capability*, *Alliance*, *Contiguity*, *Distance*, and *Major Power* while A is a fuzzy rule as explained in Chap. 5.

The neuro-fuzzy rules seem to be more complicated to interpret than the rough set rules. Using the results produced by each optimization method, the optimal known discretization points can be determined. Using these partition cuts, rough sets can be run on the particular data set and forecast with a certain plausibility, based on the rough membership function. From these rough sets, rules can also be extracted. These rules are linguistic and easy to interpret, however they state the obvious conditions for peace. Indeed, the findings as illustrated in the generated rule shown above are what one would expect. Although an analysis of attribute sensitivity does not make sense when applied to rough set theory, the rules produced provide a clear explanation of the main conditions that produce peace. Another important observation is that because of the use of rough sets, the rules can be generated without any *a priori* information.

7.8 Conclusion

The work performed in this chapter was concerned with using the static equal-width-bin and equal-frequency-bin partitioning techniques to granulize the rough set input partitions to achieve the highest forecasting accuracy produced by the rough set and apply this to interstate conflict. The rough sets produce a balance between the transparency of the model and the accuracy of conflict prediction. The results demonstrated that equal-width-bin partitioning gives better accuracy than equal-frequency-bin partitioning. However, both of these techniques were found to give less accurate results than neuro-fuzzy sets as well as provide insights that state obvious conditions for peace. However they have been found to be more transparent and easy to interpret than the neuro-fuzzy sets.

7.9 Further Work

The rough set model was implemented for modeling interstate conflict and it was found that it gives results that are more transparent than neuro-fuzzy model. For future work, methods must be developed and implemented that are intrinsically optimized for accuracy using static partitioning.

References

Araujo, E.: Improved Takagi-Sugeno fuzzy approach. In: IEEE International Conference on Fuzzy Systems, pp. 1154–1158, Hong Kong (2008)

Azadeh, A., Saberi, M., Moghaddam, R.T., Javanmardi, L.: An integrated data envelopment analysis – artificial neural network-rough set algorithm for assessment of personnel efficiency. Expert Syst. Appl. **38**, 1364–1373 (2011)

Babuska, R., Verbruggen, H.: Neuro-fuzzy methods for nonlinear system identification. Annu. Rev. Control. **27**, 73–85 (2003)

Bazan, J., Nguyen, H.S., Szczuka, M.: A view on rough set concept approximations. Fund. Inform. **59**, 107–118 (2004)

Beynon, M.: Reducts within the variable precision rough sets model: a further investigation. Eur. J. Oper. Res. **134**, 592–605 (2001)

Bi, Y., Anderson, T., McClean, S.: A rough set model with ontologies for discovering maximal association rules in document collections. Knowl. Based Syst. **16**, 243–251 (2003)

Bilski, P.: An unsupervised learning method for comparing the quality of the soft computing algorithms in analog systems diagnostics. Przeglad Elektrotechniczny **86**, 242–247 (2010)

Chanas, S., Kuchta, D.: Further remarks on the relation between rough and fuzzy sets. Fuzzy Set. Syst. **47**, 391–394 (1992)

Chen, C., Shen, J., Chen, B., Shang, C.-X., Wang. Y.-C.: Building symptoms diagnosis criteria of traditional Chinese medical science treatment on the elderly's pneumonia by the rough set theory. In: Proceedings of the 29th Chinese Control Conference, pp. 5268–5271, Beijing (2010)

Chen, R., Zhang, Z., Wu, D., Zhang, P., Zhang, X., Wang, Y., Shi, Y.: Prediction of protein interaction hot spots using rough set-based multiple criteria linear programming. J. Theor. Biol. **269**, 174–180 (2011)

Coulibaly, P., Evora, N.D.: Comparison of neural network methods for infilling missing daily weather records. J. Hydrol. **341**, 27–41 (2007)

Crossingham, B.: Rough set partitioning using computational intelligence approach. MSc thesis, University of the Witwatersrand, Johannesburg (2007)

Crossingham, B., Marwala, T.: Using optimisation techniques to granulise rough set partitions. Comput. Model. Life Sci. **952**, 248–257 (2007)

Crossingham, B., Marwala, T.: Using genetic algorithms to optimise rough set partition sizes for HIV data analysis. Stud. Comput. Intell. **78**, 245–250 (2008a)

Crossingham, B., Marwala, T.: Using optimisation techniques for discretizing rough set partitions. Int. J. Hybrid Intell. Syst. **5**, 219–236 (2008b)

Crossingham, B., Marwala, T., Lagazio, M.: Optimised rough sets for modeling interstate conflict. In: Proceedings of the IEEE International Conference on Systems, Man, and Cybernetics, pp. 1198–1204, Singapore (2008)

Crossingham, B., Marwala, T., Lagazio, M.: Evolutionarily optimized rough set partitions. ICIC Exp. Lett. **3**, 241–246 (2009)

Degang, C., Wenxiu, Z., Yeung, D., Tsang, E.C.C.: Rough approximations on a complete completely distributive lattice with applications to generalized rough sets. Inf. Sci. **176**, 1829–1848 (2006)

Deng, T., Chen, Y., Xu, W., Dai, Q.: A novel approach to fuzzy rough sets based on a fuzzy covering. Inf. Sci. **177**, 2308–2326 (2007)

Dubois, D.: Rough fuzzy sets and fuzzy rough sets. Int. J. Gen. Syst. **17**, 191–209 (1990)

Fayyad, U., Irani, K.: Multi-interval discretization of continuous valued attributes for classification learning. In: Proceedings of the 13th International Joint Conference on Artificial Intelligence, pp. 1022–1027, Los Alamos (1993)

Goh, C., Law, R.: Incorporating the rough sets theory into travel demand analysis. Tourism Manag. **24**, 511–517 (2003)

Gong, J., Yang, H., Zhong, L.: Case-based reasoning based on rough set in rare-earth extraction process. In: Proceedings of the 29th Chinese Control Conference, pp. 70–1706, Beijing (2010)

Grzymala-Busse, J.W., Hu, M.: A comparison of several approaches to missing attribute values in data mining. Lect. Notes Artif. Intell. **205**, 378–385 (2001)

Grzymala-Busse, J.W.: Three approaches to missing attribute values – a rough set perspective. In: Proceedings of the IEEE 4th International Conference on Data Mining, pp. 57–64, Brighton (2004)

Grzymala-Busse, J.W., Siddhaye, S.: Rough set approaches to rule induction from incomplete data. In: Proceedings of the 10th International Conference on Information Processing and Management of Uncertainty in Knowledge-Based Systems, vol. 2, pp. 923–930, Perugia (2004)

Hoa, N.S., Son, N.H.: Rough set approach to approximation of concepts from taxonomy. http://logic.mimuw.edu.pl/publikacje/SonHoaKDO04.pdf (2008)

Huang, C.-C., Liang, W.-Y., Shian-Hua, L., Tseng, T.-L., Chiang, H.-Y.: A rough set based approach to patent development with the consideration of resource allocation. Expert Syst. Appl. **38**, 1980–1992 (2011)

Inuiguchi, M., Miyajima, T.: Rough set based rule induction from two decision tables. Eur. J. Oper. Res. **181**, 1540–1553 (2007)

Jaafar, A.F.B., Jais, J., Hamid, M.H.B.H.A., Rahman, Z.B.A., Benaouda, D.: Using rough set as a tool for knowledge discovery in DSS. In: Proceedings of the 4th International Conference on Multimedia and Information and Communication Technologies in Education, pp. 1011–1015, Seville, Spain (2006)

Jang, J.S.R., Sun, C.T., Mizutani, E.: Neuro-Fuzzy and Soft Computing: A Computational Approach to Learning and Machine Intelligence. Prentice Hall, Toronto (1997)

Jensen, R., Shen, Q.: Semantics-preserving dimensionality reduction: rough and fuzzy-rough based approaches. IEEE Trans. Knowl. Data Eng. **16**, 1457–1471 (2004)

Komorowski, J., Pawlak, Z., Polkowski, L., Skowron, A.: A rough set perspective on data and knowledge. In: Klösgen, W., Zytkow, J.M., Klosgen, W., Zyt, J. (eds.) The Handbook of Data Mining and Knowledge Discovery. Oxford University Press, New York (1999)

Kondo, M.: On the structure of generalized rough sets. Inf. Sci. **176**, 589–600 (2006)

Leung, Y., Wu, W., Zhang, W.: Knowledge acquisition in incomplete information systems: a rough set approach. Eur. J. Oper. Res. **168**, 164–180 (2006)

Liao, S.-H., Chen, Y.-J., Chu, P.-H.: Rough-set-based association rules applied to brand trust evaluation model. Lect. Notes Comp. Sci. **6443**, 634–641 (2010)

Lin, C.-S., Tzeng, G.-H., Chin, Y.-C.: Combined rough set theory and flow network graph to predict customer churn in credit card accounts. Expert Syst. Appl. **38**, 8–15 (2011)

Liu, S., Chan, F.T.S., Chung, S.H.: A study of distribution center location based on the rough sets and interactive multi-objective fuzzy decision theory. Robot. Comput. Integrated Manuf. **27**, 426–433 (2011)

Machowski, L.A., Marwala, T.: Using object oriented calculation process framework and neural networks for classification of image shapes. Int. J. Innov. Comput, Info. Control **1**, 609–623 (2005)

Marwala, T.: Computational Intelligence for Missing Data Imputation, Estimation and Management: Knowledge Optimization Techniques. IGI Global Publications, New York (2009)

Marwala, T., Crossingham, B.: Bayesian rough sets. ICIC Exp. Lett. **3**, 115–120 (2009)

Marwala, T., Crossingham, B.: Neuro-rough models for modelling HIV. In: Proceedings of the IEEE International Conference on Systems, Man, and Cybernetics, pp. 3089–3095, Singapore (2008)

Nelwamondo, F.V.: Computational intelligence techniques for missing data imputation. Ph.D. thesis, University of the Witwatersrand, Johannesburg (2008)

Ohrn, A.: Discernibility and rough sets in medicine: tools and applications. Unpublished Ph.D. thesis, Norwegian University of Science and Technology, Trondheim (1999)

Ohrn, A., Rowland, T.: Rough sets: a knowledge discovery technique for multifactorial medical outcomes. Am. J. Phys. Med. Rehabil. **79**, 100–108 (2000)

Pawlak, Z.: Rough Sets – Theoretical Aspects of Reasoning About Data. Kluwer Academic Publishers, Dordrecht (1991)

Pawlak, Z., Skowron, A.: Rough sets and boolean reasoning. Inf. Sci. **177**, 41–73 (2007)

Pawlak, Z., Wong, S.K.M., Ziarko, W.: Rough sets: probabilistic versus deterministic approach. Int. J. Man. Mach. Stud. **29**, 81–95 (1988)

Pawlak, Z., Munakata, T.: Rough control application of rough set theory to control. In: Proceedings of the 4th European Congress on Intelligent Techniques and Soft Computing, pp. 209–218, Aachen, Germany (1996)

Quafafou, M.: α-RST: a generalization of rough set theory. Inf. Sci. **124**, 301–316 (2000)

Rowland, T., Ohno-Machado, L., Ohrn, A.: Comparison of multiple prediction models for ambulation following spinal cord injury. In Chute **31**, 528–532 (1998)

Salamó, M., López-Sánchez, M.: Rough set based approaches to feature selection for case-based reasoning classifiers. Pattern Recogn. Lett. **32**, 280–292 (2011)

Shan, N., Ziarko, W.: Data-based acquisition and incremental modification of classification rules. Comput. Intell. **11**, 357–370 (1995)

Slezak, D., Ziarko, W.: The investigation of the bayesian rough set model. Int. J. Approx Reason. **40**, 81–91 (2005)

Stefanowski, J.: On rough set based approaches to induction of decision rules. In: Polkowski, L., Skowron, A. (eds.) Rough Sets in Knowledge Discovery 1: Methodology and Applications. Physica-Verlag, Heidelberg (1998)

Terlecki, P., Walczak, K.: On the relation between rough set reducts and jumping emerging patterns. Inf. Sci. **177**, 74–83 (2007)

Tettey, T., Nelwamondo, F.V., Marwala, T.: HIV Data analysis via rule extraction using rough sets. In: Proceedings of the 11th IEEE International Conference on Intelligent Engineering Systems, pp. 105–110, Budapest (2007)

Wang, W., Yang, J., Jensen, R., Liu, X.: Rough set feature selection and rule induction for prediction of malignancy degree in brain glioma. Comput. Meth. Prog. Bio. **83**, 147–156 (2006)

Wang, J., Guo, K., Wang, S.: Rough set and tabu search based feature selection for credit scoring. Procedia Comput. Sci. **1**, 2433–2440 (2010)

Witlox, F., Tindemans, H.: The application of rough sets analysis in activity based modelling: opportunities and constraints. Expert Syst. Appl. **27**, 585–592 (2004)

Wright, S., Marwala, T.: Artificial intelligence techniques for steam generator modelling. arXiv:0811.1711 (2006)

Wu, W., Mi, J., Zhang, W.: Generalized fuzzy rough sets. Inf. Sci. **151**, 263–282 (2003)

Xie, F., Lin, Y., Ren, W.: Optimizing model for land use/land cover retrieval from remote sensing imagery based on variable precision rough sets. Ecol. Model. **222**, 232–240 (2011)

Yan, W., Liu, W., Cheng, Z., Kan, J.: The prediction of soil moisture based on rough set-neural network model. In: Proceedings of the 29th Chinese Control Conference, pp. 2413–2415, Beijing (2010)

Yang, Y., John, R.: Roughness bound in set-oriented rough set operations. In: Proceedings of the IEEE International Conference on Fuzzy Systems, pp. 1461–1468, Vancouver (2006)

Yao, J.T., Yao, Y.Y.: Induction of classification rules by granular computing. In: Proceedings of the Third International Conference on Rough Sets and Current Trends in Comput, pp. 331–338, Malvern (2002)

Zadeh, L.A.: Fuzzy sets. Inf. Control **8**, 338–353 (1965)

Zhang, L., Shao, C.: Designing fuzzy inference system based on improved gradient descent method. J. Syst. Eng. Electron. **17**, 853–857 (2006)

Zhang, Y., Zhu, J., Zhang, Z-Y.: The research of reagent adding control in anionic reverse flotation process based on rough set theory. In: Proceedings of the 29th Chinese Control Conference, pp. 3487–3491, Beijing (2010)

Zhao, Y., Yao, Y., Luo, F.: Data analysis based on discernibility and indiscernibility. Inf. Sci. **177**, 4959–4976 (2007)

Ziarko, W.: Rough sets as a methodology for data mining. In: Polkowski, L. (ed.) Rough Sets in Knowledge Discovery 1: Methodology and Applications. Physica-Verlag, Heidelberg (1998)

Zou, Z., Tseng, T.-L., Sohn, H., Song, G., Gutierrez, R.: A rough set based approach to distributor selection in supply chain management. Expert Syst. Appl. **38**, 106–115 (2011)

Chapter 8
Particle Swarm Optimization and Hill-Climbing Optimized Rough Sets for Modeling Interstate Conflict

8.1 Introduction

In Chap. 7, the rough set theory was applied to model militarized interstate disputes. An important aspect of modeling through rough sets is the issue of granulizing the input data. In Chap. 7, two granulization techniques – Equal-Width-Bin (EWB) and Equal-Frequency-Bin (EFB) partitioning – were introduced, implemented, and compared. The rough set model was also compared to the neuro-fuzzy system, introduced in Chap. 6. The results were that the EWB partitioning gives better accuracy than the EFB partitioning. For this reason, the EWB partition technique is implemented in this chapter. Both EWB and EFB partitioning were found to give less accurate but more transparent results when compared to neuro-fuzzy sets. Furthermore, it was observed that the rules generated from the rough sets were linguistic and easy-to-interpret when compared to the neuro-fuzzy model.

To acquire knowledge from data with numerical attributes, this chapter presents rough sets (Pawlak 1991). When rough sets are implemented, a step taken before the main step of rule induction or decision tree generation, called discretization, is applied (Crossingham and Marwala 2008). This important step is the focus of this chapter. Particle swarm and hill climbing optimization techniques are used to discretize the rough set partitions (Russell and Norvig 2003; Marwala and Crossingham 2008). In the case of optimizing the partition sizes of a rough set, the particular optimization technique goes through the entire search space, and creates partition sizes according to an objective criterion. The criterion used in this chapter is the maximization of the rough set's classification accuracy. The results produced by the particle swarm and the hill climbing optimization methods are compared to that of the more commonly used EWB partitioning method. The techniques were tested through modeling of militarized interstate dispute data.

Shen et al. (2010) applied particle swarm optimization for the attribute reduction of rough sets. The Cache concept was introduced to reduce the complexity of the algorithm. The experimental results demonstrated the simplicity and viability of

T. Marwala and M. Lagazio, *Militarized Conflict Modeling using Computational Intelligence*, Advanced Information and Knowledge Processing, DOI 10.1007/978-0-85729-790-7_8, © Springer-Verlag London Limited 2011

their method. Li and Zhang (2010) applied particle swarm optimization for learning the similarity measure of nominal features. Using the particle swarm optimization algorithm, the results demonstrated that the convergence was faster than that of a genetic algorithm and the accuracy was also improved.

Lim et al. (2006a) hybridized hill climbing and ant colony optimization and successfully applied this hybrid technique to reducing the bandwidth of sparse matrices through permuting rows and columns. Cano et al. (2007) successfully applied hill-climbing and branch-and-bound optimization methods for determining exact and approximate inference in credal networks. Jacobson et al. (2006) applied the hill climbing technique to determine optimal search strategies in reconnaissance, surveillance, as well as search and rescue missions. Their results indicate that, when limited computing power is available, optimal/near-optimal search strategies over multiple search platforms can be attained more efficiently using a simultaneously generalized hill climbing method instead of using other generalized hill climbing algorithms.

The main advantage of using a rough set is its ability to deal with imprecise or conflicting data, and its ability to produce easy-to-interpret and linguistic rules (Crossingham and Marwala 2008). However, its disadvantage is its classification accuracy. Rough sets compromise accuracy for rule interpretability. This is brought about in the discretization process where the granularity of the variables is decreased. A rough set technique is used for classification as it offers a balance between transparency of the rough set model and accuracy of data estimation, but it does come at the cost of a high computational effort. In this chapter the approach taken was to evaluate the effects of optimizing rough sets using the following steps (Tettey et al. 2007):

1. Create a rough set model to be used on the various data sets.
2. Using the militarized interstate dispute (MID) data set, discretize the input data into four partitions using EWB partitioning. (This regulates the classification accuracy produced).
3. Apply the particle swarm and hill climbing optimization techniques to the rough set for analysis on the MID data and, in so doing, generate the optimal partition sizes for each technique.
4. Using these newly generated optimal values, compare them with the results produced using EWB partitioning.

The focus of the method described in this chapter was the classification accuracy of the rough set, which was based on the Receiver Operating Characteristic (ROC) curve. The area under the ROC curve was used as the performance criteria for each method.

Note that, although there are many aspects involved in rough set theory – from the generation of reducts to the optimization of the number of split/discretization points – the focus of this research was to find how to optimally granulize the input data into partitions predefined as being four. For the process of knowledge acquisition, there are two discretization approaches. The first approach involves the discretization of numerical attributes during the process of knowledge acquisition. The second, the more commonly used approach, employs discretization as a preprocessing step (Mpanza and Marwala 2011).

8.2 Rough Sets

The process of rough set modeling, which was also discussed in Chap. 7, can be classified into these five stages (Crossingham 2007);

1. The first stage is to select the data to be modeled.
2. The second stage involves pre-processing the data to ensure that it is ready for analysis. This stage involves discretizing the data set and removing unnecessary data. It is this stage that this chapter focuses on, by applying the hill climbing and the particle swarm optimization methods.
3. If reducts are considered, the third stage would be to use the cleaned data to produce reducts. A reduct is the most concise way in which we can discern object classes. Stated differently, a reduct is the minimal subset of attributes that allows the same classification of elements of the universe as the whole set of attributes. To manage inconsistencies, lower and upper approximations of decision classes are defined in this stage.
4. Stage four is where the rules are extracted or generated. The rules are normally determined based on condition attribute values. Once the rules are extracted, they can be presented in an '*if CONDITION(S)-then DECISION*' format, as described in Chap. 7.
5. The fifth and final stage involves testing the newly created rules on a test set. The accuracy is noted and sent back into the optimization method used in step two. The process will continue until the optimum or highest accuracy is achieved.

The procedure for computing rough sets and extracting rules is given in Algorithm 1 (Crossingham 2007; Crossingham and Marwala 2008). Equations 8.1–8.3 are important for a full understanding of Algorithm 1. Once the rules are extracted, they can be tested using a set of test data. The classification output is expressed as a decision value which lies between 0 and 1. The accuracy of the rough set is determined using the area under the ROC curve. The equations that are relevant to this chapter and were explained in detail in Chap. 7 are Eqs. 8.1–8.3.

$$\underline{B}X = \{x \in U \,|[x]_B \subseteq X\} \tag{8.1}$$

$$\overline{B}X = \{x \in U \,|[x]_B \cap X \neq 0\} \tag{8.2}$$

$$\mu_A^x(X) = \frac{|[x]_B \cap X|}{|[x]_B|} \tag{8.3}$$

Here B is called a *B-definable* set, X is a set, μ is a plausibility and A is an attribute.

Algorithm 1: The procedure to generate a rough set model
Input: Condition and Decision Attributes
Output: Certain and Possible Rules
1   Obtain the data set to be used;
2   Repeat
3   **for** conditional_attribute ← 1 to size_of_training_data **do**
4   Pre-process data to ensure that it is ready for analysis;
5   Discretize the data according to an optimization technique;
6   Compute the lower approximation, as defined in Eq. 8.1;
7   Compute the upper approximation, as defined in Eq. 8.2;
8   From the general rules, calculate plausibility measures for which an object x belongs to set X, as defined by Eq. 8.3;
9   Extract the certain rules from the lower approximation generated for each subset;
10   Similarly, extract the possible rules from the upper approximation of each subset;
11   Remove the generated rules, for the purpose of testing on unseen data;
12   Compute the classifier performance using the AUC;
13   End
14   **until** Optimization technique termination condition.

The general framework followed in this chapter is best illustrated by referring to
Fig. 8.1. Mathematically, the procedure's outline is:

$$y = f(x, RP) \tag{8.4}$$

Here x is the input data − in this study is militarized interstate data, RP is the
rough set partition and y is the accuracy obtained when the model is tested on
unseen data. In this chapter, the aim of the optimization process is to identify the RP
parameters so that the accuracy y is maximized. To this end, optimization methods
are used. These methods are the subject of the next section.

8.3   Optimization Methods

This section of the chapter uses the particle swarm optimization technique to solve
Eq. 8.4. This is followed by the use of hill climbing. The next section compares
them.

8.3.1   Particle Swarm Optimization

This subsection uses the Particle Swarm Optimization (PSO) technique to solve
Eq. 8.4. The PSO technique uses a stochastic, population-based evolutionary

Fig. 8.1 Procedure for creating an optimized rough set model

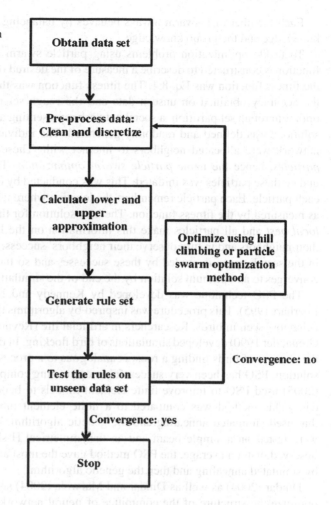

algorithm that is extensively used for the optimization of complex problems (Kennedy and Eberhart 1995; Poli 2007; Marwala 2010). It is based on socio-psychological principles that were inspired by swarm intelligence, which gives an understanding of social behavior and which has contributed to engineering applications (Marwala 2005). Society empowers an individual to sustain cognitive robustness through the influence and learning, and individuals learn to solve problems by communicating and interacting with other individuals and, in that way, cultivate a commonly similar approach of solving problems. Thus, swarm intelligence is driven by two factors (Kennedy and Eberhart 1995):

1. Group knowledge.
2. Individual knowledge.

Each member of a swarm always behaves by balancing between its individual knowledge and the group knowledge.

To tackle optimization problems using particle swarm optimization, a fitness function is constructed to describe a measure of the desired outcome. In this chapter the fitness function was Eq. 8.4. The fitness function was the relationship between the accuracy obtained on unseen data and the rough set partitions. To reach an optimum rough set partition, a social network representing a population of possible solutions was defined and randomly generated. The individuals within this social network were allocated neighbors to interact with. These individuals are called *particles*, hence the name *particle swarm optimization*. Thereafter, a process to update these particles was initiated. This was conducted by evaluating the fitness of each particle. Each particle remembers the location where it had its greatest success as measured by the fitness function. The best solution for the particle is named the *local best* and all particles make this information on the local best accessible to their neighbors and in turn observe their neighbors' success. The process of moving in the search space is guided by these successes and so the population ultimately converges to an optimum solution by the end of the simulation.

The PSO technique was developed by Kennedy and Eberhart (Kennedy and Eberhart 1995). This procedure was inspired by algorithms that model the "flocking behavior" seen in birds. Researchers in artificial life (Reynolds 1987; Heppner and Grenander 1990) developed simulations of bird flocking. In the field of optimization, the concept of birds finding a roost is analogous to a process of finding an optimal solution. PSO has been very successful in optimizing complex problems. Marwala (2005) used PSO to improve finite element models to better reflect the measured data. This method was compared to a finite element model updating approach that used simulated annealing and the genetic algorithm. The presented methods were tested on a simple beam and an unsymmetrical H-shaped structure. It was observed that, on average, the PSO method gave the most accurate results followed by simulated annealing and then the genetic algorithm.

Dindar (2004) as well as Dindar and Marwala (2004) successfully used PSO to optimize the structure of the committee of neural networks. The results obtained from the optimized networks were found to be better than both un-optimized networks and the committee of networks. Ransome et al. (2005) as well as Ransome (2006) successfully used PSO to optimize the position of a patient during radiation therapy. In this application, a patient positioning system with an integrated robotic arm was designed for proton beam therapy. A treatment image was aligned with a pre-defined reference image attained by aligning the radiation and reference field boundaries and then registering the patient's anatomy relative to the boundary. Methods for both field boundary and anatomy alignment including particle swarm optimization were implemented. It was found that the PSO was successful in overcoming problems in existing solutions.

Arumugam and Rao (2008) successfully implemented multiple-objective particle swarm optimization for molecular docking. Multi-objective PSO is a technique that aims at solving more than one objective function. Arya et al. (2007) successfully used PSO and singular value decomposition to design neuro-fuzzy networks.

This process was aimed at identifying the optimal neuro-fuzzy networks whose objective was to accurately model the data. Berlinet and Roland (2008) introduced a PSO algorithm for the permutation of flow-shop scheduling problems. Scheduling problems have design variables that are integers. If there are many of these variables, the combinatorial nature of these problems makes the process of finding solutions to these problems extremely difficult.

Jarboui et al. (2008) introduced and successfully applied PSO where a distribution vector was used for the update of the velocities of particles. Other applications of PSO include Jiang et al. (2007) who successfully applied it to a conceptual design; Kathiravan and Ganguli (2007) in power systems; Lian et al. (2008) in training radial basis functions that were trained to identify chaotic systems; Lin et al. (2008) in inverse radiation problems; Qi et al. (2008) in scheduling problems and Guerra and dos S Coelho (2008) in the modeling of nonlinear filters.

Brits et al. (2007) presented a PSO technique aimed at locating and refining multiple solutions to problems with multi-modal characteristics. Their method extended the uni-modal nature of the standard PSO approach by using many swarms from the initial population. A different solution was represented by a sub-swarm and was individually optimized. Thereby each set of particle in the swarm represented a possible solution. When implemented experimentally it was found to successfully locate all optima.

Sha and Hsu (2006) proposed a hybrid PSO for the job-shop problem which operated in discrete space rather than in continuous space. Due to the nature of the discrete space, the PSO algorithm was improved through particle position representation, particle movement, and particle velocity. The particle position was then represented based on a preference list, particle movement on the swap operator, and particle velocity on the tabu list concept. Giffler and Thompson (1960) implemented a heuristic to decode a particle position into a schedule while the tabu search improved the solution quality.

This chapter deals primarily with the application of PSO to rough sets. Zhao et al. (2010) successfully applied discrete PSO method for feature selection to optimize classification rules. Miao et al. (2010) proposed a dynamic PSO which was based on neighborhood rough set model and their results demonstrated good performance in terms of speed and computational accuracy. Filiberto et al. (2010) successfully applied PSO and rough set theory to predict the resistant capacity of connections in composite structures.

Lin et al. (2008) successfully applied PSO for attribute reduction in rough sets by converting the problem of attribute reduction into a 0–1 combinatorial optimization problem. Xu et al. (2008) successfully applied PSO and rough sets for knowledge acquisition. The results demonstrated that the grate-kiln expert technique was effective and offered significant advantages in the palletizing production process control. Other successful applications of the PSO to rough sets are for intelligent decision making (Yu et al. 2010), for rough set approximate entropy reducts (Wang et al. 2009) and for attribute reduction (Zhao 2009).

PSO is implemented by finding a balance between searching for a good solution and exploiting other particles' success. If the search for a solution is too limited, the simulation will converge to the first solution encountered, which may be a local

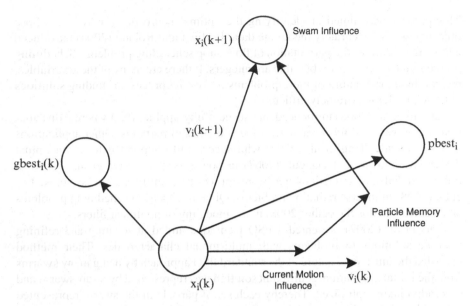

Fig. 8.2 Velocity and particle update in the particle swarm optimization

optimum position. If the successes of other particles are not exploited then the simulation will never converge. The particle swarm optimization approach has the following advantages (Kennedy and Eberhart 1995):

- It is computationally efficient.
- It is simple to implement.
- It has few adjustable parameters when compared with other competing evolutionary programming methods such as genetic algorithm.
- It can adapt to explore locally and globally.

When implementing the particle swarm optimization method the simulation is initialized with a population of random candidates which are each conceptualized as particles. Each particle is assigned a random velocity and is iteratively moved through the particle space. At each step, the particle is attracted towards a region of the best fitness function by the location of the best fitness achieved so far in the population (Fig. 8.2).

On implementing the standard particle swarm optimization, each particle is represented by two vectors (Kennedy and Eberhart 2001):

- $p_i(k)$, which is the position of particle i at Step k; and
- $v_i(k)$, which is the velocity of particle i at Step k.

The initial positions and velocities of particles are randomly generated. The subsequent positions and velocities are calculated using the position of the best solution that a particular particle has encountered thus far during the simulation called *pbest*$_i$ and the best particle in the swarm, which is called *gbest(k)*. The subsequent velocity of a particle i can be identified using the equation (Kennedy and Eberhart 2001):

$$v_i(k+1) = \gamma v_i(k) + c_1 r_1(pbest_i - p_i(k)) + c_2 r_2(gbest(k) - p_i(k)) \qquad (8.5)$$

where γ is the inertia of the particle, c_1 and c_2 are the "trust" parameters, and r_1 and r_2 are random numbers between 0 and 1.

In Eq. 8.5, the first term is the current motion, the second term is the particle memory influence and the third term is the swarm influence. The subsequent position of a particle i can be calculated using these equations (Kennedy and Eberhart 2001):

$$p_i(k+1) = p_i(k) + v_i(k+1) \qquad (8.6)$$

The inertia of the particle controls the impact of the previous velocity of the particle on the current velocity. These parameters control the exploratory properties of the simulation with a high value of inertia encouraging global exploration and a low value of the inertia encouraging local exploration.

The parameters c_1 and c_2 are trust parameters. The trust parameter c_1 indicates how much confidence the current particle has about itself while the trust parameter c_2 indicates how much confidence the current particle has on the successes of the population. The parameters r_1 and r_2 are random numbers between 0 and 1 that determine the degree to which the simulation should explore the space. It can be seen in Eq. 8.6 that the particle swarm optimization makes use of the velocity to update the position of the swarm.

The position of the particle is updated based on the social behavior of the particles' population and the position adapts to the environment by continually coming back to the most promising region identified. This process is stochastic and it can be summarized as follows (Shi and Eberhart 1998; Clerc and Kennedy 2002):

1. Initialize a population of particles' positions and velocities. The positions of the particles must be randomly distributed in the updating parameter space.
2. Calculate the velocity for each particle in the swarm using Eq. 8.5.
3. Update the position of each particle using Eq. 8.6.
4. Repeat steps 2 and 3 until convergence.

This process is represented diagrammatically in Fig. 8.3. To improve the performance of particle swarm optimization as presented above, several additions and modifications of particle swarm optimization have been presented and implemented. Liu et al. (2007) presented a combination of particle swarm optimization and evolutionary algorithms and applied this method to train recurrent neural networks for time series prediction.

Janson et al. (2007) combined particle swarm optimization with a gradient based optimization method and used this to design a composite beam which has the highest possible strength while Yisu et al. (2008) improved particle swarm optimization by introducing a crossover functionality from the genetic algorithm and applied this to controlling hybrid systems.

Fig. 8.3 Flow diagram of the implementation of particle swarm optimization

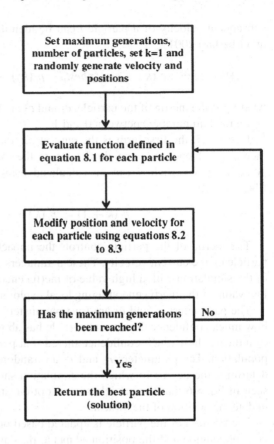

8.3.2 Hill Climbing

Hill climbing is an optimization technique that belongs to the group of local search algorithms (Marwala 2009). Essentially this means the algorithm moves from solution to solution in the search space until an optimal solution is found. The algorithm attempts to maximize the fitness function (accuracy) by iteratively comparing two solutions. It accepts the best solution and proceeds with the comparison (i.e., moves further up the hill). This iteration terminates when there are no better solutions on either side of the current solution (i.e., it has reached the true peak).

There are several variants or methods of hill climbing. The first and most basic form is *simple hill climbing*. In this method the first, closest node is chosen for evaluation. A second variant is called *steepest ascent hill climbing*. In the steepest ascent hill climbing method, all successors are compared and the closest to the solution is chosen. Other variants that can be investigated include next-ascent hill climbing and zero-temperature Monte Carlo hill climbing (Mitchell et al. 1994).

In this chapter, steepest ascent hill climbing was implemented. However, a major disadvantage of both simple and steepest ascent hill climbing is that they only find the local optimum. So the hill climbing (HC) algorithm was chosen with an initial 20 starting points. As with all the other optimization techniques, hill climbing uses the prediction accuracy (area under the receiver operation characteristics curve) as the objective/fitness function, but because it is a "greedy" algorithm, other methods or variations of hill climbing should also be investigated. (A "greedy" algorithm is an algorithm that looks at the next solution, and if the next solution is a better solution (fitter), this method will take on the position of the next solution.)

The steepest-ascent hill climbing method was implemented for this chapter. The pedigree of this method follows. Hernandez et al. (2008) applied neighborhood functions and Hill-Climbing (HC) strategies to study the generalized un-gapped local multiple alignment which is generally applied in bioinformatics. Iclanzan and Dumitrescu (2007) proposed an HC method that operates in building block space to solve hierarchical problems. Their building block hill-climber used its hill-climbing search knowledge to learn the problem structure. Then the neighborhood structure was adapted every time the latest knowledge on the building block structure was included into the search. This permitted the technique to climb the hierarchical structure by successively solving the hierarchical level by level. They showed that this technique scaled approximately linearly with the size of the problem and therefore outperformed population based re-combinative techniques such as the genetic algorithm, particle swarm optimization and simulated annealing.

Other successful implementations of HC include the study of the role of DNA transposition in enduring artificial evolution (Khor 2007); in time-delay systems (Santos and Sanchez-Diaz 2007), in credal networks (Cano et al. 2007), in decentralized job scheduling (Wang et al. 2006), in the traveling tournament problem (Lim et al. 2006a, b), for evolving robot gaits (Garder and Hovin 2006), for optimizing the 3-Joint Fish Robot (Vo et al. 2009), for solving design and manufacturing problems (Yildiz 2009), for automated grouping systems (Lewis 2009), for an adaptive optical system with a Shack-Hartmann sensor (Sheldakova et al. 2010), for tool path optimization (Du and Qi 2010) and for modeling HIV (Crossingham and Marwala 2007a, b). The pseudo-code for the implementation of hill climbing follows (Du and Qi 2010):

1. Set initial conditions.
2. Current node = Starting node = Initial configuration = S.
3. Compute $S\_Fitness$, i.e., the initial configuration fitness.
4. Repeat:

(a) Compute a neighboring configuration S' by local transformation from the current point in the search space to the next point.
(b) Compute fitness of S' ($S'\_Fitness$).
(c) If $S\_Fitness > S'\_Fitness$ then $S' = S$.

5. Until the maximum is reached

The flow chart for implementing hill climbing is given in Fig. 8.4. A variation of steepest ascent hill climbing is Random-Restart Hill Climbing (RRHC). RRHC is an algorithm built on top of the hill climbing algorithm. What it does is that it

Fig. 8.4 Flow diagram of
the implementation of hill
climbing

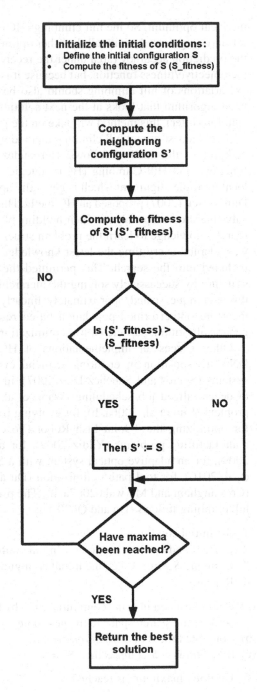

Table 8.1 Comparison of methods

Method	Particle swarm optimization	Hill climbing
General philosophy	It operates in one path. It is a global optimization method, inspired by swarm characteristics e.g., the flocking of birds.	It operates in multi-paths through the population size. It is a local optimization method.
Characteristics	It can explore the space efficiently in binary form.	Scaling this method to a higher dimension is difficult.
Advantages	It has a high probability that it will identify a global optimum point. It is computationally manageable.	It is relatively easy to implement with fewer parameters to tune
Disadvantages	It is relatively difficult to implement with many parameters to tune.	It is computationally expensive. It has a low probability of identifying a global solution.

runs an outer loop over HC, where each step chooses a random initial point (x_0) to start the HC. The best initial point is stored (x_{best}). If a new run of HC produces a better initial point than the stored one (i.e., if x_0 is better than x_{best}), then the stored one gets replaced ($x_{best} := x_0$). There are several other variations of HC but these methods were not investigated for this chapter.

8.4 Hill Climbing Versus Particle Swarm Optimization

The optimization methods outlined in the earlier chapters were compared. This comparison appears in Table 8.1 and gives the general philosophy, characteristics, advantages and disadvantages.

Table 8.1 demonstrates that the PSO seems to have more advantages than the HC optimization method. More importantly, the PSO has a higher capacity to identify a global optimum solution than the HC method and the impact of this on the solution is potentially significant.

8.5 Interstate Conflict

In this chapter rough sets were implemented with militarized interstate dispute (MID) data. Data were discretized using two optimization techniques, being particle swarm optimization and hill climbing. The MID had seven inputs and each was discretized into four bins meaning that there were 28 variables to be optimized as in Eq. 8.4. The population size of the PSO implementation chosen was 100 and the algorithm was run for 50 generations. After the HC method was implemented it was found that there was no improvement in the quality of the solutions obtained after

Table 8.2 Classification results

Method	True conflicts TC	False peaces FP	True peaces TP	False conflicts FC
Rough sets: equal width bin	272	120	291	99
Rough sets: particle swarm optimization	218	74	217	75
Rough sets: hill climbing	212	80	211	81

27 generations. The results of these implementation decisions for the MID data are shown in Table 8.2. It should be noted that the PSO and HC methods have 200 fewer cases because some were used in the optimization phase and, therefore, no longer formed part of the test set.

The results demonstrate that detection rate of conflict was 69% when the equal-width-bin rough set was used, 73% when HC was used and 75% when particle swarm optimization was used. The detection rate for peace was 75% when the equal-width-bin rough set model was used, 72.4% when HC was used and 74.5% when particle swarm optimization was used. Overall, the detection rate of a correct outcome was 71.8% when the equal-width-bin was used, 72% when HC was used and 74% when particle swarm optimization was used. Furthermore, the area under the receiver operating characteristics curves when the PSO was used was 0.79, 0.77 for when equal-width-bin rough set model was used and 0.77 when HC was used. These results demonstrate that the optimization process improves the rough set implementation. However, the improvement is marginal when compared to the results obtained by Crossingham (2007). This indicates that the equal-width-bin partitioning was not far off from the optimized partition. The PSO was found to perform better than HC, which was marginally better than the equal-width-bin partitioning. This is mainly because the PSO is a global optimization method while HC is a local optimization method.

8.6   Conclusion

The work performed in this chapter was concerned with using various optimization techniques to granulize the rough set input partitions to achieve the highest forecasting accuracy producible by the rough set and applied this to interstate conflict. The two optimization techniques used were PSO and HC. The results indicated that the optimized methods produce higher forecasting/classification accuracies than that of the static equal-width-bin (EWB) method. When comparing the optimized approaches against each other, PSO gave better results than HC. This could be because the implementation of hill climbing used allows the optimum to be found at a local rather than a global point. Note that, depending on the linearity and complexity of the data set, the optimal technique to be used to discretize the partitions will vary. The rough sets produce a balance between transparency of the rough set model and the accuracy of conflict prediction, but this does come at the cost of a high computational effort.

8.7 Further Work

The rough set model was implemented for modeling interstate conflict and standard PSO and HC were used to optimize the rough set partition. For future work, more robust variants of PSO and HC should be applied.

References

Arumugam, M.S., Rao, M.V.C.: Molecular docking with multi-objective particle swarm optimization. Appl. Soft Comput. **8**, 666–675 (2008)

Arya, L.D., Choube, S.C., Shrivastava, M., Kothari, D.P.: The design of neuro-fuzzy networks using particle swarm optimization and recursive singular value decomposition. Neurocomputing **71**, 297–310 (2007)

Berlinet, A., Roland, C.: A novel particle swarm optimization algorithm for permutation flow-shop scheduling to minimize makespan. Chaos, Solitons & Fractals **35**, 851–861 (2008)

Brits, R., Engelbrecht, A.P., van den Bergh, F.: Locating multiple optima using particle swarm optimization. Appl. Math. and Comput. **189**, 1859–1883 (2007)

Cano, A., Gomez, M., Moral, S., Abellan, J.: Hill-climbing and branch-and-bound algorithms for exact and approximate inference in credal networks. Int. J. Approx. Reason. **44**, 261–280 (2007)

Clerc, M., Kennedy, J.: The particle swarm - explosion, stability, and convergence in a multidimensional complex space. IEEE Trans. Evol. Comput. **6**, 58–73 (2002)

Crossingham, B.: Rough set partitioning using computational intelligence approach. M.Sc. thesis, University of the Witwatersrand (2007)

Crossingham, B., Marwala, T.: Using genetic algorithms to optimise rough set partition sizes for HIV data analysis. Stud. in Comput. Intell. **78**, 245–250 (2007a)

Crossingham, B., Marwala, T.: Using optimisation techniques to granulise rough set partitions. Comput. Models for Life Sci. **952**, 248–257 (2007b)

Crossingham, B., Marwala, T.: Using optimisation techniques for discretizing rough set partitions. Int. J. Hybrid Intell. Syst. **5**, 219–236 (2008)

Dindar, Z.A.: Artificial neural networks applied to option pricing. Unpublished MSc thesis, University of the Witwatersrand (2004)

Dindar, Z.A., Marwala, T.: Option pricing using a committee of neural networks and optimized networks. In: Proceedings of the 2004 IEEE International Conference on Systems, Man and Cybernetics, vol. 1, pp. 434–438. The Hague (2004)

Du, H., Qi, J.: Application of a hybrid algorithm based on genetic algorithm and hill-climbing algorithm to tool path optimization in CNC machining. Adv. Mater. Res. **102**, 681–685 (2010)

Filiberto, Y., Bello, R., Caballero, Y., Larrua, R.: Using PSO and RST to predict the resistant capacity of connections in composite structures. Stud. in Comput. Intell. **284**, 359–370 (2010)

Garder, L.M., Hovin, M.E.: Robot gaits evolved by combining genetic algorithms and binary hill climbing. In: Proceedings of the 8th annual conference on Genetic and Evolutionary Computation, pp. 1165–1170. ACM, New York (2006)

Giffler, B., Thompson, G.L.: Algorithms for solving production scheduling problems. Oper. Res. **8**, 487–503 (1960)

Guerra, F.A., dos S Coelho, L.: A particle swarm optimization approach to nonlinear rational filter modeling. Expert. Syst. with Appl. **34**, 1194–1199 (2008)

Heppner, F., Grenander, U.: A stochastic non-linear model for coordinated bird flocks. In: Krasner, S. (ed.) The Ubiquity of Chaos, 1st edn. AAAS Publications, Washington, DC (1990)

Hernandez, D., Gras, R., Appel, R.: Neighborhood functions and hill-climbing strategies dedicated to the generalized ungapped local multiple alignment. Eur. J. Oper. Res. **185**, 1276–1284 (2008)

Iclanzan, D., Dumitrescu, D.: Overcoming hierarchical difficulty by hill-climbing the building block structure. In: Thierens, D et al. (eds.) GECCO 2007: Proceedings of the 9th annual conference on Genetic and Evolutionary Computation, vol. 2, pp. 1256–1263 ACM Press, London (2007)

Jacobson, S.H., McLay, L.A., Hall, S.N., Henderson, D., Vaughan, D.E.: Optimal search strategies using simultaneous generalized hill climbing algorithms. Math. Comput. Model. **43**, 1061–1073 (2006)

Janson, S., Merkle, D., Middendorf, M.: Strength design of composite beam using gradient and particle swarm optimization. Compos. Struct. **81**, 471–479 (2007)

Jarboui, B., Damak, N., Siarry, P., Rebai, A.: The landscape adaptive particle swarm optimizer. Appl. Soft Comput. **8**, 295–304 (2008)

Jiang, Y., Hu, T., Huang, C., Wu, X.: Particle swarm optimization based on dynamic niche technology with applications to conceptual design. Adv. Eng. Soft. **38**, 668–676 (2007)

Kathiravan, R., Ganguli, R.: Particle swarm optimization for determining shortest distance to voltage collapse. Int. J. of Electr. Power & Energy Systems **29**, 796–802 (2007)

Kennedy, J., Eberhart, R.: Particle swarm optimization. In: Proceedings of the IEEE International Conference on Neural Networks, vol. 4, pp. 1942–1948. IEEE Service Center, Piscataway (1995)

Kennedy, J., Eberhart, R.C.: Swarm Intelligence. Morgan Kaufmann, San Francisco (2001)

Khor, S.: Hill climbing on discrete HIFF: exploring the role of DNA transposition in long-term artificial evolution. GECCO, Proceedings of the 9th annual conference on Genetic and Evolutionary Computation, pp. 277–284. ACM, New York (2007)

Lewis, R.: A general-purpose hill-climbing method for order independent minimum grouping problems: a case study in graph colouring and bin packing. Comput. & Oper. Res. **36**, 2295–2310 (2009)

Li, Y., Zhang, X.-L.: PSO-based method for learning similarity measure of nominal features. In: Proceedings of the International Conference on Machine Learning and Cybernetics, pp. 1868–1874 (2010)

Lian, Z., Gu, X., Jiao, B.: Multi-step ahead nonlinear identification of Lorenz's Chaotic system using radial basis neural network with learning by clustering and particle swarm optimization. Chaos, Solitons & Fractals **35**, 967–979 (2008)

Lim, A., Lin, J., Rodrigues, B., Xiao, F.: Ant colony optimization with hill climbing for the bandwidth minimization problem. Appl. Soft Comput. **6**, 180–188 (2006a)

Lim, A., Rodrigues, B., Zhang, X.: A simulated annealing and hill-climbing algorithm for the traveling tournament problem. Eur. J. Oper. Res. **174**, 1459–1478 (2006b)

Lin, W., Wu, Y., Mao, D., Yu, Y.: Attribute reduction of rough set based on particle swarm optimization with immunity. In: Proceedings of the 2nd International Conference on Genetic and Evolutionary Computation, pp. 14–17 (2008)

Lin, Y., Chang, W., Hsieh, J.: Application of multi-phase particle swarm optimization technique to inverse radiation problem. J. Quant. Spectrosc. and Radiat. Transf. **109**, 476–493 (2008b)

Liu, X., Liu, H., Duan, H.: Time series prediction with recurrent neural networks trained by a hybrid PSO–EA algorithm. Neurocomputing **70**, 2342–2353 (2007)

Marwala, T.: Finite element model updating using particle swarm optimization. Int. J. of Eng. Simul. **6**, 25–30 (2005)

Marwala, T.: Computational Intelligence for Missing Data Imputation, Estimation and Management: Knowledge Optimization Techniques. IGI Global Publications, New York (2009)

Marwala, T.: Finite Element Model Updating Using Computational Intelligence Techniques. Springer, London (2010)

Marwala, T., Crossingham, B.: HIV status estimation using optimization, rough sets and demographic data. Current Sci. **95**, 1123–1124 (2008)

Miao, A., Shi, X., Zhang, J., Jiang, W., Zhang, J., Gui, X.: Dynamic particle swarm optimization based on neighborhood rough set model. In: Proceedings of the 2nd International Asia Conference on Informatics in Control, Automation and Robotics, pp. 95–100 (2010)

Mitchell, M., Holland, J., Forest, S.: When will a genetic algorithm outperform hill climbing? Adv. in Neural Info. Process Syst. **6**, 51–58 (1994)

Mpanza, L.J., Marwala, T.: Rough set theory for HV bushings fault detection: tradeoff between accuracy and transparency. In: Proceedings of the 3rd International Conference on Machine Learning and Computing, vol. 2, pp. 121–125. Singapore (2011)

Pawlak, Z.: Rough Sets – Theoretical Aspects of Reasoning about Data. Kluwer Academic Publishers, Dordrecht (1991)

Poli, R.: An analysis of publications on particle swarm optimisation applications (Technical Report CSM-469). Department of Computer Science, University of Essex (2007)

Qi, H., Ruan, L.M., Shi, M., An, W., Tan, H.P.: A combinatorial particle swarm optimization for solving multi-mode resource-constrained project scheduling problems. Appl. Math. and Comput. **195**, 299–308 (2008)

Ransome, T.: Automatic minimisation of patient setup errors in proton beam therapy. Unpublished MSc thesis, University of the Witwatersrand (2006)

Ransome, T.M., Rubin, D.M., Marwala, T., de Kok, E.A.: Optimising the verification of patient positioning in proton beam therapy. In: Proceedings of the IEEE 3rd International Conference on Computation Cybernetics, pp. 279–284 (2005)

Reynolds, C.W.: Flocks, herds and schools: a distributed behavioral model. Comp. Graphics **2**, 25–34 (1987)

Russell, S.J., Norvig, P.: Artificial Intelligence: A Modern Approach. Prentice Hall, Englewood Cliffs (2003)

Santos, O., Sanchez-Diaz, G.: Suboptimal control based on hill-climbing method for time delay systems. IET Contr. Theory and Appl. **1**, 1441–1450 (2007)

Sha, D.Y., Hsu, C.: A hybrid particle swarm optimization for job shop scheduling problem. Comput. and Ind. Eng. **51**, 791–808 (2006)

Sheldakova, J., Rukosuev, A., Romanov, P., Kudryashov, A., Samarkin, V.: Hill-climbing algorithm for adaptive optical system with Shack-Hartmann sensor. In: Proceedings of the 5th International Conference on Advanced Optoelectronics and Lasers, pp. 157–158 (2010)

Shen, H., Yang, S., Liu, J.: An attribute reduction of rough set based on PSO. In: Rough set and knowledge technology. 5th international conference, RSKT 2010, Beijing, China, October 15–17, 2010. Proceedings Lecture Notes in Computer Science, vol. 6401, pp. 695–702. Springer (ISBN 978-3-642-16247-3), Berlin (2010)

Shi, Y., Eberhart, R.C.: Parameter selection in particle swarm optimization. In: Proceedings of the 7th International Conference on Evolutionary Programming VII, pp. 591–600. Springer-Verlag, London (1998)

Tettey, T., Nelwamondo, F.V., Marwala, T.: HIV data analysis via rule extraction using rough sets. In: Proceedings of the 11th IEEE International Conference on Intelligent Engineering Systems, vol. 29, pp. 105–110, Budapest (2007)

Vo, T.Q., Kim, H.S., Lee, B.R.: Propulsive velocity optimization of 3-joint fish robot using genetic-hill climbing algorithm. J. of Bionic. Eng. **6**, 415–429 (2009)

Wang, Q., Gao, Y., Liu, P.: Hill climbing-based decentralized job scheduling on computational grids. In: Proceedings of the First International Multi-Symposiums on Computer and Computational Science, vol. 1, pp. 705–708. IEEE Computer Society, Washington, DC (2006)

Wang, X., Wan, W., Yu, X.: Rough set approximate entropy reducts with order based particle swarm optimization. In: Proc of the 1st ACM//SIGEVO Summit on Genetic and Evol Comput: 553–559 (2009)

Xu, L., Dong, W., Wang, J., Gu, S.: A method of the knowledge acquisition using rough set knowledge reduction algorithm based on PSO. In: Proceedings of the World Congress on Intelligence Control and Automation, pp. 5317–5320 (2008)

Yildiz, A.R.: An effective hybrid immune-hill climbing optimization approach for solving design and manufacturing optimization problems in industry. J. Mater. Process Technol. **209**, 2773–2780 (2009)

Yisu, J., Knowles, J., Hongmei, L., Yizeng, L., Kell, D.B.: The landscape adaptive particle swarm optimizer. Appl. Soft Comput. **8**, 295–304 (2008)

Yu, Y., Wang, J., Zhu, J.: Method for intelligent decision making based on rough sets and particle swarm optimization. In: Proceedings of the 2010 2nd International Conference on Computer Modelling and Simulation, vol. 4, pp. 230–233. IEEE Computer Society, Washington, DC (2010)

Zhao, Y.: A complete algorithm for attribute reduction in rough set based on particle swarm optimization. In: Proceedings of the 2009 2nd International Conference on Intelligent Computation Technology and Automation, vol. 1, pp. 215–218. IEEE Computer Society Washington, DC (2009)

Zhao, Q., Zhao, J., Meng, G., Liu, L.: A new method of data mining based on rough sets and discrete particle swarm optimization. In: Proceedings of the International Conference on Computer Engineering and Technology, pp. 2424–2430 (2010)

Chapter 9
Simulated Annealing Optimized Rough Sets for Modeling Interstate Conflict

9.1 Introduction

Rough set theory is a technique that is used to extract linguistic explanations from the data (Pawlak 1991). In Chap. 6 the levels of transparency of the Takagi-Sugeno neuro-fuzzy model and the support vector machines model were investigated by applying them to conflict management. The conflict management problem is concerned with causal interpretations of results. The data set used in this investigation was the militarized interstate disputes dataset obtained from the correlates of war project. The support vector machine model was also trained to predict conflict. Knowledge from the Takagi-Sugeno neuro-fuzzy model was extracted by interpreting the model's fuzzy rules and their outcomes. It was found that the Takagi-Sugeno neuro-fuzzy model offered some transparency which assists in understanding conflict management. The Takagi-Sugeno neuro-fuzzy model was compared to the support vector machine method and it was found that even though the support vector machine showed marginal advantage over Takagi-Sugeno neuro-fuzzy model in terms of predictive capacity, the Takagi-Sugeno neuro-fuzzy model allowed for linguistics interpretation.

In Chap. 7, the rough set technique was applied to model the militarized interstate dispute. One of the aspects of modeling using rough sets was the issue of granulization of the input data. Two granulization techniques were introduced, implemented and compared and these were the equal-width-bin and equal-frequency-bin partitioning techniques. The rough set model was also compared to the neuro-fuzzy system which was introduced in Chap. 6. The results obtained demonstrated that equal-width-bin partitioning gave better results in terms of accuracy than equal-frequency partition. However, both these techniques were found to give less accurate results than neuro-fuzzy sets. However, they are found to be more transparent than neuro-fuzzy sets. Furthermore, it was observed that the rules generated from the rough sets were linguistic and easy-to-interpret when compared to the neuro-fuzzy model.

T. Marwala and M. Lagazio, *Militarized Conflict Modeling using Computational Intelligence*, Advanced Information and Knowledge Processing, DOI 10.1007/978-0-85729-790-7_9, © Springer-Verlag London Limited 2011

In this Chap. 8, methods to optimally granulize rough set partition sizes using particle swarm optimization and hill climbing techniques were proposed. The proposed methods were compared to that based on the equal-width-bin technique. The results obtained demonstrated that particle swarm optimization provided higher forecasting accuracies followed by hill climbing method which was better than the equal-width-bin technique.

In this chapter simulated annealing is applied for rough set partition and the results are compared to those obtained when particle swarm optimization technique was applied. This chapter also performs a comprehensive literature review on simulated annealing and a comparison between simulated annealing and other techniques. The next section briefly describes rough set technique within the context of simulated annealing technique.

9.2 Rough Sets

The process of rough set modeling, which was also discussed in Chaps. 7 and 8, can be classified into these five stages (Crossingham et al. 2008);

1. Choose the data to be modeled.
2. Pre-process the data to make sure it is prepared for analysis. This stage incorporates discretizing the data and removing unnecessary data. It is this stage that this chapter focuses on by applying simulated annealing optimization technique.
3. If reducts are considered, use the cleaned data to produce reducts. A reduct is the most concise way in which we can discern object classes. Differently stated, a reduct is the minimal subset of attributes that allows the same classification of elements of the universe as the whole set of attributes. To manage the inconsistencies, lower and upper approximations of decision classes are defined in this stage.
4. Extract rules. Rules are normally determined based on condition attributes values.
5. Finally test the newly created rules on a test data set. The accuracy is then calculated and noted and then sent back into the optimization method used in Step 2 and the process continues until highest accuracy is achieved.

The general framework followed in this Chapter is illustrated in Fig. 9.1.

Mathematically the procedure outlined above can be mathematically framed as follows as it was explained in Chap. 8:

$$y = f(x, RP) \tag{9.1}$$

Here x is the input data which in this book is the militirized interstate dispute data, RP is the rough set partition and y is the accuracy obtained when the model is tested on unseed data. The aim of the optimization process, in this chapter, is to

Fig. 9.1 Illustration of the procedure of creating an optimized rough set model that uses simulated annealing

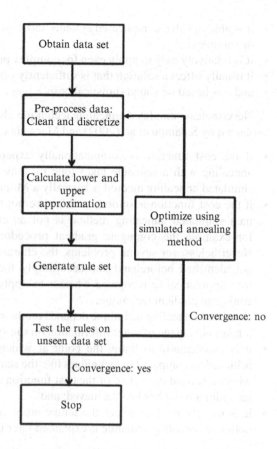

identify the rough set partition, *RP*, parameters so that the accuracy *y* is maximized. To conduct this talk, optimization methods are used and these are the subject of the next section.

9.3 Optimization Methods

9.3.1 Simulated Annealing

Simulated annealing is an optimization technique that is inspired by the natural annealing process where objects such as metals re-crystalize when cooled down according to some cooling schedule. It is basically a Monte Carlo procedure that is used to identify an optimal solution. Simulated annealing procedure has the following advantages as it was outlined by van Laarhoven and Aarts (1997) as well as Marwala (2010):

- it can statistically assures that a global optimum solution is attained despite the fact this may be after a large number of iterations;

- it is able to solve complicated systems and cost functions with arbitrary number of variables;
- it is relatively easy to apply even for complex problems;
- it usually offers a solution that is sufficiently optimal to be of practical use, and
- and it is based on sound statistical basis.

Nevertheless, simulated annealing technique also has the following drawback as explained by Salamon et al. (2002) and Marwala (2010):

- if the cost function is computationally expensive to estimate, the simulated annealing with a schedule takes time to converge. This is principally because simulated annealing method is basically a Monte Carlo simulation procedure;
- if the cost function is smooth or there are not too many local minimum points, then simulated annealing method is not as efficient as are other approaches for example the conjugate gradient procedure (Nocedal and Wright 2000). Nevertheless, for several problems, the characteristics of the cost function are not identified beforehand and accordingly for a particular class of problems it is impractical to recognize whether to apply the simulated annealing or the conjugate gradient technique;
- simulated annealing technique depends on the nature of the problem at hand and it takes advantage of other information on the system;
- it is problematic to know the point at which the optimal solution has been achieved as compared to techniques like the scaled conjugate gradient technique, where a second derivative of the cost function can be applied to decide whether an optimal point has been achieved; and
- it is usually hard to select the temperature cooling schedule technique. This notion of a cooling schedule is explained later in this chapter.

As explained before, simulated annealing method is a Monte Carlo method that is applied to find an optimal point in an optimization process. It was motivated by the procedure of annealing where entities, for example metals, recrystallize or liquids freeze. Naderi et al. (2009) presented an enhanced simulated technique for scheduling flow-shops that optimized the total completion time and the full tardiness. A method based on simulated annealing method was effectively created to achieve a compromise between intensification and diversification processes. A Taguchi method was applied to find the optimum factors using the least n number of experiments. Other illustrations of successful use of simulated anealing technique follow.

Wei-Zhong and Xi-Gang (2009) implemented simulated annealing technique for optimizing the identifying the heat-integrated distillation sequences. An encoding technique that applied an integer number series was established to substitute for and effect the flow sheet configuration of the system. This technique modeled the problem as an implied, mixed-integer, nonlinear programming problem. Simulated annealing technique was observed to be suitable for an implied, mixed-integer, nonlinear programming because when it was applied it enhanced the procedure of solving the problem.

Kannan and Zacharias (2009) successfully applied simulated annealing method to improve and optimize peptide and protein structures. Simulated annealing method was established to be significantly more efficient in attaining low energy configurations and configurations similar to the experiment when compared to continuous simulations.

Paya-Zaforteza et al. (2009) applied simulated annealing method for optimizing the design of reinforced concrete frames. In designing the reinforced concrete frames, two objective functions: the embedded carbon dioxide emissions and the economic cost were created and then optimized. The results attained from this study demonstrated that the embedded emissions and the cost were closely connected and that more environmentally compliant solutions than the lowest cost solution were obtained at a cost increment, which was practically suitable.

Cretu and Pop (2009) designed an optimized acoustic structures using simulated annealing method. This task extended the matrix technique formalism through using an auxiliary computational method based on simulated annealing method to minimize the objective function that was introduced.

Dafflon et al. (2009) successfully implemented simulated annealing method for classification of heterogeneous aquifers. A novel simulated annealing technique was introduced for the integration of high-resolution geophysical and hydrological data. This technique was successfully tested on a synthetic data set and then on data gathered at the Boise hydro-geophysical research site.

Pedamallu and Ozdamar (2008) studied a hybrid simulated annealing method and local search procedure for constrained optimization method. A hybrid simulated annealing technique with features that account for both feasibility and optimality characteristics was supplemented by a local search method. Numerical experiments demonstrated good results.

Briant et al. (2009) hybridized the greedy optimization method with multi-criteria simulated annealing method for sequencing cars. They presented a technique, which applied three criteria in decreasing order of importance and optimized each based on a criterion without permitting worsening of the objective function from an earlier optimized criterion.

Cosola et al. (2008) presented a universal structure for the identification of hyper-elastic membranes with Moire approaches and multi-point simulated annealing technique. This method was applied to mechanically characterize hyper-elastic materials. The characterization method was generalized. A multi-level and multi-point simulated annealing method that reserved the memory of all best records produced in the optimization procedure was applied to identify the unknown material properties.

Lamberti (2008) developed an efficient simulated annealing algorithm method for design optimization of truss structures. Results from numerical simulation confirmed the efficiency and robustness of the suggested technique. The technique performed well and converged rapidly to the optimum solution.

Weizhong et al. (2008) used simulated annealing method for optimal synthesis of distillation. A novel coding technique that used an integer number series was improved to signify and influence the structure of the system. Furthermore, a step-by-step technique was used for column design and cost calculation.

The synthesis problem was formulated using a mixed-integer, nonlinear programming configuration and was successfully solved using an improved simulated annealing scheme.

Sonmez (2007) implemented simulated annealing method for shape optimization of 2-dimensional structures. The results established that this method confirmed high reliability even for cases where the whole free boundary was permitted to change. Liu et al. (2007) successfully implemented a multi-path simulated annealing method to solve protein secondary structure elements. A multi-path simulated annealing technique was implemented for globally aligning the center and orientation of a particle concurrently.

He and Hwang (2006) effectively applied damage detection through an adaptive real-parameter mixture of simulated annealing and genetic algorithm while Ogura and Sato (2006) applied an automatic 3-dimensional reconstruction method using simulated annealing technique for projecting protein projections.

Crossingham et al. (2008) presented an approach to optimize rough set partition sizes using simulated annealing. The results obtained from this granulization method were compared to static granulization methods, namely, equal-width-bin and equal-frequency-bin partitioning. The results showed that the proposed optimized methods produced higher forecasting accuracies than that of the two static methods. The rules generated from the rough set were linguistic and easy-to-interpret, but this came at the expense of the accuracy lost in the discretization process where the granularity of the variables is decreased.

Xu and Qu (2011) presented a study of an evolutionary multi-objective simulated annealing (EMOSA) procedure with adjustable neighborhoods and applied this to the multi-objective multicast routing problems in telecommunications. The hybrid procedure was intended to ensure a more adaptable search in the complex space by means of features of the variable neighborhood search to discover more non-dominated results in the Pareto front. Neighborhood systems were designed to move the exploration in the direction of optimizing all objective functions at the same time. Many simulations were performed on benchmark examples and random networks with practical features. The results showed that the EMOSA procedure identifies good non-dominated answers for the problems examined. The neighborhood systems that are designed for each objective meaningfully enhanced the effectiveness of the proposed procedure when compared with alternative procedure with a single neighborhood.

Seyed-Alagheband et al. (2011) applied simulated annealing procedure for balancing the assembly line type II problem by identifying the minimum cycle time for a specified work stations. A mathematical model based on simulated annealing procedure was improved by using the Taguchi technique to identify parameters of the procedure and thus improving the standard simulated annealing procedure. The results demonstrated improved effectiveness of simulated annealing in terms of convergence rate.

Raymond et al. (2011) successfully applied simulated annealing procedure with weighted Lagrangian multipliers for overlaying small molecules. The suggested technique entailed a simple atom-based, flexible alignment. The advantage of the proposed technique is that nonlinear constraints can be easily enacted on the structural alignment simply by means of the objective function without imposing an a priori trade-off between opposing conditions.

Zhang and Wu (2011) applied simulated annealing procedure, which uses neighborhood features, based on block properties for the job shop scheduling problem with the objective of minimizing total weighted tardiness. The results demonstrated that the neighborhood significantly stimulates the search ability of the proposed method and facilitates the converge properties.

Abbasi et al. (2011) introduced a hybrid variable neighborhood search and simulated annealing algorithm to approximate the parameters of the Weibull distribution which is important modeling failure distribution. The effectiveness of the suggested procedure as measured through accuracy and computational efficiency were assessed and compared to the existing technique. The results demonstrated that the suggested technique offers accurate approximations and is computationally efficient.

Ying et al. (2011) applied simulated annealing technique for the cell formation problem in manufacturing, which is a combinatorial problem. The results demonstrated that the suggested method outperformed current state-of-the-art procedures by either surpassing or matching the best known solutions in the majority of the test problems.

Moita et al. (2006) applied simulated annealing method in the optimal design of vibration control of an adaptive laminated plate, whereas Chang (2006) applied simulated annealing method for demand side management by optimizing the chiller loading. Chang et al. (2006) applied simulated method for energy saving whereas Gomes and Oliveira (2006) applied this technique for optimal packing problems by combining simulated annealing and linear programming. Bisetty et al. (2006) applied simulated annealing to study pentacyclo-undecane cage amino acid tripeptides while McGookin and Murray-Smith (2006) applied this method in optimizing submarine maneuvering controllers. Qi (2010) applied simulated annealing method in facility layout design while Almaraashi and John (2010) applied the technique to tuning fuzzy to predict time series with added noise whereas applied the technique whereas Liu et al. (2010) applied simulated annealing in production sequencing of mixed-model assembly lines as well as Chunyu and Xiaobo (2010) who applied the technique in multi-cargo loading problem.

Because of these successful applications of simulated annealing, it is applied in this chapter for modeling interstate disputes. As indicated before, simulated annealing is inspired by the physical annealing process. In the annealing process, the object such as metal is heated until it is molten and then its temperature is slowly decreased such that the metal, at any given time, is approximately in thermodynamic equilibrium. As the temperature of the object is lowered, the system becomes more ordered and approaches a *frozen* state at $T = 0$. If the cooling process is conducted ineffectively or the initial temperature of the object is not adequately high, the system may become quenched, forming defects or freezing out in meta-stable states. This shows that the system is stuck in a local minimum energy state.

The process that is followed to simulate the annealing process was proposed by Metropolis et al. (1953) and it includes selecting an initial state (using the objective function described Eq. 9.1) and temperature, and holding temperature constant, changing the initial configuration and computing the error at the new state. If the new error is lower than the old error then the new state is accepted, otherwise if the opposite is the case, then this state is accepted with a low probability. This is fundamentally a Monte Carlo method.

Simulated annealing technique substitutes a current solution with a "nearby" random solution with a probability that depends on the difference between the corresponding objective function values and the temperature. The temperature reduces throughout the process, so as temperature starts approaching zero, there is less random changes in the solution. As it is the case in greedy search approaches, simulated annealing technique keeps converging to the best solution, except that it has the advantage of reversal in fitness. That means it can move to a solution with worse fitness than it has currently achieved, but the advantage of that is that it ensures that the solution is not a local optimum solution, but a global optimum. This is a significant advantage that simulated annealing method has over other approaches but, once again, its disadvantage is its potentially high computational time. Simulated annealing identifies the global optimum if specified, but it can take an infinite amount of time to attain this. The probability of accepting the reversal is given by Boltzmann's equation (Bryan et al. 2006):

$$P(\Delta E) = \frac{1}{Z} \exp\left(-\frac{\Delta E}{T}\right) \tag{9.2}$$

Here ΔE is the difference in error (as indicated in the objective function described in Eq. 9.1) between the old and new states. The state indicates the possible discretized partitions. T is the temperature of the system; Z is a normalization factor that ensures that when the probability function is integrated to infinity it becomes 1.

The rate at which the temperature reduces depends on the cooling schedule chosen. There are many different temperature schedules. Some of the schedules are described in this chapter. On implementing simulated annealing, the first thing to do is to choose its parameters.

9.3.1.1 Simulated Annealing Parameters

On applying simulated annealing method to rough set variable partition problem, several parameters and choices need to be stated and these are (Marwala 2010):

- the state space, which is defined in this chapter as a choice of a set of descretized partitions that improve the rough set prediction accuracy;

- the objective function described in Eq. 9.1. It should be noted that there are many ways in which this objective function could have been constructed;
- the candidate generator mechanism which is a random number generator that ensures that a set of rough partitions is selected.
- the acceptance probability function, which is a procedure through which a rough set partition is accepted or rejected; and
- the annealing temperature schedule.

The selection of these parameters has extensive implications on the efficiency of the simulated annealing technique as far as identifying an optimal solution is concerned. Nevertheless, there is no optimal method that can be applied for selecting these parameters that is best for all problems and there is no methodical process for optimally selecting these parameters for a given problem such as the rough set partition problem. Accordingly, the choice of these parameters is subjective and a technique of trial and error is extensively applied.

9.3.1.2 Transition Probabilities

When simulated annealing method is applied, a random walk process is embarked upon for a given temperature. This random walk procedure involves moving from one temperature to another. The transition probability is the probability of moving from one state to another. In this chapter, a state represents a given rough set partition. This probability is dependent on the current temperature, the order of generating the candidate moves, and the acceptance probability function. In this chapter, a Markov Chain Monte Carlo (MCMC) technique is used to make a transition from one state to another. The MCMC produces a chain of possible rough set partition and accepts or rejects them using the Metropolis algorithm (Meer 2007).

9.3.1.3 Monte Carlo Method

The Monte Carlo technique is a computational scheme that applies recurrent random sampling to compute a result (Mathe and Novak 2007; Akhmatskaya et al. 2009; Ratick and Schwarz 2009; Marwala 2010). Monte Carlo approaches have been applied for simulating systems. For instance, Lai (2009) applied the Monte Carlo technique for solving matrix and integral problems while McClarren and Urbatsch (2009) used a altered Monte Carlo technique for modeling time-dependent radiative transfer with adaptive material coupling.

Other modern applications of the Monte Carlo technique include its usage in particle coagulation (Zhao and Zheng 2009), in diffusion problems (Liu et al. 2009), for the design of radiation detectors (Dunn and Shultis 2009), for modeling bacterial activities (Oliveira et al. 2009), for vehicle detection (Jia and Zhang 2009), for modeling the bystander effect (Xia et al. 2009), and for modeling nitrogen absorption (Rahmati and Modarress 2009).

The Monte Carlo technique's confidence on recurring computation and random or pseudo-random numbers requires the use of computers. The Monte Carlo method is typically used when it is impossible or unfeasible to estimate an exact solution using a deterministic procedure.

9.3.1.4   Markov Chain Monte Carlo (MCMC)

A Markov Chain Monte Carlo (MCMC) technique is a procedure of simulating a chain of states through a process known as *random walk*. It entails of a Markov procedure and a Monte Carlo simulation (Liesenfeld and Richard 2008). Jing and Vadakkepat (2009) applied a Markov Chain Monte Carlo process for tracking of maneuvering objects while Gallagher et al. (2009) used the Markov Chain Monte Carlo process to obtain optimal models, model resolution and model choice for earth science problems and Curran (2008) implemented MCMC in DNA profiling. Other successful applications of the Markov Chain Monte Carlo method include its application in environmental modeling (Gaucherel et al. 2008), in medical imaging (Jun et al. 2008), in lake water quality modeling (Malve et al. 2007), in economics (Jacquier et al. 2007) and in statistics (Lombardi 2007).

Here a system is now considered whose evolution is described by a stochastic process consisting of random variables $\{x_1, x_2, x_3, \ldots, x_i\}$. A random variable x_l occupies a state x at discrete time i. The list of all possible states that all random variables can possibly occupy is called a state space. If the probability that the system is in state x_{i+1} at time $i + 1$ depends completely on the fact that it was in state x_i at time i, then the random variables $\{x_1, x_2, x_3, \ldots, x_i\}$ form a Markov chain. In the Markov Chain Monte Carlo, the transition between states is achieved by adding a random noise (ε) to the current state as follows:

$$x_{i+1} = x_i + \varepsilon \tag{9.3}$$

9.3.1.5   Acceptance Probability Function: Metropolis Algorithm

When the current state has been attained, it is either accepted or rejected. In this chapter the acceptance of a state is reached by using the Metropolis algorithm (Bedard 2008; Meyer et al. 2008). This algorithm which was proposed by Metropolis et al. (1953) has been applied widely to solve problems of statistical mechanics. Bazavov et al. (2009) successfully used biased Metropolis algorithms for protein simulation. Other applications of the Metropolis algorithms are in nuclear power plants (Sacco et al. 2008), in protein chains simulation (Tiana et al. 2007), and for the prediction of free Co-Pt nano-clusters (Moskovkin and Hou 2007).

In the Metropolis procedure, when sampling a stochastic process $[\{x_1\}, \{x_2\}, \ldots, \{x_i\}]$ which consists of random variables, random changes to a vector $\{x\}$ are introduced and the resulting vector is either accepted or rejected according to the following criterion:

$$if\ E_{new} < E_{old}\ accept\ state\ (s_{new})$$

$$else$$

$$accept\ (s_{new})\ with\ probability$$

$$\exp\{-(E_{new} - E_{old})\} \tag{9.4}$$

9.3.1.6 Cooling Schedule

The process of cooling scheduling is the method through which the temperature T should be decreased during simulated annealing simulation (De Vicente et al. 2003; Marwala 2010). Teachings from the physical simulated annealing process prescribe that the cooling rate should be adequately low for the probability distribution of the current state to be approximately equal to the thermodynamic equilibrium at all times during the simulation (Das and Chakrabarti 2005). The time it takes during the simulation for the equilibrium to be reinstated, which is also known as the *relaxation time,* after a change in temperature is contingent on the shape of the cost function (Eq. 9.1), the current temperature and on the candidate generator. The best cooling rate is experimentally obtained for each problem. The category of simulated annealing method which is called *thermodynamic simulated annealing* endeavors to evade this problem by removing the cooling schedule and altering the temperature at each step in the simulation, based on the difference in energy between the two states, according to the laws of thermodynamics (Weinberger 1990). The application of simulated annealing method is illustrated in Fig. 9.1 (Marwala 2010). The following cooling model is used (Salazar and Toral 2006; Marwala 2010):

$$T(i) = \frac{T(i-1)}{1+\sigma} \tag{9.5}$$

Here $T(i)$ is the current temperature; $T(i-1)$ is the previous temperature and σ is the cooling rate. It must be factored into account that the precision of the numbers utilized in the implementation of simulated annealing method can have a significant effect on the outcome. A technique to improve the computational time of simulated annealing is to apply either very fast simulated re-annealing method or adaptive simulated annealing technique (Salazar and Toral 2006).

This process is iterated such that the sampling size for the current temperature is satisfactory. Then the temperature is reduced, and the process is iterated till a frozen state is attained where $T = 0$. Simulated annealing method was initially used in optimization problems by Kirkpatrick et al. (1983). In this chapter, the current state is the current discretization bins, the energy equation is the objective function in Eq. 9.1, and the ground state is the global optimum solution (Fig. 9.2).

Fig. 9.2 The diagram for
simulated annealing
(Marwala 2010)

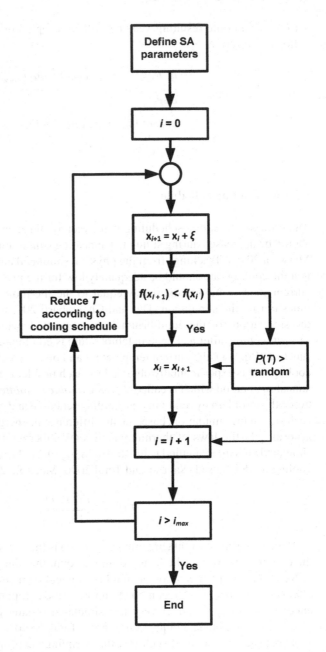

The simulated annealing procedure proposed in this chapter is compared to the
particle swarm optimization technique which was described in detail in Chap. 8.
The next section, therefore, gives a brief overview of particle swarm optimization
method.

9.3.2   Particle Swarm Optimization

As described in Chap. 8, particle swarm optimization (PSO) method is a stochastic, population-based technique for solving optimization problems. The PSO technique was invented by Kennedy and Eberhart in the mid 1990s and it is inspired by the simulation of the swarm of birds which is part of a sociocognitive study investigating the knowledge of "collective intelligence" in biological populations (Kennedy and Eberhart 1995). As mentioned in Chap. 8, PSO is based on the analogy of flocks of birds, schools of fish, and herds of animals and how they maintain an "evolutionary advantage" by either adapting to their environment, avoiding predators or finding rich sources of food, all by the process of "information sharing" (Kennedy and Eberhart 2001). PSO is implemented in this chapter as it was done in Chap. 8.

PSO has been successful and some of these successes are by Anghinolfi et al. (2011) who applied particle swarm optimization approach for the sequential ordering, which is a kind of a traveling salesman problem where precedence constraints on vertices are enforced. The technique was found to be effective in controlling a sophisticated local search in the direction of high quality regions of the search space. Other successful applications are in problems such as for system identification and control (Alfi and Modares 2011), for maximizing production rate and workload smoothing in assembly lines (Nearchou 2011) and for face recognition (Raghavendra et al. 2011).

9.4   Particle Swarm Optimization Versus Simulated Annealing

Table 9.1 shows the difference between simulated annealing and particle swarm optimization. The main difference between the two is that particle swarm optimization is an evolutionary, population-based method while simulated annealing is a statistically based optimization technique inspired by the annealing process. It is clear from Table 9.1 that simulated annealing has relatively fewer parameters to adjust and choose than the particle swarm optimization method (Marwala 2010).

Yang and Kang (2010) compared genetic algorithm, simulated annealing algorithm and particle swarm optimization Algorithm for parameter calibration of

Table 9.1 Operations, types and parameters in the implementation of SA and PSO

Operation	Parameters to select SA	Parameters to select PSO
Representation	Floating point	Floating point
Initialization	Temperature schedule, initial state	Population size, distribution of the random seed
Operations	Random walk, acceptance of samples	Mutation, crossover and reproduction type and probability

Muskingum model to solve the problem of linearization, complexity and poor accuracy. The results demonstrated that the three methods are better than traditional optimization methods.

Wang and Zeng (2010) compared genetic algorithm, ant colony optimization algorithm, particle swarm optimization algorithm and simulated annealing algorithm for task scheduling problem in computational grid. The comparison criteria included the schedule time, the make-span and the mean response time. The results demonstrated that particle swarm optimization performed better than the other methods.

Singh et al. (2010) applied biogeography based optimization method, genetic algorithm, particle swarm optimization, and simulated annealing for design of Yagi-Uda antenna and the results demonstrate similar performance.

The results obtained on comparing optimization methods demonstrate strong dependency on the problem at hand, choices made on implementation, nature of the computer code and level of understanding of the user of the method that is under consideration.

9.5 Interstate Conflict

In this chapter rough sets were implemented with militarized interstate dispute (MID) data that were discretized using two optimization techniques and these were particle swarm optimization and simulated annealing. The MID has 7 inputs and each one was discretized into for bins meaning that there were 28 variables to be optimized as in Eq. 9.1. The population size of the PSO implementation which was chosen was 100 and the algorithm was run for 50 generations and simulated annealing was run for 1,000 iterations. The results of these implementations on the MID data are shown in Table 9.2.

The results obtained in demonstrate that detection rate of conflict was 75.3% when simulated annealing was used and 74.7% when particle swarm optimization was used. The detection rate for peace was 74.0% when simulated annealing was used and 74.3% when particle swarm optimization was used. Overall the detection rate of a correct outcome was 74.7% when simulated annealing was used and 74.5% when particle swarm optimization was used. Furthermore, the areas under the receiver operating characteristics curves when the PSO and simulated annealing

Table 9.2 Classification results

Method	True conflicts TC	False peaces FP	True peaces TP	False conflicts FC
Rough sets: particle swarm optimization	218	74	217	75
Rough sets: simulated anealing	220	72	216	76

were used were both 0.79. These results demonstrate that simulated annealing is marginally better than particle swarm optimization on dealing with the data used in this book.

9.6 Conclusion

The work performed in this chapter is concerned with using various optimization techniques to granulize the rough set input partitions to achieve the highest forecasting accuracy produced by the rough set and apply this to interstate conflict. The two optimization techniques used are PSO and simulated annealing. The results indicate that simulated annealing gives marginally better results than the PSO.

9.7 Further Work

The rough set model was implemented for modeling interstate conflict and standard PSO and simulated annealing were used to optimize the rough set partition. For the future work more robust variants of PSO and simulated annealing should be applied.

References

Abbasi B, Niaki STA, Khalife MA, Faize Y (2011) A hybrid variable neighborhood search and simulated annealing algorithm to estimate the three parameters of the Weibull distribution. Expert Syst Appl 38:700–708

Akhmatskaya E, Bou-Rabee N, Reich S (2009) A comparison of generalized hybrid Monte Carlo methods with and without momentum flip. J Comput Phys 228:2256–2265

Alfi A, Modares H (2011) System identification and control using adaptive particle swarm optimization. Appl Math Model 35:1210–1221

Almaraashi M, John R (2010) Tuning fuzzy systems by simulated annealing to predict time series with added noise. UK. Workshop on Computer Intelligence, pp 1–5

Anghinolfi D, Montemanni R, Paolucci M, Maria Gambardella L (2011) A hybrid particle swarm optimization approach for the sequential ordering problem. Comput Oper Res 38:1076–1085

Bazavov A, Berg BA, Zhou H (2009) Application of biased metropolis algorithms: from protons to proteins. Math Comput Simul. doi:10.1016/j.matcom.2009.05.005

Bedard M (2008) Optimal acceptance rates for metropolis algorithms: moving beyond 0.234. Stoch Proc Appl 118:2198–2222

Bisetty K, Corcho FJ, Canto J, Kruger HG, Perez JJ (2006) Simulated annealing study of the pentacyclo-undecane cage amino acid tripeptides of the type [Ac-X-Y-Z-NHMe]. J Mol Struct THEOCHEM 759:145–157

Briant O, Naddef D, Mounie G (2009) Greedy approach and multi-criteria simulated annealing for the car sequencing problem. Eur J Oper Res 191:993–1003

Bryan K, Cunningham P, Bolshkova N (2006) Application of simulated annealing to the biclustering of gene expression data. IEEE Trans Inf Technol Biomed 10:10519–10525

Chang Y (2006) An innovative approach for demand side management - optimal chiller loading by simulated annealing. Energy 31:1883–1896

Chang Y, Chen W, Lee C, Huang C (2006) Simulated annealing based optimal chiller loading for saving energy. Energy Convers Manage 47:2044–2058

Chunyu R, Xiaobo W (2010) Study on hybrid genetic simulated annealing algorithm for multi-cargo loading problem. In: Proceedings of the International Conference on Computer, Mechatronics, Control and Electronic Engineering, pp 346–349, Changchun, China (2010)

Cosola E, Genovese K, Lamberti L, Pappalettere C (2008) A general framework for identification of hyper-elastic membranes with moire tand multi-point simulated annealing. Intl J Solids Struct 45:6074–6099

Cretu N, Pop M (2009) Acoustic behavior design with simulated annealing. Comput Mater Sci 44:1312–1318

Crossingham B, Marwala T, Lagazio M (2008) Optimised rough sets for modelling interstate conflict. In: Proceedings of the IEEE International Conference on Systems, Man and Cybernatics, pp 1198–1204, Singapore

Curran JM (2008) A MCMC method for resolving two person mixtures. Sci Justice 48:168–177

Dafflon B, Irving J, Holliger K (2009) Simulated-annealing-based conditional simulation for the local-scale characterization of heterogeneous aquifers. J Appl Geophys 68:60–70

Das, A., Chakrabarti, B.K.: Quantum annealing and related optimization methods. Lecture Notes in Physics, vol. 679, Springer, Heidelberg (2005)

De Vicente J, Lanchares J, Hermida R (2003) Placement by thermodynamic simulated annealing. Phys Lett A 317:415–423

Dunn WL, Shultis JK (2009) Monte Carlo methods for design and analysis of radiation detectors. Radiat Phys Chem 78:852–858

Gallagher K, Charvin K, Nielsen S, Sambridge M, Stephenson J (2009) Markov chain Monte Carlo (MCMC) sampling methods to determine optimal models, model resolution and model choice for earth science problems. Mar Pet Geol 26:525–535

Gaucherel C, Campillo F, Misson L, Guiot J, Boreux JJ (2008) Parameterization of a process-based tree-growth model: comparison of optimization. MCMC and particle filtering algorithms. Environ Modell Softw 23:1280–1288

Gomes AM, Oliveira JF (2006) Solving irregular strip packing problems by hybridising simulated annealing and linear programming. Eur J Oper Res 171:811–829

He R, Hwang S (2006) Damage detection by an adaptive real-parameter simulated annealing genetic algorithm. Comput Struct 84:2231–2243

Jacquier E, Johannes M, Polson N (2007) MCMC maximum likelihood for latent state models. J Econ 137:615–640

Jia Y, Zhang C (2009) Front-view vehicle detection by Markov chain Monte Carlo method. Pattern Recognit 42:313–321

Jing L, Vadakkepat P (2009) Interacting MCMC particle filter for tracking maneuvering target. Digit Signal Process. doi:10.1016/j.dsp. 2009.08.011

Jun SC, George JS, Kim W, Pare-Blagoev J, Plis S, Ranken DM, Schmidt DM (2008) Bayesian brain source imaging based on combined MEG/EEG and fMRI using MCMC. Neuroimage 40:1581–1594

Kannan S, Zacharias M (2009) Simulated annealing coupled replica exchange molecular dynamics - an efficient conformational sampling method. J Struct Biol 166:288–294

Kennedy J, Eberhart RC (1995) Particle swarm optimization. In: Proceedings of the IEEE International Conference on Neural Networks, pp 1942–1948, Piscataway

Kennedy J, Eberhart RC (2001) Swarm Intelligence. Morgan Kaufmann, San Francisco

Kirkpatrick S, Gelatt CD, Vecchi MP (1983) Optimization by simulated annealing. Sci, New Series 220:671–680

Lai Y (2009) Adaptive Monte Carlo methods for matrix equations with applications. J Comput Appl Math 231:705–714

Lamberti L (2008) An efficient simulated annealing algorithm for design optimization of truss structures. Comput and Struct 86:1936–1953

Liesenfeld R, Richard J (2008) Improving MCMC, using efficient importance sampling. Comput Stat Data Anal 53:272–288

Liu X, Jiang W, Jakana J, Chiu W (2007) Averaging tens to hundreds of icosahedral particle images to resolve protein secondary structure elements using a multi-path simulated annealing optimization algorithm. J Struct Biol 160:11–27

Liu X, Newsome D, Coppens M (2009) Dynamic Monte Carlo simulations of binary self-diffusion in ZSM-5. Microporous Mesoporous Mater 125:149–159

Liu Z, Wang C, Sun T (2010) Production sequencing of mixed-model assembly lines based on simulated annealing algorithm. Proc of the Intl Conf of Logistics Eng and Manage 387: 1803–1808

Lombardi MJ (2007) Bayesian inference for [Alpha]-stable distributions: a random walk MCMC approach. Comput Stat and Data Anal 51:2688–2700

Malve O, Laine M, Haario H, Kirkkala T, Sarvala J (2007) Bayesian modelling of algal mass occurrences - using adaptive MCMC methods with a lake water quality model. Environ Modell Softw 22:966–977

Marwala T (2010) Finite Element Model Updating Using Computational Intelligence Techniques. Springer, London

Mathe P, Novak E (2007) Simple Monte Carlo and the metropolis algorithm. J Complex 23: 673–696

McClarren RG, Urbatsch TJ (2009) A Modified implicit Monte Carlo method for time-dependent radiative transfer with adaptive material Coupling. J Comput Phys 228:5669–5686

McGookin EW, Murray-Smith DJ (2006) Submarine manoeuvring controllers' optimisation using simulated annealing and genetic algorithms. Control Eng Pract 14:01–15

Meer K (2007) Simulated annealing versus metropolis for a TSP instance. Inf Process Lett 104:216–219

Metropolis N, Rosenbluth A, Rosenbluth M (1953) A. Teller, and E. Teller, equation of state calculations by fast computing machines. J Chem Phys 21:1087–1092

Meyer R, Cai B, Perron F (2008) Adaptive rejection metropolis sampling using Lagrange interpolation polynomials of degree 2. Comput Stat Data Anal 52:3408–3423

Moita JMS, Correia VMF, Martins PG, Soares CMM, Soares CAM (2006) Optimal design in vibration control of adaptive structures using a simulated annealing algorithm. Compos Struct 75:79–87

Moskovkin P, Hou M (2007) Metropolis Monte Carlo predictions of free Co-Pt nanoclusters. J Alloys Compd 434–435:550–554

Naderi B, Zandieh M, Khaleghi A, Balagh G, Roshanaei V (2009) An improved simulated annealing for hybrid flowshops with sequence-dependent setup and transportation times to minimize total completion time and total tardiness. Expert Syst Appl 36:9625–9633

Nearchou AC (2011) Maximizing production rate and workload smoothing in assembly lines using particle swarm optimization. Int J Prod Econ 129:242–250

Nocedal J, Wright S (2000) Numerical Optimization. Springer, Heidelberg

Ogura T, Sato C (2006) A fully automatic 3D reconstruction method using simulated annealing enables accurate posterioric angular assignment of protein projections. J Struct Biol 156: 371–386

Oliveira RG, Schneck E, Quinn BE, Konovalov OV, Brandenburg K, Seydel U, Gill T, Hanna CB, Pink DA, Tanaka M (2009) Physical mechanisms of bacterial survival revealed by combined grazing-incidence X-ray scattering and Monte Carlo simulation. C R Chim 12:209–217

Pawlak Z (1991) Rough Sets, Theoretical Aspects of Reasoning about Data. Kluwer Academic Publishers, Dordrecht

Paya-Zaforteza I, Yepes V, Hospitaler A, Gonzalez-Vidosa F (2009) CO2-Optimization of reinforced concrete frames by simulated annealing. Eng Struct 31:1501–1508

Pedamallu CS, Ozdamar L (2008) Investigating a hybrid simulated annealing and local search algorithm for constrained optimization. Eur J Oper Res 185:1230–1245

Qi J-Y (2010) Application of improved simulated annealing algorithm in facility layout design. In: Proceedings of the 29th Chinese Control Conference, pp 5224–5227, Beijing

Raghavendra R, Dorizzi B, Rao A, Hemantha Kumar G (2011) Particle swarm optimization based fusion of near infrared and visible images for improved face verification. Pattern Recog 44: 401–411

Rahmati M, Modarress H (2009) Nitrogen adsorption on nanoporous zeolites studied by grand canonical Monte Carlo simulation. J Mol Struct THEOCHEM 901:110–116

Ratick S, Schwarz G (2009) Monte Carlo simulation. In: Kitchin R, Thrift N (eds) International Encyclopedia of Human Geography. Elsevier, Oxford

Raymond JW, Holsworth DD, Jalaie M (2011) The flexible alignment of molecular structures using simulated annealing with weighted lagrangian multipliers. J Comput Chem 32:210–217

Sacco WF, Lapa CMF, Pereira CMNA, Filho HA (2008) A metropolis algorithm applied to a nuclear power plant auxiliary feedwater system surveillance tests policy optimization. Prog Nucl Energ 50:15–21

Salamon P, Sibani P, Frost R (2002) Facts, Conjectures, and Improvements for Simulated Annealing (SIAM Monographs on Mathematical Modeling and Computation). Society for Industrial and Applied Mathematic Publishers, Philadelphia

Salazar R, Toral R (2006) Simulated annealing using hybrid Monte Carlo. arXiv:cond-mat/9706051

Seyed-Alagheband SA, Ghomi SMTF, Zandieh M (2011) A simulated annealing algorithm for balancing the assembly line type II problem with sequence-dependent setup times between tasks. Intl J Prod Res 49:805–825

Singh U, Kumar H, Kamal TS (2010) Design of Yagi-Uda antenna using biogeography based optimization. IEEE Trans Antennas Propag 58:3375–3379

Sonmez FO (2007) Shape optimization of 2D structures using simulated annealing. Comput Meth Appl Mech Eng 196:3279–3299

Tiano G, Sutto L, Broglia RA (2007) Use of the Metropolis Algorithm to Simulate the Dynamics of Protein Chains. Physica A: Statistical Mech and its Appl 380:241–249

van Laarhoven PJ, Aarts EH (1997) Simulated Annealing: Theory and Applications (Mathematics and Its Applications). Kluwer Academic Publishers, Dordrecht

Wang M, Zeng W (2010) A comparison of four popular heuristics for task scheduling problem in computational grid. In: Proceedings of the 6th International Conference. on Wireless Communication, Networking and Mobile Computing, pp 500–507, Chengdu

Weinberger E (1990) Correlated and uncorrelated fitness landscapes and how to tell the difference. Biol Cybernet 63:325–336

Wei-Zhong A, Xi-Gang Y (2009) A simulated annealing-based approach to the optimal synthesis of heat-integrated distillation sequences. Comput Chem Eng 33:199–212

Weizhong AN, Fengjuan YU, Dong F, Yangdong HU (2008) Simulated annealing approach to the optimal synthesis of distillation column with intermediate heat exchangers. Chin J Chem Eng 16:30–35

Xia J, Liu L, Xue J, Wang Y, Wu L (2009) Modeling of radiation-induced bystander effect using Monte Carlo methods. Nucl Instr Method Phys Res Sect B: Beam Interact Mater Atoms 267:1015–1018

Xu Y, Qu R (2011) Solving multi-objective multicast routing Problems by evolutionary multi-objective simulated annealing algorithms with variable neighbourhoods. J Oper Res Soc 62:313–325

Yang Z, Kang L (2010) Application and comparison of several intelligent algorithms on muskingum routing model. In: Proceedings of the IEEE International Conference on Information and Financial Engineering, pp 910–914, Chongqing

Ying K-C, Lin S-W, Lu C-C (2011) Cell formation using a simulated annealing algorithm with variable neighbourhood. Euro J Ind Eng 5:22–42

Zhang R, Wu C (2011) A simulated annealing algorithm based on block properties for the job shop scheduling problem with total weighted tardiness objective. Comp Oper Res 38:854–867

Zhao H, Zheng C (2009) Correcting the Multi-Monte Carlo method for particle coagulation. Powder Technol 193:120–123

Chapter 10
Genetic Algorithm with Optimized Rough Sets for Modeling Interstate Conflict

10.1 Introduction

Rough set theory, introduced by Pawlak (1991), is a mathematical tool which deals with vagueness and uncertainty. It allows for the approximation of sets that are difficult to describe with the available information. It can describe the data in terms of linguistic variables and has been successfully used to model complicated systems. The first step in rough set modeling Crossingham (2007) is to choose the data to be modeled. The second step is to pre-process the data to ensure that it is ready for analysis. This involves discretizing the data and removing unnecessary data instances. This chapter used a genetic algorithm and simulated annealing to discretize the said data. Then, if reducts are considered, the cleaned data set was used to produce reducts, which are the minimal subsets of attributes that allow the same classification of elements of the universe as the whole set of attributes Crossingham (2007). Thereafter, the rules were extracted. These were normally determined based on condition attributes values. Finally, the newly created rules were tested on a test data set. The results were used as feedback to the optimization methods which, for this chapter, were the genetic algorithm and the simulated annealing techniques.

Xie et al. (2011) successfully applied a rough set method in land use/land cover retrieval from remote sensing imagery, while Chen et al. (2011) used a rough set technique for predicting protein-interaction hot spots. Salamó and López-Sánchez (2011) applied a rough set method for the selection of features in Case-Based Reasoning classifiers while Zou et al. (2011) applied a rough set approach to select distributors in a supply chain management.

In Chap. 6, the levels of transparency of the Takagi-Sugeno neuro-fuzzy model and the support vector machines model were investigated by applying them to conflict management. The conflict management problem was concerned with the causal interpretations of results. The data set used in this investigation was the militarized interstate disputes dataset obtained from the correlates of war project. The support vector machine model was also trained to predict conflict. Knowledge from the Takagi-Sugeno neuro-fuzzy model was extracted by interpreting the

T. Marwala and M. Lagazio, *Militarized Conflict Modeling using Computational Intelligence*, Advanced Information and Knowledge Processing, DOI 10.1007/978-0-85729-790-7_10, © Springer-Verlag London Limited 2011

model's fuzzy rules and their outcomes. It was found that the Takagi-Sugeno neuro-fuzzy model offered some transparency which assisted in understanding conflict management. The Takagi-Sugeno neuro-fuzzy model was compared to the support vector machine method. It was found that even though the support vector machine showed marginal advantage over the Takagi-Sugeno neuro-fuzzy model's predictive capacity, the Takagi-Sugeno neuro-fuzzy model allowed for linguistic interpretation.

In Chap. 7, the rough set technique was applied to model the militarized interstate disputes. One aspect of modeling using rough sets was the issue of granulization of the input data. Two granulization techniques were introduced, implemented and compared: the equal-width-bin and equal-frequency-bin partitioning techniques. The rough set model was also compared to the neuro-fuzzy system introduced in Chap. 6. The results obtained demonstrated that equal-width-bin partitioning gave better accuracy than equal-frequency-bin partitioning. Both these techniques were found to give less accurate results than neuro-rough sets, even though they were found to be more transparent than neuro-fuzzy sets. Furthermore, it was observed that the rules generated from the rough sets were linguistic and easy-to-interpret when compared to the neuro-fuzzy model.

In Chap. 8, methods to optimally granulize rough set partition sizes using particle swarm optimization and hill climbing techniques were presented. The methods were compared to that based on the equal-width-bin technique, which was found to perform better than equal-frequency-bin technique in Chap. 7. The results obtained demonstrated that particle swarm optimization provided better forecasting accuracies, followed by the hill climbing method which was better than the equal-width-bin technique.

In chap. 9, approaches to optimally granulize rough set partition sizes using the simulated annealing technique were presented. The technique was applied to model the militarized interstate disputes data, and then compared to the rough set partitioning technique based on particle swarm optimization, which was found to perform better than the hill climbing optimization technique in Chap. 8. The results proved that simulated annealing provided better forecasting accuracies than the particle swarm optimization method.

In this chapter, a genetic algorithm was applied to granulize rough set partitions. This technique was then compared to the simulated annealing method, which was found to perform better than particle swarm optimization in Chap. 8. The technique presented was then applied to the modeling of militarized interstate dispute data.

10.2   Rough Sets

As indicated before, a rough set is a mathematical tool which deals with vagueness, as well as uncertainty, and it allows for the approximation of sets that are difficult to describe with the available information. A rough set is of fundamental importance to computational intelligence and cognitive science and is highly appropriate to the tasks of machine learning and decision analysis. As with many other computational intelligence techniques, the advantages of rough sets, are that they do not require rigid *a priori* assumptions about the mathematical nature of such complex relationships as do commonly used multivariate statistical techniques Garson (1991). Rough set theory is based on the assumption that the information of interest is associated with some information of its universe of discourse (Komorowski et al. 1999). An important aspect of rough set theory is its indiscernibility relation (indiscernibility means indistinguishable from one another). Rough set theory also handles inconsistent information.

For knowledge acquisition from data with numerical attributes, a special technique – called *discretization* – is applied. Several methods are currently used to perform the task of discretization and these include equal-width-bin partitioning and equal-frequency-bin partitioning, described in Chap. 7 (Jaafar et al. 2006; Grzymala-Busse 2007).

For this chapter, the optimization techniques used were the genetic algorithm and simulated annealing (Marwala 2007a). These optimization techniques were run to create a set of four partitions for the given input data. Using these partitions, the rough set model was generated and the classification accuracy was determined using the Area Under the receiver operating Characteristics (AUC) curve of the model produced against the unseen testing data. This result of the AUC was sent back to the optimizer and the partition sizes were changed accordingly to ensure that the rough set produced a better model, that is, a model with better classification accuracy. The next section describes in detail the optimization methods applied in this chapter.

10.3 Optimization Methods

A genetic algorithm is one technique used to discretize rough set partitions. Simulated annealing is another algorithm that locates a good approximation to the global optimum of a given function. This section presents the two algorithms and the next section compares the the two algorithms.

10.3.1 Genetic Algorithm

As indicated before, a genetic algorithm is one technique used to discretize rough set partitions in this chapter. Unlike many optimization procedures, a genetic algorithm has a higher probability of converging to a global optimal solution than a gradient based technique. A genetic algorithm is a population-based, probabilistic method that operates to identify a solution to a problem from a population of possible solutions (Kubalik and Lazanský 1999). It is used to identify approximate solutions to difficult problems through the application of the principles of evolutionary biology to computer science (Michalewicz 1996; Mitchell 1996; Forrest 1996;

Vose 1999). It is similar to Darwin's theory of evolution, where members of the population compete to survive and reproduce while the weaker ones die out.

Each individual is assigned a fitness value according to how well it meets the objective of solving the problem which, in this chapter, was to identify the optimal rough set partition. New and more evolutionary-fit individual solutions are produced during a cycle of generations, wherein selection and re-combination operations take place, analogous to how gene transfer applies to current individuals. This continues until a termination condition is satisfied, after which the best individual thus far is considered to be the optimal size of the rough set partition.

Genetic algorithms have successfully been applied in optimization problems. Some of these applications include Marwala (2002) who used wavelet data to update finite element models in structures, Akula and Ganguli (2003) who applied finite element model updating, based on genetic algorithms, to the design of helicopter rotor blades. Perera and Ruiz (2008) successfully applied a genetic algorithm in updating a finite element model for damage identification in large-scale structures, while Tu and Lu (2008) enhanced genetic algorithm applications by considering computational boundary conditions, and Franulović et al. (2009) implemented a genetic algorithm for the identification of material model parameters for low-cycle fatigue. Bourouni et al. (2011) applied a genetic algorithm for the design and optimization of desalination reverse-osmosis plants which are driven by renewable energy, while Gladwin et al. (2011) applied a genetic algorithm for the control of an internal combustion engine for a series of hybrid electric vehicles.

Ghosh et al. (2011) proposed a genetic algorithm to determine the optimum stacking pattern for a multi-stream plate-fin heat exchanger. Their procedure identified the stacking pattern, which offered the maximum heat load for a given number of fluid streams with particular quantified properties, the mass flow rate, and the entry temperature. The technique of area splitting and successive partitioning was applied for the estimation of the heat load. Numerous direct and indirect evaluations, including exhaustive searches, were conducted to test the optimality of the stacking pattern through inspecting the pattern of the aggregated heat load and the plate temperature profile on a plane which was normal to the exchanger. The results attained through the proposed procedure showed superb agreement with the criteria.

Marwala (2004) presented a technique based on Bayesian neural networks and genetic algorithms to control a fermentation process. The relationship between the input and output variables was modeled using a Bayesian neural network, trained using a hybrid Monte Carlo method. A feedback loop based on genetic algorithms was used to change input variables so that the output variables were as close to the desired target as possible without the loss of confidence levels of the prediction that the neural network gave. The procedure was found to considerably reduce the distance between the desired target and measured output.

Crossingham and Marwala (2008) proposed a technique to optimize rough set partition sizes, to which rule extraction was performed on HIV data. The genetic algorithm technique for optimization was used to decide the partition sizes of a rough set to maximize the rough sets' prediction accuracy. The technique was tested on a set of six demographic properties of individuals extracted from the South African antenatal survey, with the outcome being either HIV positive or negative. Rough set theory was selected based on the information that it was easy to interpret the extracted rules.

Marwala (2010) implemented a genetic algorithm for finite-element-model updating. This technique was tested on a simple beam and an unsymmetrical H-shaped structure and compared with a technique based on the Nelder–Mead simplex method. It was found, on average, that the genetic algorithm technique offered more accurate results than the Nelder–Mead (NM) simplex method.

Hlalele et al. (2009) presented a technique of imputing missing data that hybridized the principal component analysis, neuro-fuzzy modeling, and genetic algorithms. The capability of the model to impute missing data was tested using a South African HIV sero-prevalence dataset. The results indicated an average increase in accuracy from 60%, when using the neuro-fuzzy model individually, to 99% when the suggested technique was implemented.

Ozcelik and Islier (2011) applied a genetic algorithm for the generalization of unidirectional loop layout problem and its solution in manufacturing systems. This was intended to offer more efficient and effective loop layout designs. The results indicated that the genetic algorithm performed better than conventional approaches.

Patel and Marwala (2009) applied pattern classification approaches for assisting contact centers in determining caller interaction at a 'Say account' field, within an Interactive Voice Response application. Binary and real coded genetic algorithms that used normalized geometric ranking as well as tournament selection functions were used to optimize the multi-layer perceptron neural network architecture. The binary coded genetic procedure which used tournament selection functions produced the most optimal solution. However, this procedure was not the most computationally efficient but did reveal acceptable repeatability. The binary-coded genetic algorithm which used normalized geometric selection functions yielded poor repeatability capabilities. Genetic algorithm methods which employed normalized geometric ranking selection functions were computationally efficient, but produced solutions that were approximately equal. The real coded tournament selection function genetic algorithms produced classifiers that were approximately 3% less accurate than the binary-coded tournament selection function genetic algorithm.

(Marwala et al. 2001) proposed a population of committees of agents who learn by using neural networks and genetic algorithms, and implemented this to simulate the stock market. Each committee of agents bought and sold stocks. Each committee of agents was considered as a player in a game, and was optimized by continually adapting the architecture of the agents using genetic algorithms. This procedure was implemented to simulate trading of three stocks: the Dow Jones, the NASDAQ, and the S&P 500. A linear relationship between the number of players or agents versus the computational time to run the complete simulation was observed. It was also observed that no player had a monopolistic advantage.

Marwala (2007b) applied a technique inspired by the genetic algorithm in training a Bayesian neural network. This technique was tested and compared with classical methods and was observed to give better results.

Vilakazi and Marwala (2006) proposed an extension neural network for detection and diagnosis of faults in high voltage bushing. The experimentation used a dissolved gas-in-oil analysis data from bushings based on IEEEc57.104, IEC599, and used the IEEE production rates method for oil impregnated paper (OIP) bushings. The optimal learning rate for the extension neural network was selected using a genetic algorithm. The classification process was a two stage process. The first stage was the detection stage which identified if the bushing was faulty or normal. The second stage determined the nature of the fault. A classification rate of 100% and an average of 99.89% were obtained for the detection and diagnosis stages respectively. It took 1.98 s and 2.02 s to train the extension neural network for the detection and diagnosis stages respectively.

Mohamed et al. (2008) introduced a technique intended at estimating the missing data in a database using a combination of genetic algorithms and neural networks. Their method used a genetic algorithm to minimize the error function derived from an auto-associative neural-network. They employed multi-layer perceptron and radial basis function networks to create the models. They observed that there was no significant reduction in the accuracy of results as the number of missing cases in a single record increased. They also found that results of using a radial basis function network were superior to those obtained through the multi-layer perceptron network.

Tettey and Marwala (2006) applied a genetic algorithm and a neuro-fuzzy model to control interstate conflict. They showed that a neuro-fuzzy model achieved an accuracy of prediction similar to a Bayesian trained neural network. Their results indicated that a neuro-fuzzy model can be used in a genetic algorithm based control scheme to avoid 100% of the known conflict cases.

Mohamed et al. (2006) applied a genetic algorithm to enhance extension neural networks by including automatic determination of the learning rate. A genetic algorithm allowed the best network that produces the lowest classification error to be obtained. The effectiveness of this new system was proven using the Iris dataset. The system was then applied to the problem of bearing condition monitoring, where the vibration data from bearings were analyzed, diagnosed as faulty or not, and their severity classified. This system was found to be 100% accurate in detecting bearing faults with an accuracy of 95% in diagnosing the severity of the fault.

Boesack et al. (2010) applied genetic algorithms for the fuzzy logic control of large interconnected power systems. The design of fuzzy logic controllers involved a rationalization of the fuzzy inference rules, an appropriate selection of the input and output membership functions from expert knowledge of plant operation and through the appropriate selection of weighting gains.

Palaniappan and Jawahar (2011) applied a genetic algorithm for the simultaneous optimization of lot sizing and scheduling in a flow-line assembly. They applied a genetic algorithm based heuristic to evolve an optimal or near optimal solution for the flow-line assembly problem. They used an integer programming technique was to assess the performance of the presented procedure, and their results showed that the genetic algorithm could give optimal solutions.

Other successful applications include Balamurugan et al. (2008) who evaluated the performance of a two-stage adaptive genetic algorithm, enhanced with island and adaptive features in structural topology optimization while later Kwak and Kim (2009) successfully implemented a hybrid genetic algorithm, enhanced by a direct search for the optimum design of reinforced concrete frames. Canyurt et al. (2008) estimated the strength of a laser hybrid-welded joint using a genetic algorithm approach. Pasandideh et al. (2011) applied genetic algorithms for the vendor managed inventory control system of multi-product multi-constraint economic order quantity model, while Rahmani et al. (2011) used genetic algorithms to model road-traffic noise, and Onieva et al. (2011) applied genetic algorithms for automatic lateral control of unmanned vehicles.

Perera et al. (2009) applied a genetic algorithm to assess the performance of a multi-criteria damage identification system. Almeida and Awruch (2009) used a genetic algorithm and some finite element models for the optimal design of composite laminated structures. The genetic algorithm was adapted with particular operators and variables codified for the definite class of composite laminated structures.

Further notable applications of genetic algorithms for optimization structures include Paluch et al. (2008) as well as Roy and Chakraborty (2009). In addition, a genetic algorithm has also been shown to be very successful in many applications including: finite element analysis (Marwala 2003); selecting optimal neural network architecture (Arifovic and Gençay 2001); training hybrid fuzzy neural networks (Oh and Pedrycz 2006); solving job scheduling problems (Park et al. 2003); remote sensing (Stern et al. 2006); as well as for combinatorial optimization (Zhang and Ishikawa 2004).

Furthermore, the genetic algorithm method has been successful in complex optimization problems such as wire-routing, scheduling, adaptive control, game playing, cognitive modeling, transportation problems, traveling salesman problems, optimal control problems, and database query optimization (Pendharkar and Rodger 1999; Marwala and Chakraverty 2006; Hulley and Marwala 2007). The MATLAB® implementation of a genetic algorithm described in Houck et al. (1995) was used to implement the genetic algorithm for this chapter. To implement a genetic algorithm, the following steps were followed, as Fig. 10.1 shows: initialization, crossover, mutation, selection, reproduction, and termination.

For this chapter, the genetic algorithm viewed learning as a competition amongst a population of evolving candidate problem solutions. A fitness function, in this chapter represented by Eq. 10.4, evaluated each solution to decide whether it would contribute to the next generation of solutions. Through operations that are analogous to transfer of genes in sexual reproduction, the algorithm created a new population

Fig. 10.1 Flow-chart of the
genetic algorithm method

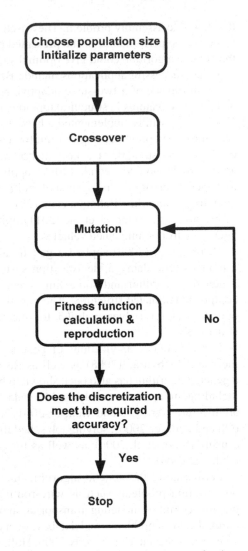

of candidate solutions (Goldberg 1989). The three most important aspects of using
genetic algorithms are:

- of the the definition objective function;
- the implementation of the genetic representation; and
- the implementation of the genetic operators.

The details of genetic algorithms are illustrated in Fig. 10.1.

10.3.1.1   Initialization

In the beginning, a large number of possible individual solutions were randomly
generated to form an initial population. This initial population was sampled so that it

covered a good representation of the rough set input solution space. In the context of this chapter, the size of the population should depend on the nature of the problem, which is determined in turn by the number of variables in the rough set model. For example, if there are two variables in the rough set model, the size of the population must be greater than when there is only one variable to be updated.

10.3.1.2 Crossover

The crossover operation mixed genetic information in the population by cutting pairs of chromosomes at random points along their length and exchanging the cut sections over. This had a potential for joining successful operations together. In this chapter, crossover is an algorithmic operation used to alter the programming from one generation to another of a potential solution to the discretization problem (Gwiazda 2006).

Crossover occurs with a certain probability. In many natural systems, the probability of crossover occurring is higher than the probability of mutation occurring. One example is a simple crossover technique (Banzhaf et al. 1998; Goldberg 1989). For a simple crossover, one crossover point is selected, a binary string from the beginning of a chromosome to the cross-over point is copied from one parent, and the rest is copied from the second parent. For example if two chromosomes in binary space $a = 11,001,011$ and $b = 11,011,111$ undergo a one-point crossover at the midpoint, then the resulting offspring is $c = 11,001,111$. However, for this chapter, arithmetic crossover was used. For the arithmetic crossover, a mathematical operation was performed to produce an offspring. For example an AND operation can be performed on $a = 11,001,011$ and $b = 11,011,111$ to form an offspring $c = 11,001,011$.

10.3.1.3 Mutation

The mutation operation picks a binary digit of the chromosomes at random and inverts it. This has a potential of introducing new information to the population, and thereby prevents the genetic algorithm simulation from being stuck in a local optimum solution. Mutation occurs with a certain probability. In many natural systems, the probability of mutation is low, usually less than 1%. In this chapter, binary mutation was used (Goldberg 1989). When binary mutation was used, a number written in binary form was chosen and one bit value was inverted. For example: the chromosome $a = 11,001,011$ may become the chromosome $b = 11,000,011$.

Furthermore, for this chapter, non-uniform mutation was used. Non-uniform mutation operates by increasing the probability of mutation in such a way that it will be close to 0 as the generation number increases sufficiently. It prevents the population from stagnating in the initial stages of the evolution process, and then permits the algorithm to refine the solution during the end stages of the evolution.

10.3.1.4   Selection

For every generation, a selection of the proportion of the existing population was chosen to breed a new one. This selection was conducted using the fitness-based process where solutions that are fitter, as measured by Eq. 10.4, were given a higher probability of being selected. Some selection methods rank the fitness of each solution and choose the best solutions, while other procedures rank a randomly chosen sample of the population for computational efficiency.

Many selection functions tend to be stochastic in nature and thus are designed in such a way that a selection process is conducted on a small proportion of less fit solutions. This ensures that the diversity of the population of possible solutions is maintained at a high level and therefore avoids convergence on poor and incorrect solutions. There are many selection methods. These include the roulette-wheel selection (Mohamed et al. 2008), which was used for this chapter.

Roulette-wheel selection is a genetic operator used for selecting potentially useful solutions in a genetic algorithm optimization process. In this method, each possible procedure was assigned a fitness function which is used to map the probability of selection with each individual solution. Suppose the fitness f_i was of individual i in the population, then the probability that this individual is selected was:

$$p_i = \frac{f_i}{\sum\limits_{j=1}^{N} f_j} \tag{10.1}$$

where N is the total population size.

This process ensures that candidate solutions with a higher fitness had a lower probability so that they might eliminate those with a lower fitness. By the same token, solutions with a low fitness had a low probability of surviving the selection process. The advantage of this was that even though a solution may have had a low fitness, it might still contain some components which may be useful in the future.

The processes described resulted in the subsequent generation of a population of solutions that was different from the previous generation and that had an average fitness that was higher than that of the previous generation.

10.3.1.5   Termination

The process described was repeated until a termination condition was achieved, either because a desired solution that satisfied the objective function in Eq. 10.4 was found or because a specified number of generations had been reached or the solution's fitness converged (or any combination of these).

Table 10.1 Operations, types and parameters in the implementation of SA and GA

Operation	Parameters to select in SA	Parameters to select in GA
Representation	Floating Point	Binary Space
Initialization	Temperature Schedule, Initial State	Population Size, Distribution of the Random Seed
Operations	Random Walk, Acceptance of samples	Mutation Crossover Reproduction

---

Algorithm 10.1. Procedure for implementing a genetic algorithm

1. Select the initial population.
2. Calculate the fitness of each chromosome in the population using Eq. 10.4:
3. Repeat
(a) Choose chromosomes with a higher fitness to reproduce.
(b) Generate a new population using crossover & mutation to produce offspring.
(c) Calculate the fitness of each offspring.
(d) Replace the low fitness section of the population with the offspring.

4. Until termination condition.

The process described above can be written in pseudo code, as shown in Algorithm 10.1 (Goldberg 1989). For example, for a genetic algorithm representation, a choice had to be made between a binary and a floating point representation. For this chapter, a binary representation was used. Given this choice, a bit size had to be chosen. For this chapter, a 16-bit binary representation was chosen.

For the initialization process, a choice had to be made for the population size.

Table 10.1 illustrates that the difficulty in the implementation of genetic algorithms is that there are many choices to be made and there is no direct methodology on how these choices must be made, so these choices tend to be arbitrary.

10.3.2 Simulated Annealing

Simulated annealing is an algorithm that locates a good approximation to the global optimum of a given function. It originated as a generalization to the Monte Carlo method and relies on the Metropolis algorithm. As is the case with genetic algorithms and hill climbing, simulated annealing continuously updates the solution until a termination criterion is reached. Simulated annealing technique is a well-established stochastic technique originally developed to model the natural process of crystallization and later adopted as an optimization technique. SA is implemented as in Marwala (2010).

10.4   Genetic Algorithm Versus Simulated Annealing

Table 10.1 shows the characteristics of simulated annealing and a genetic algorithm.

The main difference between the two is that a genetic algorithm is an evolutionary, population-based method, inspired by Darwin's theory of evolution while simulated annealing is a statistically based optimization technique inspired by the annealing process.

Wan (2010) compared the efficiency of the simulated annealing technique and a genetic algorithm for the selection of features. The results obtained demonstrated that simulated annealing is more efficient than the genetic algorithm. Jonathan et al. (2010) compared simulated annealing and a genetic algorithm in the design of the topology of a switched reluctance machine. They demonstrated that the simulated annealing algorithm performed better than the genetic algorithm.

Degertekin (2007) compared the simulated annealing and genetic algorithm techniques for the optimum design of nonlinear steel space frames. The simulated annealing performed better than a genetic algorithm, even though it took much longer to converge.

Arostegui Jr. et al. (2006) compared the Tabu search, simulated annealing, and genetic algorithms to solve facility location problems. Their results showed that the Tabu search gave better results than the simulated annealing and genetic algorithms.

Thompson and Bilbro (2000) compared a genetic algorithm with a simulated annealing algorithm for the design of a topology for an ATM network. The results demonstrated similarities even though the genetic algorithm was found to be more computationally efficient than simulated annealing.

Franconi and Jennison (1997) compared a genetic algorithm and simulated annealing in statistical images and observed that simulated annealing performed better than the genetic algorithm.

Crossingham et al. (2008) implemented an evolutionary optimization technique for rough set partition. They compared the results from this granulization method with static granulization methods, namely, equal-width-bin and equal-frequency-bin partitioning. Their results showed that all of the optimized methods presented produced higher forecasting accuracies than that of the two static methods and that the genetic algorithm method produced the best accuracy.

The results achieved in comparing optimization approaches show a strong dependency on the nature of the problem, choices made on application, the nature of the computer code and the level of understanding of the user of the technique under consideration. However, simulated annealing seems to perform better than genetic algorithm even though it is found to be more computationally expensive to implement.

10.5 Interstate Conflict

For this chapter, rough sets were implemented on the militarized interstate dispute data. The data were discretized using two optimization techniques: a genetic algorithm and simulated annealing. The militarized interstate dispute data had 7 inputs. Each was discretized into 4 bins, meaning that there were 28 variables to be optimized.

The population size of the genetic algorithm implementation was chosen to be 100. The algorithm was run for 50 generations, while simulated annealing was run for 1,000 iterations. All these details were chosen arbitrarily. The results of these implementations on the militarized interstate dispute data are shown in Table 10.2.

The results showed that the detection rate of conflict was 75.3% when simulated annealing was used and 76% when the genetic algorithm was used. The detection rate for peace was 74.0% when simulated annealing was used and 75.3% when the genetic algorithm was used. Overall, the detection rate of a correct outcome was 74.7% when the simulated annealing was used and 75.7% when the genetic algorithm was used. Furthermore, the areas under the receiver operating characteristics curves when the genetic algorithm and simulated annealing were used were 0.80 and 0.79, respectively.

These results demonstrate that genetic algorithm is marginally better than simulated annealing in dealing with the data used in this book. These results are consistent with the results obtained from a study conducted by Crossingham et al. (2008).

In comparing the optimized approaches presented in Chaps. 7–10 against each other, there is no substantial difference between the optimization techniques. Nevertheless, the hill climbing accuracy was marginally lower than the other three approaches. This could be ascribed to the fact that the used application for hill climbing permitted the optimum to be found at a local rather than a global solution and the genetic algorithm marginally outperformed simulated annealing, which in turn outperformed particle swarm optimization. It must be taken into account that, depending on the linearity and complexity of the data set, the optimal method to be used to discretize the partitions will differ. The rough sets produce a balance between the transparency of the rough set model and the accuracy of conflict prediction, but this does come at a higher cost of computational effort.

Table 10.2 Classification results

Method	True Conflicts TC	False Peaces FP	True Peace TP	False Conflicts FC
Genetic Algorithm	222	70	220	72
Simulated Annealing	220	72	216	76

10.6 Conclusion

The work performed in this chapter was concerned with using various optimization techniques to granulize the rough set input partitions to achieve the highest forecasting accuracy which was produced by the rough set and to apply this to interstate conflict. The two optimization techniques used were the genetic algorithm and simulated annealing. The results indicate that genetic algorithm gives marginally better results than the genetic algorithm.

10.7 Further Work

The rough set model was implemented for modeling interstate conflict and a standard genetic algorithm and simulated annealing were used to optimize the rough set partition. For the future work, more robust variants of genetic algorithm and simulated annealing should be applied.

References

Akula, V.R., Ganguli, R.: Finite element model updating for helicopter rotor blade using genetic algorithm. AIAA J. (2003). doi:doi:10.2514/2.1983
Almeida, F.S., Awruch, A.M.: Design optimization of composite laminated structures using genetic algorithms and finite element analysis. Compos. Struct. **88**, 443–454 (2009)
Arifovic, J., Gençay, R.: Using genetic algorithms to select architecture of a feedforward artificial neural network. Phys. Stat. Mech. Appl. **289**, 574–594 (2001)
Arostegui Jr., M.A., Kadipasaoglu, S.N., Khumawala, B.M.: An empirical comparison of tabu search, simulated annealing, and genetic algorithms for facilities location problems. Int. J. Prod. Econ. **103**, 742–754 (2006)
Balamurugan, R., Ramakrishnan, C.V., Singh, N.: Performance evaluation of a two stage adaptive genetic algorithm (TSAGA) in structural topology optimization. Appl. Soft Comput. **8**, 1607–1624 (2008)
Banzhaf, W., Nordin, P., Keller, R., Francone, F.: Genetic programming-an introduction: On the automatic evolution of computer programs and its applications. Morgan Kaufmann, San Fransisco (1998)
Boesack, CD., Marwala, T., Nelwamondo, FV.: Application of GA-Fuzzy controller design to automatic generation control. In: Proceedings of the IEEE 3rd International Workshop on Advanced Computer Intelligence, pp. 227–232 (2010)
Bourouni, K., Ben M'Barek, T., Al Taee, A.: Design and optimization of desalination reverse osmosis plants driven by renewable energies using genetic algorithms. Renew. Energ. **36**, 936–950 (2011)
Canyurt, O.E., Kim, H.R., Lee, K.Y.: Estimation of laser hybrid welded joint strength by using genetic algorithm approach. Mech. Mater. **40**, 825–831 (2008)
Chen, R., Zhang, Z., Wu, D., Zhang, P., Zhang, X., Wang, Y., Shi, Y.: Prediction of protein interaction hot spots using rough set-based multiple criteria linear programming. J Theor. Biol **269**, 174–180 (2011)

Crossingham, B.: Rough set partitioning using computational intelligence approach. M.Sc. thesis, University of the Witwatersrand (2007)

Crossingham, B., Marwala, T.: Using genetic algorithms to optimise rough set partition sizes for HIV data analysis. Studies in Comput Intelli **78**, 245–250 (2008)

Crossingham, B., Marwala, T., Lagazio, M.: Optimized rough sets for modelling interstate conflict. In: Proceedings of the IEEE Internatianal Conference on Man, Systems and Cybernatics, pp. 1198–1204 (2008)

Degertekin, S.O.: A comparison of simulated annealing and genetic algorithm for optimum design of nonlinear steel space frames. Struct. Multidisc. Optim **34**, 347–59 (2007)

Forrest, S.: Genetic algorithms. ACM Comput. Surv. **28**, 77–80 (1996)

Franconi, L., Jennison, C.: Comparison of a genetic algorithm and simulated annealing in an application to statistical image reconstruction. Stats. and Comput. **7**, 193–207 (1997)

Franulović, M., Basan, R., Prebil, I.: Genetic algorithm in material model parameters' identification for low-cycle fatigue. Comput. Mater. Sci. **45**, 505–510 (2009)

Garson, G.D.: A comparison of neural network and expert systems algorithms with common multivariate procedures for analysis of social science data. Soc. Sci. Comp. Rev **9**, 399–433 (1991)

Ghosh, S., Ghosh, I., Pratihar, D.K., Maiti, B., Das, P.K.: Optimum stacking pattern for multi-stream plate-fin heat exchanger through a genetic algorithm. Int. J Therm. Sci. **50**, 214–224 (2011)

Gladwin, D., Stewart, P., Stewart, J.: Internal combustion engine control for series hybrid electric vehicles by parallel and distributed genetic programming/Multiobjective genetic algorithms. Int. J. Syst. Sci. **42**, 249–261 (2011)

Goldberg, D.E.: Genetic Algorithms in Search, Optimization and Machine Learning. Addison-Wesley, Reading (1989)

Grzymala-Busse, J.W.: Mining numerical data - A rough set approach. In: Proceedings of the Rough Sets and Emerging Intelligence Systems Paradigms, pp. 12–21 (2007)

Gwiazda, T.D.: Genetic Algorithms Reference Vol. 1 Cross-over for Single-objective Numerical Optimization Problems. Adobe eBook, Lomianki (2006)

Hlalele, N., Nelwamondo, F.V., Marwala, T.: Imputation of missing data using PCA, neuro-fuzzy and genetic algorithms. Lect. Notes Comput. Sc. **5507**, 485–492 (2009)

Houck, C.R., Joines, J.A., Kay, M.G.:A genetic algorithm for function optimisation: a MATLAB implementation. (Tech. Rep. NCSU-IE TR 95–09). North, Carolina State: University (1995)

Hulley, G., Marwala, T.: Genetic algorithm based incremental learning for optimal weight and classifier selection. Comput. Models for Life. Sci. **952**, 258–267 (2007)

Jaafar, A.F.B, Jais, J., Hamid, MHBHA, Rahman Z.B.A., Benaouda, D.: Using rough set as a tool for knowledge discovery in DSS. Current Trends in Technology-Assisted Education, pp. 1011–1015 (2006)

Jonathan, D., Bruno, D., Hamid, B.A.: Simulated Annealing and genetic algorithms in topology optimization tools: comparison through the design of a switched reluctance machine. In: Proceedings of the International Symposium on Power Electronics, Electrical Drives, Automation and Motion, pp. 1247–1252 (2010)

Komorowski, J., Pawlak, Z., Polkowski, L., Skowron, A.: A rough set perspective on data and knowledge. In: Kloesgen, W., Zytkow, J. (eds.) The Handbook of Data Mining and Knowledge Discovery. Oxford University Press, Oxford (1999)

Kubalík, J., Lazanský, J.: Genetic algorithms and their testing. AIP Conf. Proc. **465**, 217–229 (1999)

Kwak, H.G., Kim, J.: An integrated genetic algorithm complemented with direct search for optimum design of RC frames. Comput.-Aided Des. **41**, 490–500 (2009)

Marwala, T.: Finite element updating using wavelet data and genetic algorithm. J. of Aircraft **39**, 709–711 (2002)

Marwala, T.: Control of fermentation orocess using bayesian neural networks and genetic algorithm. In: Proceedings of the African Control Conference, pp. 449–454 (2003)

Marwala, T.: Control of complex systems using bayesian neural networks and genetic algorithm. Int. J. Eng. Sim. **5**, 28–37 (2004)

Marwala, T.: Computational Intelligence for Modelling Complex Systems. Research India Publications, Delhi (2007a)

Marwala, T.: Bayesian training of neural network using genetic programming. Pattern Recogn. Lett. **28**, 452–1458 (2007b)

Marwala, T.: Finite Element Model Updating Using Computational Intelligence Techniques. Springer, London (2010)

Marwala, T., Chakraverty, S.: Fault classification in structures with incomplete measured data using autoassociative neural networks and genetic algorithm. Curr. Sci. **90**, 542–548 (2006)

Marwala, T., de Wilde, P., Correia, L., Mariano, P., Ribeiro, R., Abramov, V., Szirbik, N., Goossenaerts, J.: Scalability and optimisation of a committee of agents using genetic algorithm. In: Proceedings of the International Symposia on Soft Computer and Intelligence Syst for Industry (2001)

Michalewicz, Z.: Genetic Algorithms + Data Structures = Evolution Programs. Springer, New York (1996)

Mitchell, M.: An Introduction to Genetic Algorithms. MIT Press, Cambridge (1996)

Mohamed, A.K., Nelwamondo, F.V., Marwala, T.: Estimation of missing data: Neural networks, principal component analysis and genetic algorithms. In: Proceedings of the 12th World Multiconf on systemics, Cybernatics and Informatics, pp. 36–41 (2008)

Mohamed, S., Tettey, T., Marwala, T.: An Extension neural network and genetic algorithm for bearing fault classification. In: Proceedings of the IEEE International Joint Conference on Neural Nets, pp. 7673–7679 (2006)

Oh, S., Pedrycz, W.: Genetic optimization-drivenmMulti-layer hybrid fuzzy neural networks. Simul. Model. Pract. Th. **14**, 597–613 (2006)

Onieva, E., Naranjo, J.E., Milanés, V., Alonso, J., García, R., Pérez, J.: Automatic lateral control for unmanned vehicles via genetic algorithms. Appl. Soft Comput. J. **11**, 1303–9 (2011)

Ozcelik, F., Islier, A.A.: Generalisation of unidirectional loop layout problem and solution by a genetic algorithm. Int. J. Prod. Res. **49**, 747–764 (2011)

Palaniappan, P.K., Jawahar, N.: A genetic algorithm for simultaneous optimisation of lot sizing and scheduling in a flow line assembly. Int. J. Prod. Res. **49**, 375–400 (2011)

Paluch, B., Grédiac, M., Faye, A.: Combining a finite element programme and a genetic algorithm to optimize composite structures with variable thickness. Compos. Struct. **83**, 284–294 (2008)

Park, B.J., Choi, H.R., Kim, H.S.: A hybrid genetic algorithm for the job shop scheduling problems. Comput. Ind. Eng. **45**, 597–613 (2003)

Pasandideh, S.H.R., Niaki, S.T.A., Nia, A.R.: A genetic algorithm for vendor managed inventory control system of multi-product multi-constraint economic order quantity model. Expert Syst. Appl. **38**, 2708–2716 (2011)

Patel, P., Marwala, T.: Caller interaction classification: A comparison of real and binary coded GA-MLP techniques. Lect. Notes Comput. Sc. **5507**, 728–735 (2009)

Pawlak, Z.: Rough Sets, Theoretical Aspects of Reasoning About Data. Kluwer, Dordrecht (1991)

Pendharkar, P.C., Rodger, J.A.: An empirical study of non-binary genetic algorithm-based neural approaches for classification. In: Proceedings of the 20th International Conference on Information Systems, pp. 155–165 (1999)

Perera, R., Ruiz, A.: A multistage FE updating procedure for damage identification in large-scale structures based on multi-objective evolutionary optimization. Mech. Syst. Signal Pr. **22**, 970–991 (2008)

Perera, R., Ruiz, A., Manzano, C.: Performance assessment of multi-criteria damage identification genetic algorithms. Comput. Struct. **87**, 120–127 (2009)

Rahmani, S., Mousavi, S.M., Kamali, M.J.: Modeling of road-traffic noise with the use of genetic algorithm. Appl. Soft Comput. J. **11**, 1008–1013 (2011)

Roy, T., Chakraborty, D.: Optimal vibration control of smart fiber reinforced composite shell structures using improved genetic algorithm. J. Sound Vib. **319**, 15–40 (2009)

Salamó, M., López-Sánchez, M.: Rough set based approaches to feature selection for case-based reasoning classifiers. Pattern Recogn. Lett. **32**, 280–292 (2011)

Stern, H., Chassidim, Y., Zofi, M.: Multi-agent visual area coverage using a new genetic algorithm selection scheme. Eur. J. Oper. Res. **175**, 1890–1907 (2006)

Tettey, T., Marwala, T.: Controlling interstate conflict using neuro-fuzzy modeling and genetic algorithms. In: Proceedings of the 10th IEEE International Conference on Intelligence Engineering Systems, pp. 30–44 (2006)

Thompson, D.R., Bilbro, G.L.: Comparison of a genetic algorithm with a simulated annealing algorithm for the design of an ATM network. IEEE Commun. Lett. **4**, 267–269 (2000)

Tu, Z., Lu, Y.: Finite element model updating using artificial boundary conditions with genetic algorithms. Comput. Struct. **86**, 714–727 (2008)

Vilakazi, C.B. Marwala, T.: Bushing fault detection and diagnosis using extension neural network. In: Proceedings of the 10th IEEE International Conference on Intelligence Engineering Systems, pp. 170–174 (2006)

Vose, M.D.: The Simple Genetic Algorithm: Foundations and Theory. MIT Press, Cambridge (1999)

Wan, C.: Efficiency comparison of simulated annealing algorithm and genetic algorithm in feature selection. In: Proceedings of the 6th International Conference on Natural Computation, pp. 2330–2333 (2010)

Xie, F., Lin, Y., Ren, W.: Optimizing model for land use/land cover retrieval from remote sensing imagery based on variable precision rough sets. Ecol. Model. **222**, 232–240 (2011)

Zhang, H., Ishikawa, M.: A solution to combinatorial optimization with time-varying parameters by a hybrid genetic algorithm. Int. Congr. Ser. **1269**, 149–152 (2004)

Zou, Z., Tseng, T.-L., Sohn, H., Song, G., Gutierrez, R.: A rough set based approach to distributor selection in supply chain management. Expert Syst. Appl. **38**, 106–115 (2011)

Chapter 11
Neuro-Rough Sets for Modeling Interstate Conflict

11.1 Introduction

The levels of transparency of the Takagi-Sugeno neuro-fuzzy model and the support vector machines model were investigated in Chap. 6 by applying them to conflict management. The data set used in this investigation was the militarized interstate dispute dataset obtained from the correlates of war project. The support vector machine model was also trained to predict conflict. Knowledge from the Takagi-Sugeno neuro-fuzzy model was extracted by interpreting the model's fuzzy rules and their outcomes. It was found that the Takagi-Sugeno neuro-fuzzy model offered some transparency which assists an understanding of conflict management. The Takagi-Sugeno neuro-fuzzy model was compared to the support vector machine technique and it was found that – even though the support vector machine showed a marginal advantage over the Takagi-Sugeno neuro-fuzzy model's predictive capacity – the Takagi-Sugeno neuro-fuzzy model allowed linguistic interpretation.

Subsequently, in Chap. 7, the rough set technique was applied to model the militarized interstate dispute. The rough set model was also compared to a neuro-fuzzy system which had been introduced in Chap. 6. The results obtained showed that equal-width-bin partitioning gave a better accuracy than equal-frequency-bin partitioning. Both these techniques were found to give less accurate results than neuro-fuzzy sets did. Nevertheless, they were found to be more transparent than neuro-fuzzy sets. Additionally, it was observed that the rules generated from the rough sets were linguistic and easy-to-interpret when compared with the neuro-fuzzy model.

Chapter 8 presented techniques to optimally granulize rough set partition sizes using particle swarm optimization and hill climbing techniques. The techniques were compared to those based on the equal-width-bin technique, which was found to perform better than the equal-frequency-bin technique in Chap. 7. The results showed that particle swarm optimization provided a better forecasting accuracy, followed by the hill climbing technique, which was better than the equal-width-bin technique.

T. Marwala and M. Lagazio, *Militarized Conflict Modeling using Computational* 201
Intelligence, Advanced Information and Knowledge Processing,
DOI 10.1007/978-0-85729-790-7_11, © Springer-Verlag London Limited 2011

Chapter 9 presented approaches to optimally granulize rough set partition sizes using the simulated annealing technique. The technique was applied to model the militarized interstate dispute data. The technique was then compared to the rough set partition technique based on particle swarm optimization, which was found to perform better than the hill climbing optimization technique in Chap. 8. The results showed that simulated annealing provided a better forecasting accuracy than the particle swarm optimization technique did.

Chapter 10 presented techniques to optimally granulize rough set partition sizes using a genetic algorithm. The procedure was applied to model militarized interstate dispute data. The procedure was then compared to the rough set partition method that was based on simulated annealing, and which was observed to perform better than the particle swarm optimization in Chap. 9. The results obtained showed, for the analyzed data, that the genetic algorithm provided a better forecasting accuracy than simulated annealing did.

The main purpose of machine learning is to make predictions given a set of inputs. However, a secondary role is to extract rules that govern the interrelationships within the data. Given the input parameters, machine learning tools such as neural networks are quite good at making predictions, but are not sufficiently transparent to allow for the extraction of linguistic rules that govern the predictions they make. Machine learning tools are called 'black-box' tools as they do not give a transparent view of the rules that govern the relationships that make predictions possible.

Rough Set Theory (RST) was introduced by Pawlak (1991) and is a mathematical tool that deals with vagueness and uncertainty. It is based on a set of rules, presented in terms of linguistic variables. Rough sets are of fundamental importance in both computational intelligence and cognitive science, and are highly applicable to the tasks of machine learning and decision analysis, especially in the analysis of decisions where there are inconsistencies. Because they are rule-based, rough sets are very transparent but are not as accurate in their predictions, and most certainly are not universal approximators, as are other machine learning tools such as neural networks. It is revealed in this chapter that, in machine learning, there is always a trade-off between accuracy of prediction and transparency. This chapter presents a combined architecture that takes elements from both rough sets and multi-layered perceptron neural networks. It was therefore anticipated that this architecture will give a balanced view of the data in for both the transparency and accuracy. A rough set is based on lower and upper approximations of decision classes (Inuiguchi and Miyajima 2007) and is often contrasted to compete with a fuzzy set but, in fact, it complements it. One of the advantages of RST is that it does not require *a priori* knowledge about the data set. So it is for this reason that statistical techniques are not sufficient for determining the relationship in complex cases.

Greco et al. (2006) generalized the original idea of a rough set and introduced a variable precision rough set, which is based on the concept of relative and absolute rough membership. Marwala and Crossingham (2008) presented a neuro-rough model based on the multi-layered perceptron neural-network and rough set theory. This neuro-rough model was then tested on modeling the risk of the

Human Immunodeficiency Virus (HIV) from demographic data. The model was formulated using a Bayesian framework and trained using a Monte Carlo method and the Metropolis criterion. When the model was tested to estimate the risk of HIV infection, given the demographic data, it was found to give an accuracy of 62%. Their model combined the accuracy of the Bayesian multi-layer perceptron model with the transparency of the Bayesian rough set model.

Tettey et al. (2007) presented an analysis of HIV data obtained from a survey performed on pregnant women by the Department of Health in South Africa. The HIV data was analyzed by formulating a rough set approximation of the six demographic variables chosen for analysis. These variables were Race, Age of Mother, Education, Gravidity, Parity, and Age of Father. Of the 4.096 possible subsets in the input space it was found that the data only represented 225 of those cases with 130 cases being discernible, and 96 cases being indiscernible. The rough set analysis was suggested as a quick way of analyzing data and rule extraction for neuro-fuzzy models when it came to data driven identification. A comparison of rule extraction using rough sets and using neuro-fuzzy was conducted, and the results were in favor of the rough sets.

Nelwamondo and Marwala (2007) presented a procedure based on rough set theory for the estimation of missing data. It was envisioned for large databases, that it was more likely that the missing values could be correlated to other variables observed somewhere in the same data. Instead of approximating missing data, it might be cheaper to identify the indiscernibility relations between the observed data instances and those that contained missing attributes. Using the HIV database, the results obtained were acceptable with accuracies ranging from 74.7% to 100%. One drawback of this method is that it makes no provision extrapolation or interpolation. As a result, it can only be used if the missing case is similar or related to another case with more observations.

This chapter presents a neuro-rough model and extends this to a probabilistic domain using a Bayesian framework, trained using a Markov Chain Monte Carlo simulation and the Metropolis algorithms (Marwala and Crossingham 2008). To achieve this, the rough set membership functions' granulization and the network's weights were interpreted probabilistically as will be seen later in this chapter. The neuro-rough set that is presented exploits the generalization capacity of neural networks and the transparency advantages of rough set theory. The neuro-rough model is then compared with the results obtained from the genetic algorithm optimized rough set model for the case of modeling of militarized interstate dispute data.

11.2 Rough Sets

Rough Set Theory (RST) deals with the approximation of sets that are difficult to describe with the available information (Ohrn 1999; Ohrn and Rowland 2000). RST deals predominantly with the classification of imprecise, uncertain, or incomplete information. Some concepts that are fundamental to RST are given in the next few sections. The data is represented using an information table with each row representing a new case (or object) and each column representing the case's variables (or condition attributes). Once the information table is obtained, the data is discretised into partitions. An information system can be understood by a pair $\Lambda = (U, A)$, where U and A are finite, non-empty sets called the Universe, and the set of Attributes, respectively (Deja and Peszek 2003). For every attribute a that is an element of A, we associate a set V_a, of its values, where V_a is called the value set of a.

$$a: U \rightarrow V_a \qquad (11.1)$$

Any subset B of A determines a binary relation $I(B)$ on U, which is called an Indiscernibility relation (indiscernibility meaning indistinguishable from one another). The main concept of RST is an indiscernibility relation. Sets that are indiscernible are called *elementary sets*, and these are considered the building blocks of RST's knowledge of reality. A union of elementary sets is called a *crisp set*, while any other sets are referred to as *rough* or *vague*. More formally, for a given information system Λ, and for any subset $B \subseteq A$, there is an associated equivalence relation $I(B)$ called the B-*indicernibility* relation represented as shown below (Sakai and Nakata 2006):

$$(x, y) \in I(B) \ \textit{if abd only if } a(x) = a(y) \qquad (11.2)$$

RST offers a tool to deal with indiscernibility. The way in which it works is: for each concept/decision X, the greatest definable set containing X and the least definable set containing X are each computed. These two sets are called the *lower and upper approximation*, respectively. The sets of cases/objects with the same outcome variable are assembled together. This is done by looking at the "purity" of the particular object's attributes in relation to its outcome. In most instances, it is not possible to define cases into crisp sets, hence lower and upper approximation sets are defined. The lower approximation is defined as the collection of cases whose equivalence classes are fully contained in the set of cases we want to approximate. The lower approximation of set X is denoted $\underline{B}X$ and, it is presented mathematically as (Pawlak 1991):

$$\underline{B}X = \{x \in U : B(x) \subseteq X\} \qquad (11.3)$$

Likewise, the upper approximation is defined as the collection of cases whose equivalence classes are, at least, partially contained in the set of cases we want to approximate. The upper approximation of set X is denoted $\overline{B}X$ and is presented mathematically as (Pawlak 1991):

$$\overline{B}X = \{x \in U : B(x) \cap X = \emptyset\} \qquad (11.4)$$

It is through these lower and upper approximations that any rough set is defined. Lower and upper approximations are defined differently in the literature, but it follows that a crisp set is only defined for $\overline{B}X = \underline{B}X$. It must be noted that, for most cases in RST, reducts are generated to enable us to discard functionally redundant information (Pawlak 1991).

11.2.1 Rough Membership Function

The rough membership function is described as $\eta_A^X : U \to [0, 1]$ that, when applied to object x, quantifies the degree of relative overlap between the set X and the indiscernibility set to which x belongs. This membership function is a measure of the plausibility of which an object x belongs to set X. This membership function is defined as (Pawlak 1991):

$$\eta_A^X = \frac{|[X]_B \cap X|}{[X]_B} \tag{11.5}$$

11.2.2 Rough Set Accuracy

The accuracy of rough sets provides a measure of how closely the rough set is approximating the target set. It is defined as the ratio of the number of objects which can be positively placed in X to the number of objects that can be possibly be placed in X. In other words, it is defined as the number of cases in the lower approximation, divided by the number of cases in the upper approximation (where $0 \leq \alpha_p(X) \leq 1$) and can be written as (Pawlak 1991):

$$\alpha_p(X) = \frac{|\underline{B}X|}{|\overline{B}X|} \tag{11.6}$$

11.2.3 Rough Sets Formulation

The process of modeling the rough set can be broken down into five stages. The first stage is to select the data, while the second stage involves pre-processing the data to ensure that it is ready for analysis. The second stage involves discretizing the data and removing unnecessary instances from this data (cleaning the data).

If reducts were considered, the third stage would be to use the cleaned data to generate reducts. A reduct is the most concise way in which we can discern object classes (Witlox and Tindemans 2004). To cope with inconsistencies, lower and upper approximations of decision classes are defined. Stage four is where the rules are extracted or generated. The rules are normally determined based on condition attributes values.

Once the rules are extracted, they can be presented in an "*if CONDITION(S)-then DECISION*" format (Witlox and Tindemans 2004). The final or fifth stage involves testing the newly created rules on a test set to estimate the prediction error of the rough set model. The equation representing the mapping between the inputs x to the output γ using a rough set can be written as (Sakai and Nakata 2006; Goh and Law 2003):

$$\gamma = f(G_x, N_r, R) \tag{11.7}$$

where γ is the output, G_x is the granulization of the input space into high, low, medium etc., N_r is the number of rules, and R is the rule. So, for a given nature of granulization, the rough set model can give the optimal number and nature of rules and the accuracy of prediction. Therefore, in rough set modeling, there is always a trade-off between the degree of granulization of the input space (which affects the nature and size of rules) and the prediction accuracy of the rough set model.

11.3 Multi-layer Perceptron

The other component of the neuro-rough model is the multi-layered neural- network. This network architecture contains hidden units and output units, as well as one hidden layer. The bias parameters in the first layer are weights from an extra input having a fixed value of $x_0 = 1$. The bias parameters in the second layer are weights from an extra hidden unit, with the activation fixed at $z_0 = 1$. The model can take into account the intrinsic dimensionality of the data. The output of the jth hidden unit is obtained by calculating the weighted linear combination of the d input values to give (Bishop 1995):

$$a_j = \sum_{i=1}^{d} w_{ji}^{(1)} x_i + w_{j0}^{(1)} \tag{11.8}$$

Here, $w_{ji}^{(1)}$ indicates weight in the first layer, going from input i to hidden unit j while $w_{j0}^{(1)}$ indicates the bias for the hidden unit j. The activation of the hidden unit j is obtained by transforming the output a_j in Eq. 11.8 into z_j, as follows (Bishop 1995):

$$z_j = f_{inner}(a_j) \tag{11.9}$$

The f_{inner} function represents the activation of the inner layer. Functions such as the hyperbolic tangent may be used for this task. The output of the second layer is obtained by transforming the activation of the second hidden layer, using the second layer weights. Given the output of the hidden layer z_j in Eq. 11.9, the output of unit k may be written as (Bishop 1995):

$$a_k = \sum_{j=1}^{M} w_{kj}^{(2)} z_j + w_{k0}^{(2)} \tag{11.10}$$

Similarly, Eq. 11.10 may be transformed into the output units by using some activation function as follows:

$$y_k = f_{outer}(a_k) \tag{11.11}$$

If Eqs. 11.8, 11.9, 11.10, and 11.11 are combined, it is possible to relate the input x to the output y by a two-layered non-linear mathematical expression that may be written as follows (Bishop 1995):

$$y_k = f_{outer} \left(\sum_{j=1}^{M} w_{kj}^{(2)} f_{inner} \left(\sum_{i=1}^{d} w_{ji}^{(1)} x_i + w_{j0}^{(1)} \right) + w_{k0}^{(2)} \right) \tag{11.12}$$

Models of this form can approximate any continuous function with arbitrary accuracy if the number of hidden units M is sufficiently large. The Multi-Layered Perceptron may be expanded by considering several layers but it has been demonstrated by the Universal Approximation Theorem that a two-layered architecture is adequate for the multi-layer perceptron.

If Eqs. 11.7 and 11.12 are combined, it is possible to relate the input x to the output y by a two-layered non-linear mathematical expression that may be written as follows (Marwala and Crossingham 2008):

$$y_k = f_{outer} \left(\sum_{j=1}^{M} \gamma_{kj} (G_x, R, N_r) f_{inner} \left(\sum_{i=1}^{d} w_{ji}^{(1)} x_i + w_{j0}^{(1)} \right) + w_{k0}^{(2)} \right) \tag{11.13}$$

The biases in Eq. 11.13 may be absorbed into the weights by including extra input variables set permanently to 1, making $x_0 = 1$ and $z_0 = 1$, and giving (Marwala and Crossingham 2008):

$$y_k = f_{outer} \left(\sum_{j=0}^{M} \gamma_k (G_x, R, N_r)_{kj} f_{inner} \left(\sum_{i=0}^{d} w_{ji}^{(1)} x_i \right) \right) \tag{11.14}$$

The function $f_{outer}(\cdot)$ may be logistic, linear, or sigmoid; while f_{inner} is a hyperbolic tangent function. The equation may be represented schematically by Fig. 11.1.

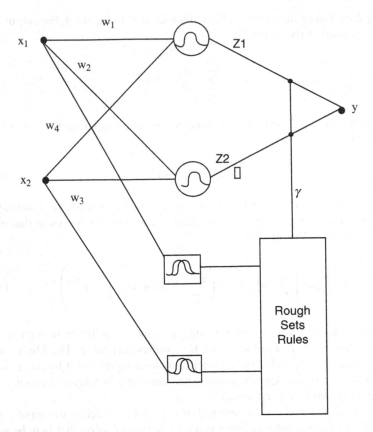

Fig. 11.1 The neuro-rough set model

11.4 Neuro-Rough Model

If Eqs. 11.7 and 11.13 are combined, it is possible to relate the input x to the output y by a two-layered non-linear mathematical expression that may be written as follows (Marwala and Crossingham 2008):

$$y_k = f_{outer} \left(\sum_{j=1}^{M} \gamma_{kj} (G_x, R, N_r) f_{inner} \left(\sum_{i=1}^{d} w_{ji}^{(1)} x_i + w_{j0}^{(1)} \right) + w_{k0}^{(2)} \right) \quad (11.15)$$

The biases in Eq. 11.15 may be absorbed into the weights by including extra input variables set permanently to 1 making $x_0 = 1$ and $z_0 = 1$, to give (Marwala and Crossingham 2008):

$$y_k = f_{outer} \left(\sum_{j=0}^{M} \gamma_k (G_x, R, N_r)_{kj} f_{inner} \left(\sum_{i=0}^{d} w_{ji}^{(1)} x_i \right) \right) \quad (11.16)$$

The function $f_{outer}(\cdot)$ may be logistic, linear, or sigmoid; while f_{inner} is a hyperbolic tangent function. The equation is represented schematically in Fig. 11.1.

11.5 Bayesian Rough Sets

Bayesian rough sets have been a subject of interest in recent times. Li et al. (2010) proposed a probabilistic rough set model with variable precision on Bayesian decisions, and discussed the elementary process of minimum risk of Bayesian decisions. Their results indicated a reduction of the error risk of the Bayesian decision.

Zhang and Wang (2010) proposed a multi-relational Bayesian classification technique with rough sets. Their results indicated that their method performed better than the traditional technique, and its efficiency is higher than that of the Bayesian classification procedures and graph methods.

Yao and Zhou (2010) proposed a naive Bayesian rough set, which is a probabilistic classifier that integrates rough set theory and Bayesian theory. The conditional probability was predicted based on the Bayes' theorem and a naive probabilistic independence assumption.

Rong et al. (2009) successfully applied a hybrid of a Bayesian network with rough sets for fault diagnosis of circuit breakers, by firstly identifying the relationship between fault symptom and fault reason sets. Thereafter, a discernible matrix procedure of attribute reduction in the rough set was used to decrease the attribute of this fault diagnosis process.

Han et al. (2009) presented a Bayesian rough set model which can deal with multiple decision classes. Their results obtained from the data for a steel plant's 150 t converter demonstrated the efficacy and applicability of this model.

Other applications of Bayesian rough sets include supporting E-learning systems by Abbas and Juan (2009), intrusion detection systems by Cheng et al. (2009), tactical decision methods for air combat by Chen et al. (2009), feature selection by Ślezak (2009), and Su and Dong (2009) for transformer fault diagnosis.

The Bayesian framework can be written as (Marwala 2007a; Marwala 2007b; Marwala and Crossingham 2008):

$$P(M|D) = \frac{P(D|M)p(M)}{p(D)} \qquad (11.17)$$

where $M = \begin{Bmatrix} w \\ G_x \\ N_r \\ R \end{Bmatrix}$.

The parameter $P(M|D)$ is the probability of the rough set model given the observed data, $P(D|M)$ is the probability of the data given the assumed rough set model (also called the likelihood function), $P(M)$ is the prior probability of the rough set model, and $P(D)$ is the probability of the data (also called the evidence). The evidence can be treated as the normalization constant. The likelihood function and the resulting error may be estimated as follows (Marwala and Crossingham 2008):

$$P(D|M) = \frac{1}{z_1} \exp(-error) = \frac{1}{z_1} \exp\{A(w, N_r, R, G_x) - 1\} \qquad (11.18)$$

$$error = \sum_{l}^{L} \sum_{k}^{K} \left(t_{lk} - \left(f_{outer} \left(\sum_{j=0}^{M} \gamma_{kj}(G_x, R)_{kj} f_{inner} \left(\sum_{i=0}^{d} w_{ji}^{(1)} x_i \right) \right) \right)_{lk} \right)^2 \qquad (11.19)$$

Here z_1 is the normalization constant, L is the number of outputs, while K is the number of training examples. In this problem, the prior probability is linked to the concept of reducts, which was explained earlier. It is the prior knowledge that the best rough set model is the one with the minimum number of rules (N_r), and that the best network is the one whose weights are of the same order of magnitude. Therefore, the prior probability may be written as follows (Marwala 2007b; Marwala and Crossingham 2008):

$$P(M) = \frac{1}{z_2} \exp\left\{-\alpha N_r - \beta \sum w^2\right\} \qquad (11.20)$$

where z_2 is the normalization constant and β is the hyperparameter of the network weights. Given the observed data, the posterior probability of the model is thus (Marwala and Crossingham 2008):

$$P(M|D) = \frac{1}{z} \exp\left\{A(N_r, R, G_x) - 1 - \alpha N_r - \beta \sum w^2\right\} \qquad (11.21)$$

where z is the normalization constant and α is the hyperparameter of the number of rules. Since the number of rules and the rules generated, given the data, depends on the nature of granulization, we shall sample in the granule space as well as the network weights using a procedure called Markov Chain Monte Carlo (MCMC) simulation (Bishop 1995).

11.6 Markov Chain Monte Carlo Simulation

The manner in which the probability distribution in Eq. 11.21 may be sampled, is to randomly generate a succession of granule-weight vectors and accepting or rejecting them based on how probable they are, using the Metropolis algorithm (Metropolis et al. 1953). This process requires a generation of a large number of samples of granules for the input space and the network weights which, in many cases, is not computationally efficient.

A Markov Chain Monte Carlo (MCMC) technique is a process of simulating a chain of states through a random-walk process. It consists of a Markov process and a Monte Carlo simulation (Liesenfeld and Richard 2008). Lau and So (2011) applied the MCMC procedure, based on the Gibbs weighted Chinese restaurant seating rule in a class of mixture-time series models. Ahmadian et al. (2011) applied the MCMC technique to decode neural spike trains. They discussed Bayesian decoding approaches based on an encoding, generalized linear model that accurately defined how stimuli were transformed into the spike trains of a group of neurons. They compared numerous MCMC procedures that permitted the calculation of general Bayesian estimators together with posterior expectations. The hybrid Monte Carlo algorithm was found to be considerably better than the MCMC approaches.

Wan et al. (2010) applied MCMC for detecting frequency-selective channels. They suggested a sequential channel approximation MCMC technique that hybridized an MCMC procedure for data detection, and an adaptive least mean square procedure for channel tracking. They applied a stochastic expectation maximization MCMC procedure to jointly identify significant samples of the transmitted data and channel impulse response. Their procedures offered a low-complexity way to estimate the optimal maximum for *a posterior* detection.

Usami (2010) applied the MCMC technique, developing a model that concurrently estimated the bias factors of raters and examinees. In particular, the MCMC technique was used to estimate the parameters of this model. This technique was tested on actual essay test data in which 4 raters assessed the essays written by 304 high school students. Good results were obtained with a stable convergence of approximates.

Polyak and Gryazina (2010) applied the MCMC technique, exploiting barrier functions with applications to control and optimization. In particular, they combined the method for interior-point approaches of convex optimization with MCMC procedures. The results obtained were promising. Von Waldenfels et al. (2010) applied the MCMC technique in radiative transfer problems by assuming that the transfer of radiation can be modeled as a Markov process.

Jiang and Wu (2009) applied a Bayesian classifier and a rough set for credit scoring. This model was applied to a German Credit Database and the results demonstrated good performance.

Jing and Vadakkepat (2009) used an MCMC process for tracking maneuvering objects, while Gallagher et al. (2009) used the MCMC process to identify optimal models, model resolution, and model choice for earth-science problems. Also, Curran (2008) applied MCMC in DNA profiling. Other successful applications of the MCMC process include its use in environmental modeling (Gauchere et al. 2008), in medical imaging (Jun et al. 2008), in lake-water quality modeling (Malve et al. 2007), in economics (Jacquier et al. 2007), and in statistics (Lombardi 2007).

The MCMC creates a chain of granules and network weights and accepts or rejects them using the Metropolis algorithm. The application of the Bayesian approach and MCMC neuro-rough sets results in the probability distribution function of the granules and network weights which, in turn, leads to the distribution of the neuro-rough model outputs. From these distribution functions, the average prediction of the neuro-rough set model and the variance of that prediction can be calculated. The probability distributions of the neuro-rough set model, represented by granules and network weights, are mathematically described by Eq. 11.21. From Eq. 11.20 and by following the rules of probability theory, the distribution of the output parameter y is written as (Marwala 2007a; Marwala 2007b; Marwala and Crossingham 2008):

$$p(y|x, D) = \int p(y|x, M)p(M|D)dM \qquad (11.22)$$

Equation 11.22 depends on Eq. 11.21, and is difficult to solve analytically due to the relatively high dimension of the combined granule and weight space. Thus the integral in Eq. 11.19 may be approximated as follows in (Marwala 2007a; Marwala 2007b; Marwala and Crossingham 2008):

$$\tilde{y} \cong \frac{1}{L} \sum_{i=I}^{Z+L-1} F(M_i) \qquad (11.23)$$

Here, F is a mathematical model that gives the output given the input, $\tilde{y}$ is the average prediction of the Bayesian neuro-rough set model (M_i), Z is the number of initial states that are discarded in the hope of reaching a stationary posterior distribution function described in Eq. 11.21, and L is the number of retained states. For this chapter, the MCMC method was implemented by sampling a stochastic process consisting of random variables $\{gw_1, gw_2, \ldots, gw_n\}$ through introducing random changes to granule-weight vector $\{gw\}$ and either accepting or rejecting the state according to the Metropolis algorithm, given the differences in posterior probabilities between two states that are in transition (Metropolis et al. 1953; Marwala and Crossingham 2008).

$$\text{If } P(M_{n+1}|D) > P(M_n|D) \text{ then accept, } M_{n+1}, \qquad (11.24)$$

$$\text{Else accept if } \frac{P(M_{n+1}|D)}{P(M_n|D)} > \xi \quad \text{where } \xi \in [0, 1] \qquad (11.25)$$

else reject and randomly generate another model M_{n+1}.

Basically, the steps described above may be summarized as follows (Marwala and Crossingham 2008):

1. Randomly generate the granule weight vector $\{gw\}_n$
2. Calculate the posterior probability p_n using Eq. 11.21 and vector $\{gw\}_n$;
3. Introduce random changes to vector $\{gw\}_n$ to form vector $\{gw\}_{n+1}$;
4. Calculate the posterior probability p_{n+1} using Eq. 11.21 and vector $\{gw\}_{n+1}$;

5. Accept or reject vector $\{gw\}_{n+1}$ using Eqs. 11.22 and 11.25;
6. Go to Step 3 and repeat the process until enough samples of distribution in Eq. 11.21 have been achieved.

11.7   Genetic Algorithm Optimized Rough Set Model

Genetic algorithms, which were explained in detail in Chap. 10, are population based search methods. Genetic algorithms are a particular class of evolutionary algorithms that use techniques inspired by evolutionary biology such as inheritance, mutation, selection, and crossover (Crossingham et al. 2008). The fitness function measures the quality of the represented solution. For this chapter it was the area under the receiver operating characteristic curve. The genetic algorithm implemented in this chapter is outlined by Crossingham et al. (2008).

The primary difference between the Bayesian neuro-rough model and a genetic-algorithm optimized rough set model is that the neuro-rough model combines neural networks with rough set theory, while the genetic algorithm optimized rough set only uses rough set theory.

11.8   Interstate Conflict

For this chapter, Bayesian neuro-rough sets were implemented to model militarized interstate dispute data and the results were compared to that obtained from rough sets discretized using a genetic algorithm.

The population size of the genetic algorithm implementation was chosen to be 100, and the algorithm was run for 50 generations. The Bayesian rough set model was trained using the MCMC method, which sampled through the granulized input state for 1000 iterations.

The genetic algorithm was run for a population of 50 and over 200 generations. The results of these implementations on the militarized interstate dispute data are shown in Table 11.1.

The results obtained demonstrated that the detection rate of conflict was 76.7% when the Bayesian neuro-rough model was used and 76% when the genetic algorithm was used. The detection rate for peace was 75.0% when the Bayesian neuro-rough model was used and 75.3% when the genetic algorithm was used.

Table 11.1 Classification results

Method	True conflict TC	False peace FP	True peace TP	False conflict FC
Genetic algorithm	222	70	220	72
Bayesian rough set model	224	68	219	73

Overall, the detection rate of a correct outcome was 75.8% when the Bayesian neuro-rough model was used and 75.7% when the genetic algorithm was used. Furthermore, the areas under the receiver operating characteristic curves, when the genetic algorithm and the Bayesian neuro-rough model were used, were 0.80–0.81, respectively.

These results demonstrate that the Bayesian neuro-rough model is marginally better than the genetic algorithm in dealing with the data used in this book.

11.9   Conclusion

This chapter presented a neuro-rough model to model interstate conflict. The model was formulated using a Bayesian framework and trained using a Monte Carlo technique and the Metropolis criterion. This technique was compared with the genetic-algorithm optimized rough sets. The presented Bayesian neuro-rough model was observed to perform better than the genetic-algorithm optimized rough set model.

11.10   Further Work

The Bayesian neuro-rough set model was implemented for modeling interstate conflict and a standard Markov Chain Monte Carlo (MCMC) model were used to train the neuro-rough set. For future work, more robust variants of Monte Carlo models, such as the hybrid Monte Carlo and genetic Monte Carlo models should be applied.

References

Abbas, A.R., Juan, L.: Supporting E-learning system with modified Bayesian rough set model. Lect. Notes Comput. Sci. **5552**, 192–200 (2009)

Ahmadian, Y., Pillow, J.W., Paninski, L.: Efficient Markov chain Monte Carlo methods for decoding neural spike trains. Neural Comput. **23**, 46–96 (2011)

Bishop, C.M.: Neural Networks for Pattern Recognition. Oxford University Press, Oxford (1995)

Chen, J., Gao, X.-G., Fu, X.-W.: Tactical decision method for BVR air combat based on rough set theory and Bayesian network. J. Syst. Sim. **21**, 1739–1742+1747 (2009)

Cheng, K., Luo, J., Zhang, C.: Rough set weighted Naïve Bayesian classifier in intrusion prevention system. In: Proceeding of the International Conference on Networks Security, Wireless Communications and Trusted Computer, pp. 25–28 (2009)

Crossingham, B., Marwala, T., Lagazio, M.: Optimised rough sets for modeling interstate conflict. In: Proceeding of the IEEE International Conference on Systems, Man and Cybernetics, pp. 1198–1204 (2008)

Curran, J.M.: A MCMC method for resolving two person mixtures. Sci. Justice **48**, 168–177 (2008)

Deja, A., Peszek, P.: Applying rough set theory to multi stage medical diagnosing. Fundamenta Informaticae **54**, 387–408 (2003)

Gallagher, K., Charvin, K., Nielsen, S., Sambridge, M., Stephenson, J.: Markov Chain Monte Carlo (MCMC) sampling methods to determine optimal models, model resolution and model choice for earth science problems. Mar. Petrol Geol. **26**, 525–535 (2009)

Gauchere, C., Campillo, F., Misson, L., Guiot, J., Boreux, J.J.: Parameterization of a process-based tree-growth model: comparison of optimization. MCMC and particle filtering algorithms. Environ. Model. Softw. **23**, 1280–1288 (2008)

Goh, C., Law, R.: Incorporating the rough sets theory into travel demand analysis. Tourism Manage **24**, 511–517 (2003)

Greco, S., Matarazzo, B., Slowinski, R.: Rough membership and Bayesian confirmation measures for parameterized rough sets. In: Proceeding of the SPIE International Society for Optical Engineering, vol. 6104, pp. 314–324 (2006)

Han, M., Zhang, J.-J., Peng, F., Xiao, Z.-Y.: Bayesian rough set model based on multiple decision classes. Control and Decision **24**, 1615–1619 (2009)

Inuiguchi, M., Miyajima, T.: Rough set based rule induction from two decision tables. Eur. J. Oper. Res. **181**, 1540–1553 (2007)

Jacquier, E., Johannes, M., Polson, N.: MCMC maximum likelihood for latent state models. J. Econometrics **137**, 615–640 (2007)

Jiang, Y., Wu, L.H.: Credit scoring model based on simple Naive Bayesian classifier and a rough set. In: Proceeding of the International Conference on Computer Intelligence and Software Engineering, pp. 1–4 (2009)

Jing, L., Vadakkepat, P.: Interacting MCMC particle filter for tracking maneuvering target. J. Digit. Signal Process. **20**, 561–574 (2009)

Jun, S.C., George, J.S., Kim, W., Pare-Blagoev, J., Plis, S., Ranken, D.M., Schmidt, D.M.: Bayesian brain source imaging based on combined MEG/EEG and fMRI using MCMC. NeuroImage **40**, 1581–1594 (2008)

Lau, J.W., So, M.K.P.: A Monte Carlo Markov chain algorithm for a class of mixture time series models. Stat. Comput. **21**, 69–81 (2011)

Li, L., Wang, J., Jiang, J.: Bayesian decision model based on probabilistic rough set with variable precision. Commun. Comput Inf. Sci. **105**, 32–39 (2010)

Liesenfeld, R., Richard, J.: Improving MCMC, using efficient importance sampling. Comput. Stat. Data Anal. **53**, 272–288 (2008)

Lombardi, M.J.: Bayesian inference for [alpha]-stable distributions: a random walk MCMC approach. Comput. Stat. Data Anal. **51**, 2688–2700 (2007)

Malve, O., Laine, M., Haario, H., Kirkkala, T., Sarvala, J.: Bayesian modelling of algal mass occurrences – using adaptive MCMC methods with a lake water quality model. Environ. Model. Softw. **22**, 966–977 (2007)

Marwala, T.: Bayesian training of neural network using genetic programming. Pattern Recogn. Lett. **28**, 1452–1458 (2007a)

Marwala, T.: Computational Intelligence for Modelling Complex Systems. Research India Publications, Delhi (2007b)

Marwala, T., Crossingham, B.: Neuro-rough models for modelling HIV. In: Proceeding of the IEEE International Conference on Systems, Man, and Cybernetics, pp. 3089–3095 (2008)

Metropolis, N., Rosenbluth, A.W., Rosenbluth, M.N., Teller, A.H., Teller, E.: Equations of state calculations by fast computing machines. J. Chem. Phys. **21**, 1087–1092 (1953)

Nelwamondo, F.V., Marwala, T.: Rough set theory for the treatment of incomplete data. In: Proceeding of the IEEE Conference on Fuzzy Systems, pp. 338–343 (2007)

Ohrn, A.: Discernibility and rough sets in medicine: tools and applications. PhD thesis, Norwegian University of Science and Technology (1999)

Ohrn, A., Rowland, T.: Rough sets: a knowledge discovery technique for multifactorial medical outcomes. Am. J. Phys. Med. Rehab. **79**, 100–108 (2000)

Pawlak, Z.: Rough Sets, Theoretical Aspects of Reasoning About Data. Kluwer Academic Publishers, Dordrecht (1991)

Polyak, B.T., Gryazina, E.N.: Markov Chain Monte Carlo method exploiting Barrier functions with applications to control and optimization. In: Proceeding of the IEEE International Symposium on Computer-Aided Control System Design, pp. 1553–1557 (2010)

Rong, Y.-J., Ge, B.-H., Zhao, J., Liu, S.: Fault diagnosis of SF circuit breaker using rough set theory and Bayesian network. High Volt. Eng. **35**, 2995–2999 (2009)

Sakai, H., Nakata, M.: On rough sets based rule generation from tables. Int. J. Innovative Comput. Inform. Control **2**, 13–31 (2006)

Ślezak, D.: Degrees of conditional (in)dependence: a framework for approximate Bayesian networks and examples related to the rough set-based feature selection. Inf. Sci. **179**, 197–209 (2009)

Su, H., Dong, H.: Transformer fault diagnosis based on reasoning integration of rough set and fuzzy set and Bayesian optimal classifier. WSEAS Trans. Circ. Syst. **8**, 136–145 (2009)

Tettey, T., Nelwamondo, F.V., Marwala, T.: HIV data analysis via rule extraction using rough sets. In: Proceeding of the 11th IEEE International Conference on Intelligent Engineering Systems, pp. 105–110 (2007)

Usami, S.: A polytomous item response model that simultaneously considers Bias factors of raters and examinees: estimation through a Markov Chain Monte Carlo algorithm. Jpn. J. Educ. Psychol. **58**, 163–175 (2010)

Von Waldenfels, W., Wehrse, R., Baschek, B.: Markov Chain Monte Carlo solutions for radiative transfer problems. Astron. Astr. (2010). doi:10.1051/0004-6361/201014070

Wan, H., Chen, R.-R., Choi, J.W., Singer, A., Preisig, J., Farhang-Boroujeny, B.: Joint channel estimation and Markov Chain Monte Carlo detection for frequency-selective channels. In: Proceeding of the IEEE Sensor Array and Multichannel Signal Process Workshop, pp. 81–84 (2010)

Witlox, F., Tindemans, H.: The application of rough sets analysis in activity based modeling: opportunities and constraints. Expert Syst. Appl. **27**, 585–592 (2004)

Yao, Y., Zhou, B.: Naive Bayesian rough sets. Lect. Notes Comput. Sci. **6401**, 719–726 (2010)

Zhang, C., Wang, J.: Multi-relational Bayesian classification algorithm with rough set. In: Proceeding of the 7th International Conference on Fuzzy Systems and Knowledge Discovery, pp. 1565–1568 (2010)

Chapter 12
Early Warning and Conflict Prevention Using Computational Techniques

12.1 Introduction

Early warning generally refers to a set of activities that aim to collect, integrate and analyze data in order to detect and identify the early signs of an emerging crisis before it explodes into violence (Alexander 2003). *Conflict prevention* instead describes the whole range of development and crisis intervention activities aimed at reconciling parties with conflicting interests, to prevent the pursuit of divergent goals from degenerating into hostilities of any intensity (Rupesinghe 1994). The concept of conflict prevention has also been extended to include the efforts and management strategies designed and implemented to prevent future relapses into violence.

Early warning and conflict prevention are closely intertwined. When carried out promptly, they can be mutually reinforcing. Indeed, early warning is carried out for the preventive purpose of: (a) anticipating the escalation of violent conflict; (b) the development of strategic responses to these crises; and (c) the presentation to critical actors of options for purposes of decision-making and preventive action (Alexander 2003). Furthermore, both of them aim at the prevention of any form of violent conflict, including war.

Early warning and conflict prevention forms a complex field with many different approaches and a broad variety of actors involved, ranging from practitioners, grassroots actors and academics. Although few people will disagree with the necessity of early warning and conflict prevention, successful early warning linked with conflict prevention has proved to be difficult. As the painful and strenuous conflict experiences in Rwanda, Iraq and Afghanistan, just to cite a few, underline, that there is still a gap between rhetoric and reality. What more can we do to bridge the gap between them? We believe that there is still a need to actively engage in crisis prevention where the first step is the diagnosis and prognosis of *when, why*

T. Marwala and M. Lagazio, *Militarized Conflict Modeling using Computational Intelligence*, Advanced Information and Knowledge Processing, DOI 10.1007/978-0-85729-790-7_12, © Springer-Verlag London Limited 2011

and *where* conflict will erupt as well as *how* to intervene. This is the same procedure as any troubleshooting process where we ask five key questions:

(a) What is the problem?
(b) How imminent is it?
(c) What are the underlying causes?
(d) What can we do about it?
(e) Is the preventive measure having an impact?

The options and activities that can be chosen and implemented are necessarily tied to an understanding of the potential conflict. In this sense, early warning becomes one of the criteria for success in conflict prevention.

This chapter critically reviews the development of the field of early warning and conflict prevention. Initially, this chapter discusses some of the challenges and problems which the international community still faces in this area, and how computational intelligence may help to address some of these issues. Our focus is on the relationship between early warning and prevention and how conflict prevention can be enhanced to spread peace. Then, the results of all our analyses are integrated into *a controlling model* to provide a possible single solution for increasing peace in the international system. We present our diagnosis and prognosis of international relations based on the final controlling model that this book has developed. Special attention is given to the three pillars of Kantian peace - democracy, economic interdependence and international organizations – and how, on the basis of our results, the international community should use these three key factors to promote the spreading of peace in the international system. It is important to note that we are not trying here to critically discuss and address all the possible challenges that the international community struggles with when preventing future conflicts, such as for instance a lack of international engagement or political will. This chapter focuses on the capability of enhancing early warning and conflict prevention. We also believe that by enhancing national and international capability for early warning and conflict prevention we will help strengthen global norms, values and institutions for peace, therefore reducing political barriers to action in the longer term.

12.2 Early Warning and Conflict Preventions: Theory, Approaches and Issues

With the end of the Cold War there was a great deal of talk about the prospect for a 'new world order' characterized by a spirit of great power cooperation that could lead to a more stable and peaceful international system. This optimistic view was empirically supported by a decline in incidence of inter-state war and a reduction in the number of civil wars after they peaked in 1992 (Wallensteen and Sollenberg 1999; Gurr 2000; Marshall 2001).

However, despite good reasons for optimism, the risk of conflict has remained a painful reality and a constant threat in the new century. Many inter-state militarized disputes have occurred in the post-cold war era. Competition for natural resources, above all for energy, has also resurfaced as a possible major drive for future inter-state wars (Klare 2002). Confrontations over nuclear capability have arisen between the West, North Korea and Iran. Developments in climate changes, population growth, poverty and inequality have brought about new insights on international security. Pressures on intra-state conflicts have also mounted since fledgling democracies could destabilize and post-conflict countries fall back into war (Gurr and Marshall 2005). Furthermore, cases such as the genocides in Rwanda, ethnic wars in Bosnia-Herzegovina, state failure in Somalia and, more recently, the Iraq war have pointed to the human and economic cost of the new century's conflicts as well as the very limited success of peace-keeping and peace-enforcing operations. Reactive interventions in a full-blown conflict are the costliest and most dangerous way of intervening and also the ones least likely to succeed (Annan 1996). As a result, the international community has started to turn towards preventative measures, which means early warning and conflict prevention, as a more effective and cost-efficient way to deal with future conflicts (Brown and Rosecrance 1999). The idea here is to resolve conflicts before they even start as experience suggests that taking early action is of great importance. Indeed, conflict prevention is now an official policy in the UN, the EU, the G8 and several other countries. It has been successfully applied in several places facing the risk of conflict, such as South Africa and Macedonia. Today, as a matter of fact, the importance of conflict prevention and early warning has been increasingly recognized and has extended as far as those responsible for devising and implementing policy. As several experts have indicated, prevention is not only highly ideal but a political option that often works (Zartman 2001; Miall 2007). In general, the factors for stimulating early warning and conflict prevention can be summarized as follows (Doom and Vlassenroot 1997; Schmid 1998):

- increased communication and growth in the complex ways of gathering, processing and analyzing information;
- new insights about international security activated by the end of Cold War;
- moderation of the concept of sovereignty and non-interference in the internal affairs of other countries;
- the rising costs of conflicts and the limited success of peace-keeping and peace-enforcing operations; and
- the high risk of transnational impacts.

12.2.1 The Development of the Field

At a very general level, conflict prevention and early warning have been distinguished from other approaches in conflict management by the timing of when they come into play rather than how they are implemented. Initially, the term *conflict prevention*, which was coined by the UN Secretary General Hammarskjold in 1960, was directed to avoid great power wars and confrontations in developing countries from escalating into global conflicts. Later, in 1992, with the end of the Cold War, the UN Secretary General Boutros-Ghali changed the focus of conflict prevention to indicate taking action when non-violent disputes were emerging but had not escalated into significant violence or armed conflict. Following this line Peck (1998) defined two further stages in the preventive phase: early and late prevention. The former seeks to improve the relationship of parties or states that are not actively fighting but who are significantly divided and estranged. This early stage is characterized by latent tensions in peaceful contexts. However, if these tensions are left unresolved, they may develop into armed conflict. The late stage indicates a subsequent stage when fighting among parties appears to be imminent. Both stages are concerned with actions and efforts taken early, when a conflict is at a low level, and as such they should be distinguished by actions taken when higher levels of violence are unfolding. Following Lund classification, we can identify four stages of peace or conflicts: Stable peace, unstable peace, crisis and war. Stable peace is characterized by peacetime diplomacy and politics. Unstable peace should be managed by conflict preventive diplomacy and activities. Crisis requires crisis management and diplomacy. Finally, war calls for peacemaking (Lund 2009).

In the initial stage of conflict, early warning is fully interlinked with conflict prevention. Indeed, early warning has been regarded as an instrument of conflict prevention strategies that should help to ascertain whether and when violent conflicts can occur and how to intervene to prevent these from happening. As defined by Alexander (2003), early warning refers to a set of activities that aim to collect, integrate and analyze data in order to detect and identify the early signs of an emerging crisis before it explodes into violence. In real terms, early warning systems operate on the basis of three steps: information gathering (data collection), processing and analysis (detection), translation and signaling (prognosis). This is because the purpose of early warning is twofold: one is to identify the potential sources of conflict and make a prognosis of how they may develop and the other is to identify the causes which lie at the root of the conflict as well as the relevant actions that can readdress these causes (Doom and Vlassenroot 1997). If the prognosis concludes that the risk of violence exists and an early response can make a difference, a warning is then sent to decision makers, who should act as recommended to prevent the latent tensions from escalating. Early responses could be of different types ranging from military to non-military actions, interventions from third actors – governmental and non-governmental – to individual mediators (Rupesinghe 1994)

Although a certain level of agreement exists around the concept of early warning, the field lacks a shared understanding of what constitutes conflict prevention. Wallensteen and Möller (2003) count eight different definitions of conflict prevention. These range from the traditional approach underlined by Boutros (1996), which utilizes traditional preventive diplomacy techniques, to a more structural approach where prevention becomes a medium and long-term proactive operational and structural strategy undertaken by a variety of actors, intended to identify and create the conditions to enable a stable and more predictable international security environment (Väyrynen 2003).

Although many researchers argue that the definition of conflict prevention should be "broad in meaning and malleable as a policy" (Carment and Schnabel 2003), the recent tendency has been to develop more precise definitions that can be easily operationalized, while still driven by policy concerns (Wallensteen and Möller 2003). As Lund argues, we should strive for a more rigorous definition that can differentiate conflict prevention from other closely related concepts, such as traditional preventive diplomacy, foreign policy and intervention. This more rigorous concept should still be applicable to different contexts and yet be specified well enough to be operationalized (Lund 1996). Definitions of prevention have also varied because the means of engagement have varied. However, a consensus has also emerged here. Tools for conflict prevention should be identified on the basis of which causes of conflict are targeted. Initially, tools for conflict preventions revolved around early warning, mediation, confidence building measures, fact-finding, preventive deployment, and peace zones (Boutros 1994). But subsequent UN policies, for instance the Agenda for Development (1997), greatly expanded preventive measures to include the institutional, socio-economic, and global environment within which conflicting actors operate. In addition, in the new millennium, long-term conflict prevention has become a new strategic option for the UN as opposed to short term activities (see Millennium Report 2000). As result, conflict prevention is now regarded as encompassing almost any policy sector, whether labeled conflict prevention or not, and involving long term strategies (Rubin 2004).

From a theoretical standpoint, there are two ways of understanding conflict prevention and its tools. Initiatives aimed at particular actors in a particular conflict are distinguished from efforts to shape underlying socio-economic, political, institutional processes and the global environment. The former understanding concerns a *direct* preventive action, which is taken when a crisis is deemed to be imminent and in a dangerous phase of military escalation. The actor involved in direct prevention is normally an independent third party, whose interests are not directly linked with the conflicting sides. The latter understanding focuses on a *structural* prevention, where the objective is to create conditions that make conflicts and disputes almost impossible. In this context, a third party could be involved in providing long term assistance for such conditions to develop. (On the two ways of prevention, see: Sriram 2003; Wallensteen 2002; Miall et al. 1999). *Direct prevention*, often called operational or light prevention is more time-sensitive and actor- or event-focused since it targets specific parties and the issues between them to avoid escalation (Miall 2004). Examples of direct prevention are: training in non-violence, military deterrence, mediation efforts, etc. *Structural prevention*, also called deep prevention, tends to be more long term, and less time-context and actor sensitive. The objective here is to create constraints or opportunities that shape what the actors do. This is because structural prevention intervenes on the key factors generating the environment where potentially contending actors operate. Examples of structural prevention are: building the governing institution, creating and implementing regimes, increasing trade, reducing regional disparity, etc. Lund (2009) argues that with structural intervention we are not just simply avoiding violence, or creating 'negative peace,' but rather aspiring to 'positive peace.' He also points out that structural prevention intervention is most appropriate in the earlier (latent) stages. During the latent stage it is easier to implement more far-reaching measures since there are lower levels of inter-party, societal and international suspicion and mistrust (Lund 2009). More recently, the UN has introduced a third category of conflict prevention, 'systemic prevention', to describe measures that address trans-national conflict risks. *Systemic prevention* seeks to reduce conflict at a global level with mechanisms that are not focused on any particular state (Rubin and Jones 2007). However, this type of prevention can be regarded as a special case of direct and structural intervention (see next paragraph on *a priori* prevention).

A further theoretical distinction, based on the mode of intervention, has been put forward in the literature (Lund 2009). This is based on the difference between *a priori* and *ad hoc* measures. The former refers to generic international principles/regimes, not-specific to any particular countries, which have been agreed upon by the majority of the states comprising the international system. International regimes have been defined as "Implicit or explicit principles, norms, rules and decision-making procedures around which actors' expectations converge in a given area of international relations." (Krasner 1983). On regime theory see: Mearsheimer (1994), Keohane and Martin (1995), and Hasenclever et al. (1997). These principles are normally codified by global and regional organizations and are treated as norms of conduct that all the states in the international system are expected to follow and comply with. *A priori* actions can both readdress structural or direct causes of conflict. *A priori* measures operating on structural conditions tend to be regarded as supranational normative regimes, such as human rights conventions, environmental regimes, World Trade organization negations, etc.; while the ones dealing with more imminent causes tend to be categorized as international regulations, such as global regulation on illegal trade or international tribunals, arms control treaties, war crimes tribunals, EU Lome and Cotonou processes on democracy, governance and human rights, etc. Differently, *ad hoc* measures are specific to countries and places and are hands-on interventions aiming to respond to a country-specific risk. *Ad hoc* measures can also be structural or direct. Examples of ad hoc structural measures include: Economic reforms and assistance, enterprise promotion, decentralization, group assimilation policies, aid for election, etc. Ad hoc direct measures are instead: inter-group dialogue and reconciliation, fact finding missions, arms embargoes, preventive deployment, economic sanctions, threat of force, preventive deployment, etc. Illustrative example of the main theoretical categories, which have been developed in the literature to differentiate different types of conflict prevention activities can be found in Lund (2009).

Practical approaches to conflict prevention have also been put forward by practitioners. Jan Eliasson, a diplomat and the first Under-Secretary General for the UN Department of Humanitarian Affairs, has suggested a ladder of increasingly coercive actions that could be undertaken by the international community to prevent a local situation from degenerating into violence (Eliasson 1996). In addition, a culture of tool boxes for conflict prevention has spread within IGOs. This has promoted the emergence of several practical tools for conflict prevention within several international and regional organizations. The UN Secretariat's 'Interagency Framework Team for Coordinating Early Warning and Information Analysis' identifies countries at risk of conflict and applicable UN preventive measures. OSCE and OAS have their own active regional mechanisms for conflict prevention, while all African sub-regional organizations have agreed to the development of toolboxes and prevention mechanisms (e.g., the AU; ECOWAS; IGAD; SADC; ECCAS).

What emerges from the literature is a variety of means and methods for conflict prevention. This underlines that rather than a single specific instrument, conflict prevention has become a multi-tooled, multi-factored and multi-leveled approach. Conflict prevention does not imply a single technique but instead a pro-active stance toward possible and emerging stages of conflict. This stance can make use of a wide range of pro-active responses aimed at avoiding disputes from escalating into violence and addressing the underlying problems affecting the conflicting sides. Furthermore, the actors involved in prevention could range from diplomats to a wide variety of third-parties: governmental and non-governmental organizations operating in the social, economic, and cultural context; international financial institutions; regional organizations; states; NGOs; the private sector; and single individuals. The extension of the scope, means and actors involved in conflict prevention has increased the complexity of operationalizing prevention and, at times, made it difficult for academics and practitioners to move from theory to practice. Some of the challenges that this inclusive concept of conflict preventions, together with the sheer number of actors involved in the process, poses for timeless, coherence, successful and effective preventive response are discussed in the next section.

12.2.2 Challenges

The need to prevent, rather than merely react to conflicts through peacekeeping and enforcement has been an on-going challenge for the international community. Notwithstanding several successes, e.g., South Africa and Macedonia, conflict prevention and early warning came under especially heavy criticism after the embarrassing failures by the UN, the USA, and other international actors to stop the massive genocide in Rwanda in 1994. This failure, together with more recent episodes of enfolding conflicts (Iraq and Afghanistan to cite only two) has revealed that there is still a gap between rhetoric and reality. What more can be done to bridge the gap between them?

To fill the gap between conflict prevention theory and practice, prevention needs to become a full-time professional and governmental endeavor. We believe that an important aspect that will lead to this commitment is to address the still pressing need to actively engage in crisis prevention. Specifically, attention should be directed to improve all the key steps involved in the prevention process, from the diagnosis and prognosis of *when*, *why* and *where* conflict will erupt to *how* to intervene. Indeed, there is still a lack of strategy and capacity for prevention efforts and inadequate local knowledge and local networks.

Some of the challenges to early warnings and conflict prevention can be found in the limited extent to which existing operational early warning systems can identify areas of potential conflicts in sufficient time for effective preventive actions to be taken. Data gathering and analysis are critical, not only in assisting in anticipating a crisis, but in determining the appropriate early response for a particular situation. As the Rwandan case underlines, international actors could not draw the appropriate conclusions on events unfolding on the ground. This was partly because there was a strategic failure to collect and analyze the data that was available and translate this wealth of information into strategic plans and actions. Indeed early warning specialists emphasize that accurate, comprehensive and systematic data on conflict is hardly available, let alone routinely analyzed (Lund 1994). Reliable data still needs to be systematically collected and integrated. Although according to a number of authors there is sufficient information, this data is only to a very limited extent reliable, accurate, meaningful, adequate, recent and validated (Walker 1989). Issues also remain about the gathering and centralizing of the data in a systematic way. Due to these shortfalls, much information is either under-used or not used at all, and there is a reliance on information which has been gathered on an *ad hoc* basis. The task of gathering accurate and reliable data in systemic fashion should perform by an integrated network, made up by international and local organizations, where early warning work is decentralized and responsibilities allocated on the basis of an appropriate division of labor (Rupesinghe 1994). Regional efforts, such as the continental early warning system that was established in 1995 by the African Union (AU) in Addis Ababa, are a step in this direction.[1]

Challenges also still exist in relation to analysis and operationalization. Different theoretical notions and models of conflicts have been developed. However, there is no agreement on which models or notions can best explain and predict different kind of conflicts. Conflicts are the consequence of historical factors which build up over a long period of time as well as of sudden dynamic accelerating triggers. They take place within societies, in other words, in complex and open systems. A feature of such systems is that they are highly adaptive and in constant transformation. An additional problem is that since societies are open, they are sensitive to factors which may be external and this makes prediction even more difficult (Shermer 1995). Predicting social processes is, however, not just a scientific challenge, but a necessity within conflict prevention, because without it all chance of anticipation is lost.

Following Gurr and Harff's typology (1994), notions and models of conflicts based upon quantitative methodologies can be classified into five main categories:

---

[1]In June 1995, the AU endorsed the establishment of a continent-wide early warning system. The system is linked with regional Economic Communities such as ECOWAS, the Southern African Development Community (SADC) and the Intergovernmental Authority on Development (IGAD), as well as research institutes and civil society organizations. The AU needs to adequately fund the system and train analysts to make it functional (on the AU continental early warning system see AU 2006).

structural models, accelerator models, threshold models, conjuncture models and *response models*. *Structural models*, also called correlation models, tend to use multiple regressions to test the relationships between a set of variables and the probability that a conflict will arise. They aim to identify the conditions and structural contexts under which violent conflict will erupt. These models use information that is gathered from past events. Therefore they post-dictate the future. As a result they need constant appraisal and refreshing based on new data. In addition they have not been successful in identifying at which point and when intervention from third party is likely to have the greatest impact on avoiding conflicts. The *accelerator models* amplify the effect of background condition, which are structural conditions, and those of intervening variable. The aim of these analyses is to examine what possible connections exist between dynamic factors which suddenly arise and historical variables, and what impact these connections have on the on-going course of events. The aim of these systems, also referred to as sequential models, is to identify the triggers and antecedent processes that spark and lead to conflict. The accelerator models look for sequences that lead from high-risk situations to conflict (Davies and Gurr 1998). Events fit more easily within a sequential model than they do in a correlation model since events typically trigger changes in a sequential fashion. For instance, if the unemployment rate in a society is rising, the level of discontent among the workers will also rise. Then if the level of discontent is high and the government drastically raises the price of bread and reduces public participation, then violence is likely to erupt. However, sequential models need solid theoretical and empirical foundation explaining the processes by which different types of violent conflict erupt to operate efficiently. Unfortunately, up to today, there is no single understanding and agreed theoretical sequences for the outbreak of violent conflicts. An example of the sequential or accelerator model is the Global Event Data Survey –GEDS (Davies and Daniel 1993). *Threshold models* use event data analysis and, although they do not try to identify the causes or processes of conflict, they try to abstract the information from other conflicts and identify similarities in the patterns formed by the event data. The assumption is that the event data will form similar clusters before there is a shift in conflict phase. Event data are "nominal or ordinal codes recording the interactions between international actors as reported in the open press" (Schrodt and Gerner 1994). An example of event data is: "Iraqi newspapers denounce Kuwait's foreign minister as a US agent." Using Boolean statements this event is coded for further analysis and comparison. *Conjectural models* represent a new development and they are still in their infancy (Brecke 2000). Similar to causal models, they operate using predefined indicators or variables but differ insofar as they do not examine the magnitude but rather the relationship between the indicators. By identifying these complex relationships among indicators present in the pre-conflict phase, they aim to identify the risk of conflict. Finally *response models* aim to assess the impact of various interventions and their appropriateness to the conflict. The main objective is to produce various hypothetical scenarios in response to different solutions and combinations of intervention. Whatever model is preferred, it is also important to note there is also a frequent statement within the field, that conflict prevention must be context-specific to be effective (Ackerman 2003; Väyrynen 2003; Lund 2002). This potentially implies a deep examination of cases which is time-consuming as well as less prone to generalization. If context is examined, it also needs to be operationalized and made comparable since preventive methods are often the same, requiring as well concepts that bring out similarities in the actual situation.

In relation to operationalization, challenges remain on establishing what types of preventive actions, both structural and direct, both *a priori* and *ad hoc* levels, in what combinations, are likely to have a positive or negative effect in different stages of conflicts and contexts. Existing response models could not fully readdress these issues yet and uncertainty still exists on what preventive actions need to be taken when an early warning has been raised (Wallensteen and Möller 2003). Once it is decided that some action should be initiated, since a conflict is likely to happen, decision makers are confronted with an extensive range of possible response. Anticipation means that in a potential conflict situation an intervention is made in such a way that there is a change for the initial position to be avoided and moved towards the desired outcome. This presupposes that the situation at the beginning can be clearly described, that the proper means are at hand and that the effects of the intervention can be easily predicted. None of these three conditions is in place at the present time. What is needed thus is a rigorous and comprehensive evaluation of how the factors that have been identified as potential causes of the onset of war can be offset by the preventive actions.

Early warning and conflict prevention must not be a mere palliative. What is still needed is a consistent and integrated approach that encompasses prediction, identification of causes and selection of successful preventive measures. This should be done in a coordinated and integrated fashion, where international and local organizations work together to achieve the same outcome. It is only when these conditions are fulfilled that thoughts can be turned towards real conflict-resolving initiatives. Information and analysis are critical, not only in assisting in anticipating a crisis, but in determining the appropriate response and strategic initiatives in a particular situation. Integration and coordination of data, analysis and strategic planning is also paramount to avoid "the *excess* of political wills paradox" (Lund 2009). As often the case, many actors are already engaged in conflict-prone places, pursuing a variety of differing policy goals that are not necessarily supportive of conflict prevention. Here the problem appears then to be less about pushing the international actors to intervene before a crisis erupts when an early warning is issued but rather making sure that everyone shares the same understanding of why a conflict may erupt and which preventive actions should be pursued.

12.3   Computational Intelligence Early Warning and Conflict Prevention

Computational techniques can help address some of the challenges that the international community is still facing when dealing with early warning and conflict prevention. We believe that computational intelligence can make an important contribution in improving the diagnosis and prognosis of *when*, *why* and *where* conflict will erupt as well as *how* to intervene. Indeed, computational techniques could play an important role in supporting the development of a consistent and integrated approach that encompasses prediction, identification of conflict causes and the selection of successful preventive measures. This is because computational techniques can easily match the complexity of the data involved in early warning as a well as provide a flexible platform for redefining theories and hypotheses on conflict causes and what constitutes successful interventions. Since computational techniques rely on knowledge discovery in databases to extract valuable information from massive amounts of data, these techniques can easily adapt their internal models to include new factors and dynamic changes that take place within societies. As mentioned in the previous section, conflicts are the consequence of historical factors which build up over a long period as well as of sudden dynamic accelerating triggers. They take place within societies, in other words, in complex and open systems. As result, any model that would like to predict and explain conflict needs to endorse adaptation and complexity. Indeed, the analyses that we have developed from Chaps. 2 to 11 demonstrate that computational intelligence does indeed offer a powerful predictive platform for early warning in interstate conflict.

However in addition to prediction, computational intelligence can also transform the newly acquired knowledge into operational insights for controlling the events analyzed. This means that computational intelligence can also help move away from mere early warning towards a unified analytical approach which links the prediction of conflict and identification of causes of conflict with a selection of the right preventive actions. In the following section we have developed a *controlling approach* using computational intelligence that fully integrates the prediction of the previous models with the need for preventive action. The model provides insights on how to control the conflict at stake by identifying which factor or combination needs to change, and the magnitude of the change required. This in turn provides a useful and direct indication of which preventive initiatives should be selected to avoid the conflict about to occur. Decision makers can use these direct insights to evaluate, case by case, which initiative will produce the required change. The selected preventive actions can then be identified on the basis of systemic information and case-by-case considerations. This allows both a rigorous examination of possible preventive actions and the flexible inclusion of context-sensitive information within the final preventive solution (Sriram and Wermester 2003; Väyrynen 2003).

12.3.1 Controlling Interstate Conflicts

There is an old saying stating that: "Revolutionaries are not just interested in understanding the world, but in changing it. However to change it, you need to understand it". Chaps. 2–11 presented different models to help understand militarized interstate disputes (MID). These models were the automatic relevance determination, the maximum likelihood multi-layer perceptron as well as the radial

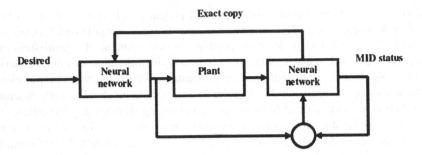

Fig. 12.1 A general adaptive controller

basis function, Bayesian multi-layer perceptrons, support vector machines, rough sets (that used equal-width-bin, equal-frequency-bin, hill climbing, particle swarm optimization, simulated annealing, and genetic algorithms), a neuro-rough model, and an auto-associative network. All the insights from the models have indicated that there is a significant strong effect running between democracy, economic inter-dependence and conflict. However, instead of exerting a constant effect, democracy and economic interdependence vary their influence as they are either enabled or not by interaction effects between themselves and with the realist variables. Above all, the realist opportunities provided by power difference, geographical proximity and lack of alliances emerge as significant in creating the pre-conditions for war. This pre-condition is then activated if the liberal constrains exerted by democracy and economic interdependence are not in place.

Now that we have used all these approaches to understand the MID, it is important to move further on to a stage where it is possible to control the outcome of the MID process, thereby moving away from mere prediction towards true conflict prevention. The objective of any rational government, as far as international relations are concerned, is to maximize peace or to minimize conflict. For this chapter, control system techniques were applied to the MID to meet the objective of maximizing peace (Crossingham and Marwala 2008; Marwala et al. 2009).

Control theory offers a reasonable method to solve many complex problems. Two distinct approaches can be applied to adaptively control a system: the direct adaptive control and the indirect adaptive control. In the *direct control method*, the parameters of the controller are directly adjusted to decrease a distance of the output error. In the *indirect control method*, the parameters of the plant are approximated as elements of a vector at any instant k, and the parameter vector of the controller is adapted based on the estimated plant vector (Marwala 2009).

The general configuration of the indirect adaptive control, as a self-tuning controller, is shown in Fig. 12.1 (Marwala 2009; Widrow and Walach 1996). At each sampling instant, the input and output of the generating unit is sampled, and a plant model is obtained by an on-line identification algorithm to represent the dynamic behavior of the generating unit at that instant in time. The required control signal is computed, based on the identified model and various control techniques can be used to compute the control signal. All control procedures assume that the identified model is a good approximation of the system that needs to be controlled. *In this chapter, a control algorithm is created using computational intelligence.*

Computational intelligence has been used successfully in medical informatics for decision making, clinical diagnosis, prognosis and prediction of outcomes (Tandon et al. 2006; Alkan et al. 2005; Sawa and Ohno-Machado 2003; Szpurek et al. 2005; Tan and Pan 2005). Computational intelligence can be understood as the aptitude of a machine or object to carry out similar purposes that characterize human thought (Kalogirou 2003).

Neural networks, which are a type of computational intelligence machines, are capable of non-linear pattern recognition with there being no necessity for an exact model based on scenarios. When applied to classification problems, neural networks learn which characteristics or combinations of characteristics are helpful for distinguishing classes. An additional purpose of a pattern recognition system is to discover a separator that partitions the classes, locating as many samples into the correct classes as possible (Hudson and Cohen 2000). Talebi et al. (1998) used neural network based control schemes for flexible-link manipulators, whereas Aziz et al. (2003) implemented a neural network inverse-model-based control technique for batch reactors. Other implementations of neural networks in control systems include: the inverted pendulum (Wu et al. 2002), DC motors (Nouri et al. 2008), temperature control (Juang et al. 2006); yeast fermentation control (Marwala 2004; Kalman 2007); mineral grinding plants (Flament et al. 1993), as well as braking control systems (Ohno et al. 1994).

Altinten et al. (2007) used genetic algorithms for the self-tuning PID control of a jacketed batch polystyrene reactor while Arumugam et al. (2005) introduced a new hybrid genetic operator for real coded genetic algorithms to identify the optimal control of a class of hybrid systems. McGookin et al. (2000) used genetic algorithms for ship steering control system optimization, while Hu and Chen (2005) used genetic algorithms based on a receding horizon control for arrival sequencing and scheduling.

Other different applications of genetic algorithms to control include water pollution (Rauch and Harremoës 1999), feed-batch reactors (Nougués et al. 2002), decentralized control system structure selection and optimization (Lewin and Parag 2003), pH control (Mwembeshi et al. 2004), inventory control (Disney et al. 2000), high rise buildings (Pourzeynali et al. 2007), internet-based systems for business-to-consumer electronic commerce (Lee and Ahn 2011), unmanned vehicles (Onieva et al. 2011), as well as flight control (El-Mahallawy et al. 2011).

Marwala (2004) presented a technique, which was based on Bayesian neural networks and genetic algorithms, to control a fermentation process. The relationship between the input and output variables was modeled using a Bayesian neural network, trained using the hybrid Monte Carlo technique. A feedback loop, based on genetic algorithms, was used to alter the input variables so that the output variables were as close to the desired target as possible, without the loss of confidence levels on the prediction that the neural network gave. The proposed technique was observed to meaningfully decrease the distance between the desired target and measured outputs.

Tettey and Marwala (2006) introduced neuro-fuzzy modeling to the problem of controlling interstate conflict. It was demonstrated that a neuro-fuzzy model attained prediction accuracy similar to Bayesian trained neural networks. It was further demonstrated that a neuro-fuzzy model can be applied in a genetic algorithm based control scheme to avoid 100% of the detected conflict cases. They observed that:

- An increase in democracy levels of interacting states reduces the likelihood of conflict.
- If interacting states become allies, the likelihood of conflict is reduced.
- Any increase in the capability of the interacting states reduces the likelihood of conflict.
- An increase in the dependency of the interacting states reduces the likelihood of conflict.

A control mechanism is now presented in this chapter, to assess the MID dyadic variables required to effectively control conflict. To control a single MID dyadic variable, a golden search method was applied, while to control more than one MID dyadic variable, simulated annealing was used. In this chapter, a brief background on Bayesian neural networks, simulated annealing, the golden search method, and control systems is thus provided now within the context of controlling conflict.

12.3.2   Control Systems

A control system is basically a process where the input of a system is manipulated to obtain a certain outcome. To achieve this, a model that describes the relationship between the input and the outcome needs to be identified. In this chapter, this model entails describing the relationship between the MID dyadic variables and the MID status, which can either be peace or conflict. Various techniques were described in this book to identify such relationships. In Chap. 3, the multi-layer perceptron and radial basis functions were used to identify such a relationship, while in Chap. 4 a Bayesian neural network trained using the hybrid Monte Carlo method was used to identify such a relationship. Furthermore, in Chap. 5, support vector machines were used to identify such a relationship, while in Chap. 6, a neuro-fuzzy system was used to identify that relationship. Chap. 7 applied a rough set model, while Chaps. 8, 9, and 10 optimized the rough sets using particle swarm optimization, hill climbing, and simulated annealing to identify this relationship. Chaps. 11 and 12 applied neuro-rough sets and an auto-associative network to model the relationship between the MID dyadic variables and the MID status.

Now that we have developed models to predict the MID status, given the MID dyadic variable, the next step is to use this procedure to identify the set of variables that make certain that conflict can be controlled, thus reducing the occurrence of war in the international context. The whole rationale behind the development of the

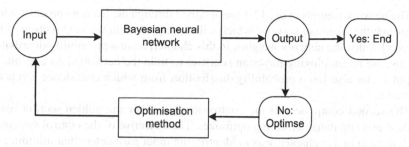

Fig. 12.2 Feedback control loop that uses Bayesian neural networks and an optimization method

interstate dispute prediction infrastructure is to maximize the occurrence of peace, whilst minimizing conflicts. This is achieved, in this chapter, by applying classical control theory to conflict resolution.

Classical control theory has been used to control many complex problems, and a literature review on the application of control systems to solving complex problems can be found in Shurgel (2001). In this article, Shurgel reviews recent developments in bioprocess engineering that include the monitoring of the product formation processes. Shurgel also reviews the advanced control of indirectly evaluated process variables by means of state estimation using structured and hybrid models, expert systems, and pattern recognition for process optimization. Control system theory has also been applied to aerospace engineering, where it has been applied to actively control the pressure oscillations in combustion chambers (Blonbou et al. 2000). Genetic algorithms and fuzzy logic have been successfully used to control the load frequency in PI controllers (Chang et al. 1998). Plant growth has been optimally controlled using neural networks and genetic algorithms (Morimoto and Hashimoto 1996) and fuzzy control has been applied for active management of queuing problems (Fengyuan et al. 2002). Other applications of control approaches to complex systems may be found in Yang et al. (2001) and Peres et al. (1999).

The control scheme applied in this chapter is illustrated in Fig. 12.2. This figure shows that there are two components of this control system:

- The Bayesian network that was used to identify the relationship between the MID dyadic variable and the MID status; and
- The optimization component that takes the difference between the MID status output and the desired output, which is peace, and identifies the set of inputs that would minimize the distance between the predicted output (from the Bayesian neural network) and the desired output, peace.

The Bayesian network component which takes the MID dyadic variables as input vector $\{x\}$ given the network weight vector $\{w\}$ and predicts the MID status as output scalar y can be mathematically written as follows (Marwala 2004):

$$y = f(\{x\}, \{w\}) \qquad (12.1)$$

The network weights in Eq. 12.1 are obtained through the learning process, which is through the Bayesian network which will be explained in the next section. It can be recalled that the network weights, in this chapter, form a probability distribution because we are employing Bayesian statistics to train the networks. As a result, the output vector also has a probability distribution from which confidence levels can be drawn.

The second component of the control loop is either the golden section search method or a simulated annealing optimizer. The objective of the control system, as implemented in this chapter, was to identify the input parameters that minimize the distance between the predicted and the desired target output. The objective function that is used to achieve this goal in this chapter was:

$$error = \sum (y - t_d)^2 \tag{12.2}$$

Here, y is the Bayesian neural network output and t_d is the desired target output. It is Eq. 12.2 in which the golden section search method and simulated annealing optimize for a single variable and multiple variables strategies, respectively.

12.3.3 Bayesian Network

For this chapter a Bayesian network was used to learn the relationship between the MID dyadic variables and the conflict status. To implement the Bayesian neural network, a Bayesian framework was applied to identify the weights (w_i) as follows (Bishop 1995; Marwala 2001):

$$P(w|D) = \frac{P(D|w)P(w)}{P(D)} \tag{12.3}$$

Here $P(w)$ is the probability distribution function of the weight-space in the absence of any data, also known as the prior distribution, and $D \equiv (y_1, \ldots, y_N)$ is a matrix containing the Militarized Interstate Dispute data. The quantity $P(w|D)$ is the posterior probability distribution after the militarized interstate dispute dyadic data have been seen and $P(D|w)$ is the likelihood function. Equation 12.3 may be expanded. Details of this expansion can be found in (Bishop 1995; Marwala 2001) to give:

$$P(w|D) = \frac{1}{Z_s} \exp\left(\beta \sum_{n}^{N} \sum_{k}^{K} \{t_{nk} \ln(y_{nk}) + (1 - t_{nk}) \ln(1 - y_{nk})\} - \frac{\alpha}{2} \sum_{j}^{W} w_j^2 \right) \tag{12.4}$$

Here, Z is the normalization function, t is the target of the MID status, α and β are hyperparameters, W is the number of weights, K is the number of input variables, and N is the number of data samples.

In this chapter, the Hybrid Monte Carlo method was used to sample Eq. 12.2 (Neal 1993). A Hybrid Monte Carlo is an algorithm that uses stochastic dynamics and the Metropolis algorithm to sample probability distribution functions. In a simple form, the Hybrid Monte Carlo can be viewed as an algorithm that combines the Monte Carlo sampling and the gradient search as implemented in methods such as conjugate gradient or scaled conjugate gradient methods (Bishop 1995).

The Hybrid Monte Carlo technique takes a series of trajectories from an initial state, *i.e.*, 'positions' and 'momentum', and moves in some direction in the state space for a given length of time and accepts the final state using the Metropolis algorithm (Metropolis et al. 1953).

On implementing the Hybrid Monte Carlo method to sample the posterior probability function shown in Eq. 12.4, for a given step size, ε_0, and the number of steps, L, the dynamic transition of the procedure is conducted as follows (Neal 1993):

1. Randomly choose the direction of the trajectory, λ, to be either -1 for backward trajectory and $+1$ for forward trajectory.
2. Starting from the initial state, (w, p), perform L steps with the step size $\varepsilon = \varepsilon_0(1 + 0.1k)$ resulting in state (w^*, p^*). Here ε_0 is a chosen fixed step size and k is the number chosen from a uniform distribution and lies between 0 and 1 and p is the momentum.
3. Reject or accept (w^*, p^*) using the Metropolis criterion (Metropolis et al. 1953). If the state is accepted, then the new state becomes (w^*, p^*). If rejected, the old state, (w,p), is retained as a new state.

After implementing step (3) the momentum vector is reinitialized before moving on to generate the subsequent state. In this chapter, the momentum vector was sampled from a Gaussian distribution before starting to generate the subsequent state. This ensured that the stochastic dynamics model samples were not restricted to regions representing local distributions.

12.3.4   Golden Section Search Method

For this chapter, the golden section search (GSS) method (Press et al. 1988; Fletcher 1987) was used for a single strategy approach (where only one MID dyadic variable was manipulated to achieve the control objective) and simulated annealing was used for the multiple strategy approach (where more than one MID dyadic variable was manipulated to achieve the control objective) (Kirkpatrick et al. 1983).

The golden ratio is when the ratio of the sum of the quantities to the larger quantity is equal to the ratio of the larger quantity to the smaller one. The golden section search is a method for identifying the optimum point of a uni-modal function by iteratively reducing the range of values inside which the optimum is identified to be present. The name of the method arises from the fact that the procedure retains the function values for triples of points whose distances form a golden ratio. This method was introduced by Kiefer (1953).

Cai et al. (2010) successfully applied the golden section search algorithm in nonlinear isoconversional calculations to determine the activation energy from non-isothermal kinetic conversion data. The results indicated that the golden section search algorithm could provide the correct activation energy values.

Tsai et al. (2010) successfully applied the GSS procedure for identifying a good shape-parameter for multi-quadrics, for the solution of partial differential equations. Their results showed that the golden section search technique was effective, and gave an acceptable shape parameter and a good solution.

Shao and Chang (2008) introduced the golden search section technique for a new maximum power point tracking method. Their results showed that the proposed technique converged fast, was resistant to noise and was robust.

Lu and Hargreaves (2008) applied the GSS to estimate the multi resolution field map for water-fat separation. Their technique was successfully tested on multi-echo sequences where long echo-spacings gave rise to difficulties in estimating reliable field map.

Other successful implementations of the GSS were in estimating the parameters of the Monod model (Rolz and Mata-Alvarez 1992) and on estimating parameters in the Robertson-Stiff non-Newtonian fluid model (Ohen and Blick 1990).

On implementing the GSS the objective function $f(x)$ is calculated at three points: x_1, x_2, and x_3 giving f_1 or f_2 and f_3, respectively. If f_2 is smaller than either f_1 or f_3, it is postulated that an optimum point lies inside the interval ranging from x_1 to x_3. The following step is to understand the function by calculating it at a new value of x_4 which is chosen to fall inside the largest interval, that is, between x_2 and x_3. If the function yields f_{4a}, then an optimum point lies between x_1 and x_4, and the new triplet of points are then x_1, x_2, and x_4. Nevertheless, if the function gives the value f_{4b}, then an optimum point is located between x_2 and x_3, and the new triplet of points will be x_2, x_4, and x_3 and, therefore, a new contracted search interval that is certain to enclose the function's optimum point can always be identified. The algorithm is terminated when the following condition, based on the bracket size in relation to its central value, is satisfied (Press et al. 1988):

$$|x_3 - x_1| < \tau \left(|x_2| + |x_4|\right) \tag{12.5}$$

Here, τ is a tolerance parameter and $|x|$ is the absolute value of x.

12.3.5   Simulated Annealing

As indicated in Chap. 9, simulated annealing is a procedure that localizes a good estimate to the global optimum point of a given function. It originated as a generalization to the Monte Carlo technique and depends on the Metropolis procedure (Kirkpatrick et al. 1983).

Simulated annealing constantly updates the solution until a termination criterion is reached. It is a well-established stochastic technique, originally developed to model the natural process of crystallization and later adopted as an optimization technique. The algorithm substitutes a current solution with a "nearby" random solution with a probability that depends on the difference between the corresponding function values and the temperature. The temperature *(T)* decreases throughout the process, so as *T* starts approaching zero, there are less random changes in the solution.

As with the case of greedy search approaches, simulated annealing keeps moving towards the best solution, except that it has the advantage of reversal in fitness. This implies that it can move to a solution with worse fitness than it currently has, but the advantage of this is that it ensures the solution is not found at a local optimum, but rather at a global optimum. This is the major advantage that simulated annealing has over most other approaches. But again, its disadvantage is that it is expensive computationally and that the algorithm will identify the global optimum point if specified but it can approach infinite time to do so. The probability of accepting the reversal is given by Boltzmann's equation (Crossingham et al. 2008; Crossingham 2008) as follows:

$$P\left(\Delta E\right) \propto e^{-\frac{\Delta E}{T}} \tag{12.6}$$

Here ΔE is the difference in energy (fitness) between the old and new states, and T is the temperature of the system. The rate at which temperature decreases depends on the cooling schedule chosen. The following cooling model was used in this chapter (Crossingham et al. 2008):

$$T(k) = \frac{T\left(k-1\right)}{1+\sigma} \tag{12.7}$$

Here $T(k)$ is the current temperature, $T\left(k-1\right)$ is the previous temperature, and σ dictates the cooling rate. It must be noted that the precision of the numbers used in the implementation of simulated annealing can have a significant effect on the outcome.

Now that the control system framework adopted in this chapter and all its components have been described, the next task is to apply these to controlling interstate conflict.

12.3.6 Controlling Democracy, Allies, Capability and Dependency

In this chapter, we use control system theory to control interstate conflict. This was done by identifying controllable variables that will produce a peaceful outcome.

To achieve this, the cost function indicated in Eq. 12.2 was defined as the difference between the Bayesian neural network prediction and the control objective (0 indicating the preference for peace). This difference should be as close as possible to zero, that is, absolute peace.

Two approaches were used in this chapter: a single strategy approach, where only one controllable variable was used, and a multiple strategy approach, where all the controllable variables were used. Of the 7 dyadic variables used in this chapter, there are only 4 that are controllable and these were: *Democracy*, *Allies*, *Capability* and *Dependency*. Therefore, only these variables were part of the *control analysis*.

As indicated before, in this chapter, the control system infrastructure consists of three components: the hybrid Monte Carlo trained Bayesian feed-forward neural network, which predicts the MID status, as well as the optimizer, which is activated only if the predicted outcome is *Dispute*, and therefore undesirable, and whose function is to identify the controllable input parameters that could produce peace. This approach is illustrated in Fig. 12.2. The optimizer can be any nonlinear function minimization method. In this chapter, the GSS technique was used for the single strategy approach and simulated annealing was used for the multiple strategy approach. The use of the GSS method was primarily because of its computational efficiency. It should be noted here that other methods, such as the conjugate gradient method, scaled conjugate method, or genetic algorithms might also be used.

On implementing the control strategy, a Bayesian network using the hybrid Monte Carlo method for training was used. This is because of its better performance on dispute prediction. The control approach was implemented to achieve peace for the dispute data in the test set. There were 392 conflict outcomes in the test set of which 286 were classified correctly by the Hybrid Monte Carlo as was indicated in Chap. 4. Therefore, in this chapter, we controlled the 286 dispute cases by identifying the controllable variables that will produce peace. Of course, in a real application we would not know which predicted conflicts are true and which are false because it is in the future, therefore we would apply the control approach to all predicted conflict cases. However, this could be problematic since the Hybrid Monte Carlo model still predicts too many false conflicts. As a result, we would control for cases that need no control, wasting valuable resources. To avoid inefficiency and to reduce the impact of false negatives on the control component of the system, the confidence levels for the predicted outcomes can then be used as further criteria to identify true predicted conflict cases. Since we found that a significant number of false conflicts predicted by the Hybrid Monte Carlo model presented low confidence levels, the inefficiency of the control system could be readdressed by disregarding predicted conflict cases with low confidence levels. When the control strategies were implemented, the results shown in Fig. 12.3 were obtained.

These results demonstrate that, for a single strategy approach, where *Democracy* is the controlling MID dyadic variable, 90% of the 286 conflicts could have been avoided. When the controlling the MID dyadic variable *Allies* as the only variable used to bring about peace, it was found that 77% of the 286 conflicts could have been avoided. When either *Dependency* or *Capability* was used as a single controlling

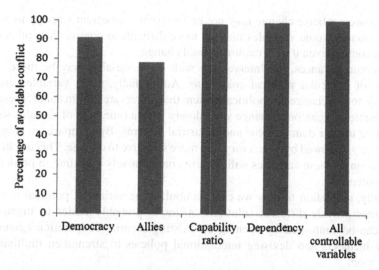

Fig. 12.3 Graph showing the proportion of past conflicts that could have been avoided

variable, 98–99% of the 286 conflicts could have been avoided, respectively. In relation to the multiple strategy approach, when all the controllable variables were used simultaneously to bring about peace, all the 286 conflicts could have been avoided.

The results of this chapter demonstrated that all the variables need to change less compared to the single approach to produce peace. This is expected since in this case, all the variables have been modified simultaneously. However, the change required for *Democracy* and *Dependency* is only marginally different from the one required by these variables in the single strategy, while *Allies* and *Capability* need to change significantly less compared with the single approach. This is a further indication of the key importance of democracy and dependency to achieve peace. Although we changed other variables, we still need to change democracy and dependency almost as much as in the single strategy to achieve peace. In addition, this result indicates that, in this case, the single approach on key variables is more efficient than the multiple one since the required change for democracy and dependency is almost similar in both approaches but the single approach does not require further changes in the other variables.

On the basis of these results, it is evident that policy makers should focus on democratization and economic cooperation to obtain peace. They should decide which approach, single or multiple, is the most convenient on the basis of how easy and cost efficient an intervention with the identified controllable variables is, and how long it would take to control them. This can be done on a case by case basis, where additional analyses, provided by local and international experts, can then help to identify the optimal control strategy out of those suggested by the control system approach.

The lowest relative change may not be the most convenient strategy to follow. This is because some variables may be more difficult to control than others in a specific context, even if they require a small change.

In certain instances, the intervention with some variable may be more costly because of particular political conditions. Additionally, some variables are less amenable to real change in a political system than others are. For instance, *capability* is a variable that can only change very slowly with a timescale of decades since it takes time to alter demographic and industrial patterns. By comparison, *allies* and *dependency*, followed by *democracy*, are more sensitive to change. This implies that intervention on these variables will require comparatively less time to produce the desire outcome.

Finally, in relation to how we can manipulate the variables, political scientists sometimes provide different solutions. *Allies* is probably easier to manipulate. *Allies* can be controlled by opening up existing security cooperation agreements to new members and devising international policies to strengthen multinational cooperation.

Dependency needs a more attentive evaluation since it involves internal changes. *Economic interdependence* can be controlled by boosting bilateral economic and trade relations, reducing gross regional disparities, eliminating protectionist barriers, increasing foreign direct investments and reforming exploitative agricultural policies to allow interdependence to grow across multiple sectors. However, all these economic initiatives need to be sensitive to internal instability and accompanied by compensatory measures towards groups that could be hard-hit by the short term effects of economic changes. This is especially true when *Economic interdependence* is pursed in the poorest and least capable states. In these contexts initiatives need to take into account the potential risk of internal conflicts since economic interdependence could initially privilege certain groups, and thus intensify intergroup rivalries (Chua 2003). International actors have sometimes found that well-intentioned actions designed to increase *Economic interdependence,* while reducing the risk of interstate tensions, may visibly affect the relative position of politically significant groups within a society and thus exacerbate the sources of internal conflict (Collier 2003).

An intervention on *Democracy* is also problematic since different approaches exist within democratization theory on how we could encourage democracy. Some authors focus on external factors and how international organizations or the international community could promote democratization through peace building initiatives, which aim at building effective governing institutions and civil society, supporting democratic movements, through foreign aid in exchange for good governance and transparency, through embargoes and even military intervention. Other authors underline the importance of internal factors and how some internal antecedent conditions, such as economic development need to be in place to trigger democracy. However, democracy may work in some states with a low economic growth and it might be cheaper and easier to achieve an initial higher level of democratization than a higher level of economic development (examples of this might be Cambodia and Nigeria). Furthermore when democratization is implemented, internal destabilization could be an unwanted byproduct of democracy building initiatives. Studies of the actual dynamics of change in particular countries show that the risk of intra-state conflict often rises during periods when authoritarian systems, characterized by exclusionary nationalism, are shifting to more pluralistic structures (Snyder 2000). Alternatively, transitioning polities may remain 'partial' or 'illiberal' democracies (Ottaway 2003; Zakaria 1997), where illiberal elites still hold onto power, political and civil rights are abridged, and representation occurs through informal power-sharing within cliques. These partial or illiberal democracies (anocracies) resisting full democratic transformation could stagnate economically and politically, therefore inviting state breakdown and violent conflict. As Russett and Oneal (2001) stress, democratization is good but it is best when complete. When selecting the right democratization intervention, it is important to consider the transition period and select strategies that allow for a "fast" transition to a high level of stable democracy in countries faced with exclusive nationalism.

As we mentioned earlier, Capability is not easy to manipulate since it requires boosting industrial and demographic development, not only military expenditure. All these options need to be evaluated, case by case, since some interventions could be feasible in the same dyad but not in others. As a result, the control approaches suggested by the system must be conjoined with political practicalities and integrated by analyses provided by local and international experts, who, by focusing on the context, can select the optimal control strategy out of the ones suggested by the system. Therefore, qualitative and context dependent analysis on which specific policy option is the most practical to achieve the variable change suggested by the system is an important part of the final decision making process.

12.4 Conclusion

In this chapter we provided an initial approach which links prediction of conflict and identification of causes of conflict with a selection of the right preventive action. The emphasis has been directed toward controlling conflicts and developing insights that can systematically use to select the right preventive action. Two control approaches were implemented to identify control strategies for maximizing peace. The single strategy approach was implemented using the golden section search method, whereas simulated annealing was used for the multiple strategy approach. It was observed that all four controllable dyadic variables could be used simultaneously to avoid all correctly identified conflict. Furthermore, it was observed that either *Dependency* or *Capability* could also be used to avoid all the correctly predicted conflicts, followed by controlling only *Democracy* and then controlling *Allies*. Finally, by comparing findings from the single and multiple approaches, it emerged that *Dependency* and *Democracy* are key variables to achieve peace since even in a multiple approach they require significant changes, which are closed to their single level requirement in comparison to the other dyadic variables. This means that significant changes in *Dependence* and *Democracy* are necessary, even if the other dyadic variables have been positively manipulated to achieve peace. It is worth noting that the methods used in this research can direct prevention policy or strategies but should not be used in isolation. A case-by-case approach needs to be integrated with the results of the controlling model. It would not be advisable to apply this model blindly without aligning the result with context-sensitive information or existing models. The neural network itself is a good model of complex input-output relationships, but considered by many as non-deterministic. However, current research is directed into better understanding the neural network so that any control system using them can be analyzed quantitatively for properties such as stability.

12.5 Further Work

In this chapter, a Bayesian neural network, golden section search, and simulated annealing were used to model and control interstate conflict. For the future, other methods such as rough set, support vector machines, and fish-school search optimization methods should be used to model and control interstate conflict. In addition our intention is to add a further capability to the controlling model, which will allow an assessment of preventive initiatives and their impact on achieving the required changes.

References

Ackerman, A.: The idea and practice of conflict prevention. J. Peace Res. **40**, 339–347 (2003)
African Union.: Meeting the challenge of conflict prevention in Africa – towards the operational-ization of the continental early warning system, meeting of governmental experts on early warning and conflict prevention, Kempton Park, 17–19 Dec (2006)
Alexander, A.: Early Warning and the Field: A Cargo Cult Science? Berghof Research Center for Constructive Conflict Management, Berlin (2003)
Alkan, A., Koklukaya, E., Subasi, A.: Automatic seizure detection in EGG using logistic regression and artificial neural network. J. Neurosci. Methods **148**, 167–176 (2005)
Altinten, A., Ketevanlioğlu, F., Erdoğan, S., Hapoğlu, H., Alpbaz, M.: Self-tuning PID control of jacketed batch polystyrene reactor using genetic algorithm. Chem. Eng. J. **138**, 490–497 (2007)
Annan, K.: The peace-keeping prescription. In: Cahill, K.M. (ed.) Preventive Diplomacy. Stopping Wars before They Start. BasicBooks, New York (1996)
Arumugam, M.S., Rao, M.V.C., Palaniappan, R.: New hybrid genetic operators for real coded genetic algorithm to compute optimal control of a class of hybrid systems. Appl. Soft. Comput. **6**, 38–52 (2005)
Aziz, N., Hussain, M.A., Mujtaba, I.M.: Implementation of neural network inverse-model-based control (NN-IMBC) strategy in batch reactors. Comp. Aid. Chem. Eng. **15**, 708–713 (2003)
Bishop, C.M.: Neural Networks for Pattern Recognition. Oxford University Press, Oxford (1995)
Blonbou, R., Laverdant, A., Zaleski, S., Kuentzmann, P.: Active adaptive combustion control using neural networks. Combust. Sci. Technol. **156**, 25–47 (2000)

Boutros, B.G.: Building peace and development. Report on the Work of the Organization from the Forty-eighth to the Forty-ninth Session of the General Assembly. New York, United Nations (1994)

Boutros, B.G.: Challenges of preventive diplomacy. The role of the United Nations and its secretary-general. In: Cahill, K.M. (ed.) Preventive Diplomacy. Stopping Wars Before They Start. BasicBooks, New York (1996)

Brecke, P.: Risk assessment models and early warning systems, Arbeitsgruppe: Internationale Politik. At http://skylla.wz-berlin.de/pdf/2000/p00-302.pdf) (2000)

Brown, M., Rosecrance, R.: The Costs of Conflict: Prevention and Cure in the Global Area. Rowman and Littlefield, Lanham (1999)

Cai, J., Han, D., Chen, C., Chen, S.: Application of the golden section search algorithm in the nonlinear isoconversional calculations to the determination of the activation energy from nonisothermal kinetic conversion data. Solid State Sci. **12**, 829–833 (2010)

Carment, D., Schnabel, A.: Introduction – conflict prevention: a concept in search of a policy. In: Carment, D., Schnabel, A. (eds.) Conflict Prevention. Path to Peace or Grand Illusion? The United Nations University Press, Tokyo (2003)

Chang, C.S., Fu, W.H., Wen, F.S.: Load frequency control using genetic-algorithm based fuzzy gain scheduling of PI controllers. Elect. Mach. Pow. Syst **26**, 39–52 (1998)

Chua, A.: World on Fire: How Exporting Free Market Democracy Breeds Ethnic Hatred and Global Instability. Doubleday, New York (2003)

Collier, P.: Breaking the Conflict Trap: Civil War and Development Policy. World Bank, Washington, DC (2003)

Crossingham, B.: Rough set partitioning using a computational intelligence approach. MSc thesis, University of the Witwatersrand (2008)

Crossingham, B., Marwala, T.: Using optimisation techniques for discretizing rough set partitions. Int. J Hybrid Intell. Syst. **5**, 219–236 (2008)

Crossingham, B., Marwala, T., Lagazio, M.: Optimised rough sets for modelling interstate conflict. In: Proceeding of the IEEE International Conference on Systems, Man, and Cybernetics, pp. 1198–1204 (2008)

Davies, J., Gurr, T.: Preventive Measures. Rowman & Littlefield, New York (1998)

Davies, J., McDaniel, C.: The global event-data system. In: Merritt, R.L., Muncaster, R.G., Zinnes, D.A. (eds.) International Event-Data Developments: DDIR Phase II. University of Michigan Press, Ann Arbor (1993)

Disney, S.M., Naim, M.M., Towill, D.R.: Genetic algorithm optimization of a class of inventory control systems. Int. J. Prod. Econ. **68**, 259–278 (2000)

Doom, R., Vlassenroot, K.: Early warning and conflict prevention: Minerva's wisdom? J. Humanitarian Assistance. http://www.jha.ac/articles/a022.htm

Eliasson, J.: Establishing trust in the healer. Preventive diplomacy and the future of the United Nations. In: Cahill, K.M. (ed.) Preventive Diplomacy. Stopping Wars before They Start. BasicBooks, New York (1996)

El-Mahallawy, A.A., Yousef, H.A., El-Singaby, M.I., Madkour, A.A., Youssef, A.M.: Robust flight control system design using H∞ loop-shaping and recessive trait crossover genetic algorithm. Expert Syst. Appl. **38**, 169–174 (2011)

Fengyuan, R., Yong, R., Xiuming, S.: Design of a fuzzy controller for active queue management. Comput. Commun **25**, 874–883 (2002)

Flament, F., Thibault, J., Hodouin, D.: Neural network based control of mineral grinding plants. Miner. Eng. **6**, 235–249 (1993)

Fletcher, R.: Practical Methods of Optimization. Wiley, New York (1987)

Gurr, T.: People vs. States: Ethnopolitical Conflict and Accommodation at the End of the Twentieth Century. US Institute of Peace, Washington, DC (2000)

Gurr, T., Harff, B.: Conceptual research and policy issues in early warning research: an overview. J. Ethno-Dev. **4**, 3–14 (1994)

Gurr, T., Marshall, M.G.: Peace and Conflict 2003: A Global Survey of Armed Conflicts, Self-Determination Movements, and Democracy. University of Maryland: Center for International Development and Conflict Research, College Park (2005)

Hasenclever, A., Mayer, P., Rittberger, V.: Theories of International Regimes. Cambridge University Press, New York (1997)

Hu, X.-B., Chen, W.-H.: Genetic algorithm based on receding horizon control for arrival sequencing and scheduling. Eng. Appl. Artef. Intell. **18**, 633–642 (2005)

Hudson, D.L., Cohen, M.E.: Neural Networks and Artificial Intelligence for Biomedical Engineering. IEEE Press, Piscataway (2000)

Juang, C.-F., Huang, S.-T., Duh, F.-B.: Mold temperature control of a rubber injection-molding machine by TSK-type recurrent neural fuzzy network. Neurocomputing **70**, 559–567 (2006)

Kalman, Z.: Model based control of a yeast fermentation bioreactor using optimally designed artificial neural networks. Chem. Eng. J. **127**, 95–109 (2007)

Kalogirou, S.A.: Artificial intelligence for the modeling and control of combustion processes: a review. Prog. Energ. Combust. Sci. **29**, 515–566 (2003)

Keohane, R.O., Martin, L.L.: The promise of institutionalist theory. Int. Security **20**, 39–51 (1995)

Kiefer, J.: Sequential minimax search for a maximum. Pro. Am. Math. Soc. **4**, 502–506 (1953)

Kirkpatrick, S., Gelatt, C.D., Vecchi, M.P.: Optimization by simulated annealing. Science **220**, 671–680 (1983)

Klare, M.: Resource Wars: The New Landscape of Global Conflict. Henry Holt, New York (2002)

Krasner, S.D.: Structural causes and regime consequences: regimes as intervening variables. In: Krasner, S.D. (ed.) International Regimes. Cornell University Press, Ithaca (1983)

Lee, S., Ahn, H.: The hybrid model of neural networks and genetic algorithms for the design of controls for internet-based systems for business-to-consumer electronic commerce. Expert Syst. Appl. **38**, 4326–4338 (2011)

Lewin, D.R., Parag, A.: A constrained genetic algorithm for decentralized control system structure selection and optimization. Automatica **39**, 1801–1807 (2003)

Lu, W., Hargreaves, B.A.: Multiresolution field map estimation using golden section search for water-fat separation. Magn. Reson. Med. **60**, 236–244 (2008)

Lund, M.: Early warning and preventive diplomacy. In: Crocker, C., Hampson, O., Aall, P. (eds.) Managing Global Chaos: Sources or and Responses to International Conflict. United States Institute of Peace, Washington, Dc (1994)

Lund, M.: Preventing Violent Conflicts. A Strategy for Preventive Diplomacy. United States Institute of Peace Press, Washington, DC (1996)

Lund, M.: Preventing violent intrastate conflicts: learning lessons from experience. In: van Tongeren, P., von de Veen, H., Verhoeven, J. (eds.) Searching for Peace in Europe and Eurasia. An overview of Conflict Prevention and Peacebuilding Activities. Lynne Rienner Publishers, London (2002)

Lund, M.: Conflict prevention: theory in pursuit of policy and practice. In: Bercovitch, J., Kremenyuk, V., Zartman, I.W. (eds.) The SAGE Handbook of Conflict Resolution, pp. 287–308. Sage, London (2009)

Marshall, M.G.: Assessing the societal and systemic impact of warfare. In: Malone, D., Hampson, O. (eds.) From Reaction to Prevention: Opportunities for the UN System in the New Millennium. Lynne Rienner, Boulder (2001)

Marwala, T.: Fault identification using neural networks and vibration data. Ph.D. thesis, University of Cambridge (2001)

Marwala, T.: Control of complex systems using Bayesian neural networks and genetic algorithm. Int. J. Eng. Simul. **5**, 28–37 (2004)

Marwala, T.: Computational Intelligence for Missing Data Imputation, Estimation and Management: Knowledge Optimization Techniques. IGI Global Publications, New York (2009)

Marwala, T., Lagazio, M., Tettey, T.: An integrated human-computer system for controlling interstate disputes. Int. J. Comput. Appl. (2009). doi:10.2316/Journal.202.2009.4.202-2410

McGookin, E.W., Murray-Smith, D.J., Li, Y., Fossen, T.I.: Ship steering control system optimisation using genetic algorithms. Control Eng. Pract. **8**, 429–443 (2000)

Mearsheimer, J.: The false promise of international institutions. Int. Security **19**, 5–49 (1994)

Metropolis, N., Rosenbluth, A., Rosenbluth, M., Teller, A., Teller, E.: Equation of State Calculations by Fast Computing Machines. J. Chem. Phys. **21**, 1087–1092 (1953)

Miall, H.: Conflict transformation: a multi-dimensional task. In: The Berghof Handbook for Conflict Transformation. Berghof Research Center, Berlin (2004)

Miall, H.: Emergent Conflict and Peaceful Change. Palgrave, Basingstoke (2007)

Miall, H., Ramsbotham, O., Woodhouse, T.: Contemporary Conflict Resolution. The Prevention, Management and Transformation of Deadly Conflicts. Polity, Oxford (1999)

Millennium Report, United Nations (2000). Website: http://www.un.org/millennium/sg/report/full. htm. Last Accessed 28 July 2011

Morimoto, T., Hashimoto, Y.: Optimal control of plant growth in hydroponics using neural networks and genetic algorithms. Acta Hortic. Process **406**, 433–440 (1996)

Mwembeshi, M.M., Kent, C.A., Salhi, S.: A genetic algorithm based approach to intelligent modelling and control of pH in reactors. Comput. Chem. Eng. **28**, 1743–1757 (2004)

Neal, R.M.: Probabilistic inference using Markov Chain Monte Carlo methods. Toronto, University of Toronto technical report CRG-TR-93-1 (1993)

Nougués, J.M., Grau, M.D., Puigjaner, L.: Parameter estimation with genetic algorithm in control of fed-batch reactors. Chem. Eng. Process **41**, 303–309 (2002)

Nouri, K., Dhaouadi, R., Braiek, N.B.: Adaptive control of a nonlinear DC motor drive using recurrent neural networks. Appl. Soft Comput. **8**, 371–382 (2008)

Ohen, H.A., Blick, E.F.: Golden section search method for determining parameters in Robertson-Stiff non-Newtonian fluid model. J. Petrol. Sci. Eng. **4**, 309–316 (1990)

Ohno, H., Suzuki, T., Aoki, K., Takahasi, A., Sugimoto, G.: Neural network control for automatic braking control system. Neural Nets **7**, 1303–1312 (1994)

Onieva, E., Naranjo, J.E., Milanes, V., Alonso, J., Garcia, R., Perez, J.: Automatic lateral control for unmanned vehicles via genetic algorithms. Appl. Soft Comput. **11**, 1303–1309 (2011)

Ottaway, M.: Promoting democracy after conflict: the difficult choices. Int. Stud. Perspect. **4**, 314–322 (2003)

Peck, C.: Sustainable Peace: The Role of the UN and Regional Organizations in Preventing Conflict. Rowman and Littlefield, Lanham (1998)

Peres, C.R., Guerra, R.E.A., Haber, R.H., Alique, A., Ros, S.: Fuzzy model and hierarchical fuzzy control integration: an approach for milling process optimization. Comput. Ind. **39**, 199–207 (1999)

Pourzeynali, S., Lavasani, H.H., Modarayi, A.H.: Active control of high rise building structures using fuzzy logic and genetic algorithms. Eng. Struct. **29**, 346–357 (2007)

Press, W.H., Flannery, B.P., Teukolsky, S.A., Vetterling, W.T.: Numerical Recipes in C. Cambridge University Press, Cambridge (1988)

Rauch, W., Harremoës, P.: Genetic algorithms in real time control applied to minimize transient pollution from urban wastewater systems. Water Res. **33**, 1265–1277 (1999)

Rolz, C., Mata-Alvarez, J.: Use of the golden section search method to estimate the parameters of the Monod model employing spread sheets. World J. Microb. Biot. **8**, 439–445 (1992)

Rubin, B.: Blood on the Doorstep: The Politics of Preventive Action. The Century Foundation Press, New York (2004)

Rubin, B., Jones, B.: Prevention of violent conflict: tasks and challenges for the United Nations. Glob. Gov. **13**, 391–408 (2007)

Rupesinghe, K.: Early warning and preventive diplomacy. J. Ethno-Dev.. **4**, 88–97 (1994)

Russett, B., Oneal, J.: Triangulating Peace. Norton, New York (2001)

Sawa, T., Ohno-Machado, L.: A neural network-based similarity index for clustering Dna microarray data. Comput. Biol. Med **33**, 1–15 (2003)

Schmid, A.P.: Thesaurus and Glossary of Early Warning and Conflict Prevention Terms. Fewer, London (1998)

Schrodt, P., Gerner, D.: Validity assessment of a machine-coded event data set for the middle east, 1982-92. Am. J. Polit. Sci. **38**, 625–654 (1994)

Shao, R., Chang, L.: A new maximum power point tracking method for photovoltaic arrays using golden section search algorithm. In: Proceeding of the Canadian Conference on Electrical and Computer Engineering, pp. 619–622 (2008)

Shermer, M.: Exorcising Laplace's demon: chaos and antichaos, history and metahistory. In: History and Theory. Studies in the Philosophy of History, vol. 34. Blackwell, Oxford (1995)

Shurgel, K.: Progress in monitoring, modeling and control of bioprocesses during the last 20 years. J. Biotechnol **85**, 149–173 (2001)

Snyder, J.: From Voting to Violence: Democratization and Nationalist Conflict. Norton, New York (2000)

Sriram, C.L.: Insights from the cases: opportunities and challenges for preventive actors. In: Sriram, C.L., Wermester, K. (eds.) From Promise to Practice. Strengthening UN Capacities for the Prevention of violent Conflict. Lynne Rienner Publishers, Boulder (2003)

Sriram, C.L., Wermester, K.: From risk to response: phases of conflict prevention. In: Sriram, C.L., Wermester, K. (eds.) From Promise to Practice. Strengthening UN Capacities for the Prevention of violent Conflict. Lynne Rienner Publishers, Boulder (2003)

Szpurek, D., Moszynski, R., Smolen, A., Sajdak, S.: Artificial neural network computer prediction of ovarian malignancy in women with Adnexal masses. Int. J. Gynaecol. Obstet. **89**, 108–113 (2005)

Talebi, H.A., Khorasani, K., Patel, R.V.: Neural network based control schemes for flexible-link manipulators: simulations and experiments. Neural Nets **11**, 1357–1377 (1998)

Tan, A.-H., Pan, H.: Predictive neural network for gene expression data analysis. Neural Nets **18**, 297–306 (2005)

Tandon, R., Adak, S., Kaye, J.A.: Neural network for longitudinal studies in Alzheimer's disease. Artif. Intell. Med. **36**, 245–255 (2006)

Tettey, T., Marwala, T.: Controlling interstate conflict using neuro-fuzzy modelling and genetic algorithms. In: Proceeding of the 10th IEEE International Conference on Intelligent Engineering, pp. 30–44 (2006)

Tsai, C.H., Kolibal, J., Li, M.: The golden section search algorithm for finding a good shape parameter for Meshless collocation methods. Eng. Anal. Bound. Elem. **34**(8), 738–746 (2010)

Väyrynen, R.: Challenges to preventive action: the cases of Kosovo and Macedonia. In: Carment, D., Schnabel, A. (eds.) Conflict Prevention: Path to Peace or Grand Illusion? United Nations University Press, New York (2003)

Walker, P.: Famine Early Warning Systems: Victims and Destitution. Earthscan Publications, London (1989)

Wallensteen, P.: Understanding Conflict Resolution. War, Peace and the Global System. Sage, London (2002)

Wallensteen, P., Möller, F.: Conflict Prevention: Methodology for Knowing the Unknown. Coronet Books, Philadelphia (2003)

Wallensteen, P., Sollenberg, M.: Armed conflict 1989-1998. J. Peace Res. **36**, 593–606 (1999)

Widrow, B., Walach, E.: Adaptive Inverse Control. Prentice Hall, Upper Saddle River (1996)

Wu, Q., Sepehri, N., He, S.: Neural inverse modeling and control of a base-excited inverted pendulum. Eng. Appl. Artif. Intell. **15**, 261–272 (2002)

Yang, C., Wu, M., Shen, D., Deconinck, G.: Hybrid intelligent control of gas collectors of coke ovens. Control Eng. Pract. **9**, 725–733 (2001)

Zakaria, F.: The rise of illiberal democracies. Foreign Aff. **76**, 22–43 (1997)

Zartman, I.W.: Preventive Negotiation. Lanham, Rowman and Littlefield et. In: Proceeding of the 7th International Conference on Fuzzy Systems and Knowledge Discovery, pp. 1565–1568 (2001)

Chapter 13
Conclusions and Emerging Topics

13.1 Introduction

The capability to scientifically comprehend the causes of militarized interstate disputes and then to apply this knowledge to build and spread peace in the international context is unquestionably a vital endeavor. Recent advances in the conflict literature have underlined the importance of handling international conflicts as complex phenomena, exhibiting non-linear and complex interactions amongst the relevant militarized interstate dispute variables. Again and again, the relationships between the characteristics of a pair of states and the probability of militarized interstate disputes have been proven to be consistent and robust across time and space. The interstate characteristics that have been observed to influence the occurrence of militarized interstate dispute include: *economic interdependence, democracy, distance, relative power* and *alliances*. For example, if two states are both highly established democracies the probability of them engaging in war is almost non-existent. Similarly, if the two states are economically interdependent the probability of them engaging in war is also quite low. Both *democracy* and *economic interdependence* provide important constraints on a state's behavior and intention to wage a war. Furthermore, if two states' capitals are located *close* together, the probability of them engaging in war is high. In addition, if one of the states is a *superpower*, the distance between the two states' capitals becomes irrelevant, since the capability of a superpower to fight a distant war is high. If the difference in power between two states is low, their willingness to use force will also be low, since equal power works as deterrent. Finally, the number of *standing alliances* also affects the probability of militarized interstate dispute, with more alliances increasing the probability of peace. On the one hand, alliances are constraining the probability of war with non-allies, providing a deterrence mechanism, similarly to relative power, but on the other are also reducing the probability of war among their members. *Distance, relative power* and *alliances* provide the state with the opportunities to wage a war. The constraints which are imposed by *democracy* and

T. Marwala and M. Lagazio, *Militarized Conflict Modeling using Computational Intelligence*, Advanced Information and Knowledge Processing,
DOI 10.1007/978-0-85729-790-7_13, © Springer-Verlag London Limited 2011

economic interdependence, and opportunities provided by *distance, relative power* and *alliances* interact among each other and create different paths to war and peace. Our analysis demonstrates that there is a significant strong effect running between *economic interdependence* and *democracy* and *conflict outcome*. However, instead of exerting a constant effect, *economic interdependence* and *democracy* vary their influence as they are either enabled or not by interaction effects between themselves and with the realist variables.

Computational intelligence models have proved to be a powerful approach in conflict analysis. All the computational intelligence techniques developed in this book have provided strong predicative results with additional insights have emerging on the complex interactions among the Kantian and realist factors. Economic interdependence and democracy were identified as key components in promoting and maintaining peace, however these two variables still need the opportunities and constraints provided by the realist variable to activate their positive influence on interstate relationships. In addition, computational intelligent techniques have proved important in enhancing conflict preventive capabilities. The flexibility of the computational intelligent approach has been exploited for developing a controlling mechanism, which can bridge the gap between theory and practice in early warning and conflict prevention. The book has suggested a controlling approach which makes use of intelligent techniques, linking prediction of conflict and identification of causes of conflict with the selection of the right preventive action. In summary, the results of each chapter follow.

Chapter 2 introduced the Bayesian and the evidence frameworks to allow automatic relevance-determination. The techniques were described in detail, relevant literature reviews were conducted, and their use was justified. The automatic relevance-determination method was then applied to determine the relevance of interstate variables that were instrumental in modeling interstate conflict. The chapter's results indicated that economic interdependence is a major factor in maintaining peace in international context. Any incremental change in *economic interdependence* between two countries produces a positive impact on peace that is almost double the impact of any incremental change produced by a reduction in the differences in *power* or an increase in *democracy*. However, *democracy, power* and *allies* also exert an important and significant impact on peace. Once again this underlines that the relationship between peace and the Kantian factors is not bi-directional. *Economic interdependence* interacts with *democracy* to enhance its influence as well as *democracy's* influence on peace. In addition the impact of the two Kantian factors is also significantly mediated by both the dyadic balance of *power* and *alliances*.

Chapter 3 presented and then compared the multi-layer perceptron neural network with the radial basis function neural network to help in understanding and estimating interstate conflict. These two approaches were described in detail and justified with a review of relevant literature and its application to interstate conflict. The results obtained from the implementation of these techniques demonstrated that the multi-layer perceptron was better at predicting interstate conflict than the radial basis function network was. This was principally due to the cross-coupled characteristics of the multi-layer perceptron's network compared to the radial basis function network.

In Chap. 4, two Bayesian techniques were explained and compared for interstate conflict prediction. These were firstly, the Bayesian method which applied the Gaussian approximation method to approximate the posterior probability for neural network weights, given the observed data and the evidence framework to train a multi-layer perceptron neural network. Secondly one was presented that treated the posterior probability as it was, and then applied the hybrid Monte Carlo procedure to train the multi-layer perceptron neural network. When these techniques were applied to model militarized interstate disputes, it was observed that training the neural network with the posterior probability as it was, and applying the hybrid Monte Carlo procedure gave better results than estimating the posterior probability with a Gaussian approximation method and then applying the evidence framework to train the neural network.

In Chap. 5, support vector machines were presented for the prediction of militarized interstate disputes and compared with the hybrid Monte Carlo trained multi-layer perceptron neural networks. The results revealed that support vector machines predicted militarized interstate dispute better than neural networks, but neural networks gave a more consistent and easy-to-interpret sensitivity analysis than support vector machines did. Democracy emerged as having the maximum effect on reducing conflicts, followed by the difference in capability between the dyads. This is consistent with the democratic peace theory which states that two democracies will never go to war even if opportunities for war are offered by the realist factors such as the dyad being contiguous or not being linked by any alliances.

Chapter 6 investigated the level of transparency of the Takagi-Sugeno neuro-fuzzy model by applying it to militarized interstate dispute prediction and comparing it to the support vector machine model. The results showed that even though the support vector machine displayed a marginal advantage over the Takagi-Sugeno neuro-fuzzy model in terms of its predictive capacity, the Takagi-Sugeno neuro-fuzzy model allowed for linguistic interpretation. The result in Chap. 6 also appears to strongly support democratic peace theory and democracy as a key and necessary factor for peace.

In Chap. 7, the rough set method was applied to model militarized interstate disputes. One of the characteristics of modeling using rough sets was the subject of granulizing the input data. Two granulization methods were introduced, applied, and compared. These were the equal-width-bin and equal-frequency-bin partitioning methods. The results obtained when this technique was compared to the neuro-fuzzy model confirmed that equal-width-bin partitioning offered better accuracy, than equal-frequency-bin partitioning. Yet, both these methods were found to give less accurate results than neuro-fuzzy sets but were found to be more transparent than neuro-fuzzy sets. In addition, it was observed that the rules generated from the rough sets were linguistic and easy-to-interpret when compared to the ones produced from the neuro-fuzzy model. Although the rules on interstate conflicts that were generated did not reveal new insights and are aligned with the more obvious statements of both Kantian and realist theory, they indicate that the rough set offers a good starting point to generate easy-to-interpret explanations of interstate conflicts.

Chapter 8 presented approaches to optimally granulize rough set partition sizes using particle swarm optimization and hill climbing techniques. These two techniques were then compared to the equal-width-bin partitioning technique. The results showed that hill climbing provided a higher forecasting accuracy, followed by the particle swarm optimization technique, which was better than the equal-width-bin technique.

In Chap. 9, approaches to optimally granulize rough set partition sizes using simulated annealing method were presented. The method was applied to model militarized interstate dispute data. The procedure was then compared to the rough set partition method based on particle swarm optimization. The results showed that simulated annealing provided higher forecasting accuracies than the particle swarm optimization method.

Chapter 10 presented approaches to optimally granulize rough set partition sizes using a genetic algorithm. The technique was applied to model the militarized interstate dispute data. The method was then compared to the rough set partition method based on simulated annealing. The results showed that, for the data being analyzed, a genetic algorithm gave higher forecasting accuracy than did simulated annealing.

In Chap. 11, a neuro-rough model (an amalgamation of a multi-layered perceptron neural-network and rough set theory) was applied to model interstate conflict. The model was formulated using a Bayesian framework and trained using a Monte Carlo technique with the Metropolis criterion. The model was then tested on militarized interstate dispute and was found to combine the accuracy of the neural network model with the transparency of the rough set model. The method presented was compared with genetic algorithm optimized rough set model. The presented Bayesian neuro-rough model performed better than the genetic algorithm optimized rough set model.

Chapter 12 reviewed the principal conclusions and their consequences for early warning and conflict prevention. The results of all our analyses were factored to offer a possible single solution for increasing peace in the international system. Initially, we evaluated different general theories and approaches to early warning and conflict prevention as well as the role that computational intelligence could play in enhancing international capabilities for early warning and conflict prevention. Lastly, we presented a control approach that linked the prediction of conflict and identification of causes of conflict with the selection of the right preventive action. Special attention was given to the three pillars of Kantian peace: *democracy*, *economic interdependence* and *international organizations*, and how on the basis of our analyses, the international community should use these three forces to promote and spread peace.

13.2   Emerging Topics in Computational Intelligence

Computational intelligence field is growing on a daily basis and some emerging techniques that can be of great benefit to the subject of interstate conflict deserve special mention in this book. One area that can benefit in the interstate conflict field is the area of unstructured data mining. Unstructured data mining field can be used to search for keywords that indicate the possibility of conflict from newspaper clippings from the periods in questions and come up with a variable representing the media's perception.

Another emerging area that will be of benefit to the interstate conflict discipline is the issue of adding adaptability to the computational intelligence techniques that are used to predict interstate conflict. For example, as each computational intelligence technique is applied to predict interstate conflict, the nature of the data being collected evolves as nations evolve and therefore there is a need to make these computational intelligence techniques to evolve. Methods for building evolving computational intelligence techniques such as neural networks and support vector machines have been presented using techniques in evolutionary computation such as genetic programming.

The methods proposed in Chaps. 3–12 were mainly used in isolation and each technique seems to give different predictive results. The emerging question that needs to be answered is how will the results look if all these techniques are then combined e.g., into a voting framework? Will the accuracy of the prediction increase? How should this hybrid of techniques be configured to increase accuracy?

Finally, further development in rule extraction methods, combined with computational intelligence techniques could be useful in further decoding and explaining the multiple and complex paths, made up of the constraints and opportunities that lead to war or peace.

13.3   Emerging Topics in Interstate Conflicts

The main concern of this book has been about the possibility of improving the predictive and explanatory power of interstate conflict analysis. We have seen that by moving away from the linear and fixed effect paradigm that has dominated the scientific approach in the conflict literature, significant progresses can be achieved. The possibilities of expressing the intricacies of international behavior, while at the same time affording a new vision of theoretical progression, offers a new venue and vision for further research and progress in conflict analysis. Research is never final and conflict analysis has been characterized by constant developments.

From a theoretical standpoint, much work has focused on developing theoretical explanations that systematically combine multiple paths to peace and war. Multiple convergent causal theories for interstate conflicts could provide the necessary insights to fully explain the complex and somewhat different dynamics involved in conflict behavior.

Another development lies in increasing the number of explanatory variables for interstate conflict. New dyadic and systemic factors could be combined. Although systemic characteristics, such as state's satisfaction with the *status quo* or the relative power of the hegemon, do not appear to eliminate the influence of the liberal and realist dyadic factors, they may still play a part in influencing militarized behavior. Furthermore, multiple convergent causal theories may provide an ideal setting to integrate these two levels of analysis. Dyadic variables, such as the level of the states' technological knowledge, membership in international organizations or the state's cultural attributes, may provide further and important insights on the working of the liberal and Kantian factors. In relation to Inter-Governmental Organizations (IGOs), new improved measures related to IGO's effectiveness may pave the way for different results and shed light on their impact on peace (if any).

Finally from a methodological perspective, controlling for temporal dependency requires a richer and a more complete approach that a simple measure of the time elapsed since the last dispute. It is important to distinguish, for example, between a dyad that enjoyed a long period of peace before experiencing a conflict and a pair of states that have been involved in conflict almost every year over the last decade. Recent work which integrates the years of peace with its splines is a promising approach in redressing the temporal dependency issue.

Biographies

Tshilidzi Marwala

Tshilidzi Marwala born in Venda (Limpopo, South Africa) is the Dean of Engineering at the University of Johannesburg. He was previously a Full Professor of Electrical Engineering, the Carl and Emily Fuchs Chair of Systems and Control Engineering, as well as the DST/NRF South Africa Research Chair of Systems Engineering at the University of the Witwatersrand. He is a professor extraordinaire at the University of Pretoria and is on boards of EOH (Pty) Ltd and City Power Johannesburg (Pty) Ltd. He is a Fellow of the following institutions: Royal Society of Arts, the Council for Scientific and Industrial Research, South African Academy of Engineering, South African Academy of Science, TWAS - The Academy of Science of the Developing World and Mapungubwe Institute of Strategic Reflection. He is a senior member of the IEEE and distinguished member of the ACM. He is a trustee of the Bradlow Foundation as well as the Carl and Emily Fuchs Foundation. He is the youngest recipient of the Order of Mapungubwe and was awarded the President Award by the National Research Foundation. He holds a Bachelor of Science in Mechanical Engineering (Magna Cum Laude) from Case Western Reserve University, a Master of Engineering from the University of Pretoria, a Ph.D. in Engineering from the University of Cambridge and completed a Program for Leadership Development at Harvard Business School. He was a post-doctoral research associate at Imperial College (London) and was a visiting fellow at Harvard University, Wolfson College (Cambridge) and a Visiting Scholar at the University of California (Berkeley). His research interests include the application of computational intelligence to engineering, computer science, finance, social science and medicine. He has successfully supervised 35 masters and 6 PhD students, published over 200 refereed papers, holds 3 patents and authored 3 books.

T. Marwala and M. Lagazio, *Militarized Conflict Modeling Using Computational Intelligence*, Advanced Information and Knowledge Processing, DOI 10.1007/978-0-85729-790-7, © Springer-Verlag London Limited 2011

Monica Lagazio

Monica Lagazio born in Italy is currently a Senior Visiting Research Fellow at the University of Johannesburg. She is also the EU Head of Insights and Analytics for Paypal Europe. Monica holds a PhD in Politics and Artificial Intelligence from Nottingham University, an MA in Politics from the University of London and a BA(Hons) in Philosophy with Economics (*Summa Cum Laude*) from the University of Lecce in Italy. In 1999 she was a Research Fellow at Yale University, from 2001 to 2002 she was a senior consultant at Anderson Consulting in London, from 2002 to 2004 she was a Lecturer in Politics at the University of the Witwatersrand, from 2004 to 2006 she was a Lecturer of Politics and International Relations at the University of Kent, from 2006 to 2008 she led customer insights offerings in leading consultancies, such as Accenture and Mouchel in London. Monica has published more than 20 refereed publications in journals, conference proceedings and book chapters as well as a book. She has consulted widely for organizations such as USAid and Developmental Bank of Southern Africa.

Index